'Rather than experiencing cultural differences as threats to be overcome, Barmeyer and Franklin challenge the reader to experience and enjoy the richness of cultural diversity with in-depth case studies that go beyond stereotypical representations of cultural differences. This book is not only a valuable resource for cross-cultural management scholars and educators, but also a useful addition to any executive's library.'

– Günter Stahl, Vienna University of Economics and Business, Austria

'*Intercultural Management* addresses one of the most important issues of the 21st century: how people from around the world can work well together. It is not a question of merely recognizing differences, but rather leveraging and appreciating global diversity. Franklin and Barmeyer guide readers through the complexities of human dynamics and offer much needed analysis and advice.'

– Nancy J. Adler, McGill University, Canada

'For the first time, a book that brings together theory, practice and reflective application homogeneously. The succinct approach and clarity of thought makes for an ideal resource for both students and academics alike.'

– Meena Chavan, Macquarie University, Australia

'For too long the treatment of culture in management research and education has remained detached from work place settings. At last we have a well–conceived, ground-breaking book that is replete with solution-oriented, up-to-date cases for students and practitioners.'

– Nigel Holden, Leeds University Business School, UK

'This is the perfect text for students and researchers who require case studies which treat culture as a complex and contextual influence. They present entertaining and engaging scenarios which get to the heart of the role of culture in today's transnational business environment and encourage the reader to explore and question a wide variety of managerial dilemmas.'

– Fiona Moore, Royal Holloway, University of London, UK

'Finally, a management book on culture that doesn't reduce this important concept to simplistic, wholistic, nomothetic, value-based dimensions that do more harm than good in guiding intercultural interactions! Taking a dynamic, non-North American perspective, this book goes far in offering authentic, reflective, and practical guidance for practitioners as well as academics who want an up-close and genuine understanding of the culture in today's complex global business context.'

– Mary Yoko Brannen, University of Victoria, Canada

'This book is a very valuable resource on culture in management - the texts, cases and examples are highly insightful not only for students, but also for executives. The book helps readers on their journey towards improving intercultural competencies.'

– Stefan Schmid, ESCP Europe Business School, Germany

Published by Palgrave:

Intercultural Interaction. A Multidisciplinary Approach to Intercultural Communication, 2009,
by Helen Spencer-Oatey and Peter Franklin

Published by other publishers:

Taschenlexikon Interkulturalität. Vandenhoeck & Ruprecht, 2012,
by Christoph Barmeyer

Management interculturel et styles d'apprentissage. PUL, 2007,
by Christoph Barmeyer

The Mindful International Manager. How to Work Effectively across Cultures. 2nd edition. Kogan Page, 2014,
by Jeremy Comfort and Peter Franklin

Multinational Enterprises and Innovation: Regional Learning in Networks. Routledge, 2012,
by Martin Heidenreich, Christoph Barmeyer, Knut Koschatzky/ Jannika Mattes, Elisabeth Baier and Katharina Krüth

Intercultural Management

A Case-Based Approach to Achieving Complementarity and Synergy

Edited by Christoph Barmeyer and Peter Franklin

First published 2016 by
PALGRAVE

Palgrave in the UK is an imprint of Macmillan Publishers Limited, registered in England, company number 785998, of 4 Crinan Street, London, N1 9XW.

Palgrave Macmillan in the US is a division of St Martin's Press LLC, 175 Fifth Avenue, New York, NY 10010.

Palgrave is a global imprint of the above companies and is represented throughout the world.

Palgrave® and Macmillan® are registered trademarks in the United States, the United Kingdom, Europe and other countries.

ISBN 978–1–137–02737–5 paperback

This book is printed on paper suitable for recycling and made from fully managed and sustained forest sources. Logging, pulping and manufacturing processes are expected to conform to the environmental regulations of the country of origin.

A catalogue record for this book is available from the British Library.

A catalog record for this book is available from the Library of Congress.

Library of Congress Cataloging-in-Publication Data

Names: Barmeyer, Christoph I., editor. | Franklin, Peter, 1955- editor.
Title: Intercultural management : a case-based approach to achieving complementarity and synergy / edited by Christoph Barmeyer, Peter Franklin.
Description: New York : Palgrave Macmillan, 2016.
Identifiers: LCCN 2015044409 | ISBN 9781137027375 (paperback)
Subjects: LCSH: Diversity in the workplace. | Intercultural communication. | Management. | BISAC: BUSINESS & ECONOMICS / International / General. | BUSINESS & ECONOMICS / Management. | BUSINESS & ECONOMICS / Workplace Culture.
Classification: LCC HF5549.5.M5 I578 2016 | DDC 658.3008 – dc23
LC record available at http://lccn.loc.gov/2015044409

Contents

List of Figures

List of Tables

Acknowledgements

Firstly, we acknowledge the contribution of the authors of the case studies in this volume. We are very grateful to them for the cooperative spirit in which they engaged with us – often in numerous iterations – in creating their case studies. They were asked to meet the challenge of buying into our ideas about the desirability of creating synergy from diversity in international management settings and not least of adhering to a structure for their cases which reflects our beliefs about how to develop intercultural management competence in tertiary educational settings. We are also extremely grateful for their patience – this book has been very long in the making!

In the second place, we acknowledge with many heartfelt thanks the unstinting and difficult work of those people involved in preparing the manuscript and managing the proofreading – Kiyo Dörrer, Marcella Poguntke and Moritz Krüger.

We are also very grateful to the following publishers and intellectual property owners for permission granted free of charge in the spirit of unhindered scientific inquiry to use the material listed below.

Publisher granting permission free of charge	**Material used**	**From which book or article**	**Used in which chapter of this book**	**Figure in chapter**
The Academy of Management Review	Acquirer's modes of acculturation	Nahavandi, A. & Malekzadeh, A. R. (1988). "Acculturation in mergers and acquisitions". In: Academy of Management Review, 13:1, 79–90.	Chapter 4: *Intercultural Challenges in International Mergers and Acquisitions: A German–Bulgarian–Romanian Case Study* by Anna Gajda and Petia Genkova	Figure 4.2

(*continued*)

Publisher granting permission free of charge	Material used	From which book or article	Used in which chapter of this book	Figure in chapter
IESE Publishing	*Japan Tobacco International (JTI): Achieving Excellence through Diversity* by Yih-teen Lee and Steven Poelmans		Chapter 18: *Japan Tobacco International: Managing and Leveraging Cultural Diversity* by Yih-teen Lee	
Linde Verlag GmbH	Translation of Abb. 3: Strategischer Fokus bei M&A-Transaktionen, p. 878.	Unger, M. (2007). Post-Merger-Integration. In: Polster-Grüll, B. (Ed.). *Handbuch Mergers & Acquisitions. Rechtliche und steuerliche Optimierung; ausgewählte Fragen der Bewertung und Finanzierung*, 871–897.	Chapter 4: *Intercultural Challenges in International Mergers and Acquisitions: A German–Bulgarian–Romanian Case Study* by Petia Genkova and Anna Gajda	Figure 4.1
WorldWork Ltd	International Competency Framework	www.worldwork.biz	Chapter 11: *adidas and Reebok: What Expatriate Managers Need to Manage M&As Across Cultures* by Matthias Kempf and Peter Franklin	Table 11.1

We acknowledge the permission granted by the following publishers on payment of a licence fee to use the material listed below:

Publisher granting permission on payment of a licence fee	Figure used	From which book or article	Used in which chapter	Figure in chapter
Pearson Education Ltd.	Figure 2.1 A model of cultural dynamics, p. 17	Usunier, J-C. & Lee, J. A. (2009). *Marketing Across Cultures.* Harlow: Pearson Education Ltd.	Chapter 8: *Smart Spacing: The Impact of Locations on Intercultural Trust Building and Decision Making* by Fritz Audebert, Thilo Beyer and Veronika Hackl	Figure 8.1
Sage Publications	Figure 1 Inclusion framework	Shore, L. M., Randel, A. E., Chung, B. G., Dean, M. A., Ehrhart, K. H. & Singh, G. (2011). "Inclusion and diversity in work groups: A review and model for future research". In: *Journal of Management*, 37:4, 1262–1289, p. 1266.	Chapter 18: *Japan Tobacco International: Managing and Leveraging Cultural Diversity* by Yih-teen Lee	Figure 18.3
Taylor & Francis	Figure 11.2 Approaches to CSR in global organizations, p. 251	Stahl, G., Pless, N. & Maak, T. (2013). "Responsible global leadership". In: Mendenhall, M. E., Osland, J., Bird, A., Oddou, G. R., Maznevski, M. L. & Stahl, G. (Eds). *Global Leadership: Research, Practice, and Development*. 2nd Edition, 240–259. London: Routledge.	Chapter 9: *IKEA's Ethical Controversies in Saudi Arabia* by Christof Miska and Michaela Pleskova	Figure 9.1
John Wiley and Sons	Figure 1 Acculturation model	Berry, J. W. (1997). "Immigration, acculturation and adaptation". In: *Applied Psychology: An International Review*, 46:1, 5–68, p. 10.	Chapter 18: *Japan Tobacco International: Managing and Leveraging Cultural Diversity* by Yih-teen Lee	Figure 18.4

Christoph Barmeyer & Peter Franklin

Foreword

Günter Stahl

Cross-cultural management education and learning has never been more critical and, at the same time, more challenging, than it is today. At no time in human history has the contact between individuals, groups and organizations from different countries and cultures been greater. As part of the globalization of businesses and societies over the past few decades, millions of managers and professionals at all levels find themselves dealing with people who grew up in a different culture and institutional environment from their own. Not surprisingly, the simplistic assumption that "one size fits all" in management practices has had to be abandoned in favour of an acknowledgement that the influence of culture is pervasive and shapes not only our social interactions, but also affects our attitudes, feelings and actions in the workplace and at home. Taken together, these developments have led to the acute need for managers and employees to understand the impact of cultural differences and to work effectively in different cultural contexts.

This is a book about managing across cultures: the threats and opportunities, the dangers and benefits, the problems and possibilities. It rejects simplistic analyses and, instead, explores the cultural dynamics of human behaviour, groups and organizations. Rather than experiencing cultural differences as threats to be overcome, Professors Barmeyer and Franklin challenge the reader to experience and enjoy the richness of cultural diversity. The book also avoids an over-reliance on the cultural dimensions models such as the ones proposed by Hofstede, Trompenaars or the GLOBE researchers, which have dominated the field of cross-cultural management research and education for decades. While these models are useful, in-depth case studies such as the ones presented in this book go beyond stereotypical representations of cultural differences by trying to make sense of a culture's internal logic and showing how collective sense-making processes can explain an individual's actions in cross-cultural situations. They thus capture the uniqueness of each cultural environment and look for specificities not found in other cultures, thereby promoting a more positive perspective on culture and cross-cultural encounters.

This leads me to my last point. While the bulk of the international business and cross-cultural management literature tends to overemphasize the "dark side" of culture, many of the case studies included in this volume highlight the positive dynamics and outcomes associated with cultural differences (giving due consideration to the challenges and risks inherent in cross-cultural contact, which are undeniable). The customary negative bias has hindered our understanding of the processes and conditions that help organizations leverage the benefits of cultural differences, and has led cross-cultural management instructors to adopt a limited set of thematic foci, pedagogical approaches and learning methods in the design and delivery of their courses. This presents a very one-sided view of culture and cultural diversity. As noted by Carlos Ghosn, who is credited with the successful turnaround of Nissan and for making the Renault–Nissan alliance a success, "cultural differences [can be] seen more as an object of cross-fertilization and innovation". A careful reading of this book may allow a thoughtful executive to combine his or her own experience, cultural values and understanding of the crucial variables associated with success in cross-cultural encounters to leverage the benefits of cultural diversity in a variety of contexts, creating cultural synergies. As such, this book is not only a valuable resource for cross-cultural management scholars and educators, but also a useful addition to any executive's library.

Introduction

From Otherness to Synergy – An Alternative Approach to Intercultural Management

Christoph Barmeyer and Peter Franklin

1 WHAT IS THE BACKGROUND OF THIS BOOK? WHAT ARE ITS AIMS?

The internationalization of economic and business activity has long challenged the simple principles of managing and working in one's home environment with people more or less like oneself and with organizations more or less similar to one's own. Professional life in organizations has become immeasurably more complicated by the encounter with the unfamiliar and dissimilar values and practices of foreign organizations, colleagues and clients. This has led to intercultural situations in which people are compelled to interact, perform and achieve management goals in conditions far more demanding than even only ten years ago. Cultural complexity is the rule in many organizations and no longer the exception.

While at the personal level such culturally complex encounters can be challenging and painful due to the differences in values, norms, identities and meanings embodied in interactants from different cultural backgrounds, they can also be inspiring and enriching, and contribute to professional and personal development. Similarly, at the organizational level, whereas the intercultural interface can lead to "frictional loss" such as dysfunctional interaction, conflict, delayed implementation, overextended budgets, culture-shocked executives and missed opportunities and objectives, the view is emerging that cultural diversity can be leveraged to achieve creativity and synergy.

The development and continuing existence of organizations depend in particular on how they manage to generate and apply effective and sustainable problem-solving practices. This is particularly challenging for organizations operating internationally and interculturally, whose members have to combine and integrate different approaches to solving problems. Different backgrounds and experiences lead to different styles of thinking and working, which affect cooperation across cultures and frequently lead to misunderstandings and conflicts. Those departments and groups affected by interculturality, especially, should be particularly interested in implementing effective and appropriate processes.

This book aims to help promote constructive, solution-oriented attitudes and to develop the intercultural competencies required for this purpose through the analysis of case studies showing human, organizational and bi- or multicultural situations in which cultural differences and discord are not merely to be overcome but can be leveraged to achieve complementarity and synergy from diversity.

Consciously adopting constructive interculturality as its approach, the book brings together 20 new and innovative case studies on diverse topics. They are the result of many years' experience of management practice gathered by scholars, researchers, consultants and management practitioners and show how organizations, interactants and culture are interrelated in work settings. They link models and concepts generated by research into interculturality with the practice of intercultural management and thus prepare the book's users for the intercultural challenges within organizations and in a broader context.

Experts on interculturality from research and practice present their approaches, insights and experience using authentic case studies in which the potential of complementarity and synergy is revealed. These case studies are not only intended as objects for theory-driven analysis but are also a source of stimulus and ideas for generating synergy in the reader's own intercultural work setting.

2 WHAT MAKES THIS BOOK DIFFERENT FROM OTHERS ON INTERCULTURAL MANAGEMENT?

2.1 A synergistic and resource-oriented approach

In the past, intercultural management has largely been preoccupied with cultural difference and the managerial difficulties it was seen to cause. It has also, but to a lesser extent, been concerned with the competencies required to handle these differences and difficulties. More recently, a paradigm change has emerged which sees cultural diversity as a resource. This is due to increasing amounts of research and experience which confirm this view. The wish to benefit from cultural difference rather than to merely handle the difficulties it may cause is more and more reflected in the diversity management programmes run within organizations and in the competence sets guiding the selection, development and actions of their leaders and managers.

This book aims to explore this change in viewpoint by investigating intercultural interaction in organizations. It is no longer enough just to know about how people and organizations differ across cultures. This is largely known or knowable. The more urgent question is: How can organizations manage these intercultural challenges and benefit from diversity?

A crucial task for international managers is to understand the dynamics of such encounters and to develop not just the cognitive but also the affective and behavioural competencies to deal with cultural differences effectively and appropriately in a synergistic way. For them, too, the key question is: How can we overcome cultural differences and conflicts and turn them into creative, synergistic solutions? This book can be used to generate answers to such questions and to develop the required competencies.

2.2 A diverse conceptual and analytical approach

Unlike many similar collections, in this book each case study includes a description of conceptual frameworks and analytical approaches useful for understanding and/or handling the complexity of the particular aspect of intercultural management that is presented. These concepts, models and frameworks serve two purposes. Firstly, they help the reader to analyse the intercultural interaction and cooperation not from a simplifying, mono-causal perspective using overfamiliar cultural dimensions but, instead, they enable readers to arrive at a finer-grained understanding which takes account of multiple perspectives and bodies of knowledge. More sophisticated solutions are thus achieved as complementarity and synergy rely not only on often intuitively generated arguments but also on a systematic and analytical approach.

Secondly, the conceptual frameworks and analytical approaches, which are derived from diverse research traditions and disciplines such as psychology, sociology and management science, serve the purpose of interdisciplinary cross-fertilization in the broadening and deepening of knowledge and competencies. For this reason each case contains recommendations for further reading for the student and – in the solutions available on the website – for the lecturer.

2.3 A focus on organizations

In this book an organization is understood as a group of interactants, each with specific competencies and resources, who, as a social system and under certain structural and strategic conditions, are engaged in joint purposeful activity and thus contribute to the achievement of certain goals. Organizations are thus a key location for interpersonal and professional action and interaction. Every organization displays specific features, which result from its history, strategy, objectives, structure and culture(s). More and more, organizations are the most central contexts of intercultural management.

Not only are people and information exchanged and transferred within an organization; management practices and tools are as well. In many cases, for example, management practices designed in the country of an organization's headquarters are introduced with more or less success in their foreign subsidiaries. Here, the intercultural challenge is that the unconscious assumptions and espoused values underlying and justifying these practices may not be shared by interactants in the host countries. To avoid creeping cultural clashes, organizations also need to devote attention to intercultural organizational development. These social systems of joint, purposeful activity are often absent as the focus of intercultural management development materials. Such a focus can be found in this book.

2.4 A more continental European take on intercultural management

Those working in management education in continental Europe are all too well aware of the problems connected with using Anglo-American materials for developing intercultural management competencies. The Anglo-centric nature of many cases may make them hard to use with success in continental European business schools. Students sometimes fail to identify with the problems and situations illustrated and, in particular, with the executives portrayed and their attitudes and actions. European priorities and concerns often receive inadequate consideration.

The cases presented here are fully contextualized and take account of country-specific characteristics. Whereas British and US authors and their views are also represented in the book, a wide spread of country cultures, organizations, functional areas and business situations viewed from a continental European perspective aims to make up for the Anglo-centric emphasis found in other collections of case studies.

Through their long history of trade and commercial integration, continental European countries have become familiar with the challenges of intercultural management posed by interaction with their "old" European neighbours, their Anglo-Saxon cousins and longer-established Asian partners: France, Germany, Spain, Sweden, the United Kingdom and the United States of America, Japan and South Korea are all to be found in this collection. Less familiar – and a deficit in the competence of executives both experienced and prospective – are the cultures of Central and Eastern Europe and beyond. However, Bulgaria and Romania feature in the case studies in this book.

In addition and increasingly, European organizations are dealing with the new and emerging economic powerhouses and markets in Asia and elsewhere, such as Brazil, Russia India, China, Vietnam and Thailand, all of which feature in the case studies presented here. These two groups of cultures and others, such as those of the developing world, are under-represented in traditional case study material, especially in their relationships with continental Europe. This book goes some way to removing this deficit.

2.5 A user-friendly approach

In contrast to similar collections of case studies and in spite of the wide variety of topics, here the reader encounters a uniform and easily recognized structure. This helps both students and lecturers to concentrate on the content and focus their discussion. Furthermore, students will find that the cases are rather more concise and, for that reason, more easily handled than many Anglo-American case studies written for native speakers of English. They are also written in more accessible language and are thus suitable for use in settings in which English is used as a foreign or second language.

3 WHAT IS THE RATIONALE OF THIS BOOK?

We assume that: 1) culturally influenced differences may lead to difficulties in interaction and management across cultures; 2) intercultural competence and competencies help to bridge these differences, overcome problems and form a basis for developing intercultural complementarity and synergy; 3) intercultural synergy can only be generated by integrating numerous contextual factors such as strategy, structures and processes and the competencies of the interactants. These considerations lead to the book being divided into three parts:

Part 1. Understanding Otherness and Discord. The first part of the book gathers case studies which deal with the special characteristics of national cultures and the problems of working interculturally. Intercultural cooperation is shown to be made difficult by differences and misunderstandings. Models and analytical approaches are presented which can help in the comprehension of these differences, difficulties and misunderstandings.

Part 2. Applying Competencies and Resources. In the second part of the book, the case studies demonstrate how the development and application of certain competencies and resources can be used to handle cultural otherness and the difficulties it may cause. These competencies and resources also enable interactants to use attitudes, skills and knowledge to shape complementary and synergistic intercultural cooperation.

Part 3. Achieving Complementarity and Synergy. The case studies of the third part of the book illustrate a systemic, collective and integrative approach to organizations and individuals which – by means of genuine cooperation among the interactants in their entire context of action and on the basis of intercultural competence – can give rise to complementarity and synergy.

Subject	Learning objectives
1. Understanding Otherness and Discord	Readers acquire an understanding of those cultural and social systems and their differences that can lead to confusion, misunderstandings and conflicts
2. Applying Competencies and Resources	Readers acquire an understanding of the competencies that facilitate interactions and the reaching of objectives with members of diverse cultures
3. Achieving Complementarity and Synergy	Readers learn to respect and integrate cultural characteristics in a resourceful and constructive way in order to generate added value

4 TO WHOM IS THIS BOOK ADDRESSED?

As this book provides a connection between various debates and countries and between theory and practice, and also represents an interdisciplinary approach, it is of interest to a wide range of potential readers. The case studies will appeal to students and scholars interested in intercultural management in business schools and universities. These students of management studies, international management and comparative management may be in their final stages of undergraduate study or undergoing postgraduate education, especially at MBA level. The book is also useful to consultants, trainers and management practitioners, e.g. HR managers or project managers, who work internationally and are confronted with intercultural challenges.

5 HOW CAN THIS BOOK BE USED?

This book has many features which support lecturers choosing it for their teaching, and can be used in a number of ways. With 20 cases on a wide variety of management topics and embracing numerous countries and sectors, the book can form the basis of an entire course. The lecturer can present the concepts and models useful for analysing the case, ask the students to work on the case and generate answers to the questions – individually or in groups – which can then be discussed in the classroom setting.

The book can also be used as supplementary material to support a course on international management. The case studies provide opportunities to illustrate and understand intercultural phenomena as expressed in the practice of management.

In spite of the wide variety of topics and the uniqueness of each case study, each case is structured in the same way. This helps lecturers to concentrate on the content and the discussion with their students. All the case studies are structured as follows:

1. Introduction
This section places the case in the international management context and describes its significance.

2. Case description
By analysing accounts of (dys)functional international management, readers learn the subjective reasons behind an individual's or organization's behaviour and are challenged to generate solutions.

3. Background knowledge

3.1 The author's point of reference
Here the author(s) describe their occupation, their disciplinary orientation and their attitude and approach to interculturality. They also describe their cultural background. This information prepares the reader for the approach which is implicit in the concepts, models and frameworks suggested for dealing with the case in the next section.

3.2 Concepts, models, frameworks

The reader is provided with a range of terms, concepts and instruments which can be used to analyse and understand the case, to generate answers to questions and derive possible actions related to the case.

3.3 Recommended reading

This section suggests and comments on texts which elaborate on the concepts, models and frameworks presented in the case study.

4. Questions on the case

Readers find three or four questions to help them analyse the case and generate solutions and recommendations.

5. References

Possible answers to the questions in this book

On the Palgrave website, registered lecturers can find possible answers to the questions posed in the book, references and further reading.

The following matrix (p. 8) gives readers an overview of the topics, concepts, countries and sectors dealt with in the case studies.

An overview of the cases

Part 1.

Understanding Otherness and Discord

Subject/Key words	Concepts/analytical approaches	Countries	Sector (e.g. IT)
Chapter 2: *Harmonizing Expectations: NSF International's Experience in Shanghai* by David A. Victor and Christine R. Day			
Market entry, HR management, culture-specific customs	LESCANT model	China, USA	Public health and environment
Chapter 3: *Planning a Sino-British Collaborative Workshop: Negotiating Preferences and Achieving Synergy* by Helen Spencer-Oatey			
Planning, intercultural collaboration and communication	Power distance; task-relationship orientation; learning approaches; Moran's 3Ps model, Hofstede's dimensions, GLOBE study	Britain, China	Higher education
Chapter 4: *Intercultural Challenges in International Mergers and Acquisitions: A German–Bulgarian–Romanian Case Study* by Petia Genkova and Anna Gajda			
M&A, organizational culture, acculturation and integration, leadership	Nahavandi and Malekzadeh's acculturation model, GLOBE study	Bulgaria, Germany, Romania	Energy
Chapter 5: *How to Implement Change in a Post-acquisition Multicultural Context: The Lafarge Experience in Britain* by Evalde Mutabazi and Philippe Poirson			

M&A, organizational culture, organizational change	Model of the M&A and alliance process	France, England	Construction
Chapter 6: *The Intercultural Challenge of Building the European eSports League for Video Gaming* by Volker Stein and Tobias M. Scholz			
Virtual and intercultural communication and interaction, bridging communities, adaptation	Scholz's virt.cube, Adler and Gundersen's synergy model	Based in Germany, worldwide	Video games/ gaming industry
Chapter 7: *Leading Change in Mergers and Acquisitions in Asia–Pacific* by Jenny Plaister-Ten			
M&A, decision making, sales and marketing, centralization v. local adaptation, change management	Cross-Cultural Kaleidoscope™	UK, Asia–Pacific, Scandinavia	IT
Chapter 8: *Smart Spacing: The Impact of Locations on Intercultural Trust Building and Decision Making* by Fritz Audebert, Thilo Beyer and Veronika Hackl			
Trust building, time and space management, context, assumptions	Hall's proxemics and chronemics dimensions	Japan, Russia, Argentina, Egypt, Germany	Automotive
Chapter 9: *IKEA's Ethical Controversies in Saudi Arabia* by Christof Miska and Michaela Pleskova			
Values, ethics, public relations, gender, organizational culture, CSR, competencies	Donaldson and Dunfei's hypernorms, Stahl et al.'s framework of transnational CSR	Saudi Arabia, Sweden	Retailing

(*Continued*)

Part 2.

Applying Competencies and Resources

Subject/Key words	Concepts/analytical approaches	Countries	Sector (e.g. IT)
Chapter 11: *adidas and Reebok: What Expatriate Managers Need to Manage M&As Across Cultures* by Matthias Kempf and Peter Franklin			
M&A, organizational culture, cultural change, transfer of management practices, expatriation, intercultural competencies	WorldWork's International Competency Framework, WorldWork's International Profiler, Kühlmann and Stahl's characteristics of successful expatriate managers	Germany, USA	Retailing
Chapter 12: *Virtual Chaos at WORLDWIDE Rx: How Cultural Intelligence Can Turn Problems into Solutions* by David Livermore and Soon Ang			
Diversity and innovation, Cultural Intelligence, global teams, intercultural (dys)communication	Ang and Van Dyne's Cultural Intelligence scale	Based in USA, Korea, Europe, South America	Pharmaceuticals
Chapter 13: *Cultural Intelligence at Work – A Case Study from Thailand* by Claus Schreier and Astrid Kainzbauer			
Multiple perspectives, family business, organizational culture, cultural change, Cultural Intelligence, intercultural competence, leadership	Earley and Ang's Cultural Intelligence, Bird et al.'s intercultural competence for global leaders	Switzerland, Thailand	Logistics
Chapter 14: *Cultural Aspects of Offshoring to India* by Craig Storti and Peter Franklin			
Challenges of offshoring, intercultural, (dys) communication, management and leadership styles, intercultural competence development	Hofstede's cultural dimensions, GLOBE study, Gudykunst and Hammer's classification of training techniques	US, India	Global business services

Part 3.

Achieving Complementarity and Synergy

Subject/Key words	Concepts/analytical approaches	Countries	Sector (e.g. IT)
Chapter 16: *Future+: Intercultural Challenges and Success Factors in an International Virtual Project Team* by Christoph Barmeyer and Ulrike Haupt			
Global teams, virtual communication, diversity and innovation, project management, product development, intercultural (dys)communication, complementarity and synergy	Barmeyer and Haupt's three-factor model, Barmeyer's model of intercultural complementarity	France, Germany	Manufacturing
Chapter 17: *A Tough Day for a French Expatriate in Vietnam: The Management of a Large International Infrastructure Project* by Sylvie Chevrier			
Project management, intercultural cooperation, risk management, intercultural synergy, ethics, transfer of management practices	Interpretative approach to culture, d'Iribarne's ideal types of ethics, Chevrier's concept of intercultural synergy	France, Vietnam	Infrastructure, construction, transport
Chapter 18: *Japan Tobacco International: Managing and Leveraging Cultural Diversity* by Yih-teen Lee			
M&A, diversity management, integration, bi- and multiculturality, international HR management, innovation, synergy	Shore et al.'s inclusion framework, Berry's acculturation framework, Javidan et al.'s global mindset concept	Based in Switzerland, worldwide	Tobacco
Chapter 19: *Leveraging the Benefits of Diversity and Biculturalism through Organizational Design* by Jasmin Mahadevan			
Diversity, multi- and biculturality, innovation, organizational design, project management, HR management	Network organization, resource-based view of the firm, Brannen and Thomas's Bicultural Identity Integration	Based in Germany, Europe	IT

(*Continued*)

Chapter 20: *Going Global versus Staying Local: The Performance Management Dilemma in the International Context* by Fons Trompenaars and Riana van den Bergh			
Transfer of management practices, HR management, diversity, performance management	Trompenaars' and Hofstede's cultural dimensions, Jackson's role of cultural values in performance management	Based in USA, Italy, Germany, Japan, UAE	Start-up
Chapter 21: *A Parcel to Spain: Reconciling Cultural and Managerial Dilemmas Caused by the Implementation of Corporate Culture Instruments* by Christoph Barmeyer, Eric Davoine and Vincent Merk			
Organizational culture, transfer of management practices, codes of conduct, subsidiaries, ethics	Hampden-Turner and Trompenaars' cultural dimensions, Hampden-Turner and Trompenaars' dilemma theory	Based in USA, Germany	Pharmaceuticals
Chapter 22: *Managing Glocally: Resolving Intercultural Challenges in the Management of Local Multicultural Teams in a Multinational Venture* by Laurence Romani			
Organizational culture, global/multicultural teams, post-merger integration, HR management, performance management	Maznevski & Di Stefano's Mapping Bridging Integrating model	France, Netherlands, Sweden	Services
Chapter 23: *Strategic Alliances and Intercultural Organizational Change: The Renault–Nissan Case* by Christoph Barmeyer and Ulrike Mayrhofer			
Strategic alliances, organizational culture, adaptation and integration, cultural synergy, organizational development measures, cultural change, multiculturality, transcultural leadership	Organizational development, Bennett's Ethnorelativism, Brannen & Thomas's concept of bi- and multiculturality, Stahl & Brannen's concept of bi- and multiculturality	Japan, France	Automotive

Part 1

Understanding Otherness and Discord

1

Understanding Otherness and Discord: A Necessary but Insufficient First Step Towards Generating Complementarity and Synergy from Cultural Diversity

Christoph Barmeyer and Peter Franklin

1 COMPARATIVE MANAGEMENT STUDIES: THE TRADITIONAL ETIC APPROACH

The pioneering culture-comparative studies of management preferences and practices in different countries by Hofstede (1980 and 2001, 1991) and Laurent (1983) first directed the attention of management scholars and practitioners to the insight that management was not – as seen up till then – a cultural universal, something "done" in the same way the world over. These studies made clear that management is indeed a culturally influenced artefact, which may differ from national culture to national culture (d'Iribarne 2002, 2009). Management was thus no different from many other practices and behaviours within a group, driven by culturally influenced values and preferences and oriented to culturally influenced norms.

It was only a short and perhaps too easy a step to make such otherness responsible for dysfunctional communication, discord and ineffective cooperation across national cultural borders (which indeed they may be but need not be). This attention to the way cultures differ and the difficulties the differences may cause in communication and cooperation has stubbornly continued to this day, although both research and management practice have moved on to tackle other more pressing questions such as how to handle the difficulties – a topic dealt with in the part of this book entitled *Applying Competencies and Resources* – and how to leverage them, a subject addressed in Part 3, *Achieving Complementarity and Synergy*.

These pioneering studies – and those published later by Trompenaars (1993) and House et al. (2004), for example – have been found especially useful by those interested in international management as a result of their *etic* nature: they are empirical; they are quantitative; they are contrastive; and they use a set of concepts which the investigators believe to be common to all cultures and which quickly become familiar to the users of the studies. They assume that all cultures can to a certain extent be described by "measuring" them with the same yardsticks and by placing them at a certain position on descriptive bipolar continua.

Hofstede's original empirical research, published in 1980 in his book *Culture's Consequences: International Differences in Work-related Values* and based on a matched sample of more than 116,000 IBM employees from more than 50 countries, together with subsequent smaller surveys by others, provides the interculturalist, whether scholar or international manager, with insights into differences in work-related values or preferences and the ways in which these values are expressed in behaviour and practices in the organizations and societies to be found in the various country cultures surveyed. Hofstede names the poles of the four basic dimensions he identified in his research: *small power distance* as opposed to *large power distance*; *collectivism* contrasting with *individualism*; *femininity* as opposed to *masculinity*; and *weak uncertainty avoidance* as opposed to *strong uncertainty avoidance*. In subsequent publications, Hofstede, using the results of the Chinese Values Survey (Chinese Culture Connection 1985; Hofstede & Bond 1988) adds a fifth dimension, namely *long-term orientation* as opposed to *short-term orientation*. And most recently, Hofstede, Hofstede and Minkov (2010) have added a sixth dimension, *indulgence* versus *restraint*. The peculiar power of these studies is intensified by the presenting of their results in tables listing scores and indicating positions from highest to lowest and in Hofstede, Hofstede & Minkov (2010) by placing national cultures in global regions leading to an occasional clustering effect.

Since the publication of his work, no examination of a cultural issue in international business or management is complete without at least a mention, either positive or negative, of Hofstede. His quantitative approach has gained many supporters among scholars and HR developers alike – it seems to offer security in a field notoriously subject to the perverting effects of stereotypes and mere individual experience and anecdote. Sometimes, indeed, this interest in applying his results is so dominant as to exclude other insights. Criticism of his insights (for example, by McSweeney (2002), Smith (2002) and Franklin and Spencer-Oatey (2011) and by international managers themselves) has grown in the last decade or more, for example, for being outdated and based on data derived from a single organization, for suggesting a no longer (if ever) current cultural homogeneity, for ignoring the dynamic nature of cultures and for promoting stereotypes.

Building on the work of Kluckhohn and Strodtbeck (1961) and Parsons and Shils (1951), Trompenaars (1993), in his etic study of international managers at Royal Dutch-Shell, generated a set of seven dimensions of cultural variability: *neutral* versus *affective* in the disclosure of feelings; *ascription* versus *achievement* in the assigning of status; *diffuse* versus *specific* in the range of interpersonal involvement; *collectivism* versus *individualism*; *universalism* versus *particularism* in behaviour in relationships with others; and the management of time (*sequential* versus *synchronic*; and *past, present and future*). Although criticism, possibly justified, of the soundness of his data and of the conclusions he has drawn from it has been made by some, in particular by Hofstede (1996), Trompenaars' insights into the dimensions of cultural variation to be found in business and management have also established themselves firmly in the field, particularly when it comes to consultancy and training.

Expanding and refining Hofstede's dimensions, The Global Leadership and Organizational Behavior Effectiveness Research program (GLOBE) (House et al. 2004) more recently investigated the relationship between culture and societal, organizational and leadership effectiveness. Some 170 scholars questioned more than 17,000 middle managers in 62 cultures. Though based on a much smaller sample, it meets some of the criticism levelled at Hofstede's pioneering work: the data was collected in companies in three industries (financial services, food processing and telecommunications) and not just one; the study was the work of a multicultural team of investigators bringing with them all the benefits of multiple, culturally influenced perspectives; and the study's insights are more recent than Hofstede's – work began on the investigation in 1994 and was published in 2004. Strangely, perhaps, despite these obvious merits, the GLOBE study has still not superseded Hofstede in the favours of many scholars, HR development specialists and trainers. And, of course, the study has been the butt of criticism, not least by Hofstede (2006) himself.

2 CRITICISM OF THE ETIC STUDIES AND ITS CONSEQUENCES

These later etic studies can be criticized in certain respects in much the same way that Hofstede's work is: the bipolar continua of the "national cultural model" attempt to describe national and organizational cultures which in their nature may contradict the tacit assumption of the studies that such cultures are homogeneous and static. As McSweeney (2009:936) remarks:

> Culture is not a pre-established monolith. An acknowledgement of internal divisions, gaps and ambiguities inserts an essential element of distance at the heart of tradition and thus the possibility of critical interpretation, action variation and unpredictability within a country.

The "national cultural model" also assumes that cultures are delimited units which reject and fail to influence each other, as if, as Wolf (1982:6) describes, they were billiard balls which merely bounce off each other:

> By endowing nations, societies, or cultures with the qualities of internally homogeneous and externally distinctive and bounded objects, we create a model of the world as a global pool hall in which the entities spin off each other like so many hard and round billiard balls.

This metaphor contrasts starkly with how national cultures, especially, are commonly experienced, appositely summed up by Hannerz (1992:266) as dynamic entities which influence and are influenced by others:

> (T)he flow of culture between countries and continents may result in another diversity of culture, based more on interconnections than on autonomy. It also allows the sense of a complex culture as a network of perspectives, or as an ongoing debate.

Hannerz (1992:266) borrows a term from linguistics when he goes on to speak of the creolization of culture in which:

> a creole culture could also stabilize, or the interplay of center and periphery could go on and on, never settling into a fixed form precisely because of the openness of the global whole.

Precisely the failure to consider this hybridity in the national cultural model is criticized, for example, by Brannen and Salk (2000). In common with others, they point to both structural and contextual factors, and also to individual cultural identities different from a putative group norm, as being critical in the development of hybrid, culturally diverse work-setting cultures and organizations. It seems to be the case that the cultural identities of individuals engaged in intercultural interactions undergo development and are redefined. Static and decontextualized notions of culture are scarcely fit for the purpose of describing and analysing intercultural processes (Primecz et al. 2011; Romani 2008; Søderberg & Holden 2002). National cultural models thus lose their significance as a result of increasing cultural complexity (Hannerz 1992; Romani 2008), increasing intercultural complexity in international management and work settings and the increasing tendency towards multiple membership by individuals of a number of different cultures (Bjerregaard et al. 2009; Zander & Romani 2004), which may in turn vary from core to peripheral membership (Wenger 1998).

Taking account of these considerations, Sackmann and Phillips (2004) distinguish three streams of research in international management:

- The *Cross-National Comparison* stream assumes an equivalence of nation-state and culture. Cultural identity is considered as a given and immutable individual characteristic. Therefore culture is tractable. Generalizations and clustering, as well as cross-national testing of organizational theories, processes and practices, are possible.
- The *Intercultural Interaction* stream considers culture as socially constructed. Nevertheless, national culture and identity are of importance; context and subcultures, as well as organizational culture, may be salient, even if at the moment of interaction new cultures emerge and are negotiated. This stream is based on anthropological theories and interpretive methods.
- The *Multiple Cultures* stream sees culture as a socially constructed collective phenomenon that recognizes the complexity of personal identity in organizational settings, e.g. the multiplicity of cultures. The salience of any

> cultural group depends on the particular case. The research focus relies on sense-making as well as taking into account cultural differences and similarities. This offers possibilities to achieve synergies by building on similar cultural identities.

In short, Sackmann and Phillips' model makes clear that the role concepts and work practices of managers and staff are increasingly shaped not merely by a single, static (national) culture. New dynamic forms of cooperation and work-setting culture result from hybrid meanings and actions (Brannen & Salk 2000) which are constructed and negotiated (Spencer-Oatey & Franklin 2009) by interactants from the various cultural groups involved.

In a controversy among scholars started by Hofstede (1996) and in accordance with this notion of dynamic negotiated culture, Hampden-Turner and Trompenaars present the more static, Hofstedian notion of culture and cultural dimensions and contrast it with their own more dynamic concept:

> Instead of running the risk of getting stuck by perceiving cultures as static points on a dual axis map, we believe that cultures dance from one preferred end to the opposite and back. (Hampden-Turner & Trompenaars 1997:27; see also Hampden-Turner 2000 and Trompenaars 1993)

3 THE EMIC APPROACH TO CULTURAL OTHERNESS IN INTERNATIONAL MANAGEMENT

The etic studies described above and typified by Hofstede's *Culture's Consequences* and the GLOBE study are quantitative and tend to be positivistic in nature (Romani 2008). They contrast with qualitative and, on the whole interpretative, *emic* studies. Like the term etic, the term emic is derived from the field of ethno-linguistics and describes a methodological, culturally adapted research approach in which the researcher takes up a position within a system (Pike 1954). What is to be investigated are system-immanent contextual features. To collect data, researchers use concepts and instruments which to the members of the culture to be investigated appear to be appropriate, relevant and reasonable (Headland et al. 1990; Triandis 1995). Triandis (1994:67–68) appositely compares the two approaches, underlining their usefulness to each other:

> Emics, roughly speaking, are ideas, behaviours, items, and concepts that are culture-specific. Etics, roughly speaking, are ideas, behaviours, items, and concepts that are culture-general – i.e., universal. [...] Emic concepts are essential for understanding a culture. However, since they are unique to the particular culture, they are not useful for cross-cultural comparisons. [...] More formally, emics are studied within the system in one culture, and their structure is discovered within the system. Etics are studies outside the system in more than one culture, and their structure is theoretical. To

develop "scientific" generalizations about relationships among variables, we must use etics. However, if we are going to understand a culture, we must use emics.

Not only methods but also the results and insights of research can display emic, that is to say, context-specific, features. International management research has yielded numerous publications which supply insights into the specifics of organizations and management. Examples are those by Barmeyer and Davoine (2013), Barmeyer and Mayrhofer (2014), Chevrier (2009), Davoine et al. (2014), Delmestri and Walgenbach (2005), Ebster-Grosz and Pugh (1996), Heidenreich at al. (2012), Jackson (2011), Primecz et al. (2011), Stewart et al. (1994), v. Helmolt (1997), Winch et al. (2000) and Witt and Redding (2009).

The French management scholar Philippe d'Iribarne (2003, 2009) and his team have developed a particular emic and contextualized approach to their management research, an approach which interestingly (but unsurprisingly as significant publications are not available in English) has scarcely found its way into the Anglo-American research literature. D'Iribarne (1994) criticizes the fact that much research into the functioning of organizations tends to stress scales of attitudes and values (Hofstede 1980, 2001; Parsons 1952), interactants' strategies (Crozier & Friedberg 1977), or the role of institutions (Maurice et al. 1986; Sorge 1996) and the fact that such studies ignore phenomena which generate continuity in cultures.

D'Iribarne (2009) chooses an ethnographic and interpretive approach and his notion of culture is anthropological in nature. Only by means of an ethnographic-type *thick* description (Geertz 1973), i.e. the most comprehensive collection of features from multiple perspectives which can explain a situation, is it possible to arrive at a comprehensible interpretation of interculturality. (Inter)cultural action is embedded in systems of reference, according to Geertz (1973), that enable interactants to make sense of the world in which they live and of their own actions:

> All cultures denote, classify, identify, evaluate, connect and order. They establish criteria for distinguishing good from evil; the legitimate from the illegitimate. They define the principles of classification by means of which society can be seen to be made up of separate groups. They provide interpretative systems that give meaning to the problems of existence, presenting them as elements in a given order that have therefore to be endured, or as the result of a disturbance of that order, that have consequently to be corrected. (1994:92)

In the same way, action is located in a context and moreover can be derived historically from societal framework conditions. Here, d'Iribarne finds explanations for culturally typical behaviour in the social history of a culture (much as Thomas (1996a, 1996b) does in explaining culture standards). Using corporate case studies, d'Iribarne (2003) impressively shows how interactants in "third-world countries" such as Argentina, Cameroon, Morocco and Mexico who are not able to apply US management methods develop and successfully employ their own contextually adapted management techniques. The interactants d'Iribarne describes question what is customary, are open to what is old and has worked in the past and to what is new and have adapted to the context. They dare to take up contradictory positions which do not accord with the decontextualized, mainstream and so-called success factors such as the best practice of US management models (d'Iribarne 2002).

4 THE CASE STUDIES

Where differences exist, difficulties can be predicted and when difficulties exist, differences can be assumed to be the cause. Those at least are the convenient conclusions which have been drawn from etic and emic studies by scholars and practitioners for many years and which indeed have some foundation in reality. Unfortunately though, this conventional approach rather leaves users of the insights in the lurch: how are they to tackle the difficulties they experience and which – thanks to the studies – they now understand better? Although the cases studies in this part of the book use these contrastive (and to a lesser extent emic) studies to explain the occurrence of cultural differences and difficulties, they in fact go one step further and offer various concepts, models and tools to handle them. The underlying assumption is that cultures are not a source of intractable problems but, indeed, are tractable (Sackmann & Phillips 2004) and that the differences and their consequences are susceptible to being handled effectively and appropriately by the use of the models and tools presented.

The US–Chinese case written by David A. Victor and Christine R. Day, "Harmonizing Expectations: NSF International's Experience in Shanghai", not only explores power distance, one of the cultural dimensions described by Hofstede in his pioneering etic study, but also – particularly crucial in this case – the contrasting behavioural orientations with respect to communication style as described by Hall (1981) in his anthropological studies. However, readers are not simply expected to discover that cultures may differ in certain categories of behaviour and to name these categories. The simple but effective tool that readers are provided with for analysing the cultural aspects of international cooperation also takes due account of the significance of broader contextual factors when it comes to explaining problematic international cooperation.

The case "Planning a Sino-British Workshop: Negotiating Preferences and Achieving Synergy" by Helen Spencer-Oatey also features power distance as a crucial cultural dimension in Chinese–Western intercultural cooperation but in addition devotes attention to the task–relationship dimension, which is well-established if under-researched in the intercultural management literature. These two dimensions (or perspectives as the author refers to them) are interestingly complemented by a discussion of how learning styles may differ across cultures (Barmeyer 2004; Hofstede 1986), with attention here being devoted to two contrasting concepts: on the one hand, that learning consists in knowledge transfer and, on the other, that learning results from a process of co-construction (Jin & Cortazzi 1998; Watkins & Biggs 1996). Borrowing further from Moran (2001), the author introduces the 3Ps (Products, Practices and Perspectives) model as a tool to analyse the dysfunctionality described in the case and to enable the reader to generate a solution.

Taking a step towards correcting the relative lack of attention given to the GLOBE study in the literature, "Intercultural Challenges in International Mergers and Acquisitions: A German–Bulgarian–Romanian Case Study" by Petia Genkova and Anna Gajda uses the results of the GLOBE study to help readers to explain the different expectations and experiences of the various participants in the merger/acquisition (M&A) concerned. Connections are elicited not only to the cultural dimensions results generated by the study but also to its taxonomy of leadership styles. Besides placing the case described against the background of a conventional stages model of M&A, the case also uses Nahavandi and Malekzadeh's (1993) acculturation model to anticipate the cultural change likely to be preferred by the various parties to the M&A.

The Anglo-French case "How to Implement Change in a Post-acquisition Multicultural Context: The Lafarge Experience in Britain" also deals with an M&A. Against the backcloth of a picture of management and working practices perhaps more reminiscent of pre-Thatcherite Britain than the turn of the century when Lafarge's acquisition actually took place, the authors, Evalde Mutabazi and Philippe Poirson, illustrate the difficulties and the confusion which a top manager may experience with diverging managerial approaches in a foreign context (manufacturing, working class, legal framework). They present their own procedural model, which helps to build up "something new" using different organizational and managerial cultures and practices and to guide the M&A process from searching for a suitable partner to integrating two companies. After conducting a cultural analysis readers trace the change process implemented by the French acquirer in the British company and are requested to make further suggestions of their own.

A further tool for handling interculturality and its potential for dysfunctionality is described by Volker Stein and Tobias M. Scholz in "The Intercultural Challenge of Building the European eSports League for Video Gaming". The case describes a truly multicultural cooperation, taking place in the undeniably demanding conditions of virtuality. International teams of the sort described here have to cope with the dual challenge to transactional effectiveness posed not just by its interculturality but also by its virtuality and the impediments this brings, in particular to communication. The virt.cube framework (Scholz 2000) presented makes it possible to assess a virtual team's progress on its way to an optimally functioning virtuality.

Just as virt.cube takes account of factors apart from interculturality which may result from international cooperation, the Cross-Cultural Kaleidoscope™ model described in "Leading Change in Mergers and Acquisitions in Asia–Pacific" by Jenny Plaister-Ten pays due attention to cultural factors but also to the organizational structure of the parties to an M&A and the external environment in which it takes place. The Cross-Cultural Kaleidoscope™ model provides both a macro and a micro view of what contributes to the formation of the values and beliefs that motivate behaviours and influence decisions in organizations operating in culturally complex contexts.

Given the cultural complexity of international work settings, the concept of trust with its function in reducing social complexity (Luhmann 1989; Rousseau et al. 1998) takes on a special significance. The role of trust as a tool for handling interculturality features in one of the case studies in this part of the book.

In the German–Russian–Japanese–Egyptian–Argentinian case "Smart Spacing: The Impact of Locations on Cross-Cultural Trust Building and Decision Making", written by Fritz Audebert, Thilo Beyer and Veronika Hackl, the reader is familiarized with Hall's insights into culturally influenced behavioural orientations with respect to time and space (Hall 1959/1990, 1990; Hall & Hall 1989) and requested to consider how these may trigger business relations and be connected to the building of trust through relationship cultivation. In the context of international business travel, the case illustrates culture-specific spaces and diverse local perspectives on when and where decisions normally take place.

The theme of ethnocentrism plays a role in "IKEA's Ethical Controversies in Saudi Arabia" by Christof Miska and Michaela Pleskova. The case study illustrates both the challenges of ethical variation across cultures and societies, as well as the potential opportunities for positive change that these differences might provide. The case focuses on the removal of women from the Saudi Arabian edition of IKEA's catalogue – a step which was held by some to stand in stark contrast to IKEA's corporate culture and core values. The dispute exposed IKEA to considerable public criticism, but pointed out the responsibilities of multinational corporations (MNCs) in addressing ethical differences across cultures and societies.

REFERENCES

Barmeyer, C. (2004). "Learning styles and their impact on cross-cultural training. An international comparison in France, Germany and Quebec". In: *International Journal of Intercultural Relations*, 28:6, 577–594.

Barmeyer, C. & Davoine, E. (2013). "'Traduttore, Traditore'? La réception contextualisée des valeurs d'entreprise dans les filiales françaises et allemandes d'une entreprise multinationale américaine". In: *Management International/International Management/Gestión Internacional*, 1:18, 26–39.

Barmeyer, C. & Mayrhofer, U. (2014). "How has the French cultural and institutional context shaped the organization of the Airbus Group?". In: *International Journal of Organizational Analysis*, 4:22, 440–462.

Bjerregaard, T., Lauring, J. & Klitmøller, A. (2009). "A critical analysis of intercultural communication research in cross-cultural management introducing newer developments in anthropology". In: *Critical Perspectives on International Business*, 5:3, 207–228.

Brannen, M. Y. & Salk, J. (2000). "Partnering across borders: Negotiating organizational culture in a German-Japanese joint venture". In: *Human Relations*, 52:4, 451–487.

Chevrier, S. (2009). "Is national culture still relevant to management in a global context? The case of Switzerland". In: *International Journal of Cross Cultural Management*, 9, 169.

Chinese Culture Connection (1987). "Chinese values and the search for culture- free dimensions of culture". In: *Journal of Cross-Cultural Psychology*, 18, 143–174.

Crozier, M. & Friedberg E. (1977). *L'Acteur et le Système*, Paris: Le Seuil.

Davoine, E., Oiry, E. & Stokes, P. (2014). "Guest editorial: Special issue on organizations and organizing in a French context". In: *International Journal of Organizational Analysis*, 22:4, 422–425.

Delmestri, G. & Walgenbach, P. (2005). "Mastering techniques or brokering knowledge? Middle managers in Germany, Great Britain and Italy". In: *Organization Studies*, 26, 197–220.

d'Iribarne, P. (1994). "The honour principle in the 'Bureaucratic Phenomenon'". In: *Organization Studies*, 15:1, 81–97.

d'Iribarne, P. (2002). "Motivating workers in emerging countries: Universal tools and local adaptations". In: *Journal of Organizational Behavior*, 23:3, 243–256.

d'Iribarne, P. (2003). *Le Tiers-monde qui Réussit*. Paris: Odile Jacob.

d'Iribarne, P. (2009). "National cultures and organisations in search of a theory: An interpretative approach". In: *International Journal of Cross Cultural Management*, 9:3, 309–321.

Ebster-Grosz, D. & Pugh, D.S. (1996). *Anglo-German Business Collaboration*. Basingstoke: Macmillan.

Franklin, P. & Spencer-Oatey, H. (2011). "Intercultural competence and international management. An overview of the received wisdom and some critical reflections". In: S. Grüninger, M. Fürst, S. Pforr & M. Schmiedeknecht (Eds), *Verantwortung in der globalen Ökonomie gestalten. Governanceethik und Wertemanagement*, 457–459. Marburg: Metropolis.

Geertz, C. (1973). *The Interpretation of Cultures*. London: Hutchinson.

Hall, E. T. (1959/1990). *The Silent Language*. New York: Anchor Books.

Hall, E. T. (1981). *Beyond Culture*. New York: Anchor Books.

Hall, E. T. (1990). *The Hidden Dimension*. New York: Doubleday.

Hall, E. T. & Hall, M. R. (1989). *Understanding Cultural Differences*. Yarmouth: Intercultural Press.

Hampden-Turner, C. (2000). "What we know about cross-cultural management after thirty years". In: D. Lynch & A. Pilbeam (Eds), *Heritage and Progress. From the Past to the Future in Intercultural Understanding*, 17–27. Bath: LTS.

Hampden-Turner, C. & Trompenaars, F. (1997). "Response to Geert Hofstede". In: *International Journal of Intercultural Relations*, 21:1, 149–159.

Hannerz, U. (1992). *Cultural Complexity. Studies in the Social Organization of Meaning*. New York: Columbia University Press.

Headland, T., Pike, K. & Harris, M. (Eds) (1990). *Emic and Etic. The Insider/Outsider Debate*. Newbury Park: Sage.

Heidenreich, M., Barmeyer, C., Koschatzky, K., Mattes, J., Baier, E. & Krüth, K. (2012). *Multinational Enterprises and Innovation: Regional Learning in Networks*. New York/London: Routledge.

Helmolt, K. (1997). *Kommunikation in Internationalen Arbeitsgruppen*. München: iudicium.

Hofstede, G. (1980). *Culture's Consequences. International Differences in Work-related Values*. London: Sage.

Hofstede, G. (1986). "Cultural differences in teaching and learning". In: *International Journal of Intercultural Relations*, 10, 301–320.

Hofstede, G. (1991). *Cultures and Organizations. Intercultural Cooperation and its Importance for Survival*. London: McGraw-Hill.

Hofstede, G. (1996). "Riding the waves of commerce: A test of Trompenaars' 'model' of national culture differences". In: *International Journal of Intercultural Relations*, 20:2, 189–198.

Hofstede, G. (2001). *Culture's Consequences: Comparing Values, Behaviors, Institutions and Organizations Across Nations*. Thousand Oaks, CA: Sage.

Hofstede, G. (2006). "What did GLOBE really measure? Researchers' minds versus respondents' minds". In: *Journal of International Business Studies,* 37, 882–896.

Hofstede, G. & Bond, M. H. (1988). "The Confucius connection: From cultural roots to economic growth". In: *Organizational Dynamics*, 16, 4–21.

Hofstede, G., Hofstede, G. J. & Minkov, M. (2010). *Cultures and Organizations, Software of the Mind. Intercultural Cooperation and its Importance for Survival.* New York: McGraw Hill.

House, R. J., Hanges, P. J., Javidan, M., Dorfman, P. W. & Gupta, V. (2004). *Culture, Leadership, and Organizations. The GLOBE Study of 62 Societies*. Thousand Oaks, CA: Sage.

Jackson, T. (2011). "From cultural values to cross-cultural interfaces: Hofstede goes to Africa". In: *Journal of Organizational Change Management*, 24:4, 532–558.

Jin, L. & Cortazzi, M. (1998). "The culture the learner brings: A bridge or a barrier?". In: M. Byram & M. Fleming (Eds), *Language Learning in Intercultural Perspective: Approaches Through Drama and Ethnography*. 98–118. Cambridge: Cambridge University Press.

Kluckhohn, F. R. & Strodtbeck, F. L. (1961/1973). *Variations in Value Orientations*. New York: Harper & Row.

Laurent, A. (1983). "The cultural diversity of Western conceptions of management". In: *International Studies of Management and Organization*, 13:1–2, 75–96.

Luhmann, N. (1989). *Vertrauen. Ein Mechanismus der Reduktion Sozialer Komplexität*. Stuttgart: Lucius & Lucius.

Maurice, M., Sellier, F. & Silvestre, J.-J. (1986). *The Social Foundation of Industrial Power: A Comparison of France and Germany*. Cambridge, MA: MIT Press.

McSweeney, B. (2002). "Hofstede's model of national cultural differences and their consequences: a triumph of faith – a failure of analysis". In: *Human Relations*, 55:1, 89–118.

McSweeney, B. (2009). "Dynamic diversity: Variety and variation within countries". In: *Organization Studies*, 30:9, 933–957.

Mishra, A. K. & Mishra K. E. (2013). *Becoming a Trustworthy Leader. Psychology and Practice*. London: Routledge.

Moran, P. (2001). "Language and culture". In: *Teaching Culture: Perspectives in Practice*, 6:1, 34–47.

Nahavandi, A. & Malekzadeh, A. (1993). *Organizational Culture in the Management of Mergers*. Westport: Quorum Books.

Parsons, T. (1952). *The Social System*. New York: Free Press.

Parsons, T. & Shils, E. A. (1951). *Toward a General Theory of Action*. Cambridge, MA: Harvard University Press.

Pike, K. (1954). *Language in Relation to a Unified Theory of the Structure of Human Behavior*. The Hague: Mouton.

Primecz, H., Romani, L. & Sackmann, S. A. (2011). *Cross-cultural Management in Practice. Culture and Negotiated Meanings*. Cheltenham: Edward Elgar Publishing.

Romani, L. (2008). *Relating to the Other. Paradigm Interplay for Cross-cultural Management Research*. Stockholm: Elanders.

Rousseau, D. M., Sitkin, S. B., Burt, R. S. & Camerer, C. (1998). "Not so different after all: A cross-discipline view of trust". In: *Academy of Management Review*, 23:3, 393–404.

Sackmann, S. A. & Phillips, M. E. (2004). "Contextual influences on culture research: Shifting assumptions for new workplace realities". In: *International Journal of Cross Cultural Management*, 4:3, 370–390.

Scholz, C. (2000). "Virtualisierung als Wettbewerbsstrategie für den Mittelstand? Erste Erfahrungen und ergänzende Überlegungen". In: *Zeitschrift für Betriebswirtschaft*, 70:2, 201–222.

Smith, P. B. (2002). "Culture's consequences: Something old and something new". In: *Human Relations*, 55:1, 119–135.

Søderberg, A.-M. & Holden, N. J. (2002). "Rethinking cross-cultural management in a globalising business world". In: *International Journal of Cross Cultural Management*, 2, 103–21.

Sorge, A. (1996). "Societal effects in cross-national organization studies: Conceptualizing diversity in actors and systems". In: R. Whitley & P. H. Kristensen (Eds), *The Changing European Firm*, 67–86. London: Routledge.

Spencer-Oatey, H. & Franklin, P. (2009). *Intercultural Interaction. A Multidisciplinary Approach to Intercultural Communication*. London: Palgrave Macmillan.

Stewart, R., Barsoux, J.-L., Kieser, A., Ganter, H. D. & Walgenbach P. (1994). *Managing in Britain and Germany*. New York: St Martin's Press.

Thomas, A. (1996a). "Analyse der Handlungswirksamkeit von Kulturstandards". In: A. Thomas (Ed.), *Psychologie interkulturellen Handelns*, 107–135. Göttingen: Hofgrefe-Verlag.

Thomas, A. (1996b). *Psychologie Interkulturellen Handelns*. Göttingen: Hogrefe-Verlag.

Triandis, H. (1995). Individualism and Collectivism. Boulder, CO: Westview Press.

Triandis, H. C. (1994). *Culture and Social Behavior*. New York: McGraw Hill.

Trompenaars, F. (1993). *Riding the Waves of Culture*. London: Nicholas Brealey Publishing.

Watkins, D. A. & Biggs, J. B. (1996). *The Chinese Learner: Cultural, Psychological and Contextual Influences*. Hong Kong: Comparative Education Research Centre & Victoria, Australia: The Australian Council for the Educational Research.

Wenger, E. (1998). *Communities of Practice. Learning, Meaning, and Identity*. Cambridge: Cambridge University Press.

Winch, G. M., Clifton, N. & Millar, C. (2000). "Organization and management in an Anglo-French consortium. The case of Transmanche-Link". In: *Journal of Management Studies*, 37:7, 663–665.

Witt, M. A. & Redding, G. (2009). "Culture, meaning, and institutions: Executive rationale in Germany and Japan". In: *Journal of International Business Studies*, 40, 859–885.

Wolf, E. R. (1982). *Europe and the People Without History*. Berkeley: University of California Press.

Zander, L. & Romani, L. (2004). "When nationality matters. A study of departmental, hierarchical, professional, gender and age-based employee groupings' leadership preference across 15 countries". In: *International Journal of Cross Cultural Management*, 4:3, 291–315.

2

Harmonizing Expectations: NSF International's Experience in Shanghai

David A. Victor and Christine R. Day

1 INTRODUCTION

In an increasingly integrated world economy, business relationships between the USA and the People's Republic of China (PRC) are among those which have grown most rapidly in the last 40 years. However, this development has been hampered by major differences in the two nations' cultural outlook and business norms. This case presents a critical incident illustrating some of the challenges businesses face in US–Chinese interaction.

At the same time as managing the problems posed by differing cultures and norms, organizations have also found that in order to remain competitive, strategies which were once local or regional must now be global. The difficulty is that often the policies and practices that work effectively in one nation or region cannot be applied to all situations globally.

This particular case describes one organization's entry into the Chinese market. Responding to considerable pressure from competitors and to strong customer demand, NSF International opened a facility in Shanghai, China. Once operational, the entire NSF International team faced several challenges and dilemmas that were unfamiliar based on their US or Chinese experience. This case describes the details of the situation and the way in which NSF International worked successfully to create harmonization in one cross-cultural challenge that arose from this new business venture.

2 CASE DESCRIPTION

2.1 The situation: company background

The organization: NSF International NSF International is a public health and environmental organization. It "provides standards development, product certification, auditing, education, and risk management for public health and the environment" (NSF 2013). NSF International provides services in more than 150 countries.

NSF was founded in 1944 as the National Sanitation Foundation (NSF). When NSF expanded services beyond sanitation and into the international market, NSF changed its name to NSF International. NSF International is "an accredited, third-party organization that tests and certifies products to verify that they meet specific public health and safety standards" (NSF 2013). Once certified, these products bear the NSF Mark, which is recognized for its value in international trade around the world and is respected by "consumers, manufacturers, retailers, and regulatory agencies at the local, state, federal, and international level" (NSF 2013). NSF International is a World Health Organization Collaborating Centre for Food and Water Safety and Indoor Environment (NSF 2013).

> Manufacturers, regulators, and consumers alike look to NSF International for the development of public health, standards and certification that help protect the world's food, water, health, and consumer products. (NSF 2013)

NSF's mission is to be:

> the leading global provider of public health and safety-based risk management solutions while serving the interests of all stakeholders, namely the public, the business community, and governmental agencies. (NSF Mission, NSF 2013)

NSF International's headquarters are in Ann Arbor, Michigan (USA).

NSF International's laboratories are ISO 17025 certified (testing and calibration), and these laboratories provide a wide range of testing, certification and technical services for home appliances and consumer product industries (e.g. children's products, beverage quality, food service equipment, nutritional supplements, drinking water treatment units and automotive aftermarket parts) food retailers, growers, processors and seafood industries. The organization tests and certifies pipes, plumbing components and treatment chemicals for the water industry, and provides analytical testing for the supplement and pharmaceutical industry (NSF 2013). Its "1,200-plus staff includes microbiologists, toxicologists, chemists, engineers, environmental and public health professionals" (NSF 2013).

The need for a laboratory in China In 2008, NSF International felt considerable pressure from competitors who had more laboratories and testing centres around the world. Additional pressure came to bear on NSF International to test products locally, nearer to their place of origin. At this time, the region with the greatest number of NSF clients was in Asia-Pacific, so it was logical for NSF International to want to focus on expanding by adding a local testing laboratory there. The business units were repeatedly asked about NSF testing capabilities in China by Chinese clients and also by US-based clients with manufacturing operations in China. Management, however, wanted to continue to send clients to the Ann Arbor site, which had recently opened expanded and updated laboratory facilities. Consequently, the attempt to start a laboratory in China was side-tracked in the initial planning phases.

At the time of the original enquiries, Kurt Kneen, NSF International's Director of Chemistry, was located at the organization's US headquarters. Kneen had previously helped plan the major expansion of the headquarters' laboratory facilities in Ann Arbor, so he had acquired considerable expertise in building laboratories. As a result of the headquarters' expansion success, he was asked to be involved in exploratory efforts to determine the needs and equipment for a possible Chinese laboratory in Shanghai. Although interest in the project had waned, in an effort to be forward thinking Kneen continued to meet with other technical experts to evaluate what the Shanghai laboratory should include. In this way, he would be prepared if it ever needed to be put in place.

Eventually NSF International experienced a change of personnel at the senior leadership level. As a result, almost a year after the initial enquiries, the new leadership wanted to revisit the possibility of a laboratory in China. Kneen retrieved his plans from the original initiative. Interestingly, the push for the laboratory started coming from the technical people who had direct client contact in China. These clients had expressed a strong desire for NSF International to provide laboratory services locally. The technical people, whose relationship with the clientele was very closely knit, also conveyed this urgency. In spite of this, the US-based senior leaders were still hesitant about building a laboratory in China.

This need was discussed with NSF International's President, Kevan Lawloer, who decided it was important for NSF International to build a laboratory in China. With Lawloer's decision came the authority to push for the additional programmes needed to offer testing capabilities. This allowed other executives, as Kneen explained it, "to give in a little bit". In other words, the reluctant executives could comfortably revise their position.

Kneen further explained:

> By early July, 2010, we started to say that we were going to have a testing facility. We selected a site and began the process of hiring a site manager to help with establishing a budget to be presented to the Board in November.

The next big hurdle was the budget process. Typically, NSF International begins its annual budgeting process in August. The final proposals are presented to the Board of Directors for approval in November, for a January implementation. This process was not as smooth with the China laboratory project. Budget timing impacted the Shanghai proposal, creating a start-and-stop development sequence. As a result, during the August to November 2008 budget sequence, the proposal was not yet in place. Eventually, in November 2009, the Shanghai Laboratory project budget was approved for 2010.

2.2 The challenge

Staffing in China With the 2010 budget approved for the Shanghai Laboratory, NSF International began to search in China for candidates to fill staff positions. Of considerable help was Sol Yusu, a Chinese consultant with Asian experience, as well as a professional staffing firm. Although Kneen did not have any recruiting experience, he drew on his ten years of management experience to help him select candidates through the interviewing process. The quality of the candidates was exceptional. One criterion that helped to serve as a filter was a certification of English proficiency.

During the staffing process, one concern that NSF International had was the concept of Chinese employee turnover: deliberate quick job changes to enhance one's career, sometimes called "job-hopping". NSF International did not want to get caught in the triangle of an employee exiting one company to work at another, only to leave a short time later to return to a former company or to move to yet a third company.

In April 2010, an excellent candidate, Dongjing Liu, was offered the position of the laboratory site manager. With this position filled and an initial specification for the lab (a result of ongoing meetings with business unit managers/ executives during the whole process), Kneen and his new team developed the design and selected a building contractor. Kneen felt that the implementation was moving forward.

The budget process, however, came back into play. As 2010 progressed, budget approval for 2011 became crucial. Nothing could proceed without budget approval. This was a strict rule at NSF International. Interviewing could not continue, and no further commitments could be made until headquarters budget approval was obtained.

Finally, November 2010 arrived, and so did the next year's budget approval. The Shanghai Laboratory could now determine the number of additional staff needed and interviewing resumed. Before, when developing the initial plans for the laboratory, Kneen had had some concern that potential employees would be unwilling to come to NSF International. Liu voiced another concern that potential employees would not be willing to leave their present position, and with it that position's expected compensation bonus. To Liu, these pressures seemed worse because it was so close to the end of the year. Liu expressed her concern (but without emphasizing her point), and spoke so indirectly that Kneen did not realize the importance of the issue.

Despite concerns, 35–40 strong candidates applied for a wide variety of positions at the laboratory, including chemists, engineers, project managers, quality assurance managers, a salesperson and others. Kneen interviewed the chemist, engineer, project manager and sales candidates, and Liu focused on hiring the technician-level employees. In all, NSF International's Shanghai Laboratory hired ten outstanding candidates as employees, including six chemists, one engineer, one project manager, one salesperson and one marketing employee. In addition, Liu hired two technicians and a caretaker (as the building owners did not provide this service).

By the end of 2010, operations at the Shanghai Laboratory had been very productive and more successful than either Kneen or Liu had expected. They had found so many solid candidates (and assigned responsibilities), construction was going well, sources for technical equipment and supplies were identified and employee benefits were determined. The site had a group of employees who had started before the end of 2010, plus another group who were scheduled to start at the beginning of January 2011. Most of the employees began work in December and continued to work through the entire month, even though they were working for an organization which would normally break during the Christmas holidays. These employees were dedicated, bright, and energetic.

In December, Liu started talking to Kneen about the upcoming Chinese New Year, which would be celebrated in February 2011. She mentioned that she felt bad that these new workers gave up bonuses to work for NSF. Only one new employee would retain her bonus, because she came from a pre-existing joint venture that NSF International had in Shanghai. Liu believed that this might cause tension with the other employees.

Liu also expressed strong concern about possible morale issues. As with many North Americans, Kneen was unfamiliar with the impact of the Chinese New Year traditions. It was his preconception that the Chinese New Year traditions were comparable to the casual, low-key New Year celebrations in North America, which are generally little more than a champagne toast and a wish of good luck. He did not understand that the Chinese New Year is the equivalent of the North American Christmas holiday, when employers give very generous gifts and employees travel extensively to visit family. In fact, the Chinese holiday is celebrated so extensively that related travel creates the largest annual movement of people in the world.

As a North American, Kneen had no cultural understanding of the implications of Chinese New Year to the employees and their families. Furthermore, he had no knowledge of the nuances regarding the Chinese New Year bonus, particularly that it is not performance-based. Kneen came to realize that the main purpose for the Chinese bonus is to provide the means by which individuals can travel home to visit their families. Providing a bonus is more about morale (while the size of the bonus is dependent on performance).

During the month of December and continuing into January, Kneen began purposefully to get to know the employees. He took them out to dinner, one at a time, so that he could learn why they came to NSF International and what was motivating them, especially since they all had left good jobs. Employees mentioned in one way or another that they came to NSF International because its core mission was to protect public health and safety. Employees had an ideological motivation and adamantly described to Kneen that they liked contributing to taking care of people. Making a contribution to health and public safety was the main driver for these employees to come to work for NSF International, which these employees saw as an "arm" of the government in its work for health and public safety.

As Kneen pointed out, "All of these employees were consistently dedicated and making significant personal sacrifice." One example was an employee who, when hired, had lived a long drive away with her parents. She moved to an apartment closer to NSF, so she could work the longer hours that she deemed necessary, even though this was not required of her. Another employee, Kneen observed, never took a "break", or a day off. On one occasion, her email autoreply said that she was out of the office. Kneen sent her a note that he was glad that she was finally taking a break. About 20 minutes later, she responded to the email – which meant she really was not off work at all!

In the beginning of January 2011, Liu began reminding Kneen that the Chinese New Year was coming in less than a month, mentioning that people had given up their bonuses to come to work at the Shanghai Laboratory.

NSF International had some very specific practices related to bonuses. First, it did not give bonuses to laboratory staff, due to the fact that it is a not-for-profit organization. There was a small portion of compensation dedicated to what is called gain share, an award directly connected to performance. The organization had very strict rules governing gain share application. Employees at NSF International did not fully participate in gain share until they had achieved one year on the job; employees with service of six months to a year would receive a portion of gain share; and employees with less than six months on the job would receive no gain share. Kneen verified with the chief financial officer (CFO) at the US headquarters that this practice was in place, and that the organization would not have any gainsharing for the new Shanghai Laboratory employees due to the fact that they had not been employed long enough.

Compensation issues Kneen was gradually becoming aware that Liu was recommending that the Shanghai Laboratory employees receive a Chinese New Year bonus. To reiterate the situation, Kneen explained the gainsharing process thoroughly to Liu and carefully pointed out that the employees were not eligible for gain share.

As January progressed, Liu talked more and more urgently about the Chinese New Year bonus. Kneen tried to listen with an open mind. When she used the comparison that it is like Christmas, the message started to dawn on Kneen. As a result of his interactions with the employees, too, Kneen began to rethink his understanding of the need for Chinese New Year bonuses.

Contributing to this, Kneen started to re-evaluate how hard these new employees were working and what they had given up to come to NSF. He wanted to reinforce to them the idea that NSF has a culture that respects and appreciates its employees. In fact, at this point, Kneen, in his own words, "started to panic a little bit". He knew he was facing a dilemma: how could he respect the cultural expectations of his Chinese employees, while still abiding by NSF International's policies?

Kneen approached the US headquarters again, but the answer remained very firm. The gainsharing policy would be applied equally across all employees. There were specific policies, and they had to be applied. Kneen was given no flexibility.

3 BACKGROUND KNOWLEDGE

3.1 The authors' point of reference

The authors, David A. Victor and Christine R. Day, are specialists in international business, international communication, conflict management and global management practices. They believe in the importance of cultural context in the global application of organizational practices. Relationship building, organizational structure, specific processes, practices and global culture have a fluid interaction that impacts the dynamics of any given situation. Resolution can often be found in the specific effort of those involved to forge a bond of harmonizing expectations.

David A. Victor is the Editor-in-Chief of the Global Advances in Business Communication Journal (http://commons.emich.edu/gabc/). He also shares global cultural information at: www.davidvictorvector.blogspot.com.

3.2 Concepts, models, frameworks

Cultural differences and their consequences at work The LESCANT approach (Borisoff & Victor 1998; Victor 1992) provides a framework for accommodating cultures in a workplace setting. The model focuses on uncovering differences in seven areas that affect the meaning of the message in a business setting.

These seven areas make up the acronym that gives the LESCANT model its name:

- **L**anguage
- **E**nvironment and technology conception (whether one attempts to control, accommodate or act in harmony with one's surroundings)
- **S**ocial organizational frame of reference (regarding views of education, family, gender, institutions, etc.)
- **C**ontexting and face-saving
- **A**uthority conception
- **N**on-verbal behaviour
- **T**ime perception

The LESCANT model encourages those using it to forgo a checklist of what to do and what not to do, but rather to ask questions regarding these seven elements to determine the culture of the individual within a national culture (e.g. US or Chinese), a subculture (e.g. African American or South Chinese), a regional culture (e.g. metropolitan Detroit or a town in rural Anhui Province), an occupational culture (e.g. a marketing manager or an accountant), a corporate culture (e.g. a Fortune 500 corporate headquarters or a ten-person call centre serving a distant regional market), and as a person with any number of other characteristics (length of experience in the position, educational experience, and so on).

All of these divisions, in turn, are affected by attitudes of culture shaped by language, environment and technology, social organization, contexting, authority conception, non-verbal behaviour and the concept of time. The LESCANT model provides a frame of reference for the assessment of culture at each level. Thus, when framing a message to send to an individual or while interpreting a message from him or her, one can adjust for culture at multiple levels through analysing the seven LESCANT elements at each.

3.3 Recommended reading

Cardon, P. W. (2009). "A model of face practices in Chinese business culture: Implications for western businesspersons". In: *Thunderbird International Business Review*, 5:11, 19–36.
Cardon reports findings of in-depth interviews about the role of face in Chinese business culture, such as giving face, protecting face, vying for face, and not considering face. Cardon provides examples of the various face practices in business situations to illustrate related behaviours. The article defines a model of dominant face practices and related strategies based on business relationships. Related recommendations are provided for business practitioners and researchers.

McGregor, J. (2007). *One Billion Customers: Lessons from the Front Lines of Doing Business in China*. New York: Free Press.
As the managing partner of a major venture capital firm in the PRC who was also formerly the China Bureau Chief for the Wall Street Journal, James McGregor brings to his book a unique perspective on the practical issues facing foreign business in the PRC. This book is a guide to doing business in China (for both the foreign and the Chinese business person) provided through a collection of explanations of business deals (both successful and failed), and of insightful stories regarding some of China's major business leaders.

Rhinesmith, S. (1993). *A Manager's Guide to Globalization*. Alexandria, VA: American Society for Training and Development/Irwin.
Rhinesmith focuses on global competitiveness, specifically on the importance of a global mindset. He describes how this understanding impacts leadership, talent retention and organizational growth. The book provides an in-depth understanding of the application of the global mindset. The dynamics of the global mindset emphasize a "predisposition to see the world in a particular way that sets boundaries and provides explanations for why things are the way they are, while at the same times establishing guidance for ways in which we should behave" (Rhinesmith 1993:24). Rhinesmith further suggests that "a mindset is a filter through which we look at the world" and he advocates that people with global mindsets drive for the bigger, broader picture; accept life as a balance of contradictory forces that are to be appreciated, pondered and managed; trust process rather than structure to deal with the unexpected; value diversity and multicultural teamwork and play as the basic forum within which they accomplish their personal, professional and organizational objectives; flow with change as opportunity and are comfortable with surprises and ambiguity; and continuously seek to be open to themselves and others by rethinking boundaries, finding new meanings and changing their direction and behaviour (Rhinesmith 1993:25–26).

Tan, J. S. & Lim, E. N. (2004). *Strategies for Effective Cross-Cultural negotiation: The F.R.A.M.E. approach*. Singapore: Mc-Graw Hill Asia.
This book focuses on effective strategies for cross-cultural negotiation, using an approach called F.R.A.M.E. Using a case study approach, the book presents an incisive analysis of the successes and failures as well as some practical

negotiation tips (dos and don'ts) for cross-cultural negotiation. The book provides a focus of multinationals in three Asian markets: China, Japan and India.

Tian, X. (2007). ***Managing International Business in China.*** **Cambridge: Cambridge University Press.**
This book provides a close look at pragmatic Chinese managerial practice from the perspective of non-Chinese business practitioners working in the PRC. Tian's work provides cases and examples along with explanation of such key Chinese business practices as the role of guanxi (influence and connections), site selection, strategic alliance management, negotiation style, human resource management, marketing concerns, intellectual property protection and corporate financial management.

Varner, I. & Beamer, L. (2010). ***Intercultural Communication in the Global Workplace,*** **5th ed. New York: McGraw-Hill.**
This book presents issues of culture and communication within the context of doing business globally. By using a variety of examples from multiple countries, the research focuses on the impact of relationships, cultural environments, communication and business practices.

Victor, D. A. (1992). ***International Business Communication.*** **New York, NY: HarperCollins.**
Using the LESCANT model, the book encourages the assessment of needs in any international business interaction by isolating and evaluating those aspects of culture most likely to affect communication. This creates a contextual framework for business to be conducted across cultures. The book also asserts that asking the right questions is crucial in global business interactions. The LESCANT model itself is an acronym for the seven areas of cultural difference most likely to arise in the workplace: **L**anguage, **E**nvironment & technology, **S**ocial organization, **C**ontexting, **A**uthority conception, **N**on-verbal behaviour and **T**emporal conception.

Verluyten, P. (2000). ***Intercultural Communication in Business and Organizations.*** **Leuven, Belgium: ACCO.**
This book focuses on topics and strategies for approaches to intercultural communication on a range of concepts such as negotiation, socialization and presentation skills.

4 QUESTIONS ON THE CASE

1. Which of the LESCANT model's factors play a role in this case and how? Use the table on the next page to record your answer.
2. What were the effects of the way in which the Chinese site manager handled the situation?
3. What other cultural factors had an impact on the decision-making process, communication issues and other features of this case?
4. What synergistic options are open to Kneen?

Table 2.1 LESCANT factors

LESCANT factors	Chinese culture	US culture	NSF International's culture
Language			
Environment and technology conception			
Social organizational frame of reference			
Contexting and face-saving			
Authority conception			
Non-verbal behaviour			
Time perception			

5 REFERENCES

Borisoff, D. & Victor, D. A. (1998). *Conflict Management: A Communication Skills Approach*. Boston: Allyn and Bacon.

NSF International (2013). NSF International history. Retrieved on 16 May 2013 from www.nsf.org/business/about_NSF

Victor, D. A. (1992). *International Business Communication*. New York: HarperCollins.

3

Planning a Sino-British Collaborative Workshop: Negotiating Preferences and Achieving Synergy

Helen Spencer-Oatey

1 INTRODUCTION

Project teams are frequently globally dispersed, but as Maznevski and Chudoba (2000) report, effective teams develop a rhythm of regular face-to-face sessions. During those face-to-face sessions, time is at a premium and it is vital for project members to maximize the benefits of being together. However, different members may have different priorities for such events, and some elements may even be out of their control. Stakeholders may have certain expectations or demands, and there can be practical constraints such as budget limitations. All of these factors require effective management if the face-to-face event is to achieve everyone's goals and aspirations. This authentic case study examines the experiences of British and Chinese collaborators as they attempt to plan a workshop at a distance.

2 CASE DESCRIPTION

"Oh dear me", "nightmare", "hijacked"! These are some of the reactions from British staff when trying to negotiate the agenda for a three-day workshop in Beijing, China. What were the problems they were experiencing and why was such a "simple event" so difficult to agree on and arrange? This case study explores these issues.

Background to the joint workshop The joint workshop in this case study was a component of the Sino-UK e-Learning (eChina–UK) Programme, which was a national-level collaborative e-learning initiative, established in the UK by the Higher Education Funding Council for England (HEFCE) and in China by the Chinese Ministry of Education (MoE). It ran from 2002 to

2009 and comprised a number of teacher training projects in which staff from British and Chinese universities worked together to develop e-learning courseware. HEFCE and the MoE hoped that, as the academics worked together on various specific tasks, the partnerships would yield a range of insights of benefit to both countries, including insights into collaborating across cultures. In fact, the project members faced a complex, interacting set of challenges and the difficulties they experienced in arranging this workshop illustrate just one of them.

The projects associated with this case study workshop are shown in Table 3.1.

Table 3.1 The projects and partnerships of the initial phase of the *eChina–UK Programme*

Topic Area		Project Name	Partner Universities	
			Chinese	British
Generic approaches and methods: teaching methodology, educational psychology and educational technology		DEfT (Developing e-Learning for Teachers) Project	Beijing Normal University (BNU)	World Universities Network. Lead = University of Manchester. Supporting = Universities of Sheffield, Southampton and Bristol
Teaching English as a Foreign Language	Secondary level	Secondary eELT (e-English Language Teaching)	Beijing Normal University (BNU)	University of Nottingham
	Tertiary level	Tertiary eELT (e-English Language Teaching)	Beijing Foreign Studies University (BFSU)	University of Nottingham
English language for Chinese university lecturers		CUTE (Chinese University Teachers of English)	Tsinghua University	Lead = University of Cambridge. Supporting = Open University

HEFCE appointed a programme manager, Marie,[1] to manage all of the projects on behalf of the UK. There was no exact counterpart programme manager in China; instead there were two programme officers in two different sections of the MoE who handled strategic matters, and a programme administrative officer in one of the Chinese partner universities (Beijing Normal University). Each project within the eChina–UK Programme had a British

[1]All personal names have been changed and department/section names in organizations anonymized.

project manager and a Chinese project manager, and three out of the four projects also had project directors in both the UK and China. The number of project members within each British and Chinese partner university ranged from about 10 to 35, and there were also a number of associates. The total number of people working on the eChina–UK projects came to over 100, not counting the stakeholders (HEFCE and MoE staff) and steering committee members.

At the beginning of phase one of the eChina-UK Programme, a workshop was held in the UK so that the staff from the various projects could meet together to share ideas and discuss progress, both within the projects and over the programme as a whole. The workshop went very smoothly and it was agreed that it would be good to hold a second one and that it should be located in Beijing.[2] This second workshop was to take place near the end of the first phase of the programme, when both British and Chinese project members had become familiar with working together and had travelled frequently to each other's locations. However, since there was to be a second phase to the collaboration, one of the main aims of the workshop was for the different project teams to learn from each other so that learning from phase one could be of benefit to phase two.

Planning the joint workshop In September 2004, one of the Chinese project directors who had good relations with the Chinese MoE proposed that the workshop take place at his university in March 2005. This was provisionally agreed upon and all the project teams started thinking about what they wanted to achieve through it. In early December 2004, HEFCE informed Marie, the British programme manager, that they and MoE representatives would like to attend Day One of the workshop and that the content and focus of that day should be oriented towards senior policy people. This was a surprise to Marie, and she commented as follows to one of the Chinese project managers:

> This will require a bit of rethinking as to how to organize the workshop. I'll discuss with the UK side next Wednesday, but we will then need quite a lot of liaison with you.
>
> (Email from Marie to one of the Chinese project managers 10 December 2004)

Marie received no further news during December, and so in early January she arranged a meeting with the British project managers to draft a provisional agenda. She then sent it to the MoE, commenting as follows: "These are the thoughts of the UK team members, but we would be pleased to have your feedback and suggestions for improvement" (Email, dated 12 January 2005). The draft agenda is shown in Table 3.2.

In mid-January, even though the workshop was only about two months away, none of the Chinese project staff members had been told anything about it by the MoE. British project members were pressing Marie for confirmation that the workshop was going ahead, as they wanted to book their plane tickets. Marie, meanwhile, had many practical questions for the Chinese side, such as

[2]As can be seen from Table 3.1, all the Chinese universities were located in Beijing.

Table 3.2 Initial draft agenda proposed by British staff

	Day One: ICT Policy and Practice (Day One to be attended by British and Chinese Policy Makers)	
09.45	Welcome	Chinese representative
09.50	Introduction	[Name], Senior member of Dept B, HEFCE
10.00	**Project Reports**	
	Introduction	Marie, British Programme Manager
	Tertiary eELT Project: BFSU and U of Nottingham	Chinese representative
	Secondary eELT Project: BNU and U of Nottingham	UK representative
11.00	Break	
11.15	DEfT Project: BNU and WUN	Chinese representative
	CUTE Project: Tsinghua U and U of Cambridge	UK representative
12.15	Lunch	
14:00	**Disseminating Good Practice**	
	Plans for dissemination	Marie, British Programme Manager
	Dissemination website	[Name], British project member responsible for dissemination plans in UK
14.45	**International ICT Issues**	
	Integrated & scalable eLanguage learning	[Name], CUTE project, British project director
	Managing learners' cognitive & affective needs in eLearning	[Name], Tertiary eELT project, British project director
15.25	Break	
15.40	**International ICT Issues (contd.)**	
	Quality assurance & eEducator training	[Name], DEfT Project, British project member
	IPR in international eLearning programmes	[Name], British project member responsible for IP issues
16.20	Response from the Stakeholders	[Name], Head of Dept A, HEFCE [Name], Head of Dept X, MoE
	Day Two: Demonstration & Discussion of Project Courseware Demonstrations by each of the projects of extended samples of their eLearning courseware, followed by questions and discussion.	
	Day Three: Research and Dissemination	
9:30	Comparing perceptions of effective environments for learning	[Name], British associate project member

(Continued)

Table 3.2 (*Continued*)

10.30	International teamworking	Marie, British Programme Manager
11.00	Break	
11.15	Team discussion of dissemination themes and narratives (within projects): • eLearning pedagogy • eLearning production processes • technical design and integration	
12.45	Lunch	
14.00	Cross-team group discussions of dissemination themes & narratives	
15.00	Plenary discussion of dissemination themes & narratives	
16.00	Close of workshop	

what the policy people attending on Day One would most likely be interested in; how long they would probably stay; whether the talks would need interpreting; who would be attending from the Chinese project teams, and so on. However, she could not get an answer from them on any of these points. The Chinese project partners were equally concerned. One emailed Marie in early January saying "We are still waiting for detailed information from the MoE about the March workshop (the organizer, the funding, etc.). I hope that they don't come at the last minute." So, on 14 January, Marie commented in an email to two HEFCE staff that she had a "very deep unease about the whole situation".

On 21 January there was a slight breakthrough: the Chinese project partners emailed to say that they had been officially informed about the workshop and that a meeting had been planned for the following week, when they would discuss and agree an agenda. Marie then emailed the MoE to explain the British project members' aspirations:

> It's very important that we have a major "working workshop" for the "team workers" (Days 2 & 3), so that we can draw out the important insights and lessons from the collaborative programme. We therefore need to make sure that appropriate people from the Chinese projects are present on Days 2 & 3. I have asked the UK teams to liaise with their partners on this, and I will send you further information when I receive it.
>
> (Email from Marie to MoE, 25 January 2005)

For budget reasons, only about 20 British project members could fly to Beijing for the workshop, and Marie was concerned that the Chinese partners would (be obliged to) send figureheads to the workshop, rather than the grassroots people who had been working with the British staff on their collaborative projects. So, on 27 January, she reiterated this in an email to a Chinese colleague on one of the projects saying, "One of the main purposes of the workshop (from the UK team's perspective) is to discuss and share things together, so it's very important that a sufficient number of Chinese team members attend."

Meanwhile, Marie had not yet had any feedback on the draft programme and she was becoming increasingly concerned that time was getting very tight. People needed to prepare their talks, and since the slides needed to have some Chinese translation included this could not be left to the last minute. On 31 January she received an email from the MoE as follows:

> We from our side are dedicated to make this workshop a very successful and interactive one. As you have already noticed, we have entrusted [Chinese name] from [name of Chinese university] to liaise on behalf of us. You may contact her for details of the workshop arrangements.
>
> (Email from MoE to Marie, 31 January 2005)

At the end of that same week, 4 February, Marie received the "tentative programme/agenda" prepared by the Chinese side – see Table 3.3.

Table 3.3 Revised draft agenda prepared by the Chinese side

Day One: ICT Policy and Practice (Day One to be attended by British and Chinese Policy Makers)		
09.00	**Opening Ceremony** Host introduces honoured participants and guests	Host – to be decided
09.10	Address	Manager, Dept. X, MoE
09.20	Address	HEFCE Senior representative
09.30	Address	[Name], MoE Dept Y, Assistant Director
09.40	Sino–UK Project summary by the person in charge of the China side of the project	[Name], Head of Dept X, MoE
10.10	Tea break	
10.30	Sino–UK Project summary by the person in charge of the UK side of the project	Marie, British programme manager
11.00	**Reports on various projects** (Key contents of the reports: progress and summary of the projects; Innovation of the projects)	Host – to be decided
11.00	A Few Thoughts regarding the Cooperation between Beijing Normal University and the University of Manchester for the development of ELT Online Resources	[Name], Chinese sub-project leader, DEfT project
12.00	Lunch	

(Continued)

Table 3.3 (*Continued*)

14.00	The Beijing Foreign Studies University – University of Nottingham Cooperation	[Name], Chinese project member, Tertiary eELT project
14.30	The Tsinghua University – University of Cambridge Cooperation. The Mode, Research, Development and Application of Online Learning – Cambridge-Tsinghua Collaboration on Chinese University Teacher Training in English-CUTE	
15.00	Tea break	
15.20	The Beijing Normal University – University of Nottingham Cooperation	[Name], Chinese project director, Secondary eELT project
15.50	Open discussion: communication of achievements and experiences between project groups	
16.50	Response from the Stakeholders: Chinese representation	[Name], Head of Dept X, MoE
17.00	Response from the Stakeholders: UK representation	[Name], Head of Dept A, HEFCE
17.15	Dinner	
19.00	Entertainment/party	
	Day Two: Discussion of Academic Issues	
09.00	Relevant Policies for the Development of Distance Education in China	[Name], Head of Dept X, MoE
09.20	**Discussion theme 1: Resource Development**	
09.20	UK Representation: Applying Social Constructionist Principles to the Design of eLearning Materials	[Name], British sub-project leader, DEfT project
10.00	Chinese Representation: Instructional Design for Blended Mode of Learning	[Name], Chinese project director, DEfT project
10.40	Tea break	
11.00	Chinese Representation: Anatomizing VLE Learning	[Name], Chinese project director, Tertiary eELT project
11.40	Lunch	
13.00	Visit to the Summer Palace	
19.00	Dinner	
	Day Three: Discussion of Academic Issues, Publication of Results	
09.00	**Discussion Theme 2: Intellectual Property in ICT**	
09.00	UK representation	[Name], British associate project member responsible for IP issues

09.40	Chinese representation	Representative from the State Intellectual Property Office of China
10.20	Tea break	
10:40	**Discussion Theme 3: Reports on 'Research' Issues**	
10.40	UK Representation	
	Comparing Perceptions of Effective Environments for Learning	[Name], British associate project member
	Integrated and scalable eLanguage learning	[Name], British project director, CUTE project
	Managing Learners' Cognitive & Affective Needs in eLearning	[Name], British project director, Tertiary eELT project
11.40	Lunch	
13.30	Chinese Representation	
	A Comparison of Decision Making in Educational Innovation in China and the UK— A Case Study of SCORM Application	[Name], Chinese project member
	Presentation by BFSU	
	Frame of Research Development in the Sino-UK Project	[Name], Chinese steering committee member
14.30	**Discussion Theme 4: Publication of Results**	
	UK Representation	[Name], British project member, responsible for leading dissemination plans in UK
15.10	Tea break	
15.30	**Discussion Theme 5: Post-Project Development**	
16.30	**Summary Speech by Chinese and UK Representatives**	
16.30	Chinese Representation	
16.40	UK Representation	
16.50	Close of the workshop	
17.10	Dinner	
18.30	Depart for the Lao She Tea House	
19.50	Show starts	
21.20	Show ends	
22:00	Back in the hotel	

Marie immediately shared the revised programme with the British project members. Everyone was greatly dismayed, as the following comments illustrate:

> It has changed very considerably from our version and is turning into the nightmare I was dreading.
>
> (Marie, 4 February 2005)

There are clearly some problems with this [...] draft.

(HEFCE staff member, 4 February 2005)

Talk about winds of change. [...] what are the degrees of freedom here, if any?

(British project member, 4 February 2005)

Oh dear me ... No idea what to suggest.

(British project member, 4 February 2005)

I can imagine you must be feeling a little put-out by this, Marie! My first reaction is that the timetable barely resembles what we collectively discussed at our meeting. [...] Overall, my first impression is that our programme has been "hijacked"!!! A "little" disappointing – but maybe we can still influence it.

(British project member, 7 February 2005)

3 BACKGROUND KNOWLEDGE

3.1 The author's point of reference

I, Helen Spencer-Oatey, am a university professor who researches, teaches and supervises in the area of intercultural communication. My interest grew out of many years of living and working in Hong Kong and Shanghai, during which time I became fascinated by the subtle (and not so subtle) differences in styles of interaction displayed by foreign and local teachers. My academic degrees are in both psychology and applied linguistics and this multidisciplinary background strongly influences my approach to intercultural interaction in that I favour an interdisciplinary perspective.

All analyses of intercultural interaction require some kind of conceptualization of culture and for me, a multi-layered perspective is particularly helpful. A framework that I use frequently in my teaching can be summarized as the 3Ps: Products, Practices and Perspectives (cf. Moran 2001). *Products*: these are the "concrete" or "codified" aspects of culture, which in this case study comprise (inter alia) the workshop agenda and the venue in which it takes place. *Practices*: these are patterns of behaviour that we display, or desire, and that influence cultural products such as agendas and venue design. They include our patterns of speaking and preferences for styles of interaction, and typically reflect the rules, conventions and norms of the social group in which we are interacting. *Perspectives*: these are the deep-seated and often unconscious attitudes, values and beliefs that we hold about life, such as respect for elders, the need for modesty, and the importance of independence and self-sufficiency. They influence our practices, but often without our awareness. There are many different perspectives and almost infinite numbers of practices; key ones for this case study are explained below. You may be able to identify additional ones.

3.2 Concepts, models, frameworks

3.2.1 The perspectives of high/low power distance and their impact

A large number of researchers (e.g. Hofstede 1991; House et al. 2004; Schwartz 1999) have found that people's attitudes to power differ significantly across cultural groups. Some are supportive of hierarchical differences and feel comfortable with it; others believe in greater egalitarianism and prefer to downplay any status differences. This perspective, or value, is particularly relevant to this case study, most notably in its influence on practices. For example, with respect to the planning of a collaborative workshop, it can influence who is invited to attend, the status of people giving presentations, how many people speak, and so on.

3.2.2 The perspectives of task and relationship orientation and their impact

Some researchers (e.g. Adler 2007; Schneider & Barsoux 2002) have argued that in international business/management contexts, the relative importance that people attach to task achievement compared with relationship development/management can vary across cultural groups. Some people are very task oriented and place goal achievement as their top priority. Others are much more relationship oriented, and want to dedicate adequate time to developing, maintaining and building relationships. This perspective, or value, is highly relevant to this case study, and again influences practices. Since it affects people's priorities for social activities compared with task goals, it influences, for example, their preferences for the scheduling of different types of events.

3.2.3 The perspectives of learning as knowledge transfer and learning as co-constructed, and their impact

Some researchers (e.g. Jin & Cortazzi 1998; Watkins & Biggs 1996) have pointed out that people's beliefs about the best ways to learn can vary considerably across cultural groups. Some people believe that highest priority should be given to the clear and explicit transfer of knowledge, while others believe that this does not lead to deep, motivated learning and for that to occur, people must engage in interaction with others. They believe that this results in the co-construction of learning, in that the outcome is greater than the separate contributions. These beliefs naturally influence practices in terms of the "events", such as presentations and discussion groups, that are organized for learning.

3.3 Recommended reading

Bowe, H. & Martin, K. (2007). *Communication Across Cultures. Mutual Understanding in a Global World.* Cambridge: CUP.
This book provides an introductory linguistic perspective on communication across cultures and is intended for interdisciplinary readers. It examines the different ways in which the spoken and written word may be interpreted, depending on the context and expectations of the participants. It has many

examples from a variety of languages and cultures – from Japan to Germany, from the Americas to Africa, and to Australia. It uses key concepts of linguistic pragmatics, discourse analysis, politeness theory and intercultural communication to analyse the examples.

www.cambridge.org/us/academic/subjects/languages-linguistics/sociolinguistics/communication-across-cultures-mutual-understanding-global-world

Spencer-Oatey, H. (Ed.) (2008). ***Culturally Speaking. Culture, Communication and Politeness Theory.*** **London: Continuum.**
This book offers a comprehensive introduction to cross-cultural and intercultural pragmatics. It includes both theoretical and empirical chapters. The former explore key issues in culture and communication and the latter report comparative and interactional studies of speakers of a variety of languages, including German, Greek, Japanese and Chinese. The final section of the book comprises practical chapters on pragmatics research, recording and analysing data, and projects in intercultural pragmatics.

www.bloomsbury.com/uk/culturally-speaking-second-edition-9780826493101/#sthash.LqIXzyKQ.dpuf

Spencer-Oatey, H. (2012). "What is culture? A compilation of quotations". In: ***GlobalPAD Core Concepts.*** **Available at GlobalPAD Open House.**
This is a collection of quotations on culture, organized by sub-topic and incorporating perspectives from a wide variety of authors.

www.warwick.ac.uk/globalpadintercultural

Spencer-Oatey, H. & Franklin, P. (2009). ***Intercultural Interaction. A Multidisciplinary Approach to Intercultural Communication.*** **London: Palgrave.**
This book "provides rapid and authoritative access to current ideas and practice in intercultural communication. Drawing on concepts and findings from a range of different disciplines and using authentic examples of intercultural interaction to illustrate points, it offers a wealth of insights into the process. Part 1 explores conceptual issues: the nature of culture and intercultural interaction competence; the impact of language and culture on understanding, rapport and impression management; cultural and adaptation processes. Part 2 deals with practical applications: how competence in intercultural interaction can be assessed and developed. Part 3 focuses on research: topic areas that can be investigated and methods and approaches for doing so. Part 4 provides a rich list of resources for further study."

www.palgrave.com/page/detail/?sf1=id_product&st1=275014

Spencer-Oatey, H. & Tang, M. (2007). "Managing collaborative processes in international projects: Programme management perspectives". In:

Spencer-Oatey, H. (Ed.), *e-Learning Initiatives in China: Pedagogy, Policy and Culture*. Hong Kong: Hong Kong University Press, 159–173.
This chapter provides further insights into the collaboration experiences of the eChina–UK teams who are the focus of this chapter's case study.

http://hongkong.universitypressscholarship.com/view/10.5790/hongkong/9789622098671.001.0001/upso-9789622098671

Ting-Toomey, S. (1999). *Communicating Across Cultures*. New York: Guildford Press.
This book takes a human communication disciplinary perspective. It "presents an identity-based framework for understanding the impact of culture on communication and for helping students develop mindful intercultural communication skills. With illustrative examples from around the globe, the book shows that communicating involves much more than transmitting a particular message – it also reflects each participant's self-image, group identifications and values, and network and relational needs."

www.guilford.com/books/Communicating-Across-Cultures/Stella-Ting-Toomey/9781572304451

4 QUESTIONS ON THE CASE

Consider the description of the 3Ps above, in particular the perspectives mentioned, and compare Tables 3.2 and 3.3. Then reflect on the following questions:

1. Why were the British members upset when they received the Chinese version of the programme draft? What elements of the programme had been changed? Which aspects of the revised programme were likely to be problematic for them, and why? The table below may help you to structure your insights.

Issue	Product/Practice	Perspective
a) Who takes an active part?		
b) What is the nature of the interaction in the workshop?		
c) Should there be a free-time activity?		

2. Why do you think the Chinese members revised the programme in this way? What might have been problematic for them in the British initial draft, and why? What do you think they were trying to achieve in their revised version? The table below may help you to structure your insights.

Issue	Product/Practice	Perspective
a) Who takes an active part?		
b) What is the nature of the interaction in the workshop?		
c) Should there be a free-time activity?		

3. What do you think the final programme looked like? How could both the British and Chinese aspirations for the workshop best be achieved? Please make a suggestion by drawing up an alternative programme.

5 REFERENCES

Adler, N. (2007). *International Dimensions of Organizational Behavior*. 5th ed. Cincinnato, Ohio: South Western College.

Hofstede, G. (1991). *Cultures and Organizations: Software of the Mind*. London: HarperCollinsBusiness.

House, R. J., Hanges, P. J., Javidan, M., Dorfman, P. W. & Gupta, V. (2004). *Culture, Leadership, and Organizations. The GLOBE Study of 62 Societies*. London: Sage.

Jin, L. & Cortazzi, M. (1998). "The culture the learner brings: A bridge or a barrier?" In: Byram, M. and Fleming, M. (Eds), *Language Learning in Intercultural Perspective*, 98–118. Cambridge: Cambridge University Press.

Maznevski, M. & Chudoba, K. (2000). "Bridging space over time: Global virtual team dynamics and effectiveness". In: *Organization Science*, 11:5, 473–492.

Moran, P. (2001). *Teaching Culture. Perspectives in Practice*. Boston: Heinle and Heinle.

Schneider, S. C., & Barsoux, J.-L. (2002). *Managing Across Cultures*. 2nd ed. London: Prentice Hall.

Schwartz, S. (1999). "A theory of cultural values and some implications for work". In: *Applied Psychology: An International Review*, 48:1, 23–47.

Watkins, D. A. & Biggs, J. B. (1996). *The Chinese Learner: Cultural, Psychological and Contextual Influences*. Hong Kong: Comparative Education Research Centre & Victoria, Australia: The Australian Council for the Educational Research.

4

Intercultural Challenges in International Mergers and Acquisitions: A German–Bulgarian–Romanian Case Study

Petia Genkova and Anna Gajda

1 INTRODUCTION

Due to globalization and increasingly connected markets, companies can no longer focus exclusively on internal growth strategies. They must also consider external growth through mergers and acquisitions (M&As). National and international M&As follow the same stages, processes and goals. However, as a result of different market structures, regulatory frameworks, cultures, and languages, the latter present more complex challenges.

M&As can be divided into three different stages: The pre-merger stage, the transaction stage and the post-merger-integration (PMI) stage. The last stage, the PMI, is especially crucial because integration determines whether anticipated synergies can be achieved or not. In this context, it is important to handle employee reactions properly. M&A may cause merger syndrome; that is, the emotional resistance of employees who fear uncertainty or changes caused by the M&A. These subjective feelings have objective effects on job outcomes such as job satisfaction, commitment, effectiveness and productivity.

In order to limit merger syndrome and to establish a willingness to change among all employees involved, it is important to analyse the expectations of the employees and to handle them properly. But what does this mean in detail? As a result of the influence of Anglo-Saxon management literature on M&A, participation and employee involvement are seen as appropriate instruments in this context. Employees receive the opportunity to contribute to the change management process and to be part of it, which, it is thought, may foster their motivation and contribute to positive job outcomes. However, such aspects, which may be regarded as key factors for success in one culture, may not necessarily be as effective for international M&As, which have to involve different cultures. Although such management techniques seem to represent success factors within Western countries, it is questionable if they are a magic bullet and work as efficiently in a different cultural context. Therefore, it is fundamental to understand culture as a complex and multi-level phenomenon.

In the following German–Romanian–Bulgarian case study, in which all names have been fictionalized, we illustrate the importance of contextual and cultural factors that can lead to a deeper understanding of international mergers and what makes them successful.

2 CASE DESCRIPTION

2.1 The situation: company background

> "We are very proud to announce to you today that our energy company is right on track regarding our mission 2015. Especially our most important goal – to gain ground in prospering regions – was reached by the end of last year in 2005 with the successful merger of big energy companies in Bulgaria and Romania. We pushed forward both M&As simultaneously and we will simultaneously integrate these new companies into our corporate group. We selected our best managers for this task and I am very confident that we will transfer our well-established management tools quickly."

Dr. Stefan Wagner threw a worried glance at Ulrike Krause, whose face showed the same expression. Both managers had known each other for quite a long time and had become good friends. It was a lucky coincidence for both to be selected as the new board members of the companies in Bulgaria and Romania: Dr. Stefan Wagner as the new CEO in Bulgaria and Ulrike Krause as the new CFO in Romania. After having spent almost ten months in their respective countries, both managers had returned to the German headquarters to participate in the annual board meeting. Their assignment had been stated very clearly and they had less than one year left to fulfil these demands.

After the board meeting, Dr. Wagner went straight to Mrs. Krause.

Dr. Wagner:

> "Hi Ulrike. Nice to see you here. Our CEO made some clear statements regarding our work in Bulgaria and Romania."

Mrs. Krause:

> "Hi Stefan. Yes, the statements are very clear. And I saw your worried face. So I guess it is not going very well in Bulgaria, right?"

Dr. Wagner:

"Well, it is not very easy to answer this question. Remember summer last year, when we were all recruited to go abroad? We had to pass so many exams and assessment centres. After I knew that I had been nominated, I even spent my vacations with my family in Varna at the Black Sea in order to get to know the country better. I was very glad to have this opportunity to become the new CEO in our Bulgarian energy company and my family supported the decision.

"At the beginning everything was great. The Bulgarians were very friendly and open to the new models and ideas which came from our German headquarters. But after a while it got very difficult. We had tried many approaches to fulfil the targets – especially the financial targets – coming from German headquarters and at the same time to share our values and our corporate culture.

"For example, we radically reduced the car pool. You won't believe how many cars, drivers, and different types of cars, the Bulgarian company used to have! At the end we kept a few drivers and equipped the car pool with small, environmentally friendly, and economical cars. We had to cut costs but we wanted to emphasize that we were more than willing to find other ways to achieve the required cost cuttings than by layoffs. Additionally, we wanted to demonstrate the importance of environmental protection which, of course, is a very important value to us and our company. However, the Bulgarians reacted very strangely. But anyway, tell me, how are you doing in Romania?"

Mrs. Krause:

"You know what? I was very surprised by the warm welcome we received when we came to Romania. Maybe you remember, at the end of the bidding process there were two big energy companies left: our biggest Italian competitor and us. I was totally astonished by the behaviour of the Romanians when we arrived. They were deeply happy that we won the bidding and not the Italians. They told us on many occasions that they felt very relieved to now be part of a German company and I truly had the feeling that they meant it and that they made some effort to adopt and to incorporate our models.

"It was very hard for all of us, especially during the first months. When we arrived – we were a total of six German managers who were in charge of the whole integration process – nothing was ready for us. We didn't have computers, we didn't even have a room or desks. The Romanians were very helpful and creative and helped us a lot. They even wanted to prepare some special offices for us, so that each German manager would have his or her own office. But we didn't want to give them the wrong impression or spread the fear that the Germans would take over everything.

Therefore, we preferred to spend the first months all together in one big room. However, the Romanians reacted very strangely to that. But anyway, what concerns me most right now is the question of how to make sure that our standardized German management tools will be implemented. What did you do in Bulgaria to apply our management tools and how did this work out?"

Dr. Wagner:

"Well, we used several standardized models which I'm sure you have tried to implement, too. Our biggest task at company level was to implement process-oriented organization. I had the feeling that it was the first time for all employees to actually work with organizational charts and to have an overview of roles and responsibilities. We also established new departments like marketing, controlling and customer services and, of course, we transferred management models like our code of conduct. We have also already started to implement our standardized employee survey as well as our performance evaluation. I deeply admire the transformational ability of our Bulgarian employees and their willingness to learn!

"In order to make sure that these instruments had been implemented and internalized, we offered several discussion platforms, training events, and workshops. As far as I know, most Bulgarians participated in these trainings and workshops. However, there seemed to be a lack of discussion – but then again, maybe there was no need for discussion and they just accepted the new models.

"Sometimes we tried to incorporate their ideas. For example, we organized really big road shows. All of the German managers participated in them and we had these kinds of events not only at our Bulgarian headquarters but also at important offices in the region. All employees were invited to these road shows, to meet the new German managers and to talk to us about their ideas. But their reactions were very strange. I have to emphasize that at every location every seat was taken and every employee was at the road show, which was a great feeling and a success for us. However, the employees didn't want to participate. We asked some questions and when nobody wanted to answer, we tried to pick some volunteers. Sometimes we even knew some employees and encouraged them by addressing them by name. As soon as somebody was singled out they answered the question and had some really good ideas but it took us a great effort to get them to open up. At the end of each road show we thanked all employees for their participation and we gave particular thanks to those who had contributed ideas, addressing them by name and taking a picture which we would later publish on our intranet. I thought this was very important to do. We hoped to encourage the others to participate more in similar events as a result.

"However, I became increasingly sceptical. On the one hand the Bulgarians seem to be really interested in our tools and eager to learn them; on the other hand I'm not quite sure if they really use these tools when we are not around supervising them.

"And then there are other situations when they totally surprise us positively. For example, we had some troubles with a major supplier. He just didn't want to sign the new contract we'd written. I really didn't understand that, because the content of the contract had remained the same – we just replaced the logos and made a few more minor adjustments. We talked about this issue with some selected Bulgarian managers and they were able to explain the situation to us. What I learnt that day was that sometimes informal arrangements are more important. The changed contract was not as much of a problem as the fact that we changed the negotiating partner. The supplier and the old negotiating partner had a verbal contract which worked as efficiently as written contracts work in Germany.

"But what about you? You said you had some trouble with the transfer of certain tools?"

Mrs. Krause:

"It's so interesting to have this conversation with you! I can totally understand what you mean and I have the same feeling about the effectiveness of the transfer.

"Basically we tried to implement the same models you've mentioned. The German headquarters developed all of these standardized management models and we tried to implement them – also the IT and reporting systems which we use in Germany. I don't have detailed knowledge about all transfer processes but I do remember that it was especially difficult to implement our feedback and problem-solving culture. As you did in Bulgaria, we also offered several participatory activities like one-to-one discussions, team workshops and training. However, I don't have the feeling that these instruments really worked in transferring the tools and especially the values which are inherent in them.

"For example, we wanted to implement the German reporting system for financial figures. We had to meet several challenges regarding this task. First of all, it was very difficult to explain what kind of figures we needed. I had the feeling that some specific company facts, like the number of employees, had never been collected. Therefore, the task was first to determine what exactly we meant by the specified figures and then to collect the data. Once we had a certain pool of data, we wanted to fill in the German reporting tools. Again we had to face many obstacles.... To cut a long story short, what was most frustrating in this process was not so much the lack of common definitions or the lack of figures but the communication difficulties. Every day before going to my office I saw the employees from the financial department standing together at the coffee machine. We greeted each other and I went straight to work. I'm sure you can imagine what I thought seeing them every day at the coffee machine instead of working! Anyway, usually later that day I would go to the team room and ask if there were any problems. I never experienced a day when one of them stood up and said something about the problems we were facing. But as soon as I was back at my office, Juliana would come and tell me about some minor irregularities they had found. Of course these always turned out to be huge problems. Until this day, I haven't figured out why Juliana is the only one who understood how our feedback and problem-solving culture works. All the other employees could come forward, too and tell me when we have a problem. I always try to react very calmly and in the end we solve that problem as a team.

"But, as you've mentioned, there are also other situations. What I truly admire about the Romanians is their 'group intelligence' – as I call it. They have a very good feeling for situations as well as for group dynamics and show a very high group loyalty. This is something I've learnt from them and I try to incorporate this in my leadership style. For example, I've introduced rewards on a group level instead of an individual level. This seems to work pretty well.

"However, there are so many things I don't understand and I don't know how to deal with."

Dr. Wagner:

"I know exactly what you mean. Sometimes everything just seems so strange ..."

Let us now leave Mrs. Krause and Dr. Wagner and travel to Bulgaria and Romania. Let's see what the Bulgarians and Romanians think about the merger.

What the Bulgarian employees are thinking ...

"I am so glad to work for a German company now. I am very eager to learn more about German quality, punctuality and objectivity. Hopefully we will receive German wages soon."

"The Bulgarian culture has a long history of adapting to other circumstances and rules. I am very open to the German culture and I am happy about this new opportunity."

"Sometimes I don't understand the German managers. Why did they sell all the cars and replace them with small cars? Now nobody can see if it's the CEO coming or just a level three manager."

"I am amazed at the German efficiency! They have only spent a few months here and we already have a totally new organization. Hristina, who used to be in charge of all HR-related issues, is now only responsible for recruiting. But of course everybody keeps calling her for any HR matter as we all know that she knows it best, or at least she knows the right person in the HR department to ask."

"The German managers are such great role models; they are like mentors. I have learnt a lot from them so far. For example, I didn't know that in order to set up a structured work and time plan, you should start at the end. I wonder if there is anything the Germans could learn from us. Well, of course the Germans are very stiff and don't know what to talk about – besides work-related topics – when you meet them at lunch or at the coffee machine."

"I really like the German managers. They are so open and calm, even in stressful situations. Bulgarian managers behave in a very authoritarian way and start shouting very quickly. But what I don't understand is this new tool. They call it performance evaluation and target agreement. They want us to tell them the targets we are supposed to achieve. But isn't it actually their job to define these targets and not ours? And why do they need this formal feedback anyway? It is very judgemental and discomfiting."

"We have so many new management tools. I can't even remember all the names. For each tool we've had at least one training event or another kind of workshop. I really like these workshops; I can meet with other colleagues I haven't seen for a while. But what really annoys me during these workshops is the German way of designing them. The Germans are very strict and have a clear schedule, even for questions. We are always supposed to ask our questions at the end of a lesson. Why can they not leave us more time during the coffee break to discuss these instruments – with other Bulgarian colleagues as well as with them?"

"Finally, a German company bought our company and will lead us to European standards. These road shows were so interesting! The German managers have many great plans for us and our company. But sometimes I don't understand why they bring in all their German tools and don't even ask us how we used to do it. The old company worked well – otherwise the Germans would not have bought us. Of course, many things have to be improved but why do they have to be so strict with their tools? For example, with the employee survey, would it not be possible to extend the questionnaire with some Bulgarian-specific questions?"

"I am very proud to work for this company – one of the world-wide biggest energy companies! And I am part of this! Really amazing! I am sure I will have a great career here, especially as I get along very well with Dr. Wagner, the German CEO. I am sure he didn't mean it in a bad way when he addressed me during the big road show and made me feel uncomfortable. I don't know why he had to pick me during this huge road show with all the other colleagues participating. And at the end, when I hoped that at least most of my colleagues had forgotten that I had stood out of the group, he repeated my name and even took a picture.... Sometimes the German managers are just very clumsy, like robots. But at least they are very good at the work they do and I want to learn those skills."

What the Romanian employees are thinking...

"When we heard the news that the Germans finally won the bidding we were all very relieved. The Germans are known for their high quality standards and they are so well organized. We are all very happy to work with them and to learn as much as possible from them."

"Romanians are not as well organized as Germans. Punctuality is a big issue. I am so glad that the Germans bought the company and not the Italians. With the Italians in charge everything would have remained the same. In the end, both of us – Italians and Romanians – share the same Roman heritage. So we are too much alike."

"The Germans are so different from the Romanian managers. They always want to hear our opinion before making a decision. This is very strange for me but I like this new way."

"I'm not the youngest any more and the changes were very tough for me. But I am glad to have this opportunity to learn. What I really like about the German managers is their way of being a 'touchable role model' – as I like to call it. Now, my doors are open all the time and the younger employees especially come to me to discuss new ideas."

"I am very proud to work closely with the German managers and I learn so much from them every day. There is not one negative thing I can say about them. Although just sometimes they behave very strangely. For example, at the beginning they all shared one big office. This is so strange. Why would they do that? They are the most important people in this company. But this was at the beginning; now there really is nothing negative I can think of."

"My father and my grandfather already worked for this company. I am very proud to continue this family tradition. I will fulfil my duties and obligations with the same effort my father and my grandfather have shown. Both were leading managers and I'm sure to have a prosperous career due to my family relationships."

"We are all very glad to have this opportunity to work with the German managers and to grow. Well, maybe at the beginning we were even more enthusiastic than we are now, but even today we are all looking forward to learning more from the Germans. It's just that sometimes they are a little strange. They didn't have their own offices which made us feel very ashamed. So we prepared other big offices so that each of them could have his or her own office but they refused. Even the CEO was sitting with the other managers in one room. I really don't understand this. The office of the former CEO was empty and it is a very nice and spacious office with a sofa, a big TV, and even a fridge."

"The Germans are very good at computers and know the different programs like PowerPoint and Excel very well. I learnt a lot from them about the set-up of analyses and techniques to put results on slides. I just don't understand why they are keeping their distance; they must see the effort we are putting into learning everything."

"The most important things at work are the talks we have around the coffee machines. We meet with colleagues from other departments and we exchange our problems and findings. Very often we discover similar challenges and we help each other. I don't understand why the German managers never join us."

"Mrs. Krause is a very good manager. Right from the start we got along very well and I helped her with many different things. My husband and I even offered to show her our city. Now we don't meet that often anymore. Mostly we just see each other in the office. Still, I think I have a very good relationship with her. That is why I always go to her when we find any problems. I know that I can trust Mrs. Krause. I just don't understand why she doesn't want to establish a good trust base with all of us. But, on the other hand, I am very happy to be someone special to Mrs. Krause."

3 BACKGROUND KNOWLEDGE

3.1 The authors' point of reference

The authors, Petia Genkova and Anna Gajda, are specialists in intercultural management, especially Eastern European–German cooperation. They have a cross-cultural psychology-oriented approach. This approach is based on the assumption that people are more similar than they are different. The focus of their empirical studies lies in searching for universal features of behaviour. The patterns are indeed universal, but their expression is different (Genkova 2012). These cultural patterns or dimensions can be found in every culture. However, their expression or specification within these dimensions depends on the culture and is always culture specific. Cultural differences lead to different expressions within these patterns and, therefore, to different thoughts and behaviours.

The authors believe that by detecting and identifying these patterns and different expressions a deeper understanding of different behaviour can be achieved which increases the success of intercultural cooperation. Cultural differences and different behaviour are in their opinion not a problem but a sign of these culture-specific expressions. More information about their approaches (and some articles) can be found on www.wiso.hs-osnabrueck.de/38933.html.

3.2 Concepts, models, frameworks

3.2.1 Post-merger integration: Nahavandi & Malekzadeh (1988) model of acculturation

The term mergers and acquisitions (M&As) describes the process and the result of a strategically motivated purchase of companies and its integration into a group of companies. In general, three different stages of M&A can be distinguished: pre-merger, transaction, and post-merger integration. The last stage, the PMI, is especially crucial because the integration determines whether anticipated synergies can be achieved or not.

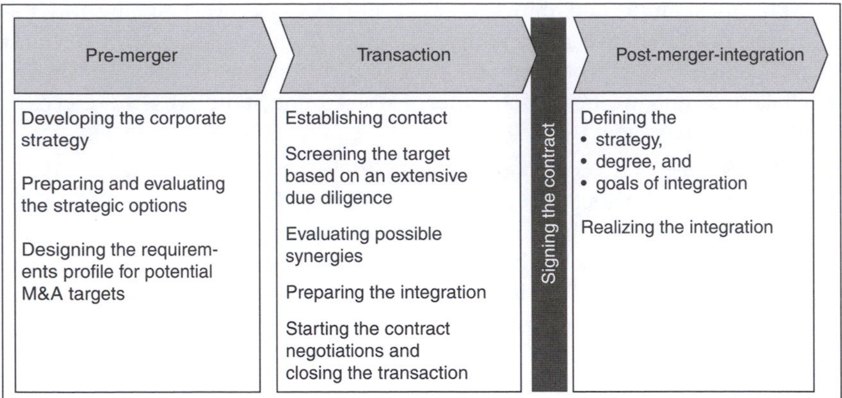

Figure 4.1 Stages of M&A

Source: Unger, 2007:878. Reproduced with permission.

National and international M&A follow the same stages, processes and goals. However, due to different market structures, regulatory frameworks, cultures and languages, the latter present more complex challenges.

Cultural differences, especially, seem to cause international M&As to fail. As the PMI is such an important stage, many models of cultural integration have been discussed in M&A literature (Stahl & Voigt 2005). These models try to shed some light on the question of how different cultures can be integrated and what should be considered.

One of these models is Nahavandi and Malekzadeh's (1988) model of acculturation. What makes the model so special is that it takes into account both sides – that of the acquired company as well as that of the buyer. For the acquired company the degree of acculturation depends on the following two factors: 1) the need of the acquired company to maintain its own culture and 2) the perceived attractiveness of the purchasing company. For the buyer the degree of acculturation depends also on two factors: 1) the diversification strategy, which has an influence on the extent of synergies achieved and 2) the cultural internationalization strategy, which determines the extent of multiculturalism of a company.

A key assumption of the model is that the closeness of the integration preferences of both companies has an influence on the culturally related perception of stress during the integration stage. This stress may lead to merger syndrome, an emotional resistance of employees who fear uncertainty or changes caused by the M&A. These subjective feelings have objective effects on job outcomes such as job satisfaction, commitment, effectiveness and productivity. Nahavandi and Malekzadeh argue that the closer the expectations and preferences are in the acquired company and the buyer, the smaller the perceived stress which in turn leads to a minimization of the merger syndrome and to a reduction of possible resistance. For these reasons, the authors emphasize that the incorporation of the expectations and preferences of both sides represents a key success factor for international M&A.

Nahavandi and Malekzadeh identify – based on the work of Berry (1983, 1984) – four different forms of acculturation: integration, assimilation, separation and deculturation.

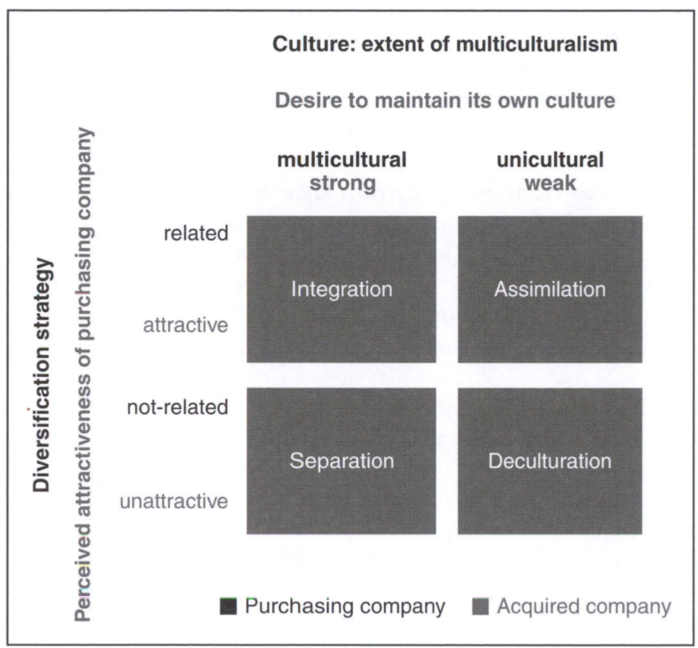

Figure 4.2 Model of acculturation

Source: Nahavandi & Malekzadeh (1988:84). Reproduced with permission.

3.2.2 Cultural patterns and expressions: the cultural dimensions of GLOBE

One of the most recent studies to measure culture is the Global Leadership and Organizational Behavior Effectiveness program (GLOBE) which was initiated by Robert House in 1991. More than 170 scientists and 17,300 managers from over 950 companies and 62 nations have been working on this study.

The initial goal of the GLOBE project was to test the generalizability of charismatic leadership in 20 different cultures. By the end of the investigation, the project had grown to become the largest research programme to identify the interrelations between national, corporate and leadership culture worldwide (House et al. 2004).

Within the GLOBE project culture is defined as "shared motives, values, beliefs, identities, and interpretations or meanings of significant events that result from common experiences of members of collectives that are transmitted across generations" (House et al. 2004:15). A standardized questionnaire was developed to measure all three types of culture (national, corporate and leadership culture), with national and corporate culture being described by the same cultural dimensions.

GLOBE's major premise and finding is that leader effectiveness is contextual; that is, it is embedded in the societal and organizational norms, values and beliefs of the people being led. As a first step to gauge leader effectiveness across cultures, GLOBE empirically established nine cultural dimensions that make it possible to capture the similarities and/or differences in norms, values, beliefs and practices among societies and organizations.

The following list gives an overview of these cultural dimensions of national and corporate culture.

Performance orientation: "Performance orientation reflects the extent to which a community encourages and rewards innovation, high standards, and performance improvement" (Javidan 2004:239).

Assertiveness: "Cultural assertiveness reflects beliefs as to whether people are or should be encouraged to be assertive, aggressive, and tough, or nonassertive, nonaggressive, and tender in social relationships" (Den Hartog 2004:395).

Power distance: "This dimension reflects the extent to which a community accepts and endorses authority, power differences, and status privileges" (Gupta & Javidan 2004:513).

Future orientation is the degree to which individuals in organizations or societies engage in future-oriented behaviours such as planning, investing in the future and delaying individual or collective gratification (House et al. 2004:12).

Gender egalitarianism is the degree to which an organization or a society minimizes gender role differences while promoting gender equality (House et al. 2004:12).

Institutional collectivism is the degree to which organizational and societal institutional practices encourage and reward collective distribution of resources and collective action (House et al. 2004:12).

In-group collectivism is the degree to which individuals express pride, loyalty, and cohesiveness in their organizations or families (House et al. 2004:12).

Uncertainty avoidance is the extent to which ambiguous situations are threatening to individuals, to which rules and order are preferred, and to which uncertainty is tolerated in a society (De Luque & Javidan 2004:602).

Humane orientation is the degree to which individuals in organizations or societies encourage and reward individuals for being fair, altrustic, friendly, generous, caring, and kind to others (House et al. 2004:13).

Based on these dimensions more than 60 societies were placed into culture clusters (see Table 4.1) which were then compared with the nine cultural dimensions (see Table 4.2).

Table 4.1 Culture clusters based on GLOBE

Culture cluster	Country	Culture cluster	Country
Anglo	Canada USA Australia Ireland England South Africa (White Sample) New Zealand	Middle Eastern	Turkey Kuwait Egypt Morocco Qatar
Germanic	Austria The Netherlands Switzerland (German Speaking) Germany	Confucian	Singapore Hong Kong Taiwan China South Korea Japan
Latin European	Israel Italy Switzerland (French Speaking) Spain Portugal France	Southeast Asian	Philippines Indonesia Malaysia India Thailand Iran
African	Zimbabwe Namibia Zambia Nigeria South Africa (Black Sample)	Latin American	Ecuador El Salvador Columbia Bolivia Brazil Guatemala Argentina Costa Rica Venezuela Mexico
Eastern European	Greece Hungary Albania Slovenia Poland Russia Georgia Kazakhstan	Nordic	Denmark Finland Sweden

Source: House et al. 2004.

Table 4.2 High-score and low-score clusters based on GLOBE

Cultural dimension	**High-score clusters**	**Low-score clusters**
Assertiveness	Eastern Europe Germanic Europe	Nordic Europe
Future orientation	Germanic Europe Nordic Europe	Eastern Europe Latin America Middle East
Gender egalitarianism	Eastern Europe Nordic Europe	Middle East
Humane orientation	Southern Asia Sub-Saharan Africa	Germanic Europe Latin Europe
Institutional collectivism	Nordic Europe Confucian Asia	Germanic Europe Latin Europe Latin America
In-group collectivism	Confucian Asia Eastern Europe Latin America Middle East Southern Asia	Anglo Germanic Europe Nordic Europe
Performance orientation	Anglo Confucian Asia Germanic Europe	Eastern Europe Latin America
Power distance	No clusters	Nordic Europe
Uncertainty avoidance	Germanic Europe Nordic Europe	Eastern Europe Latin America Middle East

Source: House et al. 2004.[1]

[1] Bulgaria and Romania were not included in the GLOBE study. But of course there are many empirical studies which deal with the Bulgarian and Romanian cultures. However, it is very difficult to compare these studies as they use different methodologies, e.g. quantitative studies (which are mostly based on the research designs of Hofstede (such as the studies of Catana & Catana 1999; Davidkov 2008; Routamaa, Hautala & Tsutzuki 2009) or GLOBE (such as the studies of Bibu & Brancu 2008; Catana & Catana 2010a) or qualitative studies (e.g. Yordanova & Davidkov 2009). Additionally, the results differ within these studies even when the same methodology has been used due to different samples (e.g. students (Catana & Catana 2010a) vs. middle managers (Catana & Catana 2010b)).

GLOBE's other major finding is how different cultures conceptualize effective leaders. The Leadership Categorization Theory (Lord & Maher 1991) states that everyone has an implicit idea of what leaders are like and how they behave. These ideas are rooted in people's early experiences with leaders and are shaped by one's culture. They then develop expectations about what good leadership is, and these expectations serve as a personal benchmark for people to determine if a leader is effective, good, and worth following – or not. GLOBE was the first study to investigate what exactly people expected of leaders on such a broad scale, and also to link them with cultural values and practices. GLOBE examined 112 leader characteristics, such as: modesty, decisiveness, autonomy and trustworthiness. The first round of analysis generated 21 leadership scales, which in turn folded into six leader styles.

The first two styles, charismatic/value based and team oriented, were seen as contributing to outstanding leadership in all cultures. However, for the other four styles, cultural variation was larger: in some cultures, they were seen as good and effective styles, while other cultures saw them as hindering outstanding leadership. Below, the six styles are listed in the order of least cultural variation to most cultural variation.

1. **The charismatic/value-based style** stresses high standards, decisiveness, and innovation; seeks to inspire people around a vision; creates a passion among them to perform, and does so by firmly holding on to core values. This includes the facets of being visionary, inspirational, self-sacrificial, decisive, performance oriented and possessing integrity.
2. **The team-oriented style** instils pride, loyalty, and collaboration among organizational members and highly values team cohesiveness and a common purpose or goals. This style includes the facets: oriented towards collaborative teams, team integrator, diplomatic, (reverse scored) malevolent, and administratively competent.
3. **The participative style** encourages input from others in decision making and implementation and emphasizes delegation and equality. This style includes the facets: (reverse scored) autocratic and (reverse scored) non-participative.
4. **The humane style** stresses compassion and generosity and it is patient, supportive, and concerned with the well-being of others. This style includes the attributes: modest and humane-oriented.
5. **The self-protective style** emphasizes procedural, status-conscious, and "face-saving" behaviours, and focuses on the safety and security of the individual and the group. This style includes the attributes: self-centred, status conscious, conflict inducing, face-saving, and procedural.
6. **The autonomous style** includes only one facet concerned with autonomy. It is characterized by an independent, individualistic and self-centric approach to leadership.

GLOBE is the most comprehensive study to date that has empirically investigated the relationship between culture and leader behaviour in so many societies, with so many different quantitative and qualitative measures and methods and in so many different organizations.

To conclude with the words of its principal investigator, Robert J. House:

> [M]y final conclusion is that we are in a position to make a major contribution to the organizational behavior and leadership literature. To date more than 90% of the organizational behavior literature reflects U.S.-based research and theory. Hopefully GLOBE will be able to liberate organizational behavior from the U.S. hegemony. (2004:xxv)

3.3 Recommended reading

Alves, J. C., Lovelace, K. J., Manz, C. C., Matsypura, D., Toyasaki, F. & Ke, G. (2006). "A cross-cultural perspective of self-leadership". In: *Journal of Managerial Psychology*, 21:4, 338–359.
The focus of this study is to explain how differences in national cultures impact on the understanding and meaning of the concept of self-leadership and its application. While self-leadership remains a valid concept, its understanding and application is likely to differ across cultures. Alves et al. (2006) showed that high power distance raises the importance of the symbolic value of tasks and correspondent covert processes of self-leadership, high uncertainty avoidance makes more explicit the importance of non-rational and intuition-based thought processes, collectivism shows the relevance of social relations, femininity reiterates the importance of social relations and non-rational processes, and long-term orientation introduces the importance of making time an explicit element.

Bibu, N. A. & Brancu, L. (2008). "Convergences of the Romanian societal culture with European culture clusters in the process of European integration: The role of intercultural teams management in increasing European cohesion". In: *Munich Personal RePEc Archive*, 9476, 1–15.
The main focus of this article is the European cohesion based on a management approach. Bibu and Brancu (2008) describe the positioning of Romania on the European map of cultures, in order to identify the convergence and divergence of its societal culture with various European cultural clusters.

Catana, G.-A. & Catana, D. (2010b). "Organizational culture dimensions in Romanian finance industry". In: *Journal for East European management studies,* 2, 128–148.
This paper explores the societal and the organizational culture of the Romanian finance industry as reflected by middle managers' opinion. As part of the GLOBE project, the two culture levels are compared across nine cultural dimensions. The differences between the cultural manifestations (practices and values) are analysed. The findings of this study show some significant differences for the majority of the cultural dimensions examined both between culture levels (organizational versus societal) and culture manifestations (practices versus values).

Routamaa, V., Hautala, T. & Tsutzuki, Y. (2009). "Values and cultures in integrating business: A comparison of Bulgaria, Finland and Japan". In: *World Journal of Management*, 1:1, 13–22.
Along with globalization, values from a cross-cultural perspective have awakened great interest and there are two different points of view. On the one hand, value types differ in different cultures, but on the other hand, it may be assumed that globalization and economic unionism may merge the values. In this article, values in terms of value types were compared in three cultures. It was found that there are culture-based stresses in the values that must be taken into consideration in international business. But it should be mentioned

that the differences were not as big as could be expected taking into consideration the large differences between the cultural, economic and religious backgrounds of the countries concerned.

4 QUESTIONS ON THE CASE

1. What are, in your opinion, the expectations of the Germans, Romanians and Bulgarians regarding the M&A? What type of acculturation would you expect the Germans, Romanians and Bulgarians to prefer and why? In your answers use the terms and concepts contained in Nahavandi and Malekzadeh's model.
2. Try to describe the work-related behaviour you can anticipate from an understanding of the nine cultural dimensions of GLOBE (high/low). In which dimension/dimensions can you detect cultural differences between the Germans and the Bulgarians as well as between the Germans and the Romanians? Please provide quotes to explain your answer.
3. Regarding the six leadership styles of GLOBE (high/low), in which style can you detect the most cultural differences between the Germans and the Bulgarians as well as between the Germans and the Romanians? Please provide quotes to explain your answer.
4. What did the Germans, Romanians and Bulgarians learn from each other? Try to incorporate the cultural dimensions of GLOBE in your answer.

5 REFERENCES

Berry, J. W. (1983). "Acculturation: A comparative analysis of alternative forms". In: Samuda, R. J. & Woods, S. L. (Eds), *Perspectives in Immigrant and Minority Education*, 66–77. Lanham, MD: University Press of America.

Berry, J. W. (1984). "Cultural relations in plural societies: Alternatives to segregation and their sociopsychological implications". In: Miller, N. & Brewer, M. B. (Eds), *Groups in Contact*, 11–27. Orlando: Academic Press.

Bibu, N. A. & Brancu, L. (2008). "Convergences of the Romanian societal culture with European culture clusters in the process of European integration: The role of intercultural teams management in increasing European cohesion". In: *Munich Personal RePEc Archive*, 9476, 1–15.

Carl, D., Gupta, V. & Javidan, M. (2004). "Power Distance". In: House, R. J., Hange, P. J., Javidan, M., Dorfman, P. W. & Gupta, V. (Eds), *Culture, Leadership, and Organizations – The GLOBE Study of 62 Societies*, 513. Thousand Oaks, CA: Sage.

Catana, G.-A. & Catana, D. (1999). "Romanian cultural background and its relevance for cross-cultural management". In: *Journal for East European Management Studies*, 3, 252–258.

Catana, G.-A. & Catana, D. (2010a). "Prospective leaders′ view on Romanian societal culture". In: *The Annals of the University of Oradea*, 639–644.

Catana, G.-A. & Catana, D. (2010b). "Organizational culture dimensions in Romanian finance industry". In: *Journal for East European Management Studies*, 2, 128–148.

Davidkov, T. (2008). "If you want to do business with Bulgarians, you should know …". In: Müller, S. (Ed.), *Management Guide Bulgaria. A Handbook for Investors and Executives*, 163–172. Birmingham: Cross-Culture.

De Luque, M. S. & Javidan, M. (2004). "Uncertainty Avoidance". In: House, R. J., Hange, P. J., Javidan, M., Dorfman, P. W. & Gupta, V. (Eds), *Culture, Leadership, and Organizations – The GLOBE Study of 62 Societies*, 602. Thousand Oaks, CA: Sage.

Den Hartog, D. N. (2004). "Assertiveness". In: House, R. J., Hange, P. J., Javidan, M., Dorfman, P. W. & Gupta, V. (Eds), *Culture, Leadership, and Organizations – The GLOBE Study of 62 Societies*, 395. Thousand Oaks, CA: Sage.

Genkova, P. (2012). "Cultural patterns and subjective culture as predictors of well-being: A cross-cultural study". In: *Psychology Research*, 2, 177–184.

House, R. J, Hanges, P. J., Javidan, M., Dorfman, P. W. & Gupta, V. (2004). *Culture, Leadership, and Organizations – The GLOBE Study of 62 Societies*. Thousand Oaks, CA: Sage.

Javidan, M. (2004). "Performance Orientation". In: House, R. J., Hange, P. J., Javidan, M., Dorfman, P. W. & Gupta, V. (Eds), *Culture, Leadership, and Organizations – The GLOBE Study of 62 Societies*, 239. Thousand Oaks, CA: Sage.

Lord, R. & Maher, K. (1991). *Leadership and Information processing: Linking Perception and Performance*. Boston: Unwin Hyman.

Nahavandi, A. & Malekzadeh, A. (1988). "Acculturation in mergers and acquisitions". In: *Academy of Management Review*, 13: 1, 79–90.

Routamaa, V., Hautala, T. & Tsutzuki, Y. (2009). "Values and cultures in integrating business: A comparison of Bulgaria, Finland and Japan". In: *World Journal of Management*, 1:1, 13–22.

Stahl, G. & Voigt, A. (2005). "The performance impact of cultural differences in mergers and acquisitions: A critical research review and an integrative model". In: Cooper, C. & Finkelstein, S. (Eds), *Advances in Mergers and Acquisitions*, 51–82. New York: JAI Press.

Unger, M. (2007). "Post-Merger-Integration". In: Polster-Grüll, B. (Ed.), *Handbuch Mergers & Acquisitions. Rechtliche und steuerliche Optimierung; ausgewählte Fragen der Bewertung und Finanzierung*, 871–897. Wien: Linde.

Yordanova, D. & Davidkov, T. (2009). "Similarities and differences between female and male entrepreneurs in a transition context: Evidence from Bulgaria". In: *Journal of Applied Economic Sciences*, 4, 571–582.

5

How to Implement Change in a Post-acquisition Multicultural Context: The Lafarge Experience in Britain

Evalde Mutabazi and Philippe Poirson

1 INTRODUCTION

Globalization and growing competition, shareholders' increased power and the everlasting focus on companies' growth and profitability have led in the last 25 years to a huge increase in the number of mergers, acquisitions and cooperations. Nowadays, this phenomenon is the most usual path companies follow to achieve external growth. In order to cope with global competition, this strategy is focused on increasing value for shareholders and tries to optimize investment, research and development (R&D), industrial efficiency and market share through synergies and complementarities.

However, as could be observed from the end of the 1980s, the reality of these processes is often more cruel than the stock exchange curves may show. Although these curves usually rise after agreements have been signed, implementation processes are often difficult. Company leaders, managers and employees have to cope with complex human and organizational change processes (Delmestri & Walgenbach 2005). Moreover, the expected advantages of these acquisitions and merging and alliance processes are difficult to achieve (Brannen & Peterson 2009). It is often a challenge to implement cooperation processes between teams or individuals who have different views of these processes and also different views of operations management and collective relationships in the workplace.

Whereas companies may initiate many acquisitions, mergers and cooperation processes, they then have to cope with cultural and managerial frictions and conflicts (d'Iribarne 2012). In all these different situations they cannot avoid such difficulties. Many company leaders or managers may feel confused by other mindsets or managerial approaches because they have to leave the markets they are acquainted with in order to find raw materials, new market segments or new business partners (shareholders, experts or employees) all around the globe. In this context, a key issue is trying to discover the processes which may enable companies to optimize their differences or at least to consider them as an "improvement factor" when acquisitions, mergers, alliances or the setting up of subsidiaries take place. They often have to modify their own policies and practices and even sometimes build up "something new" using different mentalities and organizational and managerial cultures and practices.

2 CASE DESCRIPTION

2.1 The situation: mission context and company presentation

The factory we will be considering is located in Grays in an industrial area 25 miles east of London. Founded in 1930 by a British family, this English subsidiary of LFI is owned by the French Lafarge Group, which bought it in 1980. In 1998, 70 people are on the payroll. This factory produces high-quality cement mixed with aluminium involving the usual activities in this industry sector: grinding, gravel dispatching, aggregates. This means that the plant includes an analysis laboratory, manufacturing facilities and a maintenance department.

Most of the factory's workers belong to the English "working class" and feel close to the traditional Labour Party. They are not skilled and most of them have learnt their job on the "shop floor". Almost all the foremen have gained their qualification for their work in the same way. In the late 1990s this factory had to cope with recruitment difficulties because a lot of people preferred to go and work in London. Most of the workers are unionized. They can choose to join one of three different unions: the manufacturers' union, the mechanics' union, or the electricians' union. Of course, each union defends its members' interests and in particular the wage level related to each worker's trade.

Two union leaders, who are also foremen, exert the main influence. Moreover, at this time there is "a split" (no contact) between the factory management and the workshop's production workers. Several people interviewed explain that the manufacturing director never comes to visit the workshops. To an external observer, the production workers seem to be divided into several groups: each group defends its "privileges"; for example, the electricians do not allow the production workers to do simple repairs on their machines.

From 1998 to 2002 when the events in this case study take place, the south of England is "very busy" and has to cope with a high inflation rate. Staff turnover is high, except as far as the workers on the shop floor are concerned. The average age of a staff member is 45. As the company's pensions are low, the workers are used to working until they are 65. As far as work organization is concerned, two different work schedules exist:

- Employees and managers work from 9 a.m. to 5 p.m.
- Workers work in overlapping shifts.

As external observers, we noticed two other factors: The "tea break" at nine o'clock lasts between 20 and 30 minutes. The whole staff is involved and seems to be very "relaxed" when compared with their French and German counterparts that we had observed in similar working conditions.

2.2 The challenge: André L. becomes the new factory director at Grays

When he is interviewed about the conditions that existed when he entered the position of factory director, André L. expresses the following ideas:

> "I volunteered to work abroad. It gave me an opportunity to become a factory director more quickly. This position was proposed to me as a challenge. I had been working at Lafarge for 15 years. I had worked previously in different positions, in different departments: manufacturing, maintenance, the laboratory. I replaced an Englishman who retired. When I started in this post, the major issue was quality. We had to supply the global market, the demand level was high and the French factories were unable to meet the clients' needs. During this time the British factory was coping with quantity and quality problems. Before leaving my previous position in France, I had the opportunity to be prepared technically for the new job in three different French manufacturing units in order to spend three years in England."

This is André explaining his experience at the Grays unit:

> "After two weeks, I understood everything. People had acquired bad habits a long while ago. The amount of overtime done by the maintenance staff was very high. Each year maintenance staff members were called out by phone 300 times during weekends in order to come and work (which entitled them to bonuses). In an equivalent factory in France, only 60 phone calls a year occurred. All the manufacturing staff seemed not to be committed to their work and an attitude of withdrawal could be noticed.
>
> "However, some flexibility had been introduced between some jobs and qualifications. The electricians had accepted that unskilled workers could undertake a list of 'micro-repairs'. But in practice, this agreement had not been implemented. Quality problems were very important. In the factory 3200 tonnes of sub-standard products were stored which could not be sold. This meant that two months' manufactured output was lost!
>
> "But, you know, many other points struck me when I got to know this manufacturing unit step by step. The workers felt that they belonged to a local medium-sized company although the managers felt that they were members of the Lafarge Group. I realized that this factory needed to be different, to feel different from the other factories within the LFI business unit. There was an expectation to express and to show an 'individual touch'. I also noticed that each time there were many French present in the factory, the English felt uncomfortable.

"For example, when the third Frenchman came, they used the expression 'one way system' meaning that the staff transfers were always organized in the same direction. When the French arrived, the English felt they were being handled directly by the French headquarters. They were reluctant to be monitored by Frenchmen. Although when I arrived, I noticed more curiosity than hostility."

Organization and work relations management

"In practice, my aim consisted of trying to reach the same quality level as the best French factory within a three-year period and even more quickly if it was possible. An important issue I had to cope with was the fact that some people had been promoted to a position which was too high in comparison with their real competencies. The subsidiary was living by itself, on its own resources. Moreover, its organization was very different from the French factories' organization. The manufacturing process lacked staff. Four teams consisting of three persons were in charge of the core of the process. These persons worked a great deal of overtime which cost 150,000 euros every year.

"In England the amount of overtime is not regulated by law. That is the reason why some workers on the shop floor managed to earn more money than their immediate boss. Absenteeism was also very widespread. I was very surprised to realize that in England people could take sick leave for a week without handing in a sick note signed by a doctor. Many abuses existed chiefly with respect to absences of short duration.

"In comparison with the French factories the organization of manufacturing operations was inferior, because in France many actions had been implemented in order to reduce overtime costs and to handle manufacturing uncertainties. Staff are trained in two different fields: manufacturing process monitoring and maintenance. They are numerous enough to be able to replace each other. They also usually organize themselves well enough to do most of the maintenance tasks while they are involved in the manufacturing process.

"The most shocking aspect during my mission at Grays was the fact that the managers were not available. Usually, in France, in our company, most of the manufacturing engineers I know spend time every morning visiting the workshops to check what is going on and meet foremen and workers. This is a well-established habit in our sector of industry. Engineers are supposed to show that they know the manufacturing problems and that they have some concern for people 'doing the job' and feel close to them.

"Finally, my job experience in England enabled me to understand that the English have mainly a commercial approach to business. They are pragmatic and try to find 'niches' for the products they make. The French chiefly stress the industrial rationale. They think for a long time before deciding on an investment, for example. They have a different vision from the English or Americans; as the French say: 'They do not sell the bear skin before having killed it'. Generally speaking, the French value the different jobs done by engineers and education focusing on technology whereas then English value mainly finance and commerce as the key domains of success in the business field. This may be one explanation of the lack of skilled people on the shop floor in England. I also had opportunities to observe these differences in daily life. For example, in the factory, like everywhere, the English prefer to manage instead of being close to their team members in their daily work. But is that the only reason why there were more hierarchical levels in this English factory than in the French ones?

"Paradoxically, the British seemed to me to be eager to accept my authority, with greater ease than the French, anyway! When they come to work, they usually arrive at the right time. They prepare what they have to do. They design action plans, they prepare the meetings and remain disciplined during the meetings. In England when someone sets up a process or a procedure, it lasts. For example, within a total quality framework, I chose indicators with them, and they are still in operation now. In the French factories, such procedures are obeyed, respected and last only with difficulty."

The implementation of change

"In order to reach my objectives I took into account the following principles:

- To try not to break everything
- To involve myself, to become 'a part' of the factory
- To practice openness, to observe and to listen to people

"Moreover, I gave a lot of information. Every day, especially during the first months of my mission, I spent some time in the offices and workshops. It enabled me to learn the language because I was not able at the beginning of the process to explain with nuances what I intended to get across. After several weeks I felt comfortable enough in the 'local context' to be able to set up 'improvement objectives' with them. I had understood the key elements I could rely on to fulfil my mission without creating any kind of resistance. For example, I had the idea of a competition with a French factory making the same product. But I also spoke about the survival risk for this English factory.

"When I try to understand what happened I am aware of a key point: I would not have been successful without observing, listening to people, giving information, and a permanent dialogue which enabled me to involve people in factory life. While doing this I noticed that they all expected consideration and another kind of relationship with management. To apply these principles was not difficult for me because I needed to be accepted by the factory people to achieve my mission.

"Right at the beginning most of the staff members were surprised to meet me in the workshops late in the evening or early in the morning. I used to spend some time in the workshops at the weekends in order to check if everything was all right. I was present myself at a factory 'tour' on quality control. There was some distrust, but later on it improved. People's attitudes changed and step by step people became more involved. I also believe that as far as the quality issue was concerned pride played a role. An individual or a factory cannot easily admit that their counterparts consider that they do 'bad quality' work!

"However, when I proposed organizing five shift teams (instead of four) I offended some customs and some people's interests because this decision decreased the amount of overtime. I intended, of course, to enable the company to save this money. The amount saved was significant. This was the reason why I suggested we should avoid conflicts or even strikes aimed at increasing the workers' wages. This new work organization also enabled the factory to adapt better to fluctuations in orders.

"But some people, in particular the trade union leader, had been used for many years to getting a systematic 'extra wage' related to 'overtime'. This 'extra wage' sometimes amounted to half of the real wage! In fact, my proposal was useful only for part of the workforce. For several weeks a strike took place about this new system of work organization and the ending of overtime. Only the electricians and the mechanics did not join the strike. Fortunately, first-line managers and managers did the workers' usual work. Finally, a mediator appointed by the local trade union enabled us to end this conflict. British, not involved in the factory life, but knowing the different stages of this factory story, he was able to demonstrate to the people on strike that they had a long-term interest in accepting the changes I proposed."

3 BACKGROUND KNOWLEDGE

3.1 The authors' point of reference

Evalde Mutabazi and Philippe Poirson are professors at the French Business School EM Lyon and at the same time they are consultants and accompany managers in international cooperation and merger processes. They span boundaries between theory and practice. Both pay particular attention to differences between cultures (national, regional, organizational or professional) and their positive or negative impact on the conduct of international organizational change projects. Evalde Mutabazi also has personal and professional experience of both African and Western cultures, which helps to support business development and partnerships in both "worlds" and generate benefit from cultural, organizational and managerial differences. More information about his research, publications and consulting can be found on his website: www.mutabazi.com.

3.2 Concepts, models, frameworks

Acquisitions, mergers, alliance processes: a cross-cultural model From our experiences as consultants and researchers in cross-cultural companies we learnt that managers can use leverage in several ways in order to avoid stereotypes and ethnocentric comparisons between cultural and managerial differences. In this context, a cross-cultural approach is useful and efficient at different stages throughout the acquisitions, mergers and alliances process. The following diagram represents the different stages in our theoretical model:

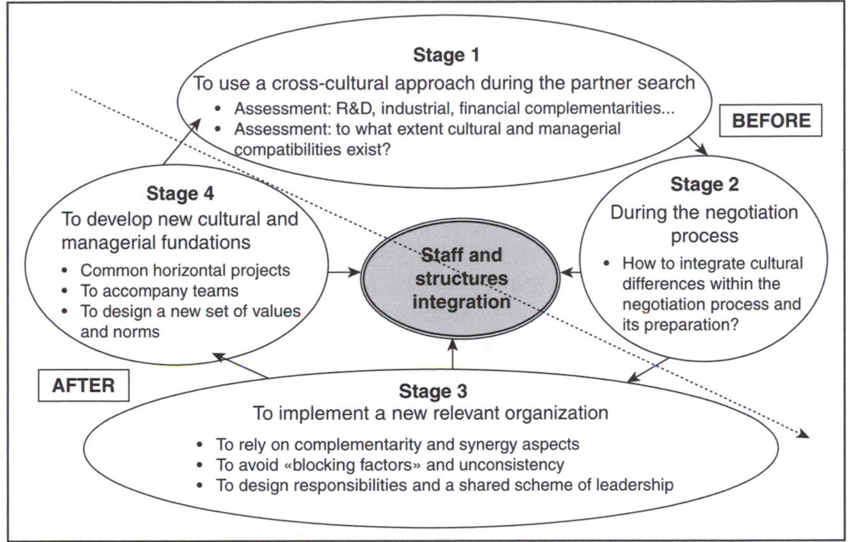

Figure 5.1 Cross-cultural approach of companies "becoming closer"

The identification and choices of the parties in decision-making processes When there is a merger as well as an acquisition or an alliance situation, it is necessary to be prepared for cultural shocks related to cultures and managerial models. This means that the companies' leaders and managers should take into account cultural and managerial differences at the strategic design stage. We suggest they use this approach when they choose their business partners and evaluate their respective input.

However, even if the quantitative aspects (financial, marketing and industrial issues) are key factors in the strategic decision-making process, they are only the "visible part of an iceberg" of the operational implementation of these acquisitions, mergers and alliance processes. Obviously, profits can be obtained by international banks or in other business situations which do not require direct, massive and permanent interactions between cross-cultural teams and individuals. But it often happens that companies that have been attracted by technological, financial or commercial complementarities do not manage to get a relevant return on investment and, even worse, have to cope with unexpected partners who may question their survival.

When the first negotiations takes place Data concerning the cultural and managerial characteristics of the chosen partners and the comparison of these characteristics with those of the company which intends to acquire, merge or set an alliance are very useful for conducting successful negotiations. To take into account cultural and managerial differences enables companies to avoid stereotypes and blunders and falling into traps set by the other party to the negotiation. It enables them also to have a clearer picture of the respective stakes, to adopt a more relevant position and attitude towards the partner, and to build up trust in order to sign acquisition, merger or alliance agreements on strong foundations.

During the implementation of human and organizational change Companies often have to cope with resistance and people issues when they implement project management or operations (Faurie 2008). When one considers the many difficulties and failures faced by companies in acquisitions, mergers and alliance processes during the last 20 years it is obvious that the quantitative analysis of technical, industrial and financial complementarities may be irrelevant and even dangerous. The companies often look for competitive advantages in different areas, for example, in procurement efficiency, sales network, manufacturing processes, logistics, R&D or cost control. In addition, they have to attract, to integrate and to foster the loyalty of highly qualified employees. Such a workforce is becoming more and more expensive and, to make things more difficult, their competitors are also seeking a similar workforce.

Moreover, the necessary changes often deal with operations management, sharing of markets and equipment, and human resource management. These changes are often complex because they have to be implemented by women and men (leaders, managers, and key decision makers) who belong to companies in the process of acquisition, merger or alliance, who have different cultural and managerial norms and practices and who are also expecting career development and often an increase in their power in this new context.

Cross-cultural management of teams designed after acquisition, merger or alliance processes A key issue is trying to know to what extent the national and corporate cultures of the different companies' staff will significantly impact on their attitudes and behaviours (d'Iribarne 1994). If one considers that their interests and behavioural patterns are inspired by specific cultures acquired before the acquisition, merger or alliance processes, it is mandatory to take these differences into account. This approach will make it possible to set up an organizational framework and a managerial model capable of avoiding cultural conflicts related to operational management and communication. This issue is problematic because every person is influenced by several cultures. One is during childhood, in a socialization process in a specific social, political and economic context; another influencing culture may be related to religion; another to vocational training; and the last to a professional experience within a specific company with its own history and skills, and also the founders', leaders' and managers' sets of values (Davel, Dupuis & Chanlat 2009).

Instead of trying to remove the cultural and managerial differences between companies after different processes such as acquisitions, mergers or alliances, the cross-cultural approach consists in considering these differences as assets and powerful resources instead of having a negative view about them as "blocking" and limiting factors (Brannen & Peterson 2009).

However, this approach is difficult. The team's effectiveness after these kinds of processes requires the real involvement of the leaders who have to spend time to accompany these cultural changes. Instead of imposing on their staff only the cultures coming from headquarters or from the leading company in the acquisition process, for example, high-performing companies often use a "positive" framework, enabling talents to emerge and develop from any origin (d'Iribarne 2012). In other words, generating competitive advantage in these acquisitions, mergers or alliance processes does not mean removing less skilled people or staff who come from the acquired company, for example. Rather, it means confronting real cultural and managerial differences and reconciling them with cross-cultural managerial practices. This involves focusing on learning processes based on cross-fertilization and aimed at the co-construction of a shared organizational and managerial culture across the different hierarchical levels and in the different functional areas.

3.3 Recommended reading

Brannen, M. Y. & Peterson, M. F. (2009). "Merging without alienating: Interventions promoting cross-cultural organizational integration and their limitations". In: *Journal of International Business*, 40, 468–489.
Foreign direct investment, particularly cross-border mergers and acquisitions, can spawn a range of individual-level outcomes from cross-cultural adjustment and synergistic learning, on the positive side, to work alienation on the negative. Unsuccessful navigation of these individual-level outcomes leads to failed integration that can seriously affect the realization of desired organizational outcomes such as successful technology transfer, knowledge sharing, and the general realization of global growth. By means of an iterative between-methods triangulation, the study identifies cross-cultural work alienation as a phenomenon that can limit the overall success of such ventures, and suggests interventions that help to promote successful post-merger integration.

Davel, E., Dupuis, J.-P. & Chanlat, J.-F. (2009). *Gestion en Contexte Interculturel*. Québec: Presse de l'Université Laval et TÉLUQ/UQAM.
In a globalization context, the cross-cultural experience is increasing in frequency and complexity and has become a reality almost no one can escape in daily life. This package (book and DVD) enables you to get a better understanding of such an experience. Written by several international experts cooperating in the management field it gives the reader an opportunity to become acquainted with several cross-cultural approaches to management, to identify problems related to companies engaged in internationalization, to be inspired by managerial practices which take cross-cultural issues into account and to discover the richness of several national cultures through immersion. Through the video environment the reader has an opportunity to immerse him- or herself in other cultures while profiting from the knowledge of experts and the experiences of international managers.

Delmestri, G. & Walgenbach, P. (2005). "Mastering Techniques or Brokering Knowledge? Middle Managers in Germany, Great Britain and Italy". In: *Organization Studies*, 26:2, 197–220.
Based on a conceptualization of knowledge as the capacity to act in response to uncertain, complex and ambiguous environmental stimuli, this article analyses the role of middle managers in Germany, Great Britain and Italy as holders of different types of knowledge in relation to national institutions such as the education system, the system of industrial relations and the career system. It identifies the common role of middle managers in the three countries as the responsibility of both maintaining a positive social environment, and handling exceptions and solving unexpected problems. German and Italian managers are directly involved in the solution of technical problems, while their British counterparts act as brokers of technical specialized competences. Italian firms differ from German ones in that the role of middle managers is less formalized.

d'Iribarne, P. (1994). "The honour principle in the bureaucratic phenomenon". In: *Organization Studies*, 15:1, 81–97.
The attempts to understand the organizational functioning of a French factory in the 1980s have been greatly assisted by the use of a model of a society governed by the honour principle, as developed by Montesquieu and extended by Tocqueville. Subsequent research encouraged d'Iribarne in his view that this model explains the French pattern of action and that it can be extended well beyond the particular sphere in which its relevance first emerged. In general, d'Iribarne claims that to manage a company successfully means respecting the national culture in which it is embedded. When management faces "absurd resistance" from employees, it is possible to understand this resistance by taking "cultural principles" into account.

d'Iribarne, P. (2012). *Managing Corporate Values in Diverse National Cultures: The Challenge of Differences*. New York: Routledge.
Philippe d'Iribarne looks at the way in which corporate values are transferred within a multinational company. His study details how these values are expressed in the employees' daily practices in a number of subsidiaries, thanks to in-depth investigations within the Lafarge Group – 'an industrial group with French roots and a humanist tradition'. In this book, d'Iribarne compares what it means to the French, the Americans, the Chinese and the Jordanians to comply with the values defined in a corporate text called "Principles of Action".

Faurie, C. (2008). *Conduite du Changement*. Editions Maxima Paris.
While the business environment has become more and more complex as a result of globalization, the traditional approaches to change processes are no longer relevant, especially in acquisitions, alliances and mergers operations. In many cases we can observe that the companies "kill" change processes, which leads to an increase in employees' stress levels. They have to bear "organizational disturbances" resulting from a brutal approach to change and/or imposed standards, which are sometimes contradictory or inappropriate to the

companies' contexts. Based on several examples mainly used to explore the different causes and consequences of change, this book is "a strategic implementation manual" which enables the reader to assess the various competencies which were acquired previously by each of the two companies concerned. Aimed mainly at top managers, managers and project leaders, this book can also be useful to people wishing to understand change mechanisms in order to become proactive "players" instead of change victims.

4 QUESTIONS ON THE CASE

1. What are the key cultural and managerial characteristics of the acquired factory? What key changes should be implemented?
2. What issues related to power and cultural differences does André L. face at the Grays factory?
3. What are the different stages of the change process implemented by André L.?
4. What would you recommend to a manager in a similar situation?

5 REFERENCES

Brannen, M.Y. & Peterson, M. F. (2009). "Merging without alienating: Interventions promoting cross-cultural organizational integration and their limitations". In: *Journal of International Business*, 40, 468–489.

Davel, E., Dupuis, J.-P. & Chanlat, J.-F. (2009). *Gestion en Contexte Interculturel.* Québec: Presse de l'Université Laval et TÉLUQ/UQAM.

Delmestri, G. & Walgenbach, P. (2005). "Mastering techniques or brokering knowledge? Middle managers in Germany, Great Britain and Italy". In: *Organization Studies*, 26:2, 197–220.

d'Iribarne, P. (1994). "The honour principle in the bureaucratic phenomenon". In: *Organization Studies*, 15:1, 81–97.

d'Iribarne, P. (2012). *Managing Corporate Values in Diverse National Cultures: The Challenge of Differences*. New York: Routledge.

Faurie, C. (2008). *Conduite du Changement*. Paris: Maxima.

6

The Intercultural Challenge of Building the European eSports League for Video Gaming

Volker Stein and Tobias M. Scholz

1 INTRODUCTION

Due to technological advancements and changed behavioural patterns, people in Western societies have become familiar with "virtual" communication and interaction. They bridge distances and time zones while working together, communicating from any place to any place, meeting in social networks and sharing their knowledge, beliefs and lives. After two decades of constant progress through internationalization and digitalization within organizations and of advances in understanding virtualization, however, persistent cultural differences among people continue to make virtual communication and interaction an intercultural challenge. The fact that communication across cultural borders is possible does not automatically mean that communication and interaction across borders will work successfully.

Globalizing companies are facing the same experience. In their international environment, they use real-time communication and interaction patterns in order to distribute their products globally (and customize them locally) among customers from different countries. Their challenges grow exponentially since competition is simultaneously taking place in different markets and cultures. And, as if this was not enough, as a result of virtualization new business models are emerging, attracting customers from different countries and allowing them to interact independently of time, space and culture.

An example of an industry with such new business model dynamics is the video gaming industry. In a highly volatile, disruptive and, therefore, demanding environment, the technical capabilities of technological virtualization in communication and interaction are used to generate profits in the recreation sector. US-American DFC Intelligence, a video gaming market research company, reported that in 2012, the growing video gaming industry generated worldwide revenues of $67 billion, forecasting this to rise to $82 billion in 2017.

A major segment of this industry focuses on competitive gaming, known as "eSports". Competitive gaming can be compared to sports on the professional level, with the only difference being that the type of sport is a combative video game. Competition among teams and game players is organized in leagues, mostly by companies on a national level. These national leagues are accepted among gamers since they provide the technological platform, organize tournaments and attract public attention as well as media coverage.

At the international and, in particular, the European level, there is still a race with regard to which company will dominate the market and in the end set the rules for most of the video gamers. While soccer established the Union of European Football Associations (UEFA) in 1954, attempts to build a similar type of video gaming federation are still ongoing. Several dominant national league operators have evolved throughout Europe; however, at the European level the competition remains undecided. From an academic perspective, this ongoing process can be seen as a "living lab" for new market development, for the diffusion of technological innovations, for the institutionalization of regulatory systems, for lobbyism, for the effectiveness of marketing and for much more.

In the case that follows, we concentrate on intercultural issues in international management. Given a specific environment, we seek ways of bringing people together in intercultural virtual gamer communities. We look for ways of interacting within a company so that intercultural synergies will emerge for the benefit of all those involved. And we seek ways of creating an internationally sustainable business model bearing in mind the dynamics of a highly volatile and disruptive market which depends on the popularity curves of the games.

2 CASE DESCRIPTION

2.1 The situation

Video gaming as an industry In recent years, the video gaming industry has become a dominant force within the entertainment industry. In several countries, the video gaming industry has surpassed the music and movie industries in annual turnover. US-American DFC Intelligence reported that in 2012, the growing video gaming industry generated worldwide revenues of $67 billion, forecasting this to grow to $82 billion in 2017.

> Video games are sophisticated products that combine advanced software technology with content and interactive qualities. (…) The games industry is similar to other creative industries in a number of ways. For instance, games require their workers (known as "developers") to perform significant amounts of creative thinking, and games need to satisfy consumers' evolving expectations. However, game development differs from the development process of other creative industries in that it needs computer programming, design, project management, and substantial amounts of testing. In addition, the design process tends to be ongoing during development, with

the design affecting other components such as the programming code (or "code") as the development proceeds. (Tschang 2007:990)

The video gaming industry is no longer a niche market but a mainstream one that has developed rapidly since affordable and fast personal computers and laptops have allowed for profitable business models (Table 6.1).

Table 6.1 Gamer demographics in the US and Europe

58% of Americans play video games, 48% in Europe.
There is an average of two gamers in each game-playing US household.
51% of US households own a dedicated game console, and those that do own an average of two. In Europe, the share is 48%.
The average age of game players in the US is 30. 32% of players are under 18 years, 32% 18–35 years and 36% 36+ years. The average age of game players in Europe is 35. 12% of players are under 19 years, 40% 19–34 years and 49% 35+ years.
55% of game players in the US and in Europe are male, 45% female.
Women aged 18 or older represent a significantly greater portion of the US game-playing population (31%) than boys aged 17 or younger (19%). In Europe, 80% of men and 61% of women in the range of 16–24 play video games on a regular basis.
The average age of the most frequent game purchaser in the US is 35.
In the US, 43% of game players believe that computer and video games give them the most value for their money, compared with DVDs, music or going out to the cinema.

Source: Based on Entertainment Software Association 2013:2–3; Interactive Software Federation of Europe 2012:5–11)

The market for video gaming is highly volatile since new companies are entering the market, mergers and acquisitions are taking place, cooperation among changing business partners is being formed, innovative games are being launched and games which are fashionable at the time of launch become outdated after a certain period of time. Companies in this industry need the capability of constant adaptation and innovation in order to keep pace with their competitors and with their customers' demands.

The value chain of the video gaming industry consists of several integrated processes (e.g. Flew 2007):

- capital raising;
- building of development teams;
- production of games, game engines, hardware and supportive tools;
- distribution, i.e. publishing/licensing of new titles;
- end-user support service, e.g. tournament organization (i.e. eSports).

Many companies in the video gaming industry only focus on one single aspect of the value chain. Successful video game production takes place in regional clusters in which highly specialized video gaming companies closely interact. The global leaders are clustered in Montreal and Los Angeles; one major European cluster is London.

Companies in this highly creative industry know that they have to attract an international workforce to match their international market. This is also essential for successful teamwork:

> Companies seeking to optimize talent management should look for culturally intelligent staff for the creative jobs like game designer, artist and animator, audio designer, community manager, and quality assurance, whereas cultural intelligence does not seem to have a significant effect on the quality of teamwork found among the analytical jobs. (Scholz 2012:85)

Recently, a new trend has been observed: game players are increasingly becoming involved in game development by modifying existing games and participating in open-source game design.

eSports as end-user support service Competitive gaming ("eSports") is a major segment of the video gaming industry. Video gaming can be compared to professional sports. By 2013, eSports had been accredited as an official sport in South Korea (where it is a national sport), China (where it was part of the supporting programme of the 2008 Olympic Games), Russia, Bulgaria, Sweden and Taiwan. eSports competitions of teams and game players are followed by a live audience via internet live-stream. As in soccer, eSports has national leagues that organize overall national tournaments by providing technological platforms and standards, setting the rules and attracting public interest and media coverage.

> Electronic sports (eSports) is a term for organized video game competitions, especially between professionals. Related terms include competitive gaming, professional gaming, and cybersport. The most common video game genres associated with electronic sports are real-time strategy, fighting, first-person shooter, and multiplayer online battle arena. Tournaments such as the World Cyber Games, the Evolution Championship Series, and the Intel Extreme Masters provide both live broadcasts of the competition, and cash prizes to competitors. (http://en.wikipedia.org/wiki/Electronic_sports)

eSports organizations focus on the end-user support service and interact with the gamers. They serve as service providers that mediate between video game developers and video gamers in order to create a shared attitude towards the game and a joint understanding of its attractiveness, shaping so-called video game communities (e.g. Burger-Helmchen & Cohendet 2011). Although eSports is an upcoming segment, only a few video gaming companies are investing in eSports or supporting eSports organizations. eSports organizations are isolated activists.

For companies in this eSports segment, the organization of gaming competitions is a difficult field in which to generate profits. Competitive gaming is even more of a young niche market than ordinary video gaming. For those gamers and companies regarding it as a real sport, it is disappointing that eSports is not accredited in most countries, as, for example, chess is. Certainly, the contents of this "sport" are constantly changing, which makes any institutionalization difficult. As to the generation of monetary returns, this is still complicated in a setting where any internet user can participate without a longer commitment. Therefore, eSports companies are heavily reliant on the money of sponsors. Countries active in the eSports segment are developed countries such as US and Canada, Australia, the European countries, South Korea and China. Japan lags behind because of its restrictive anti-gambling regulations.

eSports can be differentiated into three categories of game player involvement:

1. **Casual level**: game players play just for fun and on an irregular basis.
2. **Amateur level**: game players train on a constant basis and participate regularly in tournaments and leagues.
3. **Professional level**: game players train regularly and intensively. They get paid for playing and participate in the top leagues and at top tournaments.

All of them share a specific "gamer culture", affecting their individual and collective behavioural patterns – the ways they work, shop, eat and organize their lives (e.g. Shaw 2010). This gamer culture bridges the different game player levels:

> Because the border between amateurs and new rising pro talent is not as clear as in traditional sports, many regular players can also find themselves playing against emerging pros. This connection, between everyday leisure and fandom, between amateur and pro players, helps build strong affective attachments. (Taylor 2012:189)

Language does not play a major role: Video games are predominantly in English, but still it is possible to communicate without advanced English skills. Some games even use a specific universalistic terminology, for example in basketball games, where it is universally understood what a "foul" or a position such as "point guard", "shooting guard", "small forward", "power forward" and "centre" is.

Gamer culture: Identity for gamers, a challenge for eSports

eSports is shaped by two cultures: the national culture of contestants and game culture. In particular, the game culture layer is a very interesting one:

> For many young Koreans, their participation in online games represents one facet of a whole community and way of life. The activities

> surrounding this media ecology determine how its members navigate within their vital orientations and make choices about how they take nourishment, spend money, earn money, and even partake in courtship rituals. (Chee 2006:232)

The game culture obviously affects game players' whole way of life:

> They will devote hours upon hours to mastering it, endlessly fascinated by the intricacies of the system, its characters, its weapons, its properties. Figuring out strategies and tactics become core play activities. (Taylor 2012: 89)

What is the impact of the gamer culture on eSport? At first, the gamer culture leads to a cultural convergence at the level of gaming competition. There are the same rules, the same infrastructure, and the same game spirit. In any case, in the virtual world of online gaming, one gamer cannot be distinguished from another; it is all the same whether the gamer is Swedish or French. However – and seemingly contradictorily – national culture still matters. Since gaming is a competition with transnational tournaments – there are Swedish teams and French teams etc. – eSports sets great value upon national differences. Teams are defined by their nationality. There are only a few internationally mixed gamer teams, and even they communicate their identity by some common culture with a regional reference, for example appearing as the "Scandinavian team" or the "European team". Therefore, on top of a convergent gamer culture, eSports helps to create an "artificial cultural divergence".

> One of the interesting things about e-sports is the way it is constructed across national lines but still quite rooted and shaped by local contexts. Game culture more broadly is also located in this fashion. Game titles circulate within a global entertainment market, yet the specificities of regionality simultaneously help shape preferences and play. Neither one nor the other vector predominates but instead there is a complex interplay between a construction of the global and local. (Taylor 2012:243–244)

The Electronic Sports League (ESL) as a distinct eSports company The Electronic Sports League (ESL) is a distinct company in the European eSports industry. It was founded in 1997 in Germany and organizes national tournaments and events. In the early 2000s, the ESL expanded throughout Europe and in recent years globally, for example to China, and works with spin-offs and partners in over 40 countries. There are only a few internationally active leagues that have a similarly long history. Currently, the headquarters are in Cologne, Germany.

> The Electronic Sports League (ESL) is the largest and most important league for gamers in Europe consisting of more than three million registered

members and more than 800,000 registered teams. ESL has been operated by the company Turtle Entertainment since 2000 and offers more than 3,500 professional leagues and amateur ladders from a variety of games. Around 400,000 matches per month are played worldwide using ESL technology. (www.esl.eu)

The ESL distinguishes its leagues in Europe by the participants' level (casual, amateur and professional) and by regional level (national and continental). In addition, there are several international tournaments (e.g. Intel Extreme Masters, Blizzard World Championship Series) that are organized on a global level with European stopovers.

When the ESL was founded by members of the eSports community, it filled the need for a German tournament operator. The mission statement of the ESL is its claim to be "the league that matters". It tries to serve customers' demands at every participant and regional level. At the time of the ESL's foundation, however, the European eSports market was growing very slowly, with eSports video game providers far from any degree of professionalization. Europe-wide expansion was a long way ahead, especially since strategic, legal and technological differences occasionally turned out to be major restrictions.

The ESL has 15 franchise holders and two subsidiaries working in 41 countries around the globe. Global corporations such as Intel, BenQ, Deutsche Post, DELL, Asus, Adidas, Volkswagen and Microsoft support the ESL. In close co-operation with the Chinese ProGamerLeague, Turtle Entertainment opened the ESL Asia section in 2007. (www.esl.eu)

2.2 THE CHALLENGE

Although eSports gaming itself is similar in different countries, it is strongly influenced by regional customers' demands, interests and technologies, both on the amateur and the professional level. A European tournament operator needs to find specific solutions for each single country as well as a general solution for Europe. For example, national conditions differ in terms of internet infrastructure and legal restrictions. Sometimes, local sponsors that are visible in the games of local tournaments have to be replaced by European sponsors if it is a European tournament. In order to fit almost any potential eSports gamer in Europe, it turned out that it was not enough to be loyal to one's community and to improve eSports in general and the game culture in particular. The vision of a league suitable for everybody in Europe brought with it the necessity to overcome cultural constraints. This makes it necessary to see the similarities rather than the differences – and to utilize the differences in order to create intercultural synergies (e.g. Adler & Gundersen 2008:99–122) within that borderless "virtual" community of eSports gamers.

The first step towards intercultural synergies is intercultural communication. The ESL identified that need and the positive aspects of cultural differences by diversifying their national operations through spin-offs and partners in those countries (Table 6.2). Of course, as a Germany-based start-up, the ESL's neighbouring countries in Europe were targeted first. However, the ESL faces specific challenges in some countries, such as the underdeveloped internet infrastructure in India and Latin America or the obligation in China to form commercial partnerships with Chinese companies.

Table 6.2 Expansion of the ESL

Year	Members	New countries
2001	100,000	
2002	200,000	
2003	400,000	France
2004	600,000	Austria, Switzerland
2005	900,000	Bulgaria, Italy
2006	1,300,000	
2007	1,600,000	Romania
2008	2,000,000	Denmark, Finland, Norway, Poland, Sweden, UK, USA
2009	2,500,000	Israel
2010	3,000,000	Portugal
2011	3,600,000	
2012	4,000,000	Australia, Estonia, Latvia, Lithuania

Source: www.turtle-entertainment.com/company (last accessed 24 March 2014).

The Germany-based ESL assumes that any dominance of national tournament markets and the development of a Europe-wide eSports league will only be possible through a synergistic approach with local partners. On the one hand, the ESL still acts like a "typical German company": it tends to balance its budgets, avoids incalculable risks and has even implemented a dual education system with its own apprentices. On the other hand, however, the ESL has established international virtual teams throughout Europe for gaming community development, tournament organization, and customer service administration. Team members from different local spin-offs and partners co-operate across national and cultural borders, using the English language.

Within the international virtual teams, the international partners contribute their respective strengths, i.e. their knowledge of local tournament markets, of sponsors and gamers. Organized both by the German ESL headquarters and decentrally by the international partners, they usually have a steady communication flow, using emails, chats, Twitter, internet relay chat (IRC), forums, voice servers, and in-game communications. They talk about ideas and cooperatively decide on new regulations or sponsorship deals. If important decisions are to be made, any partner can spontaneously convene a videoconference "on demand", bringing together the partners involved. Furthermore, all partners regularly exchange recent local developments throughout the complete international ESL network so that other regions can benefit from knowing about them. They share a common ESL culture, which can be characterized as open, transparent, "technically communicative" (i.e. not too much face-to-face) and based on mutual trust. The employees involved also know each other personally from tournaments, where they help to create the required infrastructure. In addition, there is an annual "partners' conference" at which ESL employees and partners meet, talk and share new ideas. Stepwise, a convergence of tournament systems is achieved by international dialogue rather than by centralistic ESL headquarters decisions. The idea behind cooperating in international virtual teams is to collect recent trends, to identify the gamers' preference shifts at an early stage, to diversify towards regional specificities where necessary and in general to stay agile and adaptable to the volatile environment.

This ongoing internationalization is already reflected in the ESL workforce which embraces people from different countries (Table 6.3). The employees working abroad are supposed to build up international ESL subsidiaries in a polycentric network. The objective is that these international subsidiaries become capable leading the organization of major tournaments; still, however, using the ESL technology and equipment from Germany.

Table 6.3 The ESL workforce 2013

Parent country	Employees in ESL headquarters in Cologne, Germany	Employees in ESL subsidiaries abroad
Brazil		1
China	5	10
France	8	8
Germany	99	
Italy	5	15
Poland	8	10
Portugal	5	1
Russia	3	3
Spain	5	3
UK	7	
USA	5	12
Total	**150**	**63**
(of whom: women)	(8)	(3)

Source: ESL.

While the ESL is developing towards a system of interconnected local units in several countries with a coordination hub for the overall European integration tasks, it faces the typical problems that can be observed in every European integration process. The consensual selection of a broadly accepted video game for the tournaments across various countries with different traditions is still difficult. Moreover, interests of national units might dominate the overall ESL interests and, therefore, have to be negotiated.

Where should the finals take place?

In recent years it was the custom that the ESL finals – the final games of the Intel Extreme Masters Series – took place in Germany on the occasion of big fairs such as CeBit or gamescom. In 2013, the Polish ESL subsidiary suddenly claimed a bigger role, for example by asking to host some of the stops of this series in Poland. The German ESL headquarters felt uncomfortable with this request, pointing to the risk that there would be insufficient international attendance in Poland. However, the Polish ESL team prevailed against the German view, and were able to organize the stops at their own risk. These stops turned out to be extremely successful, literally "filling stadiums". In 2014, even the Intel Extreme Masters Series finals took place in Katowice, despite all concerns, and achieved record attendance figures.

Information derived from: http://de.intelextrememasters.com/season8/world-championship/ (last accessed 24 March 2014).

As one example of how the ESL's business model is sustained, mention should be made of the Intel Extreme Masters Series. This series, first held in 2005, is an international tournament season with several fixed stops in Germany and Poland and alternating stops in Ukraine, Brazil, Canada, China and the US. By visiting countries that are in the process of developing their gaming scene, local gamers have the opportunity to come into contact with the international video gaming community. They can exchange views and swap ideas on new game strategies. The ESL is very interested in assessing the potential of the emerging markets. It then repeatedly analyses its value chain for shifts in the national leagues and adapts its systems based on the new impulses from these emerging markets.

A second example is ESL-TV, a platform for broadcasting tournaments. ESL-TV shows are produced all over Europe. The usual method of video game development is that developers add "observing features" particularly for spectators right from the beginning, such as different watching perspectives and a broad range of additional real-time information. During the broadcasts of video game tournaments, commentators provide live commentaries for eSports events. The ESL not only provides interactive services to retain its customers but also tried (although without success) to establish paid eSport TV channels in order to create a business model where gaming events can still be sold if they are almost outdated or only have a limited audience – the so-called "long tail strategy".

3 BACKGROUND KNOWLEDGE

3.1 The authors' point of reference

The authors aim at combining strategic management in open systems with intercultural management:

- Strategic management in open systems means concentrating on ways of integrating people who are not formally committed to an organization and also on ways of aligning employees to common objectives even though they may work at different places and under different conditions. The underlying theoretical approach is that of virtualization and, in particular, of international virtual teams.
- Intercultural management means utilizing cultural differences in order to attain business success for the company. The underlying theoretical approach is intercultural synergy.

Both fields are relevant for up-to-date management and leave a lot of space for innovative solutions since – in spite of decades of research – conclusive answers to important questions are still missing. By combining these challenging fields with a highly specific, modern industry segment such as eSports, there will be much room for innovative ideas and fruitful discussion.

3.2 Concepts, models, frameworks

3.2.1 Cultural differences and their consequences at work: The theory of virtualization and international virtual teams

International virtual team research refers to the general theoretical concept of virtuality which is based on the original concepts of the virtual organization (e.g. Davidow & Malone 1992). The theoretical frame for virtualization used here is the "virt.cube" (Scholz 2000), which integrates specific moves along three dimensions which in combination help us to understand virtual organizations both inter-organizationally (the grouping of business units into virtual organizations) and intra-organizationally (grouping of people into virtual teams):

- Core competence differentiation as strategic dimension. Virtual structures focus on their core competencies: potential virtualization partners try to provide those capabilities where they really have unique and sustainable competitive advantages. Benchmarking and best practices lead to the selection of the best partners who combine their capabilities according to the modularity principle.
- Soft integration as organizational dimension. As differentiation always calls for integration, the second dimension concerns coupling the outcomes of the core competence partners' work and optimizing overall team performance. Since these partners work independently of each other, the formerly distributed value chain has to be re-integrated, but only by those mechanisms which do not increase dysfunctional bureaucracy and transaction

costs. For this purpose, four so-called "soft" concepts seem promising: the team members' mutual understanding of their almost symbiotic coexistence and co-destiny, their shared vision and shared goals, their fairness and trust and their commonly shared cultural values.

- Multimedia communication as technological dimension. Virtual structures are strongly linked with modern information technologies and multimedia and, in particular, with the concepts of virtual reality, social networks and cyberspace. The more information and emotions are shared via technologies without the limitations of physical attributes, the more communication will become real-time and socio-emotionally "rich", replacing physical face-to-face communication.

By applying the virt.cube framework, it is possible to assess a system's (company's, team's) progress on its road to virtuality. "Ideal" international virtual teams are highly advanced on each of the three dimensions.

Looking at international virtual teams from the intercultural perspective, two prevailing configurations can be observed. They differ in the way each of the three dimensions of virtualization is shaped (Scholz & Stein 2003):

- The first (participative) configuration is the combination of "marketplace negotiation of core competences" – "feel the suitable leader" – "federalist-type multimedia integration". In this case, the team members discuss their assignments in a rather hierarchy-free structure, negotiate timetables and deadlines and take on their collective workload in a fairly equally distributed way. Team leaders may change over time, guiding the team by means of "soft persuasion". Different multimedia supports can coexist.
- The second (hierarchical) configuration is the combination of "core competences assigned by bureaucracy and power" – "follow the imposed leader" – "monopoly-type multimedia standardization". In this case, bodies of rules dominate the collaboration. The team members expect to have a strong leader guiding them but also solving problems. It is based on one single technological platform for communication.

These configurations help in the discussion of the cultural issues of forming virtual teams. In the context of companies, the participative configuration is prevalent and more efficient in Europe; the hierarchical configuration prevalent and more efficient in the US.

3.2.2 The theory of intercultural synergy

(Inter)cultural synergy describes the process of bringing together people from two or more cultures in order to combine their strengths and ideas and create something together that they would not achieve alone.

> Cultural synergy, as an approach to managing the impact of cultural diversity, involves a process in which managers form organizational strategies, structures, and practices based on, but not limited to, the cultural patterns of individual organization members and clients. (Adler & Gundersen 2008:109)

Intercultural synergy is seen as a key resource for intercultural learning, combining "the best from different worlds". According to Adler and Gundersen (2008:112), creating cultural synergy requires three steps:

- describing the situation;
- interpreting the cultures by determining the underlying cultural assumptions and assessing the cultural overlaps;
- increasing cultural creativity and creating cultural synergy by creating culturally synergistic alternatives, selecting one and implementing it.

In the search for intercultural synergies, people have to be encouraged to stick to their own cultural identity but at the same time to be open to the otherness of their team partners. Creating intercultural synergies is a democratic, balanced process without power games.

3.3 Recommended reading

Adler, N. J. & Gundersen, A. (2008). ***International Dimensions of Organizational Behavior.*** **5th ed. Mason: Thompson-South Western.**
The basic book for understanding cultural diversity and human dynamics in international management and for managing people globally. It is one of the first books that focuses on the beneficial potential of cultural differences and states that cultural diversity can have a positive effect on teams and their creativity.

Davidow, W. H. & Malone, M. S. (1992). ***The Virtual Corporation. Structuring and Revitalizing the Corporation for the 21st Century.*** **New York: Harper Business.**
This classic is one of the first visionary contributions to explain the "virtual corporation" and to develop a picture of more flexible, more dynamic, and more media-supported ways of organizing companies in the 21st century.

Scholz, C. & Stein, V. (2003). "International Virtual Teams (IVTs): A triple 'Mission Impossible'?". In: Morley, M. J., Cross, C., Flood, P. C., Gubbins, C., Heraty, N. & Sheikh, H. (Eds), ***Exploring the Mosaic, Developing the Discipline. Full Proceedings of the 7th Conference on International Human Resource Management.*** **University of Limerick, Ireland, 4–6 June 2003, Dublin: Interesource Group, CD-ROM.**
Based on the "virt.cube" model, this article highlights alternative culture-related configurations of international virtual teams. Both the participative and the hierarchical configuration help explain the cultural dependence of the successful settings of international virtual teams. Team members can learn to cope with both configurations if they are trained accordingly.

Scholz, C. (2000). "Virtualisierung als Wettbewerbsstrategie für den Mittelstand?". In: Erste Erfahrungen und ergänzende Überlegungen. ***Zeitschrift für Betriebswirtschaft,*** **70:2, 201–222.**
This article is the first publication of the "virt.cube" model describing three dimensions of organizational virtualization. Due to the technological progress, organizations are becoming more virtual and more translucent. This change

has a major influence on the composition of an organization and its interaction with its external environment, in particular for small and medium-sized companies.

Scholz, T. M. (2012). "Talent management in the video game industry: The role of cultural diversity and cultural intelligence". In: *Thunderbird International Business Review*, 54, 845–858.
This article shows how cultural diversity helps to create advancements in the video game industry. It focuses on the video game development process in which creativity and programming are essential for success. Both aspects require a different type of job characteristic.

Taylor, T. L. (2012). *Raising the Stakes. E-Sports and the Professionalization of Computer Gaming*. Cambridge: MIT Press.
This book unfolds the world of video gaming and the recent progress of that industry. It also concentrates on gamer culture. It is the first academic research to tackle the eSports phenomenon and describes the history and development of this segment of gaming.

4 QUESTIONS ON THE CASE

1. Why does it seem to be a promising idea to build up a European eSports league rather than national eSports leagues?
2. Building a European eSports league means aligning gaming community development, tournament organization and customer service administration to the locally different preferences of the gamers. What procedural advice would you give the ESL in order to create (inter)cultural synergies among its employees? And what procedural advice would you give the ESL in order to create (inter)cultural synergies among the gamers?
3. How can the ESL use the "virt.cube" framework to stabilize its international virtual team building among its employees across the different European spin-offs?
4. How can the ESL business model become sustainable in a market where the preferences of gamers are continually changing?
5. What does the critical question "Where should the finals take place?" tell us about the ethnocentricity of the ESL strategy?

5 REFERENCES

Adler, N. J. & Gundersen, A. (2008). *International Dimensions of Organizational Behavior*. 5th ed. Mason: Thompson-South Western.

Burger-Helmchen, T. & Cohendet, P. (2011). "User communities and social software in the video games industry". In: *Long Range Planning*, 44, 317–343.

Chee, F. (2006). "The games we play online and offline: Making Wang-tta in Korea". In: *Popular Communication*, 4, 225–239.

Davidow, W. H. & Malone, M. S. (1992). *The Virtual Corporation. Structuring and Revitalizing the Corporation for the 21st Century*. New York: Harper Business.

Entertainment Software Association [ESA] (2013). *2013 Sales, Demographic and Usage Data. Essential Facts About the Computer and Video Game Industry*. Washington: ESA.

Flew, T. (2007). *New Media: An Introduction*. 3rd ed. Oxford: Oxford University Press. Interactive Software Federation of Europe [ISFE] (2012). "Video games in Europe: Consumer study". In: *European Summary Report November 2012*. Brussels: ISFE.

Scholz, C. & Stein, V. (2003): "International Virtual Teams (IVTs). A triple 'Mission Impossible'?" In: Morley, M. J., Cross, C., Flood, P. C., Gubbins, C., Heraty, N. & Sheikh, H. (Eds), *Exploring the Mosaic, Developing the Discipline. Full Proceedings of the 7th Conference on International Human Resource Management*. University of Limerick, Ireland, 4–6 June 2003, Dublin: Interesource Group, CD-ROM.

Scholz, C. (2000). "Virtualisierung als Wettbewerbsstrategie für den Mittelstand? Erste Erfahrungen und ergänzende Überlegungen". In: *Zeitschrift für Betriebswirtschaft*, 70:2, 201–222.

Scholz, T. M. (2012). "Talent management in the video game industry: The role of cultural diversity and cultural intelligence". In: *Thunderbird International Business Review*, 54, 845–858.

Shaw, A. (2010). "What is video game culture? Cultural studies and game studies". In: *Games and Culture*, 5, 403–424.

Taylor, T. L. (2012). *Raising the Stakes. E-Sports and the Professionalization of Computer Gaming*. Cambridge, MA: MIT Press.

Tschang, F. T. (2007). "Balancing the tensions between rationalization and creativity in the video games industry". In: *Organization Science*, 18, 989–1005.

7

Leading Change in Mergers and Acquisitions in Asia–Pacific

Jenny Plaister-Ten

1 INTRODUCTION

Thanks to the forces of globalization and the increased effectiveness of technology (Friedman 2005), the international business environment has become characterized by globally dispersed, multicultural project teams, virtual teamworking, and processes such as agile software development made known by the Agile Manifesto (www.agilemanifesto.org). This situation is intensified during mergers and acquisitions when each party to the merger brings differing organizational and reporting structures, matrix management structures, corporate cultures and culturally bound values, beliefs and working practices (Schein 1992). The result can be that progress is stifled, confusion is created, morale is deflated and productivity is affected.

Matrix management structures have typically been implemented as a way to break down traditional hierarchical structures (Knight 1977; Robbins 1993), and to create temporary solutions through flatter, leaner organizations. This arrangement may be quickly dismantled once new products have been introduced or projects have been completed. Other more permanent matrix structures have been built around processes, for example. Organizations can find themselves faced with complex reporting structures as the matrix grows and becomes permanent. This can actually slow decision making (Kramer 1994).

Nevertheless, the one enduring factor remains: the business imperative. As the case study that follows illuminates, without clear leadership business goals can be compromised. Simultaneously, without bias-free leadership (Glantz 2006) and an acknowledgement that different cultures can place different emphasis upon different business goals (Hofstede et al. 2010), confusion can abound. Complex business environments can provide a hotbed for frustration created by a lack of understanding of differing values, beliefs and working practices (Moran et al. 2007) and even different conceptions of self (Markus & Kitayama 1999). At their best however, they can stimulate creativity and increase responsiveness.

The following case study is situated in the Asia–Pacific region in the IT sector. It illuminates the need to be aware of the organization structure and the external environment as well as the cultural references of its corporate citizens.

2 CASE DESCRIPTION

2.1 The situation: company background

"We don't care how you do it, we just want results," Freddie Mills, Director Products UK, told Susie Wood just before she left for a two-year tenure in the Asia–Pacific region.

While the message behind this statement was clear, the company officials did not make their expectations explicit. Computers International Limited (CIL) was an established multinational company, with headquarters in the UK and operating in 70 countries around the world. It employed some 150,000 people. Susie Wood wondered what she was getting herself into.

The company had built its name in the days of the mainframe and mini-computer era of the 1960s and 1970s. It had lost ground thanks to the shift towards personal computers and solutions based on the PC platform. The company had an expensive direct sales team in the UK and needed to change its "go-to-market" strategy, in a bid to increase share in its international operations in particular. In the early 1990s it had been acquired by a Japanese company, Tojitsu, based in Toyko. Tojitsu had taken an "arm's length approach" to the acquisition so far, although there was an air of anticipation; a matter of "when" rather than "if" Tojitsu would begin to exercise control. Tojitsu executives were mainly Japanese men in their 40s and 50s.

The product division of CIL, based in the UK, was responsible for product development of a range of PCs and PC-based software, solutions and services. The division was also responsible for the worldwide marketing of these products. While it had recently gained over 50% market share for its high-end products in the UK and 40% in its main European markets of Germany, Spain and France, it had made little impact with these products in the "rest of the world"; particularly the Asia–Pacific region. The international division, also based in UK, wanted more commitment from the product division to spearhead their growth in the Asia–Pacific region. Susie Wood was the answer. She was a bright committed young marketer in her early 30s, with a previous track record of operating internationally. She had been headhunted from the market-leading company in the UK. She reported to the director of the product division in the UK.

Just as the ink was drying on Susie's contract, CIL announced a "backward merger" with a Finnish company, Konia. Konia had previously taken over a Swedish company and there was intense rivalry between the Swedes and the Finns. The backward merger meant that the product development and product marketing would be led mainly out of Helsinki, with some of the engineering out of Northern Sweden. Konia used an agile product development methodology, which meant that multicultural teams were set up and disbanded according to swift new product development methods. Konia wanted to incorporate agile methodologies throughout all of the CIL product divisions. This was a big culture shift for CIL, which had predominantly used traditional "waterfall", i.e. sequential, product development methodologies.

Susie had no time to go and visit her counterparts in Scandinavia before she left for Asia but was told that she would have to report into the product group in Helsinki and therefore she had a new boss. Phillipe van Uiderquist, 38, was a Swede who had spent several years working in the USA. He was very ambitious, finding the working practices and procedures of CIL to be a bit draconian at times. In her new role, Susie also reported to a British, male manager based in Hong Kong – Dennis Smith, aged 44, who headed up the Asia–Pacific region. Dennis saw this initiative as being critical for his career. If he became known for introducing a totally new business model in the Asia–Pacific region, he could see himself running the international division in a few years' time.

Susie was excited at the thought of being located in Hong Kong. However, at the last minute it was decided that she should be based in Singapore where there was an "international stocking unit" (ISU), responsible for the ordering and stocking of components and configuration of final items for sale by one of 12 markets. Susie had to work closely with the director of the ISU, a British-born Chinese man, who acted as a "bridge" between the locals in the region, who were typically employed on local salaries, and the "guilos", the foreigners like Susie who were employed on an expatriate basis. There was, however, an underlying tension between those employed on local contracts and those who enjoyed benefits including housing, car allowance and trips back home as well as an increase in salary to compensate for higher costs of living.

Susie was responsible for two direct reports in Singapore: a Singaporean who had been educated in Australia, Lee Ser-Hai, a male in his mid-30s, and a Chinese Malaysian, T. G. Toh, also male and in his mid-30s. While T. G. Toh appeared on the face of it to be very supportive of Susie's appointment, Ser-Hai made it clear that he believed she did not understand the local markets.

Susie was responsible for the sales activities of the PC and PC solutions product range in China, Hong Kong, Thailand, Indonesia, Singapore, Malaysia, South Korea, Taiwan, Australia and New Zealand. Each of these countries had their own local office and a salesperson was assigned to sell the new products, although they also sold other products from other product divisions. Each of these salespeople had their own boss in the local market, which was typically the country head. The country heads in each case were "traditional" CIL types: typically male, in their early 50s, who had been with the company for 20 to 30 years and were used to a direct sales model and high-margin products and solutions. They were not used to the low-margin, high-volume orientation of the PC market and were slightly apprehensive about getting into a business that they saw as risky, yet essential for the future sustainability of the business.

2.2 The challenge

One of Susie's first tasks was to create an Asia–Pacific strategy for the new product line. This entailed creating a new division called the Asia–Pacific PC division. Since she had no previous experience in any of these local markets, she did some market intelligence work. This entailed visiting the local markets and finding out what the market conditions were like. She quickly realized that no two markets were alike and each represented a different set of challenges and opportunities from a sales and marketing perspective. These ranged from price pressure in the Chinese market, to a lack of disposal income in some of the developing markets, to a lack of working space and therefore a "footprint" issue in markets like Hong Kong. It went without saying, of course, that trying to sell PCs in Asia was likely to be a challenge in itself as most of the components were sourced from Asia in the first place and sold for very little margin. PC solutions (software, services) therefore represented the highest growth potential.

Meanwhile, the product division in Helsinki had mandated that all sales operations had to sell its ergonomically designed range of PCs. Yet ergonomics was not a concept that many Asian people appreciated or desired. An exception was Singapore where aspirational purchasers realized that owning one of these PCs could set them apart. Also, in Australia, health and safety issues had started to have an impact on the desire for ergonomically designed products.

Another factor that had a bearing on the situation was that each of the local markets had a different "go-to-market" strategy. In China, Hong Kong, Malaysia and South Korea, for example, a direct sales team sold direct to the end customer. In Indonesia, Thailand and Taiwan it was through a third party. In Australia, Singapore and New Zealand it was a combination of both.

Part of the strategy was to recommend a cohesive route to market and put forward a budget to create market awareness and market penetration. After three months in post, Susie had formulated this strategy and her Asia–Pacific boss endorsed it. Now "all" she had to do was get the buy-in of the local markets and communicate the strategy back to the product centre.

Multicultural team working in a matrix environment Susie realized the magnitude of the challenge she faced at the first strategy meeting of the newly formed division. She had gathered her team for a pre-meeting meeting and they all agreed that they were going to recommend a centralized approach to marketing across the region. This meant that each local market would contribute a fund to a central marketing budget, which would be managed by the Singapore team in the interests of economies of scale. Dennis Smith was in agreement.

Nevertheless, the reality of the first strategy meeting was very different. Only Susie and Lee Ser-Hai spoke out in favour of a centralized approach. T. G. Toh voted against it, in line with the other more senior members in the room who were the country heads from the local markets. Susie was astounded that her boss, Dennis, was not openly supportive of a strategy he had previously agreed to and she was disappointed in her direct report for going against their previous agreement. Not only that, each of the country heads had different reasons for wanting local autonomy, which included a lack of belief in the need for a premium-priced ergonomic range; a desire not to upset a client or a partner by introducing a new product when they had just sold them an alternative solution; a lack of salespeople; lack of budget; lack of motivation. Mr Lam, an elderly 'statesman' from China, who had been with the company for many years, was simply focused on China alone. This surprised Susie as she would have expected senior personnel to take an enterprise-wide viewpoint. Even more surprising was an undertone that suggested a disdain for programmes run out of Singapore, particularly from the Hong Kong and Malaysian contingents.

Susie took T. G. Toh to one side and said, "Why did you do that? Why did you vote against our previous agreement?" There was no response.

Susie realized that she was caught in complexity that she did not understand. She had the ultimate responsibility for the success of this product range in the Asia–Pacific region but now she was becoming aware that she had no authority. She was confused by working practices that did not make sense to her and she felt disoriented and frustrated. She had lost trust in her team and she felt disrespected. Yet her colleagues in the UK and in the product centre were counting on her, as was her boss in Hong Kong. She started to yearn for what was familiar to her. She began to experience culture shock.

How was she going to work through all of the complexity and turn in the results expected of her? At this point she had no idea. She also had little idea of what was driving the thought patterns and decision-making processes of her colleagues in the region so she found them difficult to work with at times. She had several bosses in different parts of the world, each with different and often competing agendas. She had responsibility for growing a business across the region, but little budget or staff to help her to do this. Furthermore, her two direct reports based in Singapore seemed determined to undermine her in one way or another.

Susie was lucky. A strong leader came to rescue. Tojitsu appointed a new president from outside its own traditional culture, Mr Saitou. This new executive dismantled a lot of the complex reporting structures and streamlined product development teams. New global and multicultural project teams were established to encourage knowledge transfer and to increase creativity. More importantly, however, was a change initiative that identified new corporate values such as teamworking, openness and respect for all. To assist with the transition, the new president approved a coaching programme for all managers considered to have high potential within the company. Tangible corporate objectives were also made clear, such as to be the number one vendor of PCs and PC solutions by market share within three years.

Susie went on to achieve her objectives and is now set to become a director within the company. Mr Lam continues to do an excellent job in the China operation and Phillipe van Uiderquist left the company to pursue his career with a rival.

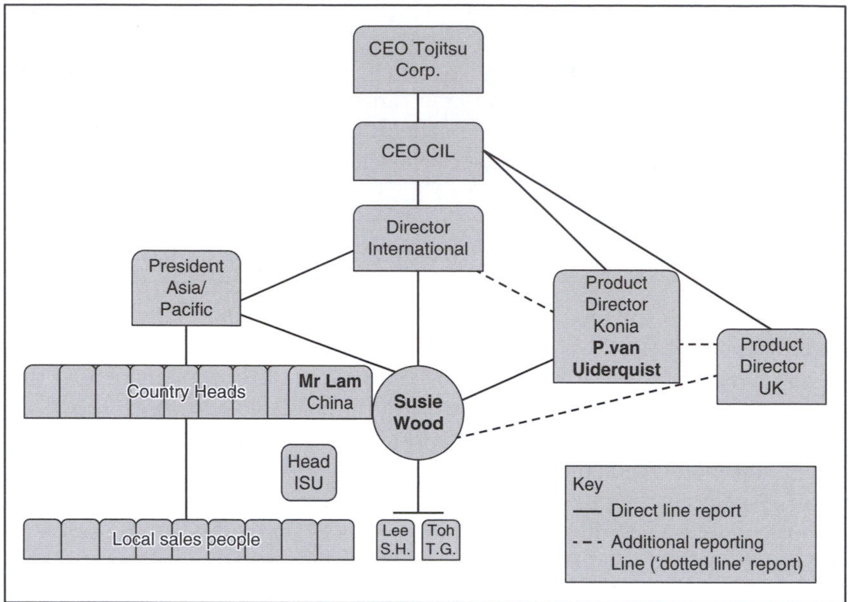

Figure 7.1 Matrix management reporting structure

3 BACKGROUND KNOWLEDGE

3.1 The author's point of reference

The author, Jennifer Plaister-Ten, is a global consultant, executive coach and trainer who develops international markets on behalf of her clients. She works with executives operating globally and with multicultural teams. She has spent many years in international roles including ten years in the Asia–Pacific region. She has run her own consultancy company based in Singapore and is now Director of 10 Consulting Ltd.

3.2 Concepts, models, frameworks

Cultural differences and their consequences at work Plaister-Ten (2013) has developed a model for intercultural working. This takes into account the culturally held values and beliefs that influence thoughts and emotions and drive behaviour as well as the external influences that impact decisions in a business context. The Cross-Cultural Kaleidoscope™ model places organizational culture at its very core. It reflects the belief that culture holds individual meanings for each and every one of its members, a concept referred to as the "cultural self", and yet is influenced by external factors such as history, economics or religious beliefs. Therefore it is not sufficient to understand cultural differences in isolation from either the organizational context, including the goals of the organization, or the external context – the contribution from the macro environment.

When working interculturally it is important to adopt a "both/and" paradigm in order to achieve synergies, rather than an "either/or" perspective. An "either/or" perspective is all too frequently perceived when working from a view of culture that suggests that cultural norms fall into opposing categories, such as individualism vs. collectivism. Such a view implies that the opposite of individualism is collectivism and vice versa. However, in reality this is unlikely to be the case. A person may exhibit signs of individualism in certain circumstances, for example when pursuing goals and objectives. Alternatively, the same person may tend toward collective behaviour when working in a team or when at home with family. Therefore, a "both/and" perspective would seek to identify a higher purpose that leverages the benefits of both approaches simultaneously.

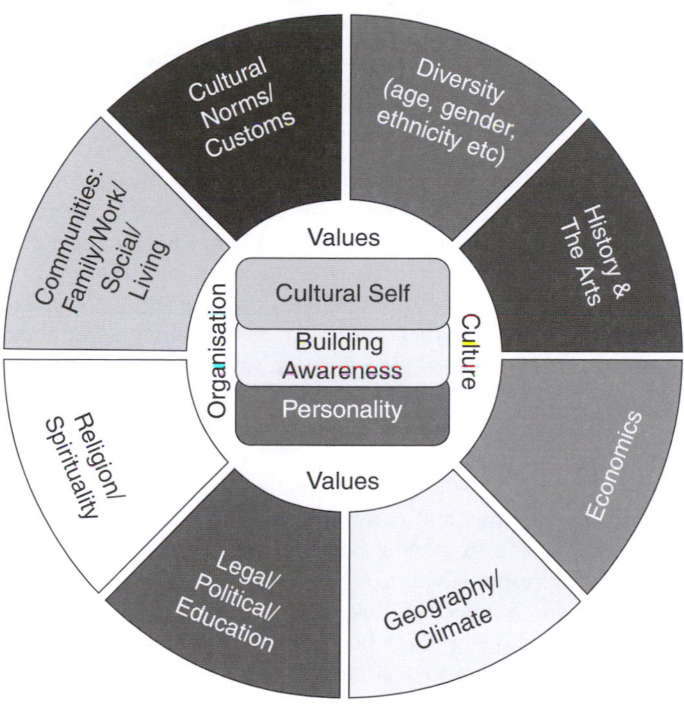

Figure 7.2 The Cross-Cultural Kaleidoscope™ model

The Cross-Cultural Kaleidoscope™ model provides a tool that enables the participant to reflect upon an intercultural situation. Thus he/she should experience raised awareness of the complexities inherent within a case such as the CIL scenario. In intercultural work, values and beliefs that are culturally constructed, either during socialization or during adult life, may be completely unconscious. This is because our cultural values and beliefs are "below the waterline", as explained in the well-known "cultural iceberg" metaphor. Yet it is below the surface of the water that most cultural clashes have their origins.

The Cross-Cultural Kaleidoscope™ model provides for both a macro and a micro view of the factors contributing to the values and beliefs that drive behaviours and contribute to decisions in a corporate environment. Much of this may have been hardwired in the past and no longer serving the person. It is therefore incumbent on the coach or facilitator of the Kaleidoscope model to reflect this back to the person. Thereafter, changes in habits or perpetual thought patterns may be initiated where practicable.

The CIL case study is explained below from the perspective of three of the participants: Susie Wood, Mr Lam and Phillipe van Uiderquist. In each case, the cultural self is explored, as distinct from personality. The concept of a cultural self, as an element of a person's internal functioning, works at the emotional level and makes meaning out of our cultural influences (Plaister-Ten 2013).

Thereafter, for the purposes of this case study, one of a possible eight external lenses is selected through which to analyse the situation further. The impact on the organizational culture is subsequently explored.

In practice, any one of a number of lenses may be selected. In a coaching session for example, the coach would use his or her intuition to select the lens through which to explore an issue. Alternatively, the coach may ask the coachee which lens or lenses have the most resonance for him or her and draw on that lens for further discussion. The Kaleidoscope model may also be used as a training or group coaching tool to elicit group meaning and purpose and to build cohesive teams. Further guidance on the range of applications to coaching practice has been identified through research (Plaister-Ten 2013).

a) Susie Wood

Cultural self

Susie is British, a Protestant and a self-starter. She believes in working hard and that with enough effort and commitment everyone can be successful, no matter where they come from. She believes she can influence the course of her career by taking responsibility for her own (high) performance. She has a strong work ethic and is a perfectionist. This means that she expects everyone she works with and who works for her to adhere to high standards of excellence. She trusts people who do what they say they are going to do and expects people to trust her in the same way.

Diversity lens

In this example, the diversity lens was selected because Susie is the only woman in the study. Susie, as a woman in a "man's world", is in a minority. However, she does not think she is and therefore does not wish to be treated as such. It is one of her core values that she is selected on merit only, not gender. Neither does she expect to get special treatment based on gender. She has been raised this way by a progressive mother and, although she was a campaigner for women's rights at university, it was in relation to oppressed and abused women.

Organizational culture

Susie works well in an organization that is transparent, holds strong ethics and a strong social purpose beyond the "profit motive". She believes in developing people to their full potential, providing they are aligned with her values. In the recent strategy meeting she realized that she is working with colleagues that are not necessarily aligned with her values and this bothers her. Furthermore, she does not respect an organization culture which is so complex that it gets in the way of getting the job done. She finds the matrix management structure cumbersome and will seek to find ways to circumnavigate it with her strong influencing skills. She may find some doors are shut to her until she understands the local culture, such as the need to respect hierarchy in China.

b) China Country Manager, Mr Lam

Cultural self

Mr Lam is from mainland China and now heads up the Beijing office. He is traditionally Chinese and so believes in the "order" of things. Since he is in his mid-50s he expects to command respect based on his age, position in the company and also his standing as a respected businessman and head of the family. He has a large network of connections that he calls upon regularly and is also proud of this.

Economic lens

In this example, the economic lens has been selected not only because of the strong economic growth enjoyed by China as a country, but also because of its past economic climate that Mr Lam has experienced and which will continue to influence him. China has been enjoying economic growth in double digits. Mr Lam has lived through almost 15 years of this buoyant economic situation although he has memories of life before the "open door policy" in the late 1970s. This means that he is still quite cautious. He considers that he should have the "largest voice" in strategy meetings although he rarely speaks up at meetings, especially when his boss is present. He just thinks that people should respect him and does not see any reason to disclose his viewpoints. He finds it strange that the European markets which are struggling for growth should be so vocal and demanding. He thinks people should respect China for its huge accomplishments.

Organizational culture

Mr Lam values an organizational culture that has the best interests of China as a priority. Although he is part of an international organization, his priority is for the long-term sustainability of the China operation. This will be good for China overall. He does not understand the need for a matrix organization structure and is not willing to accept "advice" from anyone junior to him. He does not really appreciate the appointment of Susie Wood as he thinks a local Asian person could have done the job just as well; in fact he has a young guy on his team that he wishes to get promoted to the job. His organization in Beijing works well, delivers results in the "Chinese way" and everyone understands and respects the "order of things".

C) Phillipe van Uiderquist

Cultural self
Phillipe is Swedish and from a family with connections in Sweden. His family are wealthy. Phillipe considers himself to be one of the "elite" in Sweden and has had lots of privileges, including a good education. Life therefore comes to him as reasonably easy and he sometimes has little patience for others who find life slightly more challenging. This can appear arrogant at times. He feels pressure now as he is struggling to find his place in the UK and yet he wants to provide his young kids with the advantages he had.

Social structure lens
In this example, the social structure lens has been selected because it can be useful to examine the social patterns of the country in which the person spent their formative years, and also of the countries in which he or she has spent a considerable amount of time thereafter. Phillipe has been socialized in a country with a reasonably equitable distribution of wealth and a strong consensus approach to management and equality of opportunity for all. He, however, strives for a leadership position and will not be satisfied until he has one, even if it means that he has to leave the company to get it. He now finds himself working with Finnish people again and is aware of the historic rivalry between them; but he does not let this influence him. His time in the USA has probably made him more forthright than he would have been otherwise. He has not realized that this level of directness is not valued overall in the UK and even less so in Asia. This has earned him several rivals, both in and out of the workplace.

Organizational culture
Phillipe wants a focused organization, every part of which is going in the same direction: his direction. He abhors layers of management and does not believe that a matrix management structure is of value. His preference is for an agile, lean organizational structure and his frustration with the complexity of the organization is manifested in stress and aggression. While he believes himself to be an international businessman, his approach seems to alienate people. At the moment his team are delivering results but he is exerting a lot of pressure on them to deliver more, particularly in the Asian region.

3.3 Recommended reading

Friedman, T. L. (2005). *The World is Flat*. New York: Farrar, Straus and Giroux.
A book describing globalization and the ten forces that "flattened the world", and an analysis of what this means for countries, communities and individuals.

Hofstede, G., Hofstede, G. J. & Minkov, M. (2010). *Cultures and Organizations: Software of the Mind*. New York: McGraw Hill.
This book is based on research in more than 70 countries. It looks at what sets people apart from each other and how where we grew up can determine

how we think, feel or act. It demonstrates how this in turn can impact working practices, leadership, business goals and organization structures.

Markus, H. R. & Kitayama, S. (1999). "Culture and the self: Implications for cognition, emotion and motivation". In: Baumeister, R. F. (Ed.), *The Self in Social Psychology*, 339–368. Philadelphia: Taylor & Francis.
This chapter explores the differing conceptions of self across cultures. It explores a construal of self as independent and a construal of self as interdependent and how both perceptions impact cognitions, emotions and motivation.

Moran, R. T., Harris, P. R. & Moran, S. V. (2007). *Managing Cultural Differences: Global Leadership Strategies for the 21st Century*. Oxford: Elsevier.
This book explores some of the challenges for global leaders and puts forward some strategies for the capitalization of differences and the creation of cross-cultural synergy. It also has a "doing business in" section.

Schein, E. H. (1992): *Organizational Culture and Leadership*. 2nd ed. San Francisco: John Wiley & Sons.
This book explains that it is critical for leaders to understand the role that culture plays in their efforts to effect change. It explores how to decipher cultures, create and develop them and then to manage change.

Triandis, H. C., Bontempo, R., Villareal, M. J., Asai, M., & Lucca, N. (1988): "Individualism and collectivism: Cross-cultural perspectives on self-ingroup relationships". In: *Journal of Personality and Social Psychology*, 54, 323–338.
In this article the individualism and collectivism constructs are theoretically analysed and linked to such hypothesized consequences as social behaviours and health indices. While the first study explores the meaning of these constructs within culture, the second study probes their limits with data from two collectivist samples and one individualist sample of students. A third study then replicates previous work in Puerto Rico which indicates that allocentric people perceive that they receive more and a better quality of social support than do idiocentric people.

4 QUESTIONS ON THE CASE

1. Assess the main differences between these three examples that have utilized different lenses of the Kaleidoscope model. Do you think the cultural self, the external factor or the organizational culture is the most influential in each example?
2. If you selected a different person from those mentioned in the study, such as Dennis Smith or one of Susie's direct reports, which lens of the Kaleidoscope model would you select? Why?

3. Can you see any common threads or patterns? What would be the impact of these shared characteristics across the whole organization? How could you use that synergy for further benefit?

5 REFERENCES

Friedman, T. L. (2005). *The World is Flat*. New York: Farrar, Straus and Giroux.

Glantz, J. (2006). *What Every Principal Should Know About Ethical and Spiritual Leadership*. London: Sage.

Hofstede, G., Hofstede, G. J. & Minkov, M. (2010). *Cultures and Organizations: Software of the Mind*. New York: McGraw Hill.

Knight, Kenneth (1977). *Matrix Management: A Cross-Functional Approach to Organization*. New York: PBI-Petrocelli Books.

Kramer, R. J. (1994). *Organizing for Global Competitiveness: The Matrix Design*. New York: Conference Board.

Markus, H.R. & Kitayama, S. (1999). "Culture and the self: Implications for cognition, emotion and motivation". In: Baumeister, R. F. (Ed.), *The Self in Social Psychology*, 339–368. Philadelphia: Taylor & Francis.

Moran, R. T., Harris, P. R. & Moran, S. V. (2007). *Managing Cultural Differences: Global Leadership Strategies for the 21st Century*. Oxford: Elsevier.

Plaister-Ten, J. (2013). "Raising culturally-derived awareness and building culturally-appropriate responsibility: The development of the Cross-Cultural Kaleidoscope". In: *International Journal of Evidence-Based Coaching and Mentoring*, 11:2, 54–69.

Robbins, P. R. (1993). *Organizational Behavior: Concepts, Controversies, and Applications*. New York: Prentice Hall International.

Schein, E. H. (1992). *Organizational Culture and Leadership*. 2nd ed. San Francisco: John Wiley & Sons.

8

Smart Spacing: The Impact of Locations on Intercultural Trust Building and Decision Making

Fritz Audebert, Thilo Beyer and Veronika Hackl

1 INTRODUCTION

When it comes to meetings, a recognized feature of German business culture is to first agree on a specific place to meet (meeting room) and a specific time (scheduled formal meeting), to meet there at the arranged time and then to start discussing and seeking the goal to close the scheduled deal at the end of the first agreed-upon agenda. Trust building and commitment are either assumed or achieved during this process. This stereotypical German approach completely neglects the impact in different business cultures of accompanying conditions such as time and place. In the international context, however, this way of organizing business meetings and the implied expectation of well-oiled cooperation based on a strict schedule are an exception. While decisions in non-German cultures are often made outside meeting rooms and at an unusual time (seen from a German perspective), this is not always considered when it comes to planning a programme of business trips, although decision making is often one of the major targets of such trips. In the vast majority of international decision-making processes, formal times and formal spaces are nothing more than *some* pieces of a very diverse mosaic consisting of more or less decisive times and more or less decisive spaces.

The academic discourse often suggests that the way a culture makes use of spaces implies information about its assumed cultural preferences. Mindsets relating to space become visible in choices: the manner in which rooms are organized reflect differing understandings of order. While in markedly individualistic cultures, it is very important that a certain spatial distance is maintained between participants in a meeting; this does not have to be the same distance in other cultural settings. Open doors in offices, shared offices or one-person offices, as well as distances between individuals, are expressions of these culturally learned preferences (Hall 1990).

But how can an international business traveller make use of his or her awareness of specifically marked spaces and times to generate intercultural trust and commitment? How are the size, position and function of rooms related to each other? What aspects influence the process of trust building between partners from different cultural backgrounds? Where do I meet with my partners? Do I accept it if decisions are not made in the agreed meeting room? Or can I maybe even make use of smart spacing in order to reach my business goals? In addition to the use of time, this case study therefore focuses on the decisive impact of spaces and how the language of space can be used to trigger business relations (El Kahal 1994).

If we start from the notions that certain times and spaces are more appropriate and functional for successful decision making than others, and that diverse local perspectives of *when* and *where* decisions "normally" take place depend on a high degree on specific cultural "normalities", the knowledge about these specifics can contribute to the successful design and scheduling of international business travel. The following case illustrates the impact of culture on smart timing and smart spacing in business travel. In particular, it illustrates how levels of trust are raised or reduced from the perspectives of the persons involved.

2 CASE DESCRIPTION

"Mrs. Schmitt, you really have to get things going. The building of the national training centres in Moscow, Tokyo, Cairo and Buenos Aires are pretty far behind in their schedule. Take a trip and have on-site meetings to make sure they can be inaugurated as planned."

Katrin Schmitt, 38 years old, six feet tall, blonde, German, is assigned to a task:

Position: project manager of the building department of a German premium automobile manufacturer.

Responsibility: to ensure the successful construction of national training centre buildings.

Mission: troubleshooting in Moscow, Tokyo, Cairo, and Buenos Aires.

Context: in each of these four construction projects, delays are occurring.

Stakeholders: local project partners who seem to lack commitment and a sense of urgency.

Equipment: plane tickets, business dress, schedules, contact details, project plans and documentation of progress.

Attitude: target oriented, efficient, cooperative, reliable, curious and open-minded.

Preparation: appointments have been made by email and confirmed in all Outlook calendars of the stakeholders involved; Katrin's role is clear to the local partners. She is well informed about local dos and don'ts (presents, dress code, meet and greet, body language), national holidays, key phrases in the local languages and recent political and economic developments.

Accompanied by: her team member Thomas Engelmann, 48 years old, civil engineer, senior expert in commercial constructions.

Starting position: both Katrin and Thomas are familiar to their local partners from many web conferences.

Expectations of Katrin's international hosts:

What the Russian hosts expect: "Probably happy to visit the Bolshoi. Let us see how she reacts to our Russian hospitality."

What the Egyptian hosts expect: "Probably concerned with schedules. Let us have polite and intensive conversations with her to create strong bonds."

What the Japanese hosts expect: "Probably efficient. Let us arrange a desk where she can work and discuss work issues with us."

What the Argentinian hosts expect: "Probably tough in negotiations. Let us see how we can successfully spend quality time with her."

Destination 1: Moscow When Katrin and Thomas arrive at Sheremetyevo Airport close to Moscow, their corporate driver, Vitaly, is waiting for them at the exit. When Vitaly assertively takes Katrin's trolley and puts it into the car, Katrin notices for the first time that Russian notions of hospitality and gender roles are different from those in Germany.

At the big local representative office they pass stony-faced male security guards and are then warmly welcomed by the Russian project team consisting of the team leader (Igor) and four team members. Katrin smiles when she sees various decorative pictures hanging on the walls of the construction company, even one of the last Russian tsar Nikolai with the face of Igor pasted over it, and several ones of the Russian president Vladimir Putin swimming, riding and shooting.

Igor: It is a pity that you could not come yesterday when we had our corporate party for Russian "builders' day".

Katrin: Yes, thank you so much for the invitation, but you know the restrictions in our travel scheduling when it comes to extra hotel nights which are not business related.

Igor: Well, celebrations are part of the business, aren't they?

Katrin: Maybe not so much from the perspective of our headquarters.

Igor: Anyway, for tonight, we have prepared something special for you.

Katrin: That is great. I am really curious.

The business meeting takes place in a neutral atmosphere, and Katrin is not sure how strong and genuine the commitment of the Russian partners really is because they provide construction services for many international investors, some of whom have commissioned much bigger projects in terms of volume and revenue. After the meeting, she quickly checks her smartphone for emails and has to reply to some urgent messages while the Russian business partners have a little follow-up meeting in the smokers' corner, talking intensively in low voices.

At dinner, Igor makes an announcement with great ceremony:

Igor: Now listen, dear friends, we have a suggestion. Last time, we agreed to show Thomas our favourite banya (spa). This promise will be kept tonight. As for you ladies, Svetlana can also keep a promise which we made last time: with the help of her good connections, she has been able to obtain two tickets for the Bolshoi theatre, and you are warmly invited to join her to see Tchaikovsky's "Swan Lake". I am sure you will enjoy it a lot.

Katrin: Thomas, is there any way out? I really wanted to finalize the MRD3 project plan tonight at the hotel.

Thomas: I don't think so. It doesn't sound as if we have a choice.

Local spaces: ballet performance, banya, hunting

Katrin: Svetlana, I am so glad to be here with you. I just wonder why there are so many women here and only a few men.

Svetlana: You know, this is high culture. The men in our country prefer other activities and find this rather boring, as you can see.

The next morning at the hotel breakfast, Katrin finds a text message from Thomas on her smartphone: "Sorry for the delay. We went hunting in the woods at 3 a.m., and now we are stuck in traffic back to the city."

Before Thomas falls asleep on the flight from Moscow, he and Katrin talk about their trip:

Katrin: How could you go hunting in the woods? You're a vegetarian.

Thomas: I really had no choice.

Katrin: I felt a bit uncomfortable at the Bolshoi last night, a bit of a mouse among all these incredibly dressed-up Russian ladies. I really am a bit jealous of your hunting adventure. Do you think I can join you next time?

Thomas: They said it is possible but not so common.

Katrin: You know what? I think the banya and the hunting and the ballet were all much more decisive for our success than our whole PowerPoint presentation.

Destination 2: Tokyo On their flight to Tokyo, Katrin and Thomas have a look at the agenda which they had received three weeks in advance from their Japanese partners. A meeting in the morning at 9 a.m. and a lunch at 12 p.m. are scheduled. For the afternoon and the evening no arrangements have yet been announced. In the meeting room of their local Japanese partner company, Katrin and Thomas are shown to their seats and wonder why there are 15 people representing the Japanese side.

Local spaces: golf club, karaoke bar

After the meeting and lunch, both of which Katrin and Thomas perceive as slow and formal, the Japanese partners invite Thomas to the golf club, while Katrin can choose between relaxing at the hotel and an organized sightseeing tour with a lady from the Japanese office. Later they all met again at the restaurant and continue the evening at a karaoke bar. Katrin finds it hard to get into a conversation with the locals. She perceives the atmosphere as formal, and her efforts at socializing through humour and eye contact do not seem to work very well here. When she starts to feel tired, she gets a taxi to her hotel.

The next morning, Thomas tells her how the evening continued:

> "To be honest, the atmosphere changed after you left. Some ladies came and joined our table, and encouraged us to drink and chat. Later, they all took a taxi together to their favourite hotel in the centre – you know, one of these capsule hotels where virtually all the guests are men who have decided not to return home because the public transport has already stopped for the evening. I have the impression that for our meeting this morning, we have the clear commitment of our local colleagues to negotiate detailed agreements."

Destination 3: Cairo In Cairo, Katrin and Thomas are, of course, picked up at the airport. The first golden rule the Egyptian manager mentions, after a warm welcome to Egypt, is: "Here we are not only business partners, but first and foremost hosts and guests."

The two Germans soon realize that there is absolutely no time pressure. This means that many times and spaces occur "in between" and leave room for informal conversations. Soon they lose their impatience.

Local space: outdoor lunch on the roof terrace

For lunch, the hosts have prepared a truly magnificent buffet on the rooftop of the local office. A big banquet table is prepared, and the site covered by a tent as a protection from the sun. Katrin enjoys intensive one-to-one conversations with her Egyptian hosts. Bonding works especially well with one of the female team members. When Katrin says that she enjoys these beautiful outdoor places, she replies with a smile: "You know Katrin, the prophet said, 'Whenever a man is alone with a woman the Devil makes a third.' Anyway, we are very much an outdoor culture. This fits well with our attitude of relaxed conversations which we prefer to enjoy outside those boring meeting rooms."

Destination 4: Buenos Aires On the way from the airport to the Argentinian capital, Katrin notices many huge advertising billboards promoting cosmetic products, drinks and fashion, which have one thing in common: they display a lot of female skin.

Meeting and greeting their local partner team includes hugs and kisses on the cheeks for Katrin, and hugs and back patting for Thomas. The meeting starts with a lengthy "meeting before the meeting" with drinks and sweets. Thomas at first takes this opportunity to check some emails on his smartphone, until Katrin frowns at him. He then switches to using his smartphone to share some photos with the hosts, who are genuinely curious and impressed by the snapshots from their previous destinations. The meeting itself starts with the announcement that a table has been reserved for the evening at a fashionable Buenos Aires tango bar. It continues with excuses for delays and many promises for the future. To Katrin it becomes clear from reading between the lines that many other customers have to be served during this peak business time, and that the allocation of resources is subject to intense discussion and is by and large negotiable.

Local space: tango bar

Katrin notices that the stronger eye contact and the shorter distances between people than she is used to in Germany make the conversation more intense than at her first three destinations. Physical presence and powerful facial expressions certainly play a greater role here than in the previous three cities. Katrin has a good time with the local construction experts who ask her to dance. Luckily, she can rely on some tango skills from her years as a university student, and has a good time being led and receiving compliments.

Thomas feels uncomfortable and even a little lost here, because he's never liked noise and dancing. Instead he learns in a conversation: "Isn't this beautiful, Thomas? You know, tango is not just a dance. It is an attitude, and at the same time a game you play together. It means energy and communication. Here we have a saying that a tango couple is one body with two hearts and four legs."

"Tough stuff", Thomas thinks, but admits to himself that there is something true about it, and that for the commitment of the project team it can be only a positive asset to take part in this game. And he is glad that Katrin takes on this responsibility so well.

Epilogue: back in Germany Waiting in the airport at the luggage claim, Katrin sums up their international trip:

> "Thomas, when we look back at our tour, what can we report? Can we draw a small conclusion from all our experiences? I think that we fell into many situations which were not on our agenda at all. But these activities precisely reflect our mission. How did we win the commitment of the Russians,

the Japanese, the Egyptians, and the Argentinians? For the processes, our PowerPoint meetings were important, yes. But if we're talking about commitment and real trust, this occurred outside the business meetings ..."

3. BACKGROUND KNOWLEDGE

3.1 The authors' point of reference

Dr. Fritz Audebert, CEO and founder of ICUnet.AG, Thilo Beyer and Veronika Hackl have an interest in and a mastery of intercultural management, since the business environment that surrounds them is rich in intercultural communication. Their valuable experiences and their acquisition of intercultural skills have taught them how to cope with intercultural challenges whenever business partners of different cultures meet or collaborate. To fully understand others and their culturally influenced habits and actions, mutual tolerance and a certain knowledge of cultural dimensions is required, such as time and space, and how time and space have to be interpreted given their cultural origin. By applying a proper interpretation of these cultural dimensions, intercultural trust, an indispensable component of efficient international business-to-business partnerships, can be established.

3.2 Concepts, models, frameworks

3.2.1 The cultural dimension of space – "space speaks"

In the Renaissance, Filippo Brunelleschi invented the central perspective of space. Henceforth, space was conceptualized as something fixed and linear, a static item. When Edward T. Hall, a pioneer in intercultural research, began to explore cultural differences, the word "space" received an entirely new, less visible and rather dynamic connotation. In his first work *The Silent Language* (1959/1990), Hall gives space a cultural meaning. When it comes to the individual, each human being is in possession of a personal sense of space and a conception of space, be it the social, public, personal or private space that surrounds him- or herself. Hall claims that "space speaks" (Hall 1990: 158). To describe the study of the culturally influenced use of space, Hall coined the term "proxemics" (Hall 1990:131).

Proxemics and the use of space Proxemics deals with the amount of space that people prefer to set between themselves and others. In other words, the proximity or the physical space an individual prefers to have between him- or herself and others depends on personality and cultural background. Proxemics characterizes a culturally specific perception of and behaviour within space, i.e. how people use physical space, or a territory to a certain degree. "Territoriality" (Hall 1990:44) incorporates behaviour in space and individual claims. Defending one's territory is a habit inherent to every human being as determined by human evolution, born out of the instinct for survival and thus it cannot be denied. A sense of territory has continued to develop since then and is, of course, deeply rooted in culture (Hall 1990; Hall & Hall 1989). In the work setting, for instance, differing divisions of territory may be manifested in the way an office is structured and decorated, either rather personally or impersonally. One office may have open doors with a desk turned to the entrance, ready to welcome any visitor, while another one may have a closed door and a crowded desk with a huge monitor or piles of files waiting behind it, obviously screaming out: "Do not enter unless invited" (Liu et al. 2011). Proxemics differentiates between two levels of space: a macro level and a micro level (Barmeyer et al. 2011). In the *Katrin Schmitt Case*, the macro-space is of less importance and does not have to be further outlined.

The micro-space in cultural patterns The micro level is concerned with the personal interpretation of space, a form of territoriality. According to Hall, every individual is encircled by a kind of invisible bubble that expresses a protective distance from others, depending on the relationship to them, the cultural roots, feelings etc.

In subsequent research, Hall detected four different zones of distance that reflect the micro level of space: (1) intimate (2) personal (3) social and (4) public distance (Hall 1990:113–129). Any individual may feel uncomfortable or disturbed whenever someone penetrates their personal space and exceeds a certain distance although that person may not even notice that he or she has crossed a critical line. Comprehension of and behaviour in space function as personal means of non-verbal communication. Space communicates as people interact with others. Interaction, in turn, can be translated according to a distinct cultural context. There are cultures, mainly in Southern Europe, such as Italy or France which are more sociable, and rich in physical contact and bodily proximity. It could be said that these cultures possess small bubbles. On the other hand, northern Europeans such as Germans, Scandinavians or British people have large bubbles as they prefer to keep a greater distance from others (Hall & Hall 1989).

> Each person has around him an invisible bubble of space which expands and contracts depending on a number of things: In Northern Europe, the bubbles are quite large and people keep their distance. In Southern France, Italy, Greece, and Spain, the bubbles get smaller so that the distance that is perceived as intimate in the North overlaps normal conversational distance in the South. (Hall & Hall 1989)

As a result, whenever there is a lack of know-how about any culturally specific use of space or territory, "cross-cultural communication barriers" (Hofstede et al. 2007:17) impede mutual intercultural cohesion, even if the people concerned may be skilled enough to speak the foreign language demanded. Apart from space, Hall further states that "time talks" (Hall 1990:1).

3.2.2 The cultural dimension of time – "time talks"

> Time talks. It speaks more plainly than words. The message it conveys comes through loud and clear. Because it is manipulated less consciously, it is subject to less distortion than the spoken language. It can shout the truth where words lie. (Hall 1990:1)

Apart from space, time figures as a further instrument of non-verbal communication just as effective as language.

Chronemics and the use of time "Chronemics" (Liu et al. 2011:147) signifies the study of the culturally specific use of time. Time is defined and scheduled individually and varies from one culture to another. It appears that a culturally derived time pattern determines the rhythm of life and private and public activities. Time orders social life, for instance when measuring how much time is spent with others on a special occasion, whether privately or professionally. Hall categorizes a culture's time orientation into monochronism and polychronism (Hall & Hall 1989).

A monochronic use of time can be displayed as a linear time system. Time is comparable to a future-oriented line ranging from one point to another. In business terms, this means that tasks are managed according to a set of priorities ranging from high to less important while only one task is dealt with at a time. A monochronic use of time is specific to north-west European and North American cultures. Constantly observing the clock is absolutely essential since time can be either saved or wasted. It relies on a set schedule and is highly sensitive to interruptions (Hall & Hall 1989; Liu et al. 2011).

In contrast, in polychronic cultures time functions less as a line but rather as a cycle. Not just one person but several people may deal with more than one task at a time. Priorities are of secondary importance. Discontinuities are not rare and are not taken as a source of irritation. Polychronic people put emphasis on human relationships rather than adhering to a strict schedule. They tend to change plans spontaneously. Polychronic cultures are predominant in southern European cultures, but are also present in Arab countries. Italians or Spanish people are well known for being time flexible (Hall & Hall 1989; Liu et al. 2011; Usunier & Lee 2009).

One result of a monochronic use of time is action chains structured according to a set system and aimed at achieving a distinct goal. The sequence of any event such as a lecture, a negotiation or a dinner, for example, possesses a typical action chain. Action chains differ across cultures as to their flow and duration and are thus considered culturally specific. As a consequence, possible confusion may be caused by a lack of synchronization in the action chains present in different cultures (Hall & Hall 1989; Barmeyer et al. 2011). In contrast to monochronic people, polychronic people are not disturbed by any interference and may even break up any action chain on purpose simply because they do not like it (Hall & Hall 1989).

The relationship between time and space In monochronic cultures people and departments are strictly subdivided according to their function. Offices are regarded as private and are structured accordingly. On the other hand, polychronic people feel excluded and shut off by a high degree of privacy which prevents a proper flow of information. They prefer large reception rooms, flexible appointments that can be individually changed or cancelled and they seek to have a close relationship with their customers (Hall & Hall 1989).

Time talks and space speaks and both function as languages. Therefore, it is absolutely mandatory to study the local language of time and space and not to impose our sense of time and space division on others. Tempo, rhythm or scheduling tasks vary from culture to culture (Hall & Hall 1989) and so do the definitions of space, private and public spheres, territoriality or distances. Being able to embed a given use of time or of space in a certain cultural context and comprehend the cultural meaning beyond can be described as smart timing and smart spacing, i.e. being smart enough to move in time and space in an interculturally appropriate manner.

The model of cultural dynamics proposed by Usunier and Lee visualizes how the perception of time and space shapes the concept of the self and others, in other words how people see themselves in relation to others. Therefore, time and space also have a vital influence on the way in which people interact with others (Usunier & Lee 2009:17, 37ff). Offices, for instance, can be either subdivided into small individual rooms with one or two desks each, promising a lot of privacy, or the opposite: being organized into large rooms with shared desks for more than one employee at a time. Both designs of private and public dimensions imply two opposite interaction models among employees in the office. While the first office organization shows clear elements of an individualized society, like Germans are to a certain degree, the second design represents community orientation typical of most Asian countries.

A key premise of every interaction aimed at forming a functioning relationship is trust.

3.2.3 Intercultural trust building

> The ability to build trust and to network is increasingly acknowledged as a critical factor for long-term organizational success. (Schwegler 2009)

As an undeniable guiding principle of society and civilization, trust shapes the foundation of every relationship or partnership. Trust fosters empathy between two stakeholders. A relationship of trust brings with it effective cooperation and hence is responsible for a very high degree of business viability. Although research into trust in intercultural contexts is rather young, some valuable insights have been generated (Barmeyer et al. 2011). Trust has been detected as a crucial component of success for intercultural business-to-business partnerships (Doney et al. 1998). Unfamiliarity with the culture of cooperation partners arouses a higher degree of uncertainty. Spacial distance and rare personal contact for members of some cultures increase the uncertainty of the cooperation and decrease trust. It is obvious that generating trust that functions across cultures is a most complex challenge (Schwegler 2009). The formation of trust is conditional on a principle called reciprocity of trust relations. Only persons perceived as trustworthy are met with trust. A lack of trust may stir up conflicts and the opposite of trust, mistrust, such as is manifested in stereotypes, for instance. Sources of irritation are located in the absence of necessary know-how about culturally specific characteristics

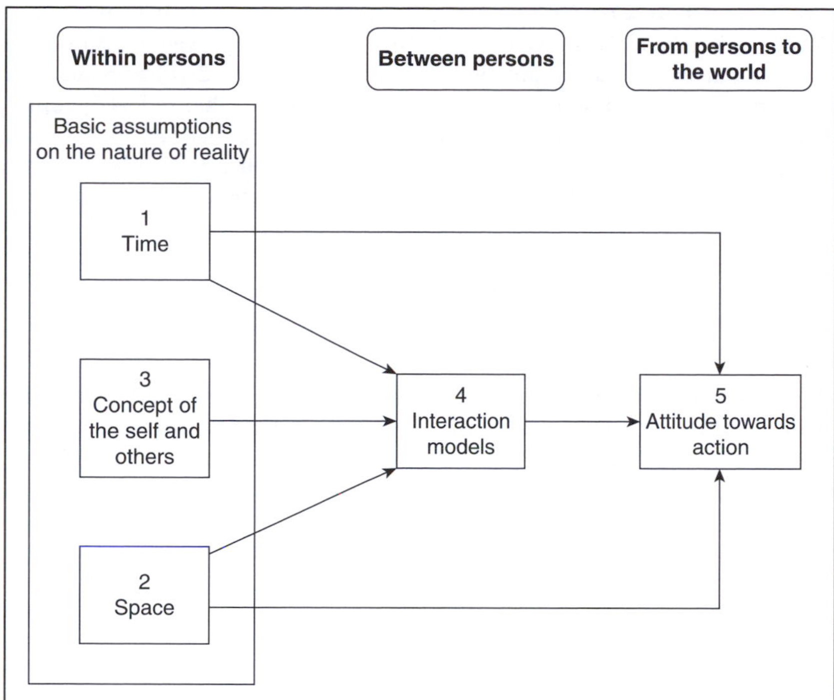

Figure 8.1 A model of cultural dynamics

Source: Usunier & Lee 2009:17. Reproduced with permission.

and how they are to be interpreted in interaction (Busch 2008). It can be concluded that intercultural business partnerships based on trust can only be established and maintained when partners are open-minded, appreciative and acquainted with cultural differences and cultural dimensions such as those of time and space.

3.3 Recommended reading

Hall, E. T. (1959/1990). ***The Silent Language.*** **New York: Anchor Books.** This work by Edward T. Hall proposes a crucial theory about differing intercultural communication styles. Hall states that culture is communication and communication is culture. He makes special tribute to time and space as two major cultural dimensions. Analysing American society, Hall illustrates how time and space differ according to various cultural patterns. He outlines the "vocabulary of culture" portraying the "voices of time" and how "space speaks". In this way, time and space develop individual means of non-verbal communication. This is the first work by Hall that laid crucial foundations for further analysis in the use of time and space influenced by the cultural system beyond.

Hall, E.T. (1990). *The Hidden Dimension*. New York: Doubleday.
This book builds on the previous work *The Silent Language*. Hall reinforces his theory about space as a cultural dimension which creates individual patterns of communication. He describes the "dynamism of space" that reflects people's perception and use of personal, social, architectural and urban spaces. Forming theory from research of animals' territorial behaviour, Hall describes a person's individual perception of territory by introducing four critical distance phases: (1) intimate (2) personal (3) social and (4) public distance. The work introduces the term "proxemics", coined by Hall. Proxemics relates space to a cultural specific use. Hall gives vivid examples of how public and private space are used in Germany, England, France, Japan and in the Arab world to a varying degree and how this influences business relations, cross-cultural exchanges and more.

Schwegler, U. (2009). "Herausforderungen der Vertrauensforschung in interkulturellen Kooperationsbeziehungen". In: Forum Qualitative Sozialforschung/ Forum: Qualitative Social Research, 10:1, Art. 48.
This article analyses the importance of trust building as a main component for success in international business relationships. First, Schwegler theorizes about trust in general as the overall basis of every kind of relationship. She relates trust to the intercultural context, pointing to important challenges that arise out of a lack of research into the matter. Schwegler emphasizes major conditions for cross-cultural trust building. This work is very important for understanding the necessity of mutual appreciation of cultural diversity in the cross-cultural trust construction that is the basis of a functioning international business partnership.

Usunier, J.-C. & Lee, J. A. (2009). *Marketing Across Cultures*. Harlow: Pearson Education.
This book provides a more current view on cross-cultural business relations. It takes up Hall's point about the cultural dynamics of time and space and describes the term "chronemics" to draw parallels with its cultural varying perception and use. The work stresses the importance of recognizing cultural differences in an increasingly linked business world. It deals with multinational companies and proposes cross-cultural marketing strategies that are de-centred and can adapt to local diversities. The book focuses on a cross-cultural and an intercultural approach to international marketing.

4 QUESTIONS ON THE CASE

1. Which of the actions of Katrin, Thomas and their business partners in Moscow, Tokyo, Cairo and Bunenos Aires can be described as monochronic or polychronic?
2. What expectations do the various parties in the case study have when it comes to the spaces in which trust can be created?
3. For Thomas and Katrin on the one hand, and their international colleagues on the other, what is the basis of the trust that they all desire?
4. Can smart spacing be a strategy for trust building?

5 REFERENCES

Barmeyer, C., Genkova, P. & Scheffer, J. (2011). "Kulturdimensionen und Kulturstandards." In: Barmeyer, C., Genkova, P. & Scheffer, J. (Eds), *Interkulturelle Kommunikation und Kulturwissenschaft. Grundbegriffe, Wissenschaftsdisziplinen, Kulturräume*. Passau: Verlag Karl Stutz, 94–127.

Busch, D. (2008). "Wie kann man Vertrauensbildungsprozesse in sprachlicher Interaktion beobachten und beschreiben?" In: Jammal, E. (Ed.), *Vertrauen im interkulturellen Kontext*, 27–50. Wiesbaden: VS-Verlag.

Doney, P. M., Cannon, J. P. & Mullen, M. R. (1998). "Understanding the influence of national culture on the development of trust". In: *Academy of Management Review*, 23:3, 601–620.

El Kahal, S. (1994). *Introduction to International Business*. New York: McGraw-Hill.

Hall, E. T. (1959/1990). *The Silent Language*. New York: Anchor Books.

Hall, E. T. (1990). *The Hidden Dimension*. New York: Doubleday.

Hall, E. T. & Hall, M. R. (1989). *Understanding Cultural Differences*. Yarmouth: Intercultural Press.

Hofstede, G. J., Pedersen P. B. & Hofstede, G. (2007). *Exploring Culture. Exercises, Stories and Synthetic Cultures*. Boston: Intercultural Press.

Liu, S., Volčič, Z. & Gallois, C. (2011). *Introducing Intercultural Communication. Global Cultures and Contexts*. Los Angeles: Sage.

Rothlauf, J. (2012). *Interkulturelles Management. Mit Beispielen aus Vietnam, China, Japan, Russland und den Golfstaaten*. München: Oldenbourg Verlag.

Schwegler, U. (2009). "Herausforderungen der Vertrauensforschung in interkulturellen Kooperationsbeziehungen". *In: Forum Qualitative Sozialforschung/ Forum: Qualitative Social Research*, 10:1, Art. 48.

Usunier, J.-C. & Lee, J. A. (2009). *Marketing Across Cultures*. Harlow: Pearson Education.

9

IKEA's Ethical Controversies in Saudi Arabia

Christof Miska and Michaela Pleskova

1 INTRODUCTION

As multinational companies (MNCs) and their managers operate across different cultures and societies, they are confronted as a matter of course with local variations in ethical standards. Cultures will generally tend towards determining a set of basic ethical norms and principles, and this can lead to differences across countries in terms of what is considered right or wrong (Buller et al. 1991). For international managers working within a cross-cultural context, this implies a number of potential dilemmas, challenges, and difficulties. MNCs customarily develop, apply, and enforce codes of conduct to safeguard good corporate citizenship among their managers and employees; such codes often aim to convey strong universal ethical principles, such as the avoidance of bribery and corruption, or the guarantee of basic human rights, including equality and personal freedom. However, these principles may not be shared by all the cultures and societies in which an MNC operates, which may instead reflect their own unique ethical notions and standards. In other words, international managers need to carefully analyse, understand, and define when ethical variations across cultures and societies simply imply differences which should be acknowledged and accepted, and when these variations are unacceptable and need to be addressed (Donaldson 1996).

While this issue can be seen as a potential obstacle or difficulty, differences in ethical standards across cultures and societies can equally be leveraged and used to determine the true responsibilities of MNCs, and can help define the ethical missions for international managers. MNCs have become powerful in influencing and determining the political, social and economic environments in the countries in which they operate (Chandler & Mazlish 2005), tending to possess the necessary resources, means and capabilities to effect positive change and development. Systematically contrasting ethical variations across cultures and societies in order to determine basic moral standards can help MNCs recognize the important universal principles they might aim to represent and enact. These, in turn, can benefit countries and societies in their development and advancement. While MNCs may voluntarily and proactively work towards such goals, often they are also confronted with high expectations and pressure from various stakeholders, including governments, the media and the general public.

IKEA's ethical controversies in Saudi Arabia illustrate both the challenges of ethical variation across cultures and societies, and the potential opportunities for positive change that these differences might provide. The case focuses on the removal of women from the Saudi Arabian edition of IKEA's catalogue – a step which was held by some as standing in stark contrast to IKEA's corporate culture and core values. The dispute exposed IKEA to considerable public criticism, but pointed to the responsibilities of MNCs in addressing ethical differences across cultures and societies. Such ethical variations can therefore be viewed as important foundations for determining MNCs' responsibilities in the global context.

2 CASE DESCRIPTION

2.1 The situation: company background

"IKEA raderar kvinnorna" (IKEA erases women) was the headline on the front page of Sweden's free newspaper, *Metro*, on 1 October 2012. Above the title, two pictures from IKEA's home furniture catalogue were shown. At first sight they both appeared to show a family in a bathroom fitted with IKEA interiors. A closer look, however, revealed a striking difference. The pictures were indeed identical, save that the one on the right-hand side did not show a woman in her pyjamas in front of the bathroom mirror. It only showed a man kneeling while wrapping a child in a towel and another child in front of the mirror. In contrast, the picture on the left-hand side of the page showed the woman as well as the man and the children. This was from the Swedish edition of IKEA's catalogue, while the father-only picture was from the Saudi Arabian edition. *Metro* revealed that throughout the Saudi Arabian version of the catalogue similar adjustments had been made – women were airbrushed from the catalogue. In another picture in the Swedish version, a woman and three men were depicted in a room full of colourful IKEA furnishings; in the Saudi Arabian edition, the picture was identical – except for the absence of the woman. Other pictures showing women were fully removed or replaced by alternative images.

IKEA's catalogue is an important marketing tool and is shipped all over the world. Several million copies appear annually in dozens of different versions. These, though, are largely identical, with some exceptions and adaptations according to local standards and preferences. However, the fact that in Saudi Arabia women were excluded sparked global media attention and considerable criticism. International news reports followed up on *Metro*'s coverage, as shown in the examples in Table 9.1:

Table 9.1 International news reports

Medium	Headline	Excerpt
AlJazeera (AlJazeera 2012)	Swedish firm erases women in Saudi catalogue	Furniture giant IKEA criticised after women and girls were airbrushed out of its Saudi Arabian catalogue.
BBC (BBC 2012)	IKEA "regrets" removal of women from Saudi catalogue	Swedish furniture company IKEA has said it regrets that images of women are missing from the Saudi version of its catalogue.
The Guardian (Malik 2012)	No women please, we're Saudi Arabian IKEA	Women being airbrushed out of catalogues is par for the course in Saudi Arabia – but what does it say about the Swedish brand?
The Telegraph (The Telegraph 2012)	Ikea criticised for airbrushing women out of Saudi catalogue	IKEA, the Swedish furniture retailer, has been criticised for deleting images of women from the Saudi version of its catalogue.
The Wire (Abad-Santos 2012)	Women Don't Exist at Saudi Arabia's IKEA	IKEA's Saudi Arabian catalogue looks like any other IKEA catalogue –weird beds with names you can't pronounce, merchandise that looks way better in photos than it will in your living room – except for one thing: there are no women. They've disappeared ... poof! Like they were never there.
Time (Pollak 2012)	IKEA Edits Women Out of Saudi Arabian Catalogue	Swedish furniture retailer IKEA is known for its uniformity across the world. But one nation is noting a stark difference between its IKEA ads and the ones seen in the other 37 countries that have IKEA stores: where are the women? The home goods company is taking heat for Photoshopping, airbrushing out, and otherwise erasing photos of women from the Saudi Arabian version of their advertising catalogue.

IKEA is an icon of Sweden, commonly associated with its liberal lifestyle and values. These include, in particular, gender egalitarianism and equality. In fact, according to IKEA's 2012 sustainability report 47% of its managers are women (IKEA 2012a). Consequently, *Metro*'s report sparked critical reactions not only from the international media, but also from Swedish politicians, including equality minister Nyamko Sabuni, who was quoted as saying:

> "For IKEA to remove an important part of Sweden's image and an important part of its values in a country that more than any other needs to know about IKEA's principles and values, that's completely wrong." (Quinn 2012)

Similarly, Sweden's trade minister Ewa Björling declared that women cannot be deleted from society, and Swedish European Union minister Birgitta Ohlsson, via the social networking site Twitter, called the case "medieval" (Ringstrom 2012).

IKEA apologized, and shortly after *Metro*'s disclosure published an official press statement on its website, accepting fault:

> We have, during the course of the day, been in dialogue with Al Sulaiman, our franchisee operating IKEA stores in Saudi Arabia. It is not the local franchisee that has requested the retouch of the discussed pictures. The mistake happened during the work process occurring before presenting the draft catalogue for IKEA Saudi Arabia. We take full responsibility for the mistakes made.
>
> We have reviewed several of the discussed pictures, for example the women in front of the bathroom mirror and the female designer of the PS2012 design collection. Those pictures could very well have been included in the Saudi Arabian catalogue.
>
> We will naturally review our routines and working process, to ensure that this will not happen again. We deeply regret that mistakes have been made in this instance. (IKEA 2012b)

This situation reflects fundamental cultural differences and opposing positions: on the one hand, IKEA's Swedish legacy and the company's core values promoting egalitarianism and equality; on the other hand, Saudi Arabia's cultural traditions, influenced by conservative Islamic values. These differences can be summarized in more detail, below:

IKEA's Swedish legacy IKEA has become the world's largest multinational furniture retailer, designing and selling household interiors and equipment. The IKEA trademark represents the leading home furnishings brand in the world, with more than 360 stores in 45 countries, and achieved €29.2 billion in sales turnover in 2013 (Bengtsson 2014). Inter IKEA Systems B.V. is the owner of the IKEA Concept and is the worldwide IKEA franchisor.

IKEA's corporate culture is distinct, due to its strong core values. These have their roots in the Småland region of Sweden, where IKEA's founder, Ingvar Kamprad, was born in 1926 (IKEA 2014a). As a set, IKEA's values form a pattern or common culture – usually referred to as doing things "the IKEA way":

- Togetherness and enthusiasm
- Constant desire for renewal
- Cost-consciousness across all areas of IKEA operations
- Willingness to accept and delegate responsibility
- Humbleness and willpower
- Simplicity
- Leadership by example
- Daring to be different
- Striving to meet reality
- The importance of constantly being "on the way"

(Bengtsson 2014)

IKEA is also commonly associated with Sweden's liberal lifestyle and values. According to the World Values Survey (WVS 2014), more than 80% of the Swedish respondents state that the same rights for women and men are an essential characteristic of democracy. Similarly, more than 80% find that there is "fairly much" respect or "a great deal of" respect for individual human rights in their country.

This importance of diversity and inclusion is reflected in IKEA's culture, as described in its 2012 sustainability report:

> The way our customers live is different in every country, region and even from family to family. The more we can reflect this diversity in our workforce, the better we can meet our customers' needs. (IKEA 2012a)

In terms of sustainability, IKEA has various environmental and societal targets. For example, IKEA aims "to create a better everyday life for the many people", working through numerous collaborations with organizations and charities like UNICEF, the UN Refugee Agency (UNHCR), and Save the Children (IKEA 2014b). With these partners, IKEA has raised large sums as part of the company's community development programme.

Saudi Arabia's cultural traditions IKEA has been operating in Saudi Arabia since the early 1980s (Jonsson & Foss 2011). The country, with close to 30 million inhabitants, is governed by King Salman bin Abdulaziz al-Saud. The oil industry has a considerable impact on the country's economic development, as Saudi Arabia is one of the world's major oil exporters. In 2012, Saudi Arabia ranked 12 on the World Bank's ease-of-doing-business list (The World Bank 2012). Consequently, foreign enterprises seeking to operate in Saudi Arabia hope to leverage promising business opportunities.

However, culturally the country can be challenging for Western companies. In particular, the stringent way in which Islamic sharia law is interpreted and applied dominates society and makes everyday life substantially different from Western lifestyles. Importantly, for women this results in considerable limitations on personal freedom. As Human Rights Watch (2013) reported, Saudi Arabian women are not allowed to travel, conduct official business, or undergo certain medical treatment without consent from their male guardians. Overall, Saudi Arabia's cultural traditions are characterized by deeply held conservative Islamic values which affect everyday life, especially for women.

2.2 The challenge

The issue that IKEA faced was in fact a matter of greater magnitude than may be suggested by their acceptance of error during the catalogue production process. As an MNC, IKEA was seen as adapting – whether intentionally or unintentionally – to the local Saudi culture, a culture frequently criticized for the way it regards women. By leaning towards local Saudi sensibilities, IKEA challenged several of its own core values and became drawn into a human rights controversy. The displacement of women was also in stark contrast to IKEA's Swedish heritage, which typically tends to be associated with values of egalitarianism and equality.

These perceptions were considerably strengthened by the hefty international media coverage. By removing women from its Saudi Arabian catalogue, the company also became subject to questions about MNCs' responsibilities as they operate within and across various cultures and societies, despite IKEA's efforts towards societal and environmental sustainability. In fact, IKEA found itself in an acute dilemma between the need to clearly determine when different is different and when different is simply wrong. The Western public had a clear expectation of action, and IKEA responded accordingly; the company announced a review of its routines, seeking to ensure that the different versions of the catalogue do not compromise its human rights and anti-discrimination policies. The company released a statement saying: "We should have reacted and realised that excluding women from the Saudi Arabian version of the catalogue is in conflict with the Ikea Group values" (Quinn 2012).

3 BACKGROUND KNOWLEDGE

3.1 The authors' point of reference

The authors are especially interested in how ethical differences across cultures and societies affect the responsibilities of MNCs. This includes questions about when MNCs should adapt to the specific requirements of certain cultural contexts, and when they should represent and promote universal values and principles. The authors contend that cultural differences are solely a complication when it comes to determining appropriate approaches towards Corporate Social Responsibility (CSR), but can help MNCs reflect upon their existing strategies and approaches, and support them in identifying their universal responsibilities. In other words, by carefully leveraging the differences in ethical standards across cultures and societies, MNCs can broaden and revise their perspectives on their own responsibilities.

3.2 Concepts, models, frameworks

The following concepts can be applied separately, but equally in combination. The first concept is a distinction between different types of responsibilities – "doing good" and "avoiding harm". By analysing ethical differences across cultures and societies in this light, companies can determine the scope of their responsibilities and how their CSR-related efforts may be perceived across countries. The second concept – hypernorms – can help MNCs determine certain foundational ethical standards when they operate in a cross-cultural context. Thus, ethical differences across cultures and societies can be used to identify common denominators. The third framework, which relates to the notion of transnational CSR, showcases the prototypical approaches along the dimensions of global CSR integration and local CSR responsiveness. Rather than focusing on and emphasizing just one of these dimensions, analysing and interpreting ethical differences across cultures and societies can help determine how to best balance and reconcile the two dimensions.

"Doing good" and "avoiding harm" The distinction between "doing good" and "avoiding harm" behaviours of companies and managers is being increasingly applied in recent research (e.g. Crilly et al. 2008; Miska et al. 2014; Stahl & Sully de Luque 2014). The first relates to realizing goals which actively contribute to society, e.g. the safeguarding of fair wages, the development of local communities, and donations to charity. The second emphasizes the circumvention of harmful activities, such as environmental protection, the shunning of corruption and the guarantee of safe products. While within one culture and society both dimensions may be clearly distinct, across cultures and societies they may or may not be considered equally germane or clear-cut. For example, in continental Europe philanthropic activities are often compulsory by law (the principle of "avoiding harm"), whereas in emerging economies they are important discretionary actions ("doing good") (Crane & Matten 2010; Visser 2008). Similarly, companies might have a tendency to focus on one set of activities while neglecting another. Therefore, looking at ethical differences across cultures and societies through the lens of "doing good" and "avoiding harm" can help companies understand the scope of responsibility across the countries in which they operate.

Hypernorms Another important concept is the idea of hypernorms. These are part of Integrative Social Contracts Theory (ISCT) (Donaldson & Dunfee 1994) and represent desired transcultural values. In essence, hypernorms determine lower-level moral norms which transcend cultures. Such norms could be the basic human rights most commonly found in most societies. Therefore, hypernorms, although they can be challenging to derive and determine, are a useful point of reference for analysing multiple cultures and societies in terms of their ethical standards in order to establish certain minimum principles of responsibility. Hypernorms may potentially conflict with a society's basic norms and practices, which can make it difficult for managers to determine how hypernorms specifically apply to certain contexts. In such cases, however, they can serve as starting points for the development of strategies which in creative ways seek to reconcile transcultural values with a society's particular local norms.

Prototypical CSR approaches A helpful model along these lines is Stahl, Pless and Maak's (2013) framework of transnational CSR. It depicts the prototypical ways in which companies can respond to the simultaneous need for global integration and local flexibility in the context of CSR. According to Argandoña and von Weltzien Hoivik (2009), one global standard of CSR is unlikely to exist. Matten and Moon (2008) describe how CSR differs among countries and changes within them. In this regard, the framework of transnational CSR builds on previous work in the area of international management (Bartlett & Ghoshal 1998; Prahalad & Doz 1987) and international CSR (Arthaud-Day 2005), and postulates that companies need to have universal ways of addressing stakeholder claims, but equally are required to respond to the unique demands of local stakeholders. From this framework three prototypical strategies can be derived: a global CSR approach, a local CSR approach and a transnational CSR approach.

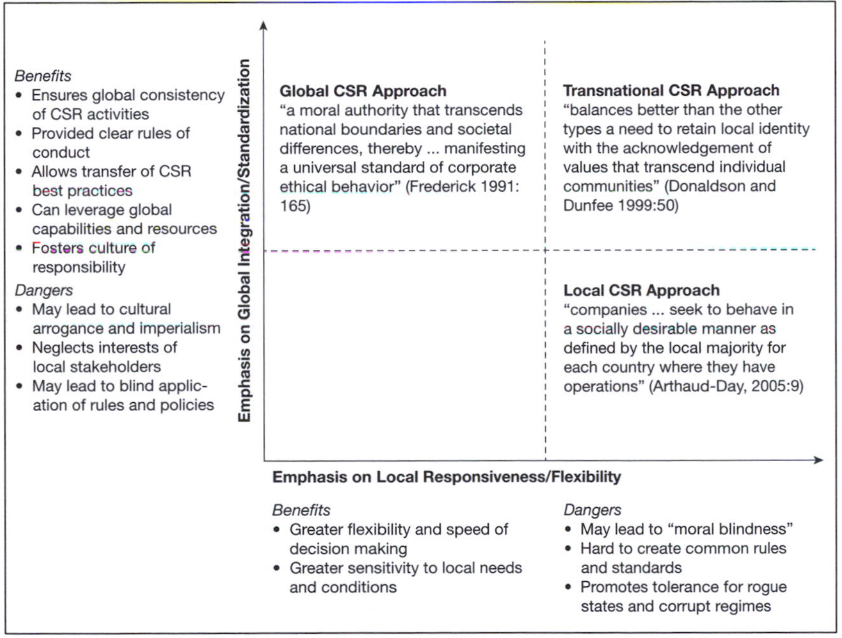

Figure 9.1 Three strategies of the framework of transnational CSR

Source: Stahl, Pless & Maak (2013). Reproduced with permission.

- **Global CSR approach**: This strategy establishes strong universal values as guidelines for companies and managers as they operate across countries and cultures. A global approach to CSR applies to all contexts in which a company operates. It provides managers with clear guidelines of which CSR principles are relevant, and thus safeguards consistency in all countries of operation. The potential downsides of such an approach are that local stakeholder demands may not be met and companies may be perceived as arrogant towards local cultures and societies.

- **Local CSR approach**: This approach can be seen as the mirror opposite of the global CSR strategy. It assumes that a company adapts to the particular needs and demands of local stakeholders. Consequently, CSR practice differs according to the country and culture in which a company operates. Companies try to behave in a socially desirable way in order to meet the demands of local stakeholders. A potential risk of such an approach is the multiplicity of different standards and resulting diversity in approaches to CSR.
- **The transnational CSR approach**: This strategy is a blend of the previous two and aims to reconcile global CSR integration and local CSR responsiveness, assuming that the two are not mutually exclusive. In essence, this approach implies that global companies provide a CSR template which establishes the foundational guidelines for managers to enact CSR. Within certain boundaries they have flexibility to adapt these guidelines according to the requirements of local contexts.

3.3 Recommended reading

Buller, P. F., Kohls, J. J., & Anderson, K. S. (1991). "The challenge of global ethics". *Journal of Business Ethics*, 10:10, 767–775.
In view of increasing globalization and the amplified concerns about ethics, the authors analyse and discuss opportunities to develop global ethics. They propose a conceptual model which describes globalization and global ethics and provide several strategies which can help deal with ethical conflicts.

Donaldson, T. & Dunfee, T. W. (1994). "Toward a unified conception of business ethics: Integrative social contracts theory". *The Academy of Management Review*, 19:2, 252–284.
In this article the authors present Integrative Social Contracts Theory (ISCT) with its various components, including the concept of hypernorms. In this vein, the authors also discuss the linkages between normative and empirical business ethics research. While influential, ISCT has received much criticism, which Thomas Dunfee addresses in detail in a 2006 *Journal of Business Ethics* article (Dunfee 2006).

Stahl, G. K., Pless, N. M. & Maak, T. (2013). "Responsible global leadership". In: Mendenhall, M. E., Osland, J. S., Bird, A., Oddou, G. R., Maznevski, M. L., Stevens, M. J. & Stahl, G. K. (Eds), *Global Leadership: Research, Practice, and Development*. 2nd ed. 240–259. New York: Routledge.
In this book chapter, the authors take on a contemporary leadership perspective and under the notion of responsible global leadership describe several CSR-related challenges that business leaders face in the global context. The authors also describe the transnational CSR framework, with various prototypical CSR strategies, and elaborate on how global organizations can promote responsible global leadership.

4 QUESTIONS ON THE CASE

1. In the table below, analyse how the distinction between "doing good" and "avoiding harm" applies to the case. In view of this distinction, how can the cultural differences between its Swedish home culture and Saudi Arabian culture help IKEA determine the scope of its responsibilities?

Doing good
Avoiding harm

2. In the table below, analyse to what extent the idea of hypernorms in the form of basic human rights such as equality and personal freedom is reflected in IKEA's, Swedish politicians', and international media's reactions. Also, consider to what extent these reactions reflect the notion that the differences between IKEA's Swedish home culture and Saudi Arabian culture are considered in view of potential synergies rather than difficulties. Does the case provide sufficient information about the Saudi Arabian perspective?

	Extent to which human rights are addressed
IKEA	
Swedish politicians	
International media	

3. Which elements of global, local, and transnational CSR are illustrated in this case? Use the table below to record your thoughts. Which approach is likely to be most promising for IKEA after the incident and its strong media exposure?

Global CSR
Local CSR
Transnational CSR

4. Which intercultural competencies do you think managers need to possess if they want to enact a global, local, and transnational CSR approach? Record your thoughts in the table below.

	Intercultural competencies required
Global CSR	
Local CSR	
Transnational CSR	

5 REFERENCES

Abad-Santos, A. (2012). "Women don't exist at Saudi Arabia's Ikea". Retrieved on 20 October 2014 from www.theatlanticwire.com/global/2012/10/womendont-exist-saudi-arabias-ikea/57464/

AlJazeera. (2012). "Swedish firm erases women in Saudi catalogue". Retrieved on 20 October 2014 from www.aljazeera.com/news/europe/2012/10/2012101151825462437.html

Argandoña, A. & von Weltzien Hoivik, H. (2009). "Corporate social responsibility: One size does not fit all. Collecting evidence from Europe". In: *Journal of Business Ethics*, 89, 221–234.

Arthaud-Day, M. L. (2005). "Transnational corporate social responsibility: A tri-dimensional approach to international CSR research". In: *Business Ethics Quarterly*, 15:1, 1–22.

Bartlett, C. A. & Ghoshal, S. (1998). *Managing Across Borders: The Transnational Solution*. Boston, MA: Harvard Business Press.

BBC (2012). "Ikea 'regrets' Saudi catalogue slip". Retrieved on 20 October, 2014 from www.bbc.co.uk/news/world-europe-19786862

Bengtsson, N. (2014). Interview via email with Niclas Bengtsson, Media Relations Manager at Inter IKEA Systems B.V., on 10 October 2014.

Buller, P. F., Kohls, J. J. & Anderson, K. S. (1991). "The challenge of global ethics". In: *Journal of Business Ethics*, 10:10, 767–775.

Chandler, A. D. & Mazlish, B. (2005). *Leviathans: Multinational Corporations and the New Global History*. Cambridge: Cambridge University Press.

Crane, A. & Matten, D. (2010). *Business Ethics: Managing Corporate Citizenship and Sustainability in the Age of Globalization*. Oxford: Oxford University Press.

Crilly, D., Schneider, S. & Zollo, M. (2008). "Psychological antecedents to socially responsible behavior". In: *European Management Review*, 5:3, 175.

Donaldson, T. (1996). "Values in tension: Ethics away from home". In: *Harvard Business Review*, 74:5, 48–62.

Donaldson, T. & Dunfee, T. W. (1994). "Toward a unified conception of business ethics: Integrative Social Contracts Theory". In: *The Academy of Management Review*, 19:2, 252–284.

Donaldson, T. & Dunfee, T. W. (1999). "When ethics travel: the promise and peril of global business ethics". In: *California Management Review*, 41:4, 45–63.

Dunfee, T. W. (2006). "A critical perspective of integrative social contracts theory: recurring criticisms and next generation research topics". In: *Journal of Business Ethics*, 68:3, 303–328.

Frederick, W. C. (1991). "The moral authority of transnational corporate codes". In: *Journal of Business Ethics*, 10:3, 165–177.

Human Rights Watch (2013). "World Report 2013: Saudi Arabia". Retrieved on 20 October 2014 from www.hrw.org/world-report/2013/country-chapters/saudi-arabia

IKEA (2012a). "Sustainability report 2012 – IKEA". Retrieved on 20 October 2014 from www.ikea.com/ms/en_JP/about_ikea/facts_and_figures/sustainability_report/sustainability_report_2012.html

IKEA (2012b). "Statement from Inter IKEA Systems B.V. regarding the IKEA catalogue in Saudi Arabia – IKEA". Retrieved on 20 October 2014 from www.ikea.com/dk/da/about_ikea/newsitem/Saudi_Arabia

IKEA (2014a). "History – IKEA". Retrieved on 20 October 2014 from www.ikea.com/ms/en_AU/about_ikea/the_ikea_way/history/

IKEA (2014b). "People & Communities – IKEA". Retrieved on 20 October 2014, from www.ikea.com/ms/en_US/this-is-ikea/people-and-planet/people-and-communities/index.html

Jonsson, A. & Foss, N. J. (2011). "International expansion through flexible replication: Learning from the internationalization experience of IKEA". *In: Journal of International Business Studies*, 42:9, 1079–1102.

Malik, N. (2012). "No women please, we're Saudi Arabian Ikea". In: *The Guardian*. Retrieved on 20 October 2014 from www.theguardian.com/commentisfree/2012/oct/02/no-women-saudi-arabian-ikea

Matten, D., & Moon, J. (2008). "'Implicit' and 'explicit' CSR: A conceptual framework for a comparative understanding of corporate social responsibility". *In: The Academy of Management Review*, 33:2, 404–424.

Miska, C., Hilbe, C. & Mayer, S. (2014). "Reconciling different views on responsible leadership: A rationality-based approach". In: *Journal of Business Ethics*, 125:2, 349–360.

Pollak, S. (2012). "IKEA edits women out of Saudi Arabian catalog". In: *Time*. Retrieved on 20 October 2014 from http://newsfeed.time.com/2012/10/01/ikea-edits-women-out-of-saudi-arabian-catalog/

Prahalad, C. K. & Doz, Y. (1987). *The Multinational Mission*. New York: The Free Press & London: Collier-Macmillan.

Quinn, B. (2012). "Ikea apologises over removal of women from Saudi Arabia catalogue". In: *The Guardian*. Retrieved on 20 October 2014 from www.theguardian.com/world/2012/oct/02/ikea-apologises-removing-women-saudiarabia-catalogue

Ringstrom, A. (2012). "Swedes slam IKEA for its female-free Saudi catalogue". In: *Reuters. Stockholm*. Retrieved on 20 October 2014 from www.reuters.com/article/2012/10/02/us-ikea-saudiarabia-idUSBRE8910O320121002

Stahl, G. & Sully de Luque, M. (2014). "Antecedents of responsible leader behavior: A research synthesis, conceptual framework, and agenda for future research". In: *The Academy of Management Perspectives*, amp–2013.

Stahl, G. K., Pless, N. M. & Maak, T. (2013). "Responsible global leadership". In: Mendenhall, M. E., Osland, J., Bird, A., Oddou, G. R., Maznevski, M. L., Stevens, M. & Stahl, G. K. (Eds). *Global Leadership: Research, Practice, and Development*, 240–259. 2nd ed. New York: Routledge.

The Telegraph (2012). "Ikea criticised for airbrushing women out of Saudi catalogue". Retrieved on 20 October 2014 from www.telegraph.co.uk/news/worldnews/europe/sweden/9578979/Ikea-criticised-for-airbrushingwomen-out-of-Saudi-catalogue.html

The World Bank (2012). "Doing business 2012: Doing business in a more transparent world". Retrieved on 20 October 2014 from www.doingbusiness.org/reports/global-reports/doing-business-2012

Visser, W. (2008). "Corporate social responsibility in developing countries". In: Crane, A., Matten, D., McWilliams, A., Moon, J. & Siegel, D. S. (Eds), *The Oxford Handbook of Corporate Social Responsibility*, 473–479. Oxford: Oxford University Press.

WVS (2014). "World Values Survey database". Retrieved on 20 October 2014 from www.worldvaluessurvey.org/wvs.jsp

Part 2

Applying Competencies and Resources

10

Applying Competencies and Resources: Handling Cultural Otherness as the Second Step Towards Generating Complementarity and Synergy from Cultural Diversity

Christoph Barmeyer and Peter Franklin

1 COMPETENCIES AS RESOURCES

The introduction to the first part of this book and the case studies that follow it illustrate the long-established insight that the behaviour, practices and institutions to be found in particular business and management settings may (but need not) be causally related to values shared by members of that culture and oriented towards the norms generated in that culture.

Knowledge and understanding of these regularities are often still considered as sufficient preparation for the "cultural side" of international management – wrongly, in our view, as cognition alone cannot guarantee the onset of the behavioural change necessary to deal effectively and appropriately with culturally driven otherness and discord.

In – intercultural – work and everyday settings, people draw on a certain repertoire of knowledge and abilities which help them to master the challenges of social activity and interaction. These resources are core means for implementing action and interaction. The term "resources" originally described tangible resources such as raw materials, capital, energy or human resources. Increasingly, however, the term is used in the social sciences to refer to intangible resources such as people's characteristics, their attitudes and abilities. The resources people draw on in intercultural contexts are known as intercultural competencies. In management studies, the resource-based view (RBV) is a widespread approach and is seen as a basis for the competitive advantage of an organization (Colbert 2004), which lies primarily in the application of a bundle of valuable tangible or intangible resources at the organization's disposal. RBV can thus be seen as providing a theoretical basis for regarding intercultural competencies as a possible source of competitive advantage.

2 INTERCULTURAL COMPETENCE AND INTERCULTURAL COMPETENCIES

The belief that there was more to effective intercultural interaction than mere knowledge of other cultures and the resulting research into what this might constitute were triggered by experiences of individual and organizational intercultural failure and by the desire to succeed, which were felt especially strongly in mainly Western, individualistic and performance-oriented cultures. Unsurprisingly, such research and the development interventions they led to were conducted first in the USA after the Second World War and much later in Europe (Bennhold-Samaan 2004; Pusch 2004; Rogers et al. 2002). This intercultural ability has been variously and inconsistently referred to in the literature as intercultural competence (Bartel-Radic 2009; Thomas 2003a), intercultural effectiveness (Cui & van den Berg 1991), intercultural communication competence (Chen & Starosta 1996; Kim & Korzenny 1991), transcultural communication competence (Ting-Toomey 1999), cross-cultural communication competence (Ruben 1989), intercultural readiness (Van Der Zee & Brinkmann 2004) and international competency (WorldWork Ltd n.d.), to name just a few examples.

The recurring and crucial aspect of most conceptualizations of this competence is the belief that the competence to communicate and interact with members of other cultures requires that behaviour (including communication) should be both effective and appropriate. Whereas effectiveness refers to the transactional nature of the intercultural encounter, i.e. the degree to which the interactants achieve their goals, appropriateness refers to the relational, situational and contextual nature of the interaction (Spencer-Oatey & Franklin 2009), i.e. the degree to which the interaction is congruent with the relationship of the interactants and the situation and context in which they find themselves.

The numerous and varied conceptualizations contain more similarities than differences and in the attempt to introduce an all-embracing concept Spencer-Oatey and Franklin (2009:51) created (yet) another term, namely, "intercultural interaction competence" (ICIC), defining it as the ability "not only to communicate (verbally and non-verbally) and behave effectively and appropriately with people from other cultural groups, but also to handle the psychological demands and dynamic outcomes that result from such interchanges".

Such terms and conceptualizations were nourished by the increasing amount of empirical research conducted from the 1960s onwards by psychologists and communication scholars into what sub-competencies constitute the whole because only that knowledge could potentially improve the success, however measured, of those at the cultural interface – for example, by supporting their selection and professional development. Among the sub-competencies identified in these empirical investigations, which have typically recurred over a long period of time and over a large number of studies (reported on, for example, by Arasaratnam and Doerfel (2005), Dinges and Baldwin (1996), Hammer (1989), Spencer-Oatey and Franklin (2009), Spitzberg (1989) and Spitzberg & Chagnon (2009)), are openness to new ideas, behaviours and people, non-judgmentalness, empathy, tolerance for ambiguity and frustration, flexibility in behaviour, self-awareness, knowledge of one's own and other cultures, resilience to and ability to manage stress, message communication skills (including foreign language proficiency and meta-communicative skills), relationship skills and self-confidence. Such insights were based on data collected about individuals' experience with interactants from a large variety of cultures and are thus considered to be applicable generally across cultures or culture-general in nature. Other research focused on interactions with particular cultures and, as well as revealing similar sub-competencies, also made clear that sub-competencies may be culture-specific in nature (Barmeyer 2000; Bartel-Radic 2013). For example, a sensitivity to power inequalities and a rapport management competence may be especially important in management interaction with Asians (Spencer-Oatey & Xing 2004; Spencer-Oatey & Xing 2008).

3 COMPETENCE FRAMEWORKS

This mass of insights led naturally to the generation of various frameworks which attempt to harness the countless sub-competencies discovered by the research into a more manageable whole. Among the most familiar frameworks, later much imitated, adapted and refined, are those by Chen & Starosta (1996), Gudykunst (2004) and Ting-Toomey (1999). These numerous frameworks in turn have led to a further simplifying and helpful categorization of insights, for example those by Landis and Bhagat (1996), Byram (1997), Barmeyer (2000) and Bolten (2001), into what have become known as the ABC components of intercultural interaction competence (Spencer-Oatey & Franklin 2009:79):

- A: affective sub-competencies expressed in the form of attitudes and personal characteristics
- B: behavioural sub-competencies expressed in the form of skills
- C: cognitive sub-competencies embodied in the form of knowledge and understanding

Such terms and frameworks of sub-competencies perhaps serve the purpose of conceptual clarification and orderliness but they do not actually provide much help to practitioners, in that they do not indicate how these sub-competencies are actually expressed in intercultural action and interaction. How does one actually "do", for example, meta-communicative skills or non-judgmentalness or flexibility? Research by Stahl (2001), reported on by Kempf and Franklin in the case study "adidas and Reebok: What Expatriate Managers Need to Manage M&As Across Cultures" (Chapter 11 of this volume), is one of the few studies which indicate how international managers – in this case returning expatriate managers – demonstrate such competencies.

In an attempt to overcome this lack of meat on the bones of competence frameworks, Spencer-Oatey and Franklin (2009) create (yet) another framework of sub-competencies which not only takes account of the long and rich history of empirical research in psychology and communication studies described above but which also draws on insights into intercultural communication and language use generated by applied linguists. More interestingly, their framework overcomes the shortcomings of many predecessors by not merely naming but also describing and exemplifying the sub-competencies. It relies in the main on descriptions of "doing" competencies, i.e. of how the sub-competence is enacted and thus observable – a factor which is useful in intercultural professional development, competence assessment and selection activities. Spencer-Oatey and Franklin (2009) divide the competencies identified into four main areas: *message communication competencies*, *rapport management competencies*, *intercultural cognitive competencies* and *intercultural competencies – emotional strength*. To give an example of this approach, in Table 10.1 we list Spencer-Oatey and Franklin's description of message communication competencies:

Table 10.1 Message communication competencies

Message attuning	Picks up meaning from indirect signals such as paralanguage (e.g. intonation, speaking volume and speed, pausing) and non-verbal communication (e.g. eye contact and other elements of body language), and uses these signals to draw inferences about people's message meanings
Active listening	Does not assume understanding – checks and clarifies the meaning of words and phrases, and tests own understanding
Building of shared knowledge	Discloses and elicits key information, including the intentions and broader context as to why something is said or requested, in order to help build trust and mutual understanding and to reduce uncertainty
Linguistic accommodation	Adapts use of language (e.g. choice of words, speed of delivery, clarity of pronunciation, use of colloquial expressions) to the proficiency level of the recipient(s)
Information structuring and highlighting	Structures and highlights information by using discourse markers to "label" language, by using visual or written aids, and by paying attention to the sequencing of information
Stylistic flexibility	Uses different language styles and conventions flexibly to suit different purposes, contexts and audiences

Source: Spencer-Oatey & Franklin, (2009:83).

4 INTERCULTURAL MANAGEMENT COMPETENCIES

The data underpinning the frameworks and competencies described in this chapter come from a wide variety of samples, often US university students. What exactly makes one *international manager* more able than another to handle cultural otherness and its consequences effectively and appropriately is a topic which has occupied management scholars ever since the premature return home of expatriate managers became a thorn in the flesh of MNCs from the 1960s onwards. Attempts were made to discover the causes of what became known as expatriate failure.

The relatively unsophisticated results of the consequent questionnaires – e.g. "The manager's personality or emotional immaturity" or "Other family-related problems" (Tung 1987:117) – were succeeded by more research on the profile of figures such as the successful expatriate (e.g. Harzing & Pinnington 2014; Stahl 2001), the international manager (e.g. Leslie et al. 2002), the international team member, the responsible international leader (e.g. Miska et al. 2013) and their implicit intercultural competencies. This type of work aimed to improve selection and development procedures and increase intercultural success.

Four approaches have been found by management scholars to be useful:

- the "survey of international managers" approach: investigating international managers themselves (e.g. Hampden-Turner & Trompenaars 2000; Leslie et al. 2002; Shi & Franklin 2014);
- the "survey of specialists" approach: asking representatives of companies (for example, human resource specialists) to describe the characteristics of their successful international managers (e.g. Barham & Devine 1991; Marx 1999);
- the "impressionistic" approach: generating the characteristics of effective international managers on the basis of a reading of the management literature, surveys, and anecdotal and experiential evidence derived from the business press (e.g. Schneider & Barsoux 2003);
- the "Big Five" approach: relating the Big Five personality characteristics of extroversion, agreeableness, conscientiousness, emotional stability and openness or intellect (e.g. Caligiuri 2000a, 2000b) to intercultural management effectiveness.

The results of the research that applied these approaches have proved congruent with the results of the earlier studies conducted in psychology and communication studies in that they also bring out more overtly personality-related characteristics of the effective intercultural interactant; for example, behavioural, cognitive and interpersonal openness, flexibility, adaptability, self-reliance, tolerance of uncertainty and ambiguity, emotional strength and cognitive complexity, as well as the distinctly communicative and relational competencies harnessed in the Spencer-Oatey and Franklin (2009) framework.

5 THE CASE STUDIES

Such insights have flowed into the models of intercultural competence contained in tools which are used (and some of which were especially created) to assess and develop the intercultural competencies of international managers. Such tools and models form the common thread in three of the cases presented in this part of the book. Whereas Kelley and Meyers' Cross-Cultural Adaptability Inventory (1993), with its dimensions of emotional resilience, flexibility/openness, perceptual acuity and personal autonomy, and Bennett and Hammer's Intercultural Development Inventory, based on Bennett's (1986, 1993) Developmental Model of Intercultural Sensitivity, are well-known (also in Europe), as long-established assessment and development tools, they are not explicitly related to the international management setting. Among more recent and more management-oriented assessment and development tools are the Intercultural Readiness Check, most recently presented by Brinkmann and van Weerdenburg (2014), and The International Profiler, based on WorldWork Ltd.'s International Competency Framework.

This last competency framework, together with that originated by Kühlmann and Stahl (1998) and Stahl (2001), is put to the test in the first case in this part of the book, "adidas and Reebok: What Expatriate Managers Need to Manage M&As across Cultures", written by Matthias Kempf and Peter Franklin. The case examines the experiences of a German expatriate manager in the USA given the task of handling the HR aspects of the post-merger integration of adidas and Reebok. The case compares the competencies expected and demanded of the manager prior to expatriation with the competencies the manager in fact felt were useful and necessary during his assignment. The comparison shows how little priority was given in the job description to intercultural competencies before the assignment began and how significant they turned out to be.

A further model of intercultural interaction competence is based on the theory of multiple intelligences and embodied in the notion of Cultural Intelligence, originated by Earley and Ang (2003). As with the results of the empirical research described above, Cultural Intelligence describes how interculturally more successful individuals differ from the less successful. In contrast to other approaches, which capture a mix of ABC competencies, Earley and Ang choose to describe the features which make up these differences as a form of intelligence. How Cultural Intelligence (or CQ as it is also described) is related to intercultural management and leadership settings and how it may be developed – thereby incidentally putting it at odds with conventional beliefs about IQ, which is seen as constant – is described in a more accessible style by Earley et al. (2006), by Livermore (2011) and Livermore et al. (2012). "Virtual Chaos at WORLDWIDE Rx: How Cultural Intelligence Can Turn Problems into Solutions" by David Livermore and Soon Ang is a case study that describes work in a culturally diverse team which the authors demonstrate needs to be handled with Cultural Intelligence if its diversity is not to obstruct participation and innovation.

The CQ conceptualization of intercultural competence, together with Bird et al.'s (2010) notion of Intercultural Competence for Global Leaders, which identified 17 intercultural competency dimensions for global leaders, is also the focus of "Cultural Intelligence at Work – A Case Study from Thailand" by Claus Schreier and Astrid Kainzbauer, who present for analysis a critical incident experienced by a Swiss expatriate manager working in Thailand for a local, family-owned company. As the case makes clear, the practical relevance of such competence concepts lies in the desired individual and organizational outcomes, such as improved business performance and cultural adjustment.

It is a matter of some discussion whether, and if so, to what extent, the various sub-competencies of intercultural interaction competence can actually be developed in international managers. Whereas greater awareness and increased knowledge and understanding are probably relatively easy to achieve, skills take longer to develop, attitudes probably even longer and personal characteristics may not be susceptible to change at all. Nevertheless, intercultural development interventions of various kinds (for more or less comprehensive accounts, see, for example, Spencer-Oatey & Franklin 2009: 199–241; Fowler & Blohm 2004; Fowler & Mumford 1995; Landis et al., 2004) are firmly established in the repertoire of management development activities, such as intercultural training (Barmeyer 2004) or intercultural coaching (Barmeyer 2000).

The selection of suitable development measures for the two sides in a virtual intercultural cooperation and the results of these measures form one of the topics in the case "Cultural Aspects of Offshoring to India" by Craig Storti and Peter Franklin. The case, which also portrays cultural otherness and the discord it can lead to, is included in this part of the book because it draws attention to the much neglected competence areas of what Spencer-Oatey and Franklin in their framework refer to as message communication competencies and rapport management competencies. This case makes clear that such outdated notions of communication as the transfer of messages from sender to receiver (Shannon & Weaver (1948) and Berlo (1960), and still present in some standard works on intercultural communication (Jandt 2013: 42–44) and cross-cultural management (Thomas & Peterson 2014: 112–113)) are deceptively simple and do not necessarily lead to effective and appropriate intercultural interaction. The inability of both sides in the case to co-construct understanding (rather than simply the inability of one side to receive and decode meaning as in Shannon and Weaver) leads to transactional and relational conflict, to the detriment of desired management outcomes.

REFERENCES

Arasaratnam, L. A. & Doerfel, M. L. (2005). "Intercultural communication competence: Identifying key components from multicultural perspectives". In: *International Journal of Intercultural Relations*, 29:2, 137–163.

Barham, K. & Devine, M. (1991). *The Quest for the International Manager. A Survey of Global Human Resource Strategies*. London: Ashridge Management Guide/Economist Intelligence Unit.

Barmeyer, C. (2000). *Interkulturelles Management und Lernstile. Studierende und Führungskräfte in Frankreich, Deutschland und Québec*. Frankfurt/New York: Campus.

Barmeyer, C. (2002). "Interkulturelles Coaching". In: Rauen, C. (Ed.), *Handbuch Coaching*, 199–231. Göttingen: Hogrefe Verlag.

Barmeyer, C. (2004). "Learning styles and their impact on cross-cultural training. An international comparison in France, Germany and Quebec". In: *International Journal of Intercultural Relations*, 28:6, 577–594.

Bartel-Radic, A. (2009). "La compétence interculturelle: état de l'art et perspectives". In: *Management International*, 13:4, 11–26.

Bartel-Radic, A. (2013). "'Estrangeirismo' and flexibility: Intercultural learning in Brazilian MNCs". In: *Management International/International Management/Gestión Internacional*, 17:4, 239–253.

Bennett, M. J. (1993). "Towards Ethnorelativism: A Developmental Model of Intercultural Sensitivity". In: Paige, R. M. (Ed.): *Education for the Intercultural Experience*, 21–71. Yarmouth: Intercultural Press.

Bennett, M. J. (1986). "A developmental approach to training for intercultural sensitivity". In: *International Journal of Intercultural Relations*, 10, 179–186.

Bennhold-Samaan, L. (2004). "The evolution of cross-cultural training in the Peace Corps". In: Landis, D., Bennett, J. M. & Bennett, M. J. (Eds), *Handbook of Intercultural* Training, 363–394. London: Sage.

Berlo, D. (1960). *Process of Communication: An Introduction to Theory and Practice*. New York: Holt, Rinehart & Winston.

Bird, A., Mendenhall, M. E., Stevens, M. J. & Oddou, G. (2010). "Defining the content domain of intercultural competence for global leaders". In: *Journal of Managerial Psychology*, 25:8, 810–828.

Bolten, J. (2001). "Interkulturelles Coaching, Mediation, Training und Consulting als Aufgaben des Personalmanagements internationaler Unternehmen." In: Clermont, A., Schmeisser, W. & Krimphove, D. (Eds), *Strategisches Personalmanagement in Globalen Unternehmen*, 1–16. München: Vahlen.

Brinkmann, U. & Van Weerdenburg, O. (2014). *Intercultural Readiness: Four Competences for Working Across Cultures*. Houndmills: Palgrave Macmillan. Byram, M. (1997). *Teaching and Assessing Intercultural Communicative Competence*. Clevedon: Multilingual Matters.

Caligiuri, P. (2000a). "The big five personality characteristics as predictors of expatriate success". In: *Personnel Psychology*, 53, 67–88.

Caligiuri, P. (2000b). "Selecting expatriates for personality characteristics: A moderating effect of personality on the relationship between host national contact and cross-cultural adjustment". In: *Management International Review*, 40,61–80.

Chanlat, J.-F., Davel, E. & Dupuis, J.-P. (2013). *Cross-Cultural Management. Culture and Management Across the World*. London: Routledge.

Chen, G.-M. & Starosta, W. J. (1996). "Intercultural communication competence: A synthesis". In: *Communication Yearbook*, 19, 353–384.

Colbert, B. A. (2004). "The complex resource-based view: Implications for theory and practice in strategic human resource management". In: *Academy of Management Review*, 29:3, 341–358.

Cui, G. & van den Berg, S. (1991). "Testing the construct validity of intercultural effectiveness". In: *International Journal of Intercultural Relations*, 15, 227–241.

Dinges, N. G. & Baldwin, K. D. (1996). "Intercultural competence. A research perspective". In: Landis, D. & Bhagat, R. S. (Eds), *Handbook of Intercultural Training*, 106–123. 2nd ed. Thousand Oaks, CA: Sage.

Earley, P. C. & Ang, S. (2003). *Cultural Intelligence: An Analysis of Individual Interactions Across Cultures*. Palo Alto, CA: Stanford University Press.

Early, P. C., Ang, S. & Tang, J. (2006). *CQ: Developing Cultural Intelligence at Work*. Palo Alto, CA: Stanford University Press.

Fowler, S. M. & Blohm, J. M. (2004). "An analysis of methods for intercultural training". In: Landis, D., Bennett, J. M. & Bennett, M. J. (Eds), *Handbook of Intercultural Training*, 37–84. Thousand Oaks, CA: Sage.

Fowler, S. M. & Mumford M. G. (1995). *Intercultural Sourcebook: Cross-Cultural Training Methods*, Vol. 1. Yarmouth: Intercultural Press.

Gudykunst, W. B. (2004). *Bridging Differences. Effective Intergroup Communication*. 4th ed. London: Sage.

Hammer, M. R. (1989). "Intercultural communication competence". In: Asante, M. R., Gudykunst, W. B. & Newmark, E. (Eds), *Handbook of International and Intercultural Communication*, 247–260. Newbury Park: Sage.

Hampden-Turner, C. & Trompenaars, F. (2000). *Building Cross-Cultural Competence. How to Create Wealth from Conflicting Values*. Chichester: John Wiley.

Harzing, A. W. & Pinnington A. (2014). *International Human Resource Management*. 4th ed. London: Sage.

Jandt, F. E. (2013). *An Introduction to Intercultural Communication: Identities in a Global Community*. Thousand Oaks, CA: Sage.

Kolb, D. & Kolb, A. (2005). "Learning styles and learning spaces: Enhancing experiential learning in higher education". In: *Academy of Management Learning & Education*, 4:2, 193–212.

Kelley, C. & Meyers, J. E. (1993). *The Cross-Cultural Adaptability Inventory*. Yarmouth: Intercultural Press.

Kim, Y. Y. & Korzenny, F. (1991). "Intercultural communication competence. A systems-theoretic view". In: Ting-Toomey, S. & Korzenny, F. (Eds), *Cross-Cultural Interpersonal Communication (International and Intercultural Communication Annual)*, *15*, 259–275. London: Sage.

Kühlmann, T. & Stahl, G. (1998). "Diagnose interkultureller Kompetenz: Entwicklung und Evaluierung eines Assessment-Centers". In: Barmeyer, C. & Bolten, J. (Eds), *Interkulturelle Personalorganisation (Intercultural Personnel Management)*, 213–224. Sternenfels: Verlag für Wissenschaft und Praxis.

Landis, D., Bennett, J. M. & Bennett, M. J. (2004). *Handbook of Intercultural Training*. Thousand Oaks, CA: Sage.

Landis, D. & Bhagat, R. S. (1996). *Handbook of Intercultural Training.* 2nd ed. Thousand Oaks, CA: Sage.

Leslie, J. B., Dalton, M., Ernst, C. & Deal, J. (2002). *Managerial Effectiveness in a Global Context. A Working Model of Predictors.* Greensboro: Centre for Creative Leadership.

Livermore, D. (2011). *The Cultural Intelligence Difference: Master the One Skill You Can't Do without in Today's Global Economy.* New York: AMACOM.

Livermore, D., Van Dyne, L. & Ang, S. (2012). "Cultural intelligence: Why every leader needs it". In: *Intercultural Management Quarterly,*13:2, 18–21.

Marx, E. (1999). *Breaking Through Culture Shock.* London: Nicholas Brealey.

Miska, C., Stahl, G. K. & Mendenhall, M. E. (2013). "Intercultural competencies as antecedents of responsible global leadership". In: *European Journal of International Management,* 7:5, 550–569.

Pusch, M. (2004). "Intercultural training in historical perspective". In: Landis, D., Bennett, J. M. & Bennett, M. J. (Eds), *Handbook of Intercultural Training,* 13–36. London: Sage.

Rogers, E., Hart, W. & Miike, Y. (2002). "Edward T. Hall and the history of intercultural communication: The United States and Japan". In: *Keio Communication Review,* 24, 3–26.

Ruben, B. D. (1989). "The study of cross-cultural competence: Traditions and contemporary issues". In: *International Journal of Organizational Behaviour,* 13, 229–240.

Schneider, S. C. & Barsoux, J.-L. (2003). *Managing Across Cultures.* 2nd ed. London: Prentice Hall.

Shannon, C. E. (1948). "A mathematical theory of communication". In: *Bell System Technical Journal,* 27, 379–423.

Shi, X. & Franklin, P. (2014). "Business expatriates' cross-cultural adaptation and their job performance". In: *Asia Pacific Journal of Human Resources,* 52:2, 193–214.

Spencer-Oatey, H. & Franklin, P. (2009). *Intercultural Interaction.* London: Palgrave Macmillan.

Spencer-Oatey, H. & Xing, J. (2004). Rapport management problems in Chinese–British business interactions: A case study. In: House, J. & Rehbein, J. (Eds), *Multilingual* Communication, 197–221. Amsterdam: John Benjamins.

Spencer-Oatey, H. & Xing, J. (2008). A problematic Chinese business visit to Britain: Issues of face. In: Spencer-Oatey, H. (Ed.), *Culturally Speaking. Culture, Communication and Politeness Theory,* 258–273. 2nd ed. London: Continuum.

Spitzberg, B. H. (1989). "Issues in the development of a theory of interpersonal competence in the intercultural context". In: *International Journal of Intercultural Relations,* 13, 241–268.

Spitzberg, B. H. & Chagnon, G. (2009). "Conceptualizing Intercultural Competence". In: Deardorff, D. K., *The SAGE Handbook of Intercultural Competence,* 2–52. Thousand Oaks, CA: Sage.

Stahl, G. (2001). "Using assessment centers as tools for global leadership development: An exploratory study". In: Mendenhall, M., Kühlmann, T. & Stahl, G. (Eds), *Developing Global Business Leaders: Policies, Processes and Innovations,* 197–210. Westport: Quorum Books.

Thomas, A. (2003a). "Interkulturelle Kompetenz: Grundlagen, Probleme, Konzepte [Intercultural competence: Principles, problems, concepts]". In: *Erwägen, Wissen, Ethik,* 14:1, 137–150.

Thomas, D. & Peterson, M. F. (2014). *Cross-Cultural Management. Essential Concepts.* 3rd ed. Thousand Oaks, CA: Sage.

Ting-Toomey, S. (1999). *Communicating Across Cultures.* New York: The Guilford Press.

Tung, R. L. (1987). "Expatriate assignments. Enhancing success and minimizing failure". In: *Academy of Management Executive,* 1:2, 117–126.

Van der Zee, K. I. & Brinkmann, U. (2004). "Construct validity evidence for the intercultural readiness check against the multicultural personality questionnaire". In: *International Journal of Selection and Assessment,* 12:3, 285–290.

WorldWork (no date). International competencies. Retrieved on 24 October 2008 from www.worldwork.biz/legacy/www/docs2/competencies.phtml

11

adidas and Reebok: What Expatriate Managers Need to Manage M&As Across Cultures

Matthias Kempf and Peter Franklin

1 INTRODUCTION

Mergers and acquisitions (M&As) are a notoriously difficult and risky undertaking even when conducted in the reassuring environment of one's home market. Not only do the initial business benefits frequently fail to materialize to the extent predicted in the commercial and financial due diligence process conducted prior to the M&A going ahead (Cooper & Finkelstein 2010; Mayrhofer 2013), but managing the acquired company, let alone integrating it into the organization and culture of the acquiring company (should that be the strategy decided on) can be a management challenge too great for the acquirer.

As soon as a merger or acquisition takes place across national cultural borders, the difficulty of integrating the acquired company increases, not least at the human level (Buckley & Ghauri 2002). Those involved in managing the integration process are not only confronted with handling a different organizational culture; this challenge is magnified by the need to handle a different national culture as well (Brannen & Peterson 2009; Stahl & Voigt 2008). This is an extremely demanding task for the managers concerned at the operational and, in particular, at the psychological level. When those involved are actually immersed as expatriate managers in both the unfamiliar organizational culture and also the unfamiliar national culture, the challenges are very considerable and demand a special range of competencies (personal qualities and attitudes, as well as skills and knowledge) if the assignment is not to end in tears. This is what Benedikt Paul, the manager featured in the following case study, came to realize when he was sent as an expatriate human resources (HR) manager from Germany to the USA to manage from the HR standpoint the acquisition and integration of Reebok into the adidas Group.

2 CASE DESCRIPTION

2.1 Company background

The adidas Group currently employs more than 53,000 people in over 160 countries. It produces more than 650 million product units every year and generates sales of € 14.5 billion (all figures relate to 2014). But the adidas story started much more modestly in a small town in Bavaria, Germany, when Adi Dassler set up the Gebrüder Dassler Schuhfabrik in 1924. Twenty-five years later, he registered a shoe that included the three stripes that were soon to become so unmistakably connected with adidas and famous all over the world. adidas became known for its product innovation, its strength in technical product development and its closeness to athletes, and for decades it has been the leading sports brand in the global – especially European – football business.

While adidas continued to grow, two Britons by the names of Joe and Jeff Foster gave their grandfather's company J. W. Foster and Sons, founded in 1895, a new name: Reebok. Thirty years after this renaming, Reebok was a leading sports goods company. Under the leadership of the American Paul Fireman, Reebok dominated the fitness and aerobics wave in the 1980s with ground-breaking products and marketing. However, mainly because it failed to focus but instead "did everything but not right", over the next few years Reebok lost its credibility and slowly turned into a cheap brand.

In 2006 adidas acquired the Reebok brand. The merger was aimed at achieving various goals. The most obvious one was to become bigger in the USA as one of the most significant markets in the sports industry, which was then very much dominated by adidas's biggest competitor. Another promising prospect for the adidas Group was also to become even more attractive in lifestyle products, to gain additional momentum through US celebrities such as rappers and actors, but also to include other sports in their portfolio by using Reebok's experience and history with American sports such as American football and basketball. Overall, it was, of course, also the opportunity to gain even more influence and power over external vendors and partners by just being a bigger sports goods corporation. It was announced that after three years the company expected overall savings in this new constellation of about USD 150 million.

The power of Reebok in the US and that of adidas in Europe and Asia made the merger for both companies a very promising marriage. Reebok's strength in retro fashion and their existing licence agreements with the American professional sports leagues were also important reasons to go for this huge project. Given Reebok's focus on fashion trends such as hip-hop and adidas's focus on sports performance and technical innovations, the strategy appeared from the overall company perspective to offer a very good match. It was not about saving money but allowing expansion, especially in growing markets such as China and Russia.

adidas's competitors aimed to keep their main competitor busy on their home turf in the US and win market share, and in so doing reduced their investment opportunities in the growing markets which from the long-term perspective was even more important. The adidas Group clearly realized that they had to become more successful in the US to be able to achieve the overarching global company goal – to be "the leading sports brand in the world".

In this context it is important to remember that both companies were actually competitors in the sports goods market, which had been a challenge but became a conscious strategy as they now focus on different customer groups. While adidas mainly targets the performance athlete, Reebok focuses on its fitness roots, because "if it is already in your DNA, why reinvent the wheel?" as an adidas manager put it.

Reebok signed a long-term partnership with CrossFit, a core strength and conditioning programme, in 2011. Two years later, the studio categories of yoga, dance and aerobics followed and Reebok was back on track to becoming the leading fitness brand with the goal of empowering consumers to be fit for life.

In this merger, one interesting opportunity and, indeed, challenge, for adidas was to learn how to steer and manage a huge global company effectively and also how to incorporate a brand with a very US feel into an originally German brand. Internally, it was also obvious for everybody that the main reason for the merger was a strategic one: the merger was not aimed at reducing headcount. However, there was of course a lot of uncertainty, especially among the Reebok employees, about the future.

2.2 Looking ahead to the assignment

The human resources perspective, and in particular the training and development side, was of special significance after the merger of these two big sports companies. Why? In a global corporation like the adidas Group with different brands and sub-brands (for example, adidas, Reebok, Rockport, Taylor-Made, Hockey CCM, NEO) it is crucial to work with the same performance, succession and people-development tools and processes. The numerous brands make it necessary not just to use the same language but to have the same understanding of how to grow the employees and how to live the values of the company.

The task for the German HR manager Benedikt Paul, who was sent to Reebok's US headquarters in Canton, MA, to be Director of Development & Training for the Region Americas, was to support the merger especially from the organizational development perspective. The implementation of the key corporate processes for talent management was seen as crucial to achieve the mid- and long-term goals. Benedikt Paul had joined the adidas company two years previously and had since then been located in the German headquarters of the Group. He had clearly proven his skills and potential and was personally thrilled about this new task abroad, as this was regarded both by him and by the company as a significant step in his career development.

In Benedikt Paul's job description the task for him and for the team he had to build was formulated as follows:

> The task is to run the Competence Centre Development & Training for the Region Americas that provides internal consultancy and services to HR

management, line management and employees across brands and functions within the adidas Group. The three organizational pillars are Training, Development (Executive and Talent Development) and Emerging Employees (functional trainee programme, business management programme). The main focus is to implement, drive and sustain concepts, tools, processes and systems related to the strategic HR pillar "Instil a Culture of Performance" covering the three success drivers Leadership Excellence, Performance Management and Talent Management. Key responsibilities are:

1. Ensure that business needs and priorities of the respective customers are covered within the Business Plan D&T Region Americas by taking into account the overall HR business strategy and objectives.
2. Liaise closely with HRM and Senior Management in the different locations and establish mutually agreed business plans together with the respective D&T responsible for the location. This includes ad hoc projects and specific initiatives for the different lines of business.
3. Monitor and support target achievement and the overall service provided by the respective local D&T department (based on the targeting).
4. Be part of the D&T Core Team of the adidas Group that determines the D&T strategy for the Group.
5. Design and develop an implementation strategy for concepts, tools and processes decided upon by the Development & Training Core Group including adapting them to meet local and business needs to ensure implementation success (while ensuring Group standards). An effective strategy will include plans to communicate effectively with HR-M, line management and dedicated D&T resources within the Region.
6. Assure high quality realization of D&T concepts, tools and processes by defining KPIs and developing an effective evaluation process focusing on quality and results.
7. Recruit and develop an effective D&T Regional staff capable of successfully managing the D&T function within their location.

adidas Group HR at headquarters summed up Benedikt Paul's tasks and what was expected of him in the following way:

1. Support the merger between these different cultures from the people side (change, coach, provide guidance, open doors in HQ, build relationships, show the network, and connect people from both sides ...).
2. Provide transparency for the Group about existing talents within the Reebok world.

3. Also provide insights for these talents on global career opportunities within the adidas Group.
4. Implement our corporate guidelines, standards, processes and tools designed by the German headquarters and build up the trust and belief in their value, so that Reebok management buys into them and is open to experience these benefits. This counts specifically for the local HR departments, as at the end of the day, they have to execute in this corporate spirit.

Before he left for the US, Benedikt received the following additional briefing, guidance and "good advice" from the corporate senior HR leadership:

> "This is a newly acquired company in the US – so we have to implement and train them in the Group standards and procedures. Be aware that you are our local guy and corporate representative. Of course you are not alone, but you have to make sure that you are supported and accepted by the local HR organizational units and that you have their commitment. Don't accept too many exceptions, as they have to understand that Reebok is now part of an international group. It's also important that you build up a team which breathes and supports the American spirit. And don't forget, we are supporting you in gaining this international experience in preparation for your next career step."

The job description and the advice he received from corporate senior HR leadership gave Benedikt Paul a lot of food for thought. Read his reflections, given in an interview, about the situation he was in when he took up his job.

2.3 Handling the assignment

How were you received when you took up your position?

> "I was one of the first three German managers now living and working in the American and Reebok environment. It quickly became obvious that there was some scepticism about me. People wondered if a German HR manager was really able to run the development & training department in an American company and even in the Region Americas, which included Canada, South and Central America. The Americans were clearly expected to give up their old tools and processes and to accept our corporate ones – for example, their newly implemented appraisal system, which was not necessarily a failure actually. But why should they?"

How did you see your task at the beginning? What did you feel were your main challenges?

> "What was demanded of me was loud and clear: help us to recognize our benefit as well. The need for the so-called 'Wiifm' ('What's in it for me?')

was always tangible. I had to find out very quickly who I could trust, and also how I could make sure that they trusted me! When I started it was a one-man show, meaning there was not a single team member left in the development and training department: in the past Reebok always fired these colleagues as soon as there was pressure from poor company results."

How did the Reebok people feel about the changes that were going on?

"The good news for the integration project was that in general the offerings for people development and talent management were received with open arms. There was a keen appetite for these topics, both among employees and their managers, but for a lot of reasons there were different expectations in quite some cases. And the big question was how our offering portfolio would match local circumstances and culture. Reebok had just implemented their own appraisal process and tool and was not amused that they were now forced to accept a new one to achieve global consistency in the Group. Also it was not clear how the training content, which had proved to be successful in Germany and other countries, would really help the organization. They were invited to participate in, and to nominate their talents for, the global leadership development programmes, but they didn't really understand the culture, the expectations of the future leaders and the intention behind the programmes of the adidas Group as the new owner."

2.4 Looking back on the assignment

In retrospect, how would you describe the way you went about things?

"My approach was mainly appreciating what was done in the past – reflecting critically but openly – and also showing them the benefits if they adopted our approach. So I asked myself for example: What are the quick gains? What does it make sense to start with so that it's meaningful for the Reebok human resources team and the line management? How can we build up the team, for example, by also taking into account diversity aspects?"

To what extent was communication a key success factor?

"Language of course was a challenge. Yes, the company language within the adidas world is English, but quite often nuances were critical when it came to specific expressions, especially when the takeover led to a sensitive or emotional situation. It was also very important to become aware of and understand the intercultural differences. There was not a particularly great interest on the part of the Americans to understand the German culture, which made it even more important for us to make additional efforts."

But there is more to effective communication across cultures than just language and culture, isn't there?

"We in adidas learned how important it was always to show the big picture and the 'why', which was, of course, completely unknown to the

Reebok colleagues who had just joined a global corporation. And especially when we faced resistance, it was crucial to communicate and even 'over-communicate', to repeat messages consistently. Telling 'the ugly truth' and being very transparent was almost always much better and respected than saying nothing or telling only bits and pieces. Another very important contribution was that our communication team did a great job from the beginning by communicating very transparently in both companies. There were regular news and updates about the progress in getting together and also regular pulse checks with over 400 nominated key people. And then it was crucial to work immediately with the results and adjust approaches. So the integration of the two companies remained a topic for a long time in all the internal media and newsletters."

How did you "play" your role?

"Key was not to show up as 'the police' from headquarters or as the guys who know everything better. It was important to show we were willing to learn as well, in particular as we were in the position that we had acquired the company. Even when there was scepticism on our part about how Reebok wanted to approach the topics and whether Reebok's thinking was the right one, we chose sometimes to do it their way first or at least to show an open mind, which gave us enough time to explore and also to learn! We were then able to adjust rather than simply force through what we were told by headquarters. And realizing and acknowledging in public that there were also a lot of things we could learn from the Reebok past and present added high respect and value and clearly made our life easier. The attitude of 'less is more', less structure while still having processes in place, the recognition of achievements and successes and celebrating even small successes on the way are additional important points I want to mention. Not always a template for everything, following process guidelines, death by PowerPoint, statistics and KPIs, but observe, appreciate and be open and curious, learn from their success in the past."

How did this go down with your Reebok colleagues?

"The greatest and nicest feedback was actually that Reebok's head of HR, who of course played a major role in this integration project, stated in the third year of the journey that the biggest benefit and value for the Reebok brand resulting from this acquisition was the fact that they gained great people development initiatives and other related tools and processes. And – these programmes allowed both sides to build relationships and networks."

What role did the relational side play?

"Building up trustworthy relationships was key. Of course, they were asking 'What's actually his interest? Why is he really here? Is this just an important step in his career? Does he only want to show that he can fulfil the expectations of HQ? Is he really here to help us?' But the fact that there

> was an authentic and real interest in Reebok's history and also an honest appreciation for some things they had done over the past years helped a lot. The openly – sometimes even loudly – asked question about 'What's in it for me?' was heard the whole time, so it was important to listen to the managers and to fulfil their needs. And that was the balance we had to find, as German headquarters expected delivery on corporate goals only. The simple fact that I was able to use my relationships with the German decision makers was of course another quick and important gain. I had the chance to open some doors for the Reebok guys and for that reason they then did the same for me in the US environment. The training we purposely organized with mixed teams from both companies showed a major benefit in terms of building up networks and also creating common understanding for the different situations."

What advice would you give to expatriates?

> "Every expatriate needs to be aware that adaptation to the host country's communication conventions is important for developing positive working relations. And there is yet another aspect to consider when it comes to cultural adaptation. Many behaviours that seem to be simple to change are deeply anchored in national character, so it is very problematic to expect people to adopt behaviours that contradict their traditions and values. Tensions can be built because of smaller differences, too – for example the tendency of US business people to describe even serious problems in positive terms as challenges tends to irritate their German colleagues, for whom 'problem solving' is evidence of professional expertise. The most important aspects to pay attention to are communication style and conflict behaviour – how colleagues interact with each other, how they deal with differences and how they share information. My advice would be that you should thoroughly prepare for the new assignment, country and culture. And actively include your family in this. Take an initial trip to the new location, gather information about the environment, the expectations of the new boss and so on. And then start to devote the necessary attention not only to relationships, but also to your cultural adaptation."

3 BACKGROUND KNOWLEDGE

3.1 The authors' points of reference

Matthias Kempf: "There are truly benefits and learning experiences for both sides when the integration of a new people development philosophy is expected for a new company resulting from a merger. This can be mainly achieved by being open for different approaches and incorporating the past. Switching behaviours and cultural codes, but also mind and attitude, are the success factors for dealing with tangible scepticism and overcoming resistance."

As a result of his work both as a scholar and as a consultant frequently involved in developing the competence profile of managers and leaders involved in intercultural assignments, Peter Franklin believes that a complex set of affective, behavioural and cognitive competencies, which express themselves in attitudes, skills and knowledge, are required to handle effectively and appropriately the challenges of working at the organizational and national cultural interface. What that profile looks like in an individual case will depend on the particular managerial task and its context.

3.2 Concepts, models, frameworks

Competencies in intercultural management Although an understanding of culturally influenced differences can undoubtedly make the practice of managing across cultures easier (as cognition may in time lead to behavioural change), the acquisition of knowledge and the achievement of understanding can be a relatively lengthy path to enhanced competence. It has thus long been realized that such culturally influenced differences as those described above might require special competencies in addition to knowledge and understanding in the individuals involved if differences are to be dealt with effectively and appropriately.

This history of research in this area means that there exists sound evidence about which knowledge and skills and, in particular, which attitudes and personal qualities contribute to intercultural interaction competence (ICIC). Empirical research in psychology and communication science in particular comes up again and again with components of what emerges as a set of sub-competencies which constitutes intercultural interaction competence. This set of sub-competencies, which, though intuitively plausible, has been criticized for lacking terminological and conceptual rigour (Spencer-Oatey & Franklin 2009; Spitzberg 1989; Spitzberg & Chagnon 2009), contains competencies such as openness of various kinds, non-judgmentalness, empathy, tolerance for ambiguity, persistence, behavioural flexibility, self-awareness, knowledge of one's own and other cultures, resilience to stress, a sense of adventure, message communication skills and relationship skills.

Despite the plethora of evidence, a major weakness of these studies is that the reader is left with little or no impression as to how these competencies are expressed in behaviour generally, let alone in work and management settings. This is a crucial weakness when it comes to selecting and developing people to work internationally, as observable behaviour and desirable behaviour are more useful for selection and HR development respectively than a list of rather vague abstract qualities open to numerous, possibly also culturally influenced, interpretations: one person's flexibility may be the next person's lack of persistence.

One of the few empirical studies of management behaviour which has contributed to our picture of what goes to make up ICIC but which does not omit to give evidence of how people "do" the competencies named is that reported on by Kühlmann and Stahl (1998) and Stahl (2001). These scholars are critical of the majority of studies of ICIC because they frequently do not explore the actual "determinants of success" of intercultural encounters, but rather simply record the respondents' personal theories of suitability. Investigating the experiences of 246 German managers who had just returned from an expatriate assignment or were still on assignment, Kühlmann and Stahl (1998:217–218) in their qualitative study employ a modified critical incident method (Flanagan 1954) (see Franklin 2007:274–275 for an overview of the method) to generate a number of characteristics of the successful expatriate, which Stahl (2001:201) lists as follows:

Tolerance for ambiguity – the ability to function effectively in a foreign environment where the expatriate experiences ambiguity, complexity, and uncertainty.

Behavioural flexibility – the capacity to vary one's behaviour according to the immediate requirements of the situation and the demands of the foreign culture.

Goal orientation – the ability and desire to achieve one's task goals despite barriers, opposition or discouragement.

Sociability and interest in other people – a willingness to establish and maintain meaningful social relationships, combined with a genuine interest in other people.

Empathy – the capacity to accurately sense other people's thoughts, feelings, and motives, and to respond to them appropriately.

Nonjudgmentalness – the willingness to critically re-examine one's own values and beliefs, and to avoid judging people against one's own norms.

Meta-communication skills – the capacity to clarify culturally different perceptions and to sensibly "guide" the intercultural communication process.

Kühlmann and Stahl (1998) regard these characteristics as necessary but not sufficient for success on assignments abroad: task-, company- or culture-related factors also need to be taken into account. (Interestingly they note that goal-orientation that is either too high or too low can be counter-productive for an expatriate assignment.)

Especially valuable is Stahl's unpacking of these characteristics by listing behavioural indicators for each of the categories, which become observable (for example, on the job or in an assessment centre) and imitable, and thus useful in recruitment and HR development activities:

Tolerance for ambiguity – Feels comfortable in ambiguous or highly complex situations; doesn't push for a particular solution; reacts patiently toward foreign business partners; stays calm in difficult situations; etc.

Behavioural flexibility – Rapidly changes behaviour if given appropriate feedback; finds creative solutions to problems; compromises; shows readiness to revise former decisions; statements match gesticulations; etc.

Goal orientation – Actively takes part in meetings; doesn't withdraw if faced with difficulties; tries to overcome language barriers; pays attention to time restrictions; struggles to overcome obstacles; etc.

> **Sociability** – Initiates contact with foreign partner; makes new appointments; asks about the partner's personal background; is talkative; smiles at partner; exchanges "conversational currency"; etc.
>
> **Empathy** – Considers the local partner's situation; shows appropriate discretion; argues from the position of the host national; picks up on the partner's contribution sympathetically; etc.
>
> **Non-judgmentalness** – Expresses approval of the host culture; avoids stereotypes; avoids making jokes about host nationals; discusses the uniqueness of the host country in a factual manner; etc.
>
> **Meta-communication skills** – Tries to dissolve ambiguities and misunderstandings; provides appropriate feedback; asks if he or she has been understood; negotiates rules of play for the conversation; summarizes contributions; etc. (Stahl 2001:202)

The results of such studies have flowed into a number of conceptual frameworks which operationalize intercultural interaction competence. One such framework is the International Competency Framework (see www.worldwork.biz) generated by WorldWork Ltd, London, which forms the basis of the International Profiler development tool. It comprises a set of ten competencies consisting of 22 dimensions which research shows tend to lead to effectiveness in international transitions, such as expatriate assignments. In Table 11.1, the ten dimensions and 22 competencies are listed and where appropriate their relationship to the Kühlmann and Stahl study indicated:

Table 11.1 Intercultural competencies

Worldwork Ltd.'s International Competency Framework*	Competencies*	Description*	Related to Kühlmann & Stahl's taxonomy
1. Openness	1.1 New Thinking	Receptive to new ideas, and typically seeks to extend understanding into new and unfamiliar fields. Likes to work internationally as they are exposed to ideas and approaches with which they are unfamiliar.	Tolerance of ambiguity
	1.2 Welcoming Strangers	Keen to initiate contact and build relationships with new people, including those who have different experiences, perceptions, and values to themselves. Often takes a particular interest in strangers from different and unfamiliar cultural backgrounds.	Sociability

	1.3 Acceptance	Not only tolerates but also positively accepts behaviour that is very different from their own. In an international context they rarely feel threatened by, or intolerant of, working practices that conflict with their own sense of best practice.	Tolerance for ambiguity
2. Flexibility	2.1 Flexible Behaviour	Adapt easily to a range of different social and cultural situations. Have either learned or are willing to learn a wider range of behaviour patterns. Ready to experiment with different ways of behaving to find those that are most acceptable and most successful.	Behavioural flexibility
	2.2 Flexible Judgement	Avoid coming to quick and definitive conclusions about the new people and situations they encounter. Can also use each experience of people from a different culture to question assumptions and modify stereotypes about how such people operate.	Non-judgmentalness
	2.3 Learning Languages	Motivated to learn and use the specific languages of important business contacts, over and beyond the lingua franca in which they conduct their everyday business activities. Ready to draw on key expressions and words from the languages of these international contacts to build trust and show respect.	
3. Personal Autonomy	3.1 Inner Purpose	Hold strong personal values and beliefs that provide consistency or balance when dealing with unfamiliar circumstances, or when facing pressures that question judgement of challenge sense of worth. Such values also give importance and credibility to the tasks that they have to perform.	

(*continued*)

Table 11.1 (*Continued*)

Worldwork Ltd.'s International Competency Framework*	Competencies*	Description*	Related to Kühlmann & Stahl's taxonomy
	3.2 Focus on Goals	Set specific goals and tasks in international projects, combined with a high degree of persistence in achieving them regardless of pressures to compromise, and distractions on the way. Believe they have a strong element of control over their own destiny, and can makes things happen in the world around them.	Goal orientation
4. Emotional Strength	4.1 Resilience	Usually tough enough to risk making mistakes as a way of learning. Able to overcome any embarrassment, criticism or negative feedback they may encounter. Have an optimistic approach to life and tend to "bounce back" when things go wrong.	
	4.2 Coping	Able to deal with change and high levels of pressure even in unfamiliar situations. They remain calm under pressure, and have well-developed means of coping even without their normal support networks. Have the personal resources necessary to deal effectively with the stress from culture shock.	Tolerance for ambiguity
	4.3 Spirit of Adventure	Ready to seek out variety, change and stimulation in life, and avoid safe and predictable environments. Push themselves into uncomfortable and ambiguous situations, often unsure whether they have the skills required to be successful.	Tolerance for ambiguity
5. Perceptiveness	5.1 Attuned	Highly focused on picking up meaning from indirect signals such as intonation, eye contact and body language. Adept at observing these signals of meaning and reading them correctly in different contexts – almost like learning a new language.	

	5.2 Reflected Awareness	Very conscious of how they come across to others; in an intercultural context particularly sensitive to how their own "normal" patterns of communication and behaviour are interpreted in the minds of international partners.	
6. Listening Orientation	6.1 Active Listening	Check and clarify, rather than assume understanding of others, by paraphrasing and exploring the words that they use and the meaning they attach to them.	Meta-communication skills
7. Transparency	7.1 Clarity of Communication	Conscious of the need for a "low-risk" style that minimised the potential for misunderstandings in an international context. Able to adapt to "how a message is delivered" (rather than just "what is said") to be more clearly understood by an international audience.	Meta-communication skills
	7.2 Exposing Intentions	Able to build and maintain trust in an international context by signalling positive intentions, and putting needs into a clear and explicit context.	Meta-communication skills
8. Cultural Knowledge	8.1 Information Gathering	Take time and interest to learn about unfamiliar cultures, and deepen their understanding of those they already know. Employ various information-gathering strategies for understanding the specific context they require.	
	8.2 Valuing Differences	Like to work with colleagues and partners from diverse backgrounds, and are sensitive to how people see the world differently. Keen not only to explore and understand others' values and beliefs, but also communicate respect for them.	Non-judgmentalness

(*continued*)

Table 11.1 (*Continued*)

Worldwork Ltd.'s International Competency Framework*	Competencies*	Description*	Related to Kühlmann & Stahl's taxonomy
9. Influencing	9.1 Rapport	Exhibit warmth and attentiveness when building relationships in a variety of contexts. Put a premium on choosing verbal and non-verbal behaviours that are comfortable for international counterparts, thus building a sense of "we". Able in the longer-term to meet the criteria for trust required by their international partners.	Empathy, sociability
	9.2 Range of Styles	Have a variety of means for influencing people across a range of international contexts. This gives greater capacity to "lead" an international partner in a style with which he or she feels comfortable.	
	9.3 Sensitivity to Context	Good at understanding where political power lies in organisations and keen to figure out how best to play to this. Put energy into understanding the different cultural contexts in which messages are sent and decisions are made.	
10. Synergy	10.1 Creating New Alternatives	Sensitive to the need for a careful and systematic approach to facilitating group and team work to ensure that different cultural perspectives are not suppressed, but are properly understood and used in the problem solving process.	Meta-communication skills, tolerance for ambiguity, behavioural flexibility

*The first three columns are reproduced with permission of Worldwork Ltd., London.

3.3 Recommended reading

Caligiuri, P. & Tarique, I. (2007). "International assignee selection and cross-cultural training and development". In: Stahl, G. & Björkman, I. (Eds), *Handbook of Research in International Human Resource Management*. Northampton: Edward Elgar Publishing Ltd., 321–342.

Spencer-Oatey, H. & Franklin, P. (2009). ***Intercultural Interaction. A Multi-Disciplinary Approach to Intercultural Communication.*** **London: Palgrave Macmillan.**
Chapter 3 of this book presents a critical overview of the results of theorizing and research into intercultural competence generated in various disciplines. It emphasizes the need for conventional competence conceptualizations to be extended to include the notion of situational and relational appropriateness. Chapter 8 is devoted to assessing intercultural interaction competence and chapter 9 to developing it in various settings. Both may be useful in answering question 3 below.

Stahl, G. & Voigt, A. (2005): "The performance impact of cultural differences in mergers and acquisitions: A critical research review and an integrative model". In: Cooper, C. & Finkelstein, S. (Eds), ***Advances in mergers and acquisitions.*** **New York: JAI Press, 51–82.**

Stahl, G. K. & Voigt, A. (2008). "Do Cultural Differences Matter in Mergers and Acquisitions? A Tentative Model and Examination". In: ***Organization Science*****, 19: 1, 160–176.**
"A substantive body of theory and research on the role of culture in mergers and acquisitions (M&A) suggests that cultural differences can create major obstacles to achieving integration benefits. However, the opposite view – that differences in culture between merging firms can be a source of value creation and learning – has also been advanced and empirically supported. In an attempt to reconcile these conflicting perspectives and findings, we present a model that synthesizes our current understanding of the role of culture in M&A, and we develop a set of hypotheses regarding mechanisms through which cultural differences affect M&A performance." (From the abstract of the article.)

4 QUESTIONS ON THE CASE

1. On the basis of Section 2.2, "Looking ahead to the assignment" only and using the terms and definitions of the Kühlmann and Stahl (1998) study and the International Competency Framework described above, seek evidence of which intercultural competencies were demanded of Benedikt Paul in the job description and advice given.
2. Now, on the basis of Sections 2.3, "Handling the assignment" and 2.4, "Looking back on the assignment" and using the results of the Kühlmann and Stahl (1998) study and the International Competency Framework described above, decide which competencies Benedikt Paul actually applied and which could have especially benefited his work. Insert the indicators (i.e. quotations) you find in the interview in the following framework. You will not be able to find evidence of all the competencies.

International Competency	Indicators found in Sections 2.3 "Handling the assignment" and 2.4 "Looking back on the assignment"
1.1 Openness: New Thinking	
1.2 Openness: Welcoming Strangers	
1.3 Openness: Acceptance	
2.1 Flexibility: Flexible Behaviour	
2.2 Flexibility: Flexible Judgement	
2.3 Flexibility: Learning Languages	
3.1 Personal Autonomy: Inner Purpose	
3.2 Personal autonomy: Focus on Goals	
4.1 Emotional Strength: Resilience	
4.2 Emotional Strength: Coping	
4.3 Emotional Strength: Spirit of Adventure	
5.1 Perceptiveness: Attuned	
5.2 Perceptiveness: Reflected Awareness	
6.1 Listening Orientation: Active Listening	

7.1 Transparency: Clarity of Communication	
7.2 Transparency: Exposing Intentions	
8.1 Cultural Knowledge: Information Gathering	
8.2 Cultural knowledge: Valuing Differences	
9.1 Influencing: Rapport	
9.2 Influencing: Range of Styles	
9.3 Influencing: Sensitivity to Context	
10.1 Synergy: Creating New Alternatives	

Headings based on WorldWork Ltd's International Competency Framework. Reproduced with permission.

3. What implications do the results of tasks 1 and 2 above have for the recruitment and selection of expatriates and others working internationally? Which of the International Competency Framework competencies would seem to be especially important for those working as expatriates rather than for those merely working internationally while based at home? Consider and discuss whether the competencies required for a successful expatriate assignment such as those generated by the Kühlmann and Stahl study and those described in the International Competency Framework can in fact be a) assessed and b) developed.

5 REFERENCES

Brannen, M. Y. & Peterson, M. F. (2009). "Merging without alienating: Interventions promoting cross-cultural organizational integration and their limitations". *Journal of International Business Studies*, 40, 468–489.

Buckley P. J. & Ghauri P. N. (2002). *International Mergers and Acquisitions*. London: Thomson.

Cooper, C. L. & Finkelstein, S (2010). *Advances in Mergers and Acquisitions.* Bingley: Emerald Group.

Flanagan, J. C. (1954). "The critical incident technique". In: *Psychological Bulletin,* 51:4, 327–358.

Franklin, P. (2007). "Differences and difficulties in intercultural management interaction". In: Kotthoff, H. & Spencer-Oatey, H. (Eds), *Handbook of Intercultural Communication,* 263–284. Berlin: Mouton de Gruyter.

Kühlmann, T. & Stahl, G. (1998). "Diagnose interkultureller Kompetenz: Entwicklung und Evaluierung eines Assessment-Centers". In: Barmeyer, C. & Bolten, J. (Eds), *Interkulturelle Personalorganisation [Intercultural Personnel Management]* , 213–224. Sternenfels: Verlag für Wissenschaft und Praxis.

Mayrhofer U. (2013). *Management of Multinational Companies. A French Perspective.* Basingstoke: Palgrave Macmillan.

Spencer-Oatey, H. & Franklin, P. (2009). *Intercultural Interaction. A Multi-Disciplinary Approach to Intercultural Communication.* London: Palgrave Macmillan.

Spitzberg, B. H. & Chagnon, G. (2009). "Conceptualizing intercultural competence". In: Deardorff, D. K., *The SAGE Handbook of Intercultural Competence,* 2–52. Thousand Oaks, CA: Sage.

Spitzberg, B. H. (1989). "Issues in the development of a theory of interpersonal competence in the intercultural context". In: *International Journal of Intercultural Relations,* 13, 241–268.

Stahl, G. (2001). "Using assessment centers as tools for global leadership development: An exploratory study". In: Mendenhall, M., Kühlmann, T. & Stahl, G. (Eds), *Developing Global Business Leaders: Policies, Processes and Innovations,* 197–210. Westport: Quorum Books.

Stahl, G. K. & Voigt, A. (2008). "Do cultural differences matter in mergers and acquisitions? A tentative model and examination". *Organization Science,* 19:1, 160–176.

12

Virtual Chaos at WORLDWIDE Rx: How Cultural Intelligence Can Turn Problems into Solutions

David Livermore and Soon Ang

1 INTRODUCTION

Cultural diversity provides one of the greatest opportunities for global innovation. An organization that learns how to utilize the diverse perspectives, knowledge and skills represented by multicultural teams has a tremendous opportunity to dynamically reach a more global audience. In fact, diversity is one of the greatest resources for coming up with innovative ways of doing things. Many organizations that understand this reality are working hard to inspire their diverse workforce to "speak up" and offer their ideas. Whether it's troubleshooting ongoing problems, offering creative solutions, or simply gaining diverse viewpoints on a new initiative, many multinationals are running campaigns to promote the importance of everyone "speaking up".

But diversity by itself doesn't guarantee innovation (Williams & O'Reilley, 1998). In fact, the more diverse a team is, the less likely participants are to offer their input and perspective. The effort to get people to speak up must be coupled with improved levels of Cultural Intelligence (CQ). Cultural diversity can actually be one of the biggest roadblocks to gathering participation and innovative ideas if the diversity isn't handled with Cultural Intelligence. In many organizations, the Europeans and North Americans dominate meetings while the Asians and Latin Americans remain quiet or get talked over. And the whole idea of "speaking up" is interpreted differently depending on your cultural background. For many Western leaders, asking people to "speak up" is a very positive thing. It's management's way of saying "your input is important and we want to hear from you". But language, power distance, assertiveness, uncertainty avoidance (House et al., 2004), and much more can make a big difference in whether someone views "speaking up" positively or not.

2 CASE DESCRIPTION

2.1 The situation

WORLDWIDE Rx is a global pharmaceutical company headquartered in Indianapolis, USA, that develops, manufactures and distributes over-the-counter medications and nutritional products across the Americas, Europe, and Asia. The company has been on a steady growth trajectory for the last decade, with the greatest growth occurring in Asia.

Jake McDonald is an information technology (IT) project manager at WORLDWIDE Rx. He's been with the company for 12 years and really enjoys the organization's global footprint. He was recently appointed as the project lead for TABLE – a new logistics software that will integrate WORLDWIDE's global distribution system.

Previously, each WORLDWIDE regional office developed and used its own IT infrastructure based upon the unique needs and logistics of that region. But headquarters has decided that an integrated, aligned system is necessary to enhance efficiency for distributing its products globally.

Jake's project team consists of co-workers from around the world who have a similar function to his. He was excited when he was asked to take the lead on this project because he was looking for a new challenge, he loves problem-solving and he enjoys working with international colleagues. There haven't been any promises made to Jake but his supervisor told him that if this project goes well, he will be the lead candidate for the open vice-president position in IT.

But this assignment comes with challenges. Jake doesn't have any formal authority over the individuals on his team so he has to work primarily through influence and consensus to get things done. The geographically dispersed nature of the team combined with its vast cultural differences results in a variety of different perspectives based upon what is important to each region. Jake has had to take an innovative approach in order to guide and influence his diverse team toward a successful result.

2.2 The challenge

It's been a long day but Jake goes to bed feeling pretty good about himself. Tonight's conference call lasted longer than usual but everybody reached agreement that TechKnow in London is the best vendor to use for integrating all the existing systems to TABLE. Others at headquarters had warned Jake how challenging it would be to get everyone on board but he did it. And this happened just in time for his meeting tomorrow morning with senior management when he will update them on the project.

The next morning, Jake scans his email before walking into the meeting with senior management. He decides he had better read the "urgent" email from Chang Su, his colleague in Seoul. Chang Su copies his response to everyone on the project team as well as his entire team in Korea. He writes:

> Dear Jake,
>
> I've spoken with others and we're concerned about working with TechKnow. I think it's better that we use TechKnow's competitor Jung & Co. to handle the integration. They've served us very well here. And I don't need to remind you that we're WORLDWIDE's largest region. What do you think?
>
> Regards,
>
> Chang Su

"What do I think?!" Jake mutters to himself. "I think this is so typical of Chang Su and I think he should have brought this up last night." This just annoys Jake. But why should it surprise him? If he says "A", Chang Su says "Z". But it's never to his face. He was extremely supportive when he was at headquarters last month and he sounded agreeable last night on the call. At least, he never raised any concerns. But the push-back always comes in the form of an email after the fact, and often through very lengthy, elaborate emails. Jake defers to Chang Su when he can, so that he can be tough when he has to be.

This isn't only undermining Jake's informal leadership. The entire project team agreed last night and Jake's very last statement was that he would be updating senior management tomorrow and signing the contract with TechKnow. Why didn't Chang Su speak up then? And how does Jake tell Chang Su that the European and South American teams have confided in him that they are very opposed to using Jung & Co.? They aren't convinced Jung & Co. will understand the unique issues they face in their regions. But they knew they couldn't say that on the call without upsetting Chang Su.

Jake decides to ignore the email from Chang Su for the moment and he goes into the senior management meeting to provide an update on the project. When asked to update everyone, Jake provides them with a brief description of the process they used over the last several weeks to vet the various vendors. And then he says, "I'm happy to report that as of last night, our team decided unanimously to select TechKnow as our partner. There are still a few problems for me to solve before I communicate that information to TechKnow so please don't begin discussing or communicating this publicly. But I believe TechKnow is going to be an ideal partner for getting us to a uniform logistics system globally." The senior leaders congratulated Jake and asked a few minor questions. Just as he got up to walk out of the boardroom, Diane Sully, Sr. Vice President of Sales for Asia–Pacific said, "Oh Jake. Just to confirm. Chang Su is on board with this too – right? We want to make sure his team feels well supported by the new system." Jake replied confidently, "Yes – I completely understand, Diane. Well, as you know, it takes a while for Chang Su to get enthused about anything that involves change; but I think it will be fine."

As he leaves the meeting, Jake decides he had better just pick up the phone and call Chang Su. But his call goes straight to voicemail. As he's preparing to leave a message, he sees a new email come in from Chang Su. This one is copied to Diane Sully and flagged "high priority". Chang Su writes,

> Dear Jake,
>
> I haven't heard back from you yet regarding the urgent email I sent you after last night's call. I'm hearing from more and more people on the team who are very opposed to moving forward with TechKnow.
>
> I think I have a great solution for you though. I believe Jung & Co. would do this whole project for us for 10% less than what TechKnow quoted. Perhaps I could set up a call for all of us with them.
>
> What do you think?
>
> Regards,
>
> Chang Su

3 BACKGROUND KNOWLEDGE

3.1 The authors' point of reference

Our research and work are focused upon Cultural Intelligence, or CQ – "the capability to function effectively across various national, ethnic and organisational cultures" (Ang & Van Dyne, 2008:3; Livermore, 2015). Soon is from Nanyang Technological University in Singapore where she pioneered the conceptualization of Cultural Intelligence. She worked with Linn Van Dyne at Michigan State University to create and validate the Cultural Intelligence Scale (Ang & Van Dyne, 2005). David is from the Cultural Intelligence Center in the US and his research focused upon global leadership and the experience of individuals who travel widely but not deeply (e.g. business travellers, study abroad students, charitable volunteers, etc.). Most of Dave's professional life has been in leading various global organizations. Soon's primary orientation is as an academic researcher who is concerned with rigour, thoroughness, and precision. David's primary orientation is as a practitioner who is concerned with evidence-based, best practices that are relevant. Together, we work to bring rigorous, academic findings on Cultural Intelligence to the practical needs faced by businesses, governments and non-profit organizations.

3.2 Concepts, models, frameworks

Cultural Intelligence is a critical management capability needed by people like Jake and Chang Su. An individual's CQ is a reliable predictor of one's effectiveness and adjustment in a multicultural team like Jake's (Ang & Van Dyne, 2008; Ward et al. 2009).

Some studies indicate that homogenous teams actually outperform diverse teams when it comes to collaborating together, speaking up, and providing innovative solutions (Ilgen et al., 2005; Ng et al. 2011,). This is because team members are freer to interact, challenge ideas, and offer solutions of their own when they are among similar colleagues. Homogenous teams provide a more psychologically safe environment. At a surface level, it would be much more efficient and productive for Jake (or Chang Su!) to convene a group of like-minded people in order to reach a creative solution about the best vendor to use.

However, when diverse teams have higher levels of CQ, they significantly outperform homogenous teams because they have the benefit of a much broader range of perspectives. A diverse team comprised of individuals with high CQ and facilitated by a leader with high CQ can utilize the benefit of everyone's input and perspective. Diversity by itself does not ensure innovative ideas. But diversity plus high CQ does (Ng et al. 2011).

Getting diverse teams to function at the highest levels requires a facilitator (e.g. Jake) and team members (e.g. Chang Su) with high CQ. Both are needed. When we use cases like this one with executives and students, we're interested to see whether the participants solely focus upon how one individual needs to adapt (e.g. Jake) or whether they look at both parties. Culturally intelligent teams and innovative outcomes are most likely when there is high CQ from everyone involved. Cultural Intelligence includes four capabilities: CQ Drive, Knowledge, Strategy, and Action (Earley & Ang, 2003; Livermore 2015).

CQ Drive is your level of interest, motivation and confidence to adapt cross-culturally. This refers to whether or not you have the confidence and drive to work through the challenges and conflict that often accompany intercultural work. The ability to be personally engaged and to persevere through intercultural challenges is one of the most novel aspects of Cultural Intelligence. Many intercultural training approaches simply *assume* that people are motivated to gain cross-cultural capabilities. Yet employees often approach diversity training apathetically, and employees headed out on international assignments are often more concerned about moving their families overseas and getting settled than they are about developing cultural understanding. Without ample motivation, there's little point in spending time and money on training.

CQ Knowledge is the cognitive dimension of Cultural Intelligence. It refers to your level of understanding about culture and culture's role in shaping the way to interact when different cultures are involved. Your CQ Knowledge is based upon the degree to which you understand the idea of culture and how it influences the way you think and behave. It also includes your overall understanding of the ways cultures vary from one context to the next.

CQ Strategy or metacognition refers to your level of awareness and ability to strategize when crossing cultures. This capability involves slowing down long enough to carefully observe what's going on inside our own and other people's heads. It's the ability to think about your own thought processes and draw upon your cultural knowledge to understand a different cultural context and solve problems in that situation. It includes whether we can use our cultural knowledge to plan an appropriate strategy, accurately interpret what's going on in an intercultural situation and check to see if our expectations are accurate or need to be adjusted.

CQ Action is your ability to act appropriately in a wide range of cultural situations. It influences whether we can actually accomplish our performance goals effectively in light of different cultural situations. One of the most important aspects of CQ Action is knowing when to adapt to another culture and when *not* to do so. An individual with high CQ learns which actions will and won't enhance effectiveness and acts upon that understanding. Thus, CQ Action involves flexible behaviours tailored to the specific cultural context.

3.3 Recommended reading

Brislin, R., Worthley R. & Macnab, B. (2006). "Cultural intelligence: Understanding behaviors that serve people's goals". In: *Group & Organization Management*, 31:1, 40–55.
Cultural Intelligence has various meanings that can be looked on as complementary. On one hand, it refers to understanding and being able to adapt to behaviours that are considered the norm from the point of view of people in specific cultures. Such behaviours can include quick application of previously learned information in some cultures, getting along with kin in other cultures, and slow and deliberate consideration of alternative courses of action in still other cultures. More specifically, Cultural Intelligence refers to the skills of people who adjust quickly, with minimal stress, when they interact extensively in cultures other than the ones where they were socialized. It is a scientific measurement of how to predict the way one will interact in culturally diverse contexts. The two uses of the term are related because people who want to be sensitive to others can examine intelligence as it is defined and demonstrated in other cultures and can make adjustments in their own behaviours during their cross-cultural experiences.

Ang, S. & Van Dyne, L. (Eds) (2008). *Handbook on Cultural Intelligence: Theory, Measurement and Applications*. Armonk, NY: M.E. Sharpe.
With contributions from scholars from around the world, this book provides the most comprehensive publication of Cultural Intelligence research. Because Cultural Intelligence capabilities can be enhanced through education and experience, this handbook emphasizes the measurement and development of those individual capabilities – specific characteristics that allow people to function effectively in culturally diverse settings. The Handbook covers conceptual and definitional issues, assessment approaches, and application of Cultural Intelligence in the domains of international and cross-cultural management as well as management of domestic activity.

Livermore, D. (2015). *Leading With Cultural Intelligence: The Real Secret to Success*. New York: AMACOM.
The second edition of this book provides the most up-to-date research on Cultural Intelligence and its relevance to leaders. In addition to explaining the findings and the CQ model, each chapter includes suggestions for how leaders can improve CQ in themselves and others. The book concludes with a summary of the research on the results for leaders and organizations with enhanced CQ.

Livermore, D. (2016). *Driven by Difference: How Global Companies Fuel Innovation Through Diversity*. New York: AMACOM
This book draws upon the latest research on Cultural Intelligence to describe how to leverage the power of cultural differences to drive innovation. Based on extensive research and filled with examples and case studies from around the world, it includes a five-step, research-based strategy for culturally intelligent innovation.

4 QUESTION ON THE CASE

Using your understanding of CQ, suggest what Jake and Chang Su should do to handle this situation. Refer in your answer to the CQ capabilities.

5 REFERENCES

Ang, S. & Van Dyne, L. (2005). *Cultural Intelligence Scale (CQS)*. East Lansing, MI: Cultural Intelligence Center.

Ang, S. & Van Dyne, L. (2008). *Handbook on Cultural Intelligence: Theory, Measurement and Applications*. Armonk, NY: M.E. Sharpe.

Earley, C. & Ang, S. (2003). *Cultural Intelligence: Individual Interactions Across Cultures*. Stanford, CA: Stanford University Press.

House, R. J., Hanges, P. J., Javidan, M., Dorfman, P. W. & Gupta, V. (2004). *Culture, Leadership, and Organizations: The GLOBE Study of 62 Societies*. Thousand Oaks, CA: Sage.

Ilgen, D. R., Hollenbeck, J. R., Johnson, M. & Jundt, D. (2005). "Teams in Organizations: From input-process-output models to IMOI models". In: *Annual Review Psychology*, 56, 571–543.

Livermore, D. (2015). *Leading with Cultural Intelligence: The New Secret to Success*. New York: AMACOM.

Ng, K. Y., Ang, S. & Van Dyne, L. (2011, August). "Speaking up in the culturally diverse workplace: The role of cultural intelligence and language self-efficacy." Paper presented at the American Psychological Association. Washington, DC.

Williams, K. Y. & O'Reilley, C. A. III (1998). "Demography and diversity in organizations: A review of 40 years of research". In: *Research in Organizational Behavior, Vol.* 20, 77–140. Greenwich, CT: JAI Press.

Ward C., Fischer, R., Lam, F. S. & Hall, L. (2009). "The convergent, discriminant, and incremental validity of scores on a self-report measure of cultural intelligence". In: *Educational and Psychological Measurement,* 69:1, 85–105.

13

Cultural Intelligence at Work – A Case Study from Thailand

Claus Schreier and Astrid Kainzbauer

1 INTRODUCTION

In today's global workplace, intercultural competence, i.e. the ability to successfully function in culturally diverse environments, is increasingly important. As more organizations require people to work abroad or with colleagues from different cultural backgrounds, cultural sensitivity becomes increasingly critical to achieving business objectives.

But what exactly is it that makes one successful in dealing with people from other cultures? This question has been discussed extensively and researchers have looked at the topic from different angles (expatriate adjustment, global leadership, intercultural sensitivity, intercultural development, and so on). For the purpose of this case study, we have selected two texts which represent different strands of literature, namely *Cultural Intelligence* (Earley & Ang 2003) and "Defining the content domain of intercultural competence for global leaders" (Bird et al. 2010).

In 2003, Earley and Ang introduced the construct of Cultural Intelligence (CQ). Their work was guided by the question: "Why is it that some people adjust relatively easily, quickly and thoroughly to new cultures but others cannot seem able to do so?" (Earley & Ang 2003:4). The underlying idea is that there are certain individual capabilities that allow people to be effective in intercultural settings. Earley and Ang define CQ as "a person's adaptation to new cultural settings and capability to deal effectively with other people with whom the person does not share a common cultural background and understanding" (Earley & Ang 2003:12).

Based on the theory of multiple intelligences, Earley and Ang (2003) conceptualized CQ as a set of four capabilities: cognition, metacognition, motivation and behaviour. Cultural Intelligence includes knowing about cultural differences, reflecting on one's own cultural conditioning and being motivated and able to adapt behaviour so that it is appropriate for the cultural context. CQ is seen as a multi-dimensional intelligence which includes both mental (cognitive, metacognitive, motivational) and behavioural capabilities. In other words, understanding cultural differences is only one side of the picture and must be complemented by the ability to choose appropriate actions which fit the cultural context.

Another strand of literature focuses on global leaders and what makes them effective. Bird et al. (2010) reviewed the existing global leadership and expatriation literatures and subsequently identified 17 intercultural competency dimensions for global leaders. Their list of competencies refers to stable personal competencies, which are also often defined as predispositions and personality traits (as opposed to the Cultural Intelligence construct which focuses on capabilities). These personal competencies can serve as "building blocks" in the development of other global leadership capabilities (Bird et al. 2010: 821).

The practical relevance of these concepts lies in the desired individual and organizational outcomes, such as improved business performance and cultural adjustment (personal well-being). In our globalized world, companies increasingly regard intercultural competence as a necessity, and screen as well as train leaders for their respective competencies and capabilities.

Finally, it is important to point out that the positive contribution of Cultural Intelligence/intercultural competence goes beyond adapting to another culture in order to fit in, and aims at shaping and creating a positive environment which allows synergistic interactions with people from other cultures.

In the following case study we aim to illustrate the importance of CQ and intercultural competence for global leaders by giving an example of how these contribute to a leader's cross-cultural effectiveness.

2 CASE DESCRIPTION

Arguably, few industries are as internationalized as global logistics. In this industry, key management issues are information and communication technology, people skills and customer orientation. For the global logistics company, small localized businesses are critical components in their business offerings. Our case study focuses on a company called TLC,[1] a small family-owned business in Thailand which was founded 40 years ago. The business is highly successful in its niche and has gained a positive image with its international clients. Although the company's history has been rocky at times, for example in the aftermath of the 1997 Asian financial crisis, the international clientele has maintained its loyalty over the years. The industry has been steadily growing and, as a result, new competitors have entered the logistics marketplace in South East Asia.

Markus joined the company 13 years ago having built a personal reputation in the industry in many countries. A Swiss national, he was hired after the CEO saw him present at an international logistics conference in Zurich. Coincidentally, Markus had already worked in Thailand and South East Asia at an earlier stage of his career. On joining the company, Markus discovered

[1]This case is based on a real situation. All names and personal details have been changed to ensure confidentiality.

that he was the only foreigner working in this family business, and that he was also the oldest employee.

Markus's CV

Markus, born and raised in Basel, is now 63 years old and a senior manager. He stands out by virtue of his expat activities in the logistics industry in many countries. Markus's career started with a logistics apprenticeship in Switzerland, and this experience eventually led him into different areas of the industry in several countries worldwide. In addition to Zurich, New York and Accra (Ghana), his profession directed him to South East Asia. Due to his wealth of international experience and his familiarity with the Thai culture, TLC offered Markus a senior position within their family business. This is quite unusual given that most other senior positions are held by family members only.

With his knowledge and capabilities it is Markus's task to position TLC so that it can compete in the international market. In his role as vice president of operations it is clear for Markus that, like in every industry in the 21st century, the difference between a successful and a less successful business are the skills of employees and their willingness to bring their knowledge into the organization.

Markus's view of the situation at TLC From his broad experiences with South East Asia in general and especially with Thailand, Markus understands that TLC is a traditional family-run business with a hierarchical structure. Middle and upper management control relevant knowledge and give specific instructions to their employees. They rarely delegate decision-making power to their employees. Instead, according to Thai tradition, the owners take the ultimate decisions. Moreover, members of the family hold relevant management positions. Open discussions are traditionally perceived as a disturbance of group harmony and tend to be avoided. Promotions are mostly decided according to the principle of seniority.

Khun Somchai's CV

Khun Somchai (53) is the CEO of TLC. He comes from a family of entrepreneurs in Bangkok. His father founded TLC 40 years ago and Somchai, the oldest son, took over the company from his ageing father. Even though his own university background was in chemistry and he had envisaged a career in this field, he saw it as his obligation to support the family business and therefore he did not hesitate when his father asked him to step in and take the lead at TLC. He admires his father for all the hard work he put in to set up the company and feels committed to making it grow.

Khun Somchai's view of TLC TLC is shaped by Thai culture. Good employees follow the orders of their superiors and are characterized by their loyalty, solidarity and reliability. Superiors give orders and "care" about their employees. In return, they receive loyalty and trust. As in many Thai businesses, the environment resembles a family atmosphere and employees are therefore considered a part of the family. If they do not achieve the desired performance, they have simply not been guided well enough or have been positioned in the wrong job by their superior. The responsibility for the results lies with the management.

It is clear to Markus that the success of his task depends on achieving cultural change. Markus is convinced that cultural change at TLC can only be accomplished with the "right" team. His main focus is on the performance of the employees. The most capable employee in every corporate function is needed to ensure the success of the company.

For the upcoming round of promotions, TLC's CEO Khun Somchai has nominated Prasit, an experienced TLC employee, to be promoted into a strategic management position.

Prasit's CV

Prasit (45) has been working for TLC for more than 20 years. He started when he was quite young and over the years has worked in several departments at TLC. His father, a well-known figure in Thai society, had also worked for TLC right from the foundation of the company 40 years ago. Prasit has a degree from the reputable Chulalongkorn University in Bangkok. The CEO of TLC, Khun Somchai, likes him because he is loyal, friendly and a good team player.

Nevertheless, from Markus's point of view, Prasit does not seem to have the competencies which Markus requires someone holding this position to contribute in order to achieve his ambitious objectives. According to Markus, Prasit lacks ambition and drive and does not see productivity as his top priority.

Markus, who would rather fire Prasit than give him a promotion, asks for a meeting with Khun Somchai – the Thai CEO – and on this occasion he names an alternative candidate for promotion: Winai, who is younger than Prasit, but who shows high potential and has the necessary knowledge.

Their meeting takes place in the CEO's office.

Khun Somchai: Markus, how have you been? How was your holiday?

Markus: Khun Somchai, thank you for taking the time to meet with me. Business is good and we are moving ahead. I came to talk to you about the upcoming promotion decisions. I think it is important to put the right people in the right jobs.

Khun Somchai: I'm happy to hear we are on the right track. And I am sure the upcoming promotion of Prasit will be good for the department.

Markus: That's exactly what I wanted to talk to you about. I don't think Prasit is the best person for the position of director of procurement. He does not have the necessary qualifications for this job. I would suggest promoting Winai instead. He is very capable and has shown his talent for managing people during a project he recently worked on. I think he is ready for a new challenge.

Khun Somchai: Prasit has been with us for many years; he is very trustworthy and has been loyal to us. With his experience, he will do a good job as a director. He more than deserves this position. And rest assured that he will carry out your instructions to your full satisfaction.

Markus: But that is exactly the problem. We need somebody in this job who does not just follow instructions but brings in new ideas and takes responsibility. I think Winai would be the perfect person for this position. His performance record shows he is highly capable and eager to succeed.

Khun Somchai: Continuity is important for the company. We need people who have experience and know how the company works. This helps to guarantee our long-term success. But Markus, you still haven't told me how your holidays went …

After a few more minutes of small talk, Markus leaves the conversation somehow annoyed and frustrated. It is obvious to Markus that Prasit is not the right person for the promotion. However, he has not reached his objective of convincing the Thai CEO to promote the person he considers the most capable candidate for the director position.

After a few days of reflection, Markus asks for another appointment with the CEO to resume the discussion. This time Markus changes his approach.

Markus: I have thought about the conversation we had last week and I can see your point. Continuity is important and we have to take care of our loyal employees.

Khun Somchai: I am happy to hear you are with me on this.

Markus: I think we can use the upcoming promotions to put the right people in positions where they can best use their talents to support the company.

Khun Somchai: That is exactly my philosophy. And this should help us to secure TLC's long-term success.

Markus:	I was thinking about Prasit. He has been with us for a long time and he is part of our family. We need to find a position for him that suits his talents. He has worked in several departments and has a good overview of internal operations. He is also very detail-oriented and good at following up on projects. I think he would be a perfect person to head the new department on internal quality control.
Khun Somchai:	I see ...
Markus:	On the other hand, I would suggest that Winai could take care of the procurement department. He is very talented and has the right skills to be in this position. People in the department seem to like him and even though he is still young, he has already made good suggestions on how to improve the department.
Khun Somchai:	Hmmm, interesting suggestion. Well Markus, you are my most senior manager and I trust your recommendations. I am sure that under your guidance Winai will do a good job. As for Prasit, I can see his potential in quality control – this would be a good position for him to help us improve our operations. Let's offer him this opportunity.

This solution seems reasonable to Markus. They seem to have found a good compromise. Later on he observes that Prasit does well in his role as a quality manager and helps TLC to cut costs and increase quality. For Markus, this episode shows yet again that after all his years in South East Asia he needs to remind himself to keep the Thai perspective in mind in order to achieve positive results. Combining different perspectives offers opportunities for learning and for the success of all participants.

3 BACKGROUND KNOWLEDGE

3.1 The authors' point of reference

Claus Schreier (based in Switzerland) and Astrid Kainzbauer (based in Thailand), both specialize in intercultural management. The authors understand leadership as culturally contingent, meaning that leaders need to be aware of the cultural context for their actions. In an intercultural context, leadership requires culture-specific knowledge as well as the ability to adapt one's behaviour to the cultural context. This perspective is linked to the literatures on intercultural competence and Cultural Intelligence which propose qualities leaders should have in order to be successful in a global work environment.

3.2 Concepts, models, frameworks

Cultural Intelligence Along with Emotional Intelligence (EQ), which is widely recognized as an important leadership characteristic, Cultural Intelligence (CQ) is a complementary form of intelligence needed in intercultural settings. Cultural Intelligence is different from emotional intelligence in that it takes the cultural context into account. Emotional intelligence addresses a person's capability to emphasize and interact with others, but assumes familiarity with the cultural context. Cultural Intelligence on the other hand is relevant when interacting with people from a different cultural background. In intercultural interactions, emotional cues may be misleading. "Thai smiles", which have a dozen different meanings, form an example that fits the context of this case. For foreigners who are not accustomed to the subtle nuances of Thai smiles, the signal may be misleading. Thus, high emotional intelligence in one's native culture does not necessarily transfer to another culture. And this is where the concept of Cultural Intelligence comes into play. CQ refers to the ability to adapt across cultures; in other words, it reflects a person's capability to perceive, understand, and act upon culturally different cues in order to function effectively across cultural settings (Earley & Ang 2003; Earley & Mosakowski 2004).

Earley and Ang (2003) identified four factors that are critical to Cultural Intelligence and divided them into mental and behavioural capabilities. Cultural Intelligence combines knowledge about cultural differences with the motivation and capability to reflect on one's own and others' cultural conditioning and adapt one's behaviour to the cultural context.

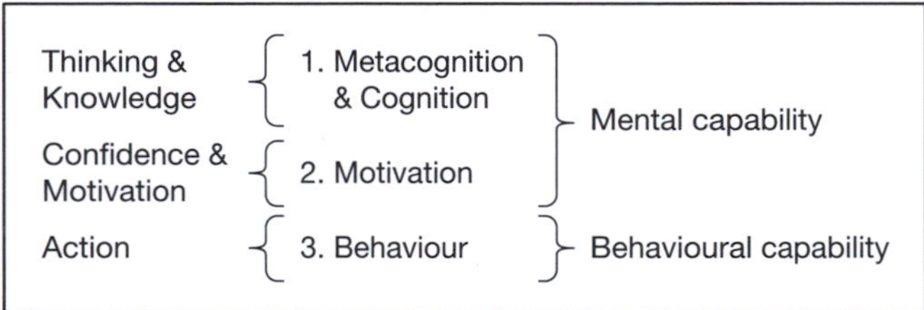

Figure 13.1 Cultural Intelligence framework

Source: Authors' illustration based on Earley & Ang (2003) and Earley & Mosakowski (2004).

Table 13.1 provides an overview of the four main components of Cultural Intelligence:

Table 13.1 Overview of Cultural Intelligence

Factors	Components
Cognition	CQ-Cognition is ... 1. **knowledge** of norms, values and practices in different cultures learned during educational and professional experiences 2. knowledge of **cultural differences** 3. knowledge about the **individual's self** as a basis of reflection.

Metacognition	CQ-Metacognition is the ability ... 1. **to think** about thinking 2. to **acquire cross-cultural knowledge** and to **question/adjust one's own cultural assumptions** prior to, during and after interaction with people from other cultures 3. to develop **learning strategies** to collect relevant information about other cultures 4. to develop **cultural intuition** (a feeling for what is happening and why) in cross cultural interactions.
Motivation	CQ-Motivation is seen as ... 1. an **inner source of drive** that helps to adapt to new cultural environment 2. someone's **confidence** and **motivation** to adapt 3. complementary to the knowledge about cultural differences (enabling knowledge / "can do") that leads to the "**will do**".
Behaviour	CQ-Behaviour is seen as ... 1. the final facet of Cultural Intelligence that refers to a person's **actions** 2. the ability to **act appropriately** in a range of cross-cultural situations 3. the **ability** to **adapt** both **verbal and nonverbal communication** to the cultural context 4. the capability to be flexible and to **know when to adapt and when NOT to adapt** in a cross-cultural encounter.

Sources: Earley & Ang 2003, Earley & Mosakowski 2004 and Ang & Van Dyne 2008.

This four-factor Cultural Intelligence model makes it possible to analyse intercultural leadership from the perspectives of both mental and behavioural capabilities (in other words, reflection and action). An important component in this model is called metacognition, a leader's meta-competence to observe, question and adapt his or her leadership behaviour based on a reflection of his or her own cultural values and those of others.

3.3 Recommended reading

Bird, A., Mendenhall, M., Stevens, M. J. & Oddou, G. (2010). "Defining the content domain of intercultural competence for global leaders". In: *Journal of Managerial Psychology*, 25:8, 810–828.
This article aims at giving a comprehensive definition of intercultural competence in the context of global leadership. The authors review the literature related to intercultural competence and suggest 17 competency dimensions (organized into three broad categories) associated with global leadership.

Earley, C. P. & Ang, S. (2003). *Cultural Intelligence: Individual Interactions Across Cultures*. Stanford: Stanford University Press.
This book introduces the concept of Cultural Intelligence. It provides a comprehensive review of existing literature in this field and explains the relationship to other models of intelligence such as social intelligence. The book

also gives insights into how Cultural Intelligence can be assessed, trained and developed.

Earley, C. P. & Mosakowski, E. (2004). "Towards cultural intelligence: Turning cultural differences into a workplace advantage". In: *The Academy of Management Executive*, 18:3, 151–157.
This article identifies the "Cultural Intelligence" approach as an individual research approach (individual level of analysis) as opposed to an aggregate approach (typologies of countries' cultural values). It briefly explains the concept of Cultural Intelligence and gives an overview of Cultural Intelligence profiles (typical combinations of Cultural Intelligence). The authors' recommendation for companies is to either train managers to enhance their CQ or to select managers for their CQ attributes.

Niffenegger, P., Kulvivat, S. & Engchanil, N. (2006). "Conflicting cultural imperatives in modern Thailand: Global perspectives". In: *Asia Pacific Business Review*, 12:4, 403–420.
The article examines conflicting cultural values between Thai and Western culture, but also between old and new value perspectives in Thailand (Buddhist perspective versus capitalist perspective). The authors give an in-depth view of Thai culture by using Thai Buddhist principles and local cultural perspectives to take Hofstede's general dimensions of culture to a deeper level of explanation.

4 QUESTIONS ON THE CASE

1. Assess Markus's Cultural Intelligence according to the four capabilities (metacognition, cognition, motivation and behaviour):

   Cognition aspect: Which values influence Markus's behaviour? Which values drive Khun Somchai's behaviour?

   Metacognition aspect: Please describe Markus's reflection process and adjustment of cultural assumptions.

   Motivation aspect: What is Markus's "inner source of drive" that helps him to manage the situation successfully?

   Behaviour aspect: How does Markus's communication change? How does he adapt to the situation?

2. How did Markus manage to overcome the cultural differences and turn them into a synergistic solution? Which aspects of "intercultural competence" helped him to achieve this? (Please read the article by Bird et al. 2010, which should help you answer this question.)

3. To what extent are Thai and Swiss leadership approaches different? Which mutual learning opportunities for Thai and Swiss leaders can you identify? (Please read the article by Niffenegger et al. 2006, which should help you answer this question.)

5 REFERENCES

Ang, S. & Van Dyne, L. (2008). "Conceptualization of cultural intelligence: Definition, distinctiveness, and nomological network". In: Ang, S. & Van Dyne, L. (Eds), *Handbook on Cultural Intelligence: Theory, Measurement and Applications*, 3–15. Armonk, NY: M. E. Sharpe.

Bird, A., Mendenhall, M., Stevens, M. J. & Oddou, G. (2010). "Defining the content domain of intercultural competence for global leaders". In: *Journal of Managerial Psychology*, 25:8, 810–828.

Earley, C. P. & Ang, S. (2003). *Cultural Intelligence: Individual Interactions Across Cultures*. Stanford: Stanford University Press.

Early, C. P. & Mosakowski, E. (2004). "Towards cultural intelligence: Turning cultural differences into a workplace advantage". In: *The Academy of Management Executive*, 18:3, 151–157.

Niffenegger, P., Kulvivat, S. & Engchanil, N. (2006). "Conflicting cultural imperatives in modern Thailand: Global perspectives". In: *Asia Pacific Business Review*, 12:4, 403–420.

14

Cultural Aspects of Offshoring to India

Craig Storti and Peter Franklin

1 INTRODUCTION

Since the 1980s numerous companies in developed countries have taken advantage of cost savings to locate or move certain functions or business processes offshore or to augment local staff with additional staff overseas, usually in economically less-developed countries. While India was the first choice of many companies, the menu of choices has expanded considerably to include locations in Europe, Latin America and Africa. But India remains very popular for a number of reasons: (1) it has a large pool of well-educated professionals, especially in the information technology (IT) sector; (2) labour costs are still comparatively low (albeit increasing); (3) English is widely used; and (4) over the last 25 years the skillset of the Indian workforce has matured considerably, due in part to its head start as an outsourcing location.

During the first wave of outsourcing, the type of work sent offshore was usually in the IT arena – labour-intensive, repetitive, relatively unskilled work (e.g., data entry) that needed an English-speaking, technically trained work force but was not complex and did not require sophisticated skills. Later, of course, many companies moved their call centres and computer helpdesks to India – and a few moved them back home. Today, a variety of increasingly sophisticated work has followed the path blazed by IT and call centres, including manufacturing, research and development (R&D), distribution and the ever-growing body of services collectively known as "back office" or business process outsourcing (BPO).

As the type of work sent offshore has evolved, so have the reasons for doing it. A recent survey by Statistic Brain identified the top five as:

1. To reduce or control costs	44%
2. To gain access to IT resources unavailable internally	34%
3. To free up internal resources	31%
4. To improve business or customer focus	28%
5. To accelerate company reorganization/transformation	22%

(Statistic Brain, n.d., www.statisticbrain.com)

Other reasons cited were to accelerate the project (15%), to gain access to management expertise unavailable internally (15%) and to reduce time to market (9%).

Along the way, companies have used a variety of different models to structure their offshore operations, running the gamut from vendors to partnerships/joint ventures to wholly owned subsidiaries/divisions. Different relationships have proven effective for different types of work and for different corporate entities and many companies use several approaches simultaneously.

And it has worked. The annual growth rate in the IT and BPO sectors in India was regularly in the 13–18% range in the period 2000–2008, and, although slowing somewhat more recently, growth was 12% for BPO in 2011 and is projected to be 11–14% for IT in 2013. Total revenue for IT and BPO in 2012 will top $132 billion.

2 CASE DESCRIPTION

2.1 The situation

A large US-based global business services company (hereafter GBS) has nearly 60,000 employees in North America and operations in more than 100 countries. In 2011, GBS total revenue exceeded $30 billion.

Some ten years ago GBS concluded that staying competitive in its industry required, among other things, outsourcing certain tasks to lower-cost locations overseas. While GBS considered a number of destinations, including Ireland and Mexico, the available labour pool was much larger in India, a key consideration in view of GBS's long-term master plan eventually to have as many as 15,000 offshore employees (a number it is now approaching in 2012). Moreover, the cost savings in India (at the time) were estimated to be in the area of 60%.

Competitive pressures notwithstanding, the decision of this more than 125-year-old company to move a significant percentage of its work (and its workforce) to a foreign country some 12,000 miles and more than nine time zones away occasioned a great deal of internal head shaking, soul searching, hand wringing – and resistance. The move offshore, in short, would have to be aggressively "sold" in the face of considerable scepticism and widespread anxiety. It may have been a financial "no brainer", but it would need to have considerably more momentum behind it.

At the core of the selling strategy, not surprisingly, was an intensive effort to make the case that nothing is really going to change, also known as the "you-won't-notice-any-difference" argument. The idea here was that sending certain tasks offshore, thereby creating the need for Americans to work closely with Indian colleagues half a world away, would actually not be any different than working with colleagues and direct reports just down the hall.

But to make this case, GBS would have to address and somehow neutralize three common concerns: we won't understand them (the language issue); they're sleeping when we're working and vice versa (the time difference issue); and they don't think or work the way we do (the cultural issue). Another possible challenge – they don't know the GBS way of doing things – was a non-starter, as a comprehensive 14-week orientation and training programme was developed for all Indian new hires.

The language issue was not about Indians' ability to speak fluent English but whether or not Americans could understand the Indian accent. While this has turned out to be a lingering concern, it has not proven to be a deal-breaker, largely because most Americans, after some initial frustration and confusion, have become used to the Indian accent. The issue of the time difference was most commonly addressed by scheduling three daily shifts, so that there were always staff available during US working hours. The time difference was in fact an advantage in those cases where the Americans could assign tasks at the end of the US workday and the Indians would complete the work overnight.

The third concern, the cultural issue, was not addressed but, rather, ultimately dismissed. This may sound odd on the surface – surely cultural differences would influence US–India work relationships – but it is actually somewhat common that both parties in an offshore venture tend to underestimate the role of culture. While there is no doubt a self-serving motive at work here – it is in neither side's interest, after all, to suggest that working with Indians is any different from working with Americans – there are at least two other factors that come into play. One is the common Indian sentiment that having worked with Westerners before, perhaps having worked only with Western clients or partners, Indians are very familiar with Western culture and easily adapt. The other, related, factor is that while both sides accept that there may be cultural differences, they consider them to be minor and, more importantly, they are far outweighed by the similarities. The differences are superficial, this logic holds, whereas the similarities are profound.

Whatever the explanation, GBS's senior management was either persuaded or persuaded itself that culture was not going to be a problem. While this was certainly convenient and completely consistent with GBS's "you-won't-notice-any-difference" theme, it does appear in retrospect that GBS came by this sentiment honestly, that there was not in fact any attempt on either side (India or the US) to deliberately minimize or ignore possible cultural differences, tempting as that might have been. Culture was discussed in headquarters, although clearly not with any cultural experts, and GBS concluded it would not cause any significant problems. In short, there was not a cultural "issue".

Work in India began with a number of trials, mostly in the tax division of GBS, lasting between three and six months. The results validated many aspects of the offshore model, and with some adjustment of other features, the company began to expand what came to be known as GBS India.

2.2 The challenge

Some 18 months into the experience, three major recurring challenges were still not responding to any of the traditional fixes. Americans complained that:

1. Indians fall behind on their work, but they don't tell us and then they miss their deadlines.

2. Indians say they understand something when in fact they do not, and as a result much of their work has to be redone.
3. Indians don't tell us when they think something we have asked for is not possible, won't work, or when they know a better way of doing it; they don't give honest feedback.

Initially, GBS responded with the standard expectations-setting approach: bring the parties involved together, describe the disconnects, lay out and get agreement on expectations going forward, and then wait for the necessary behaviour changes to start showing up.

But when Indians were made aware of the three complaints, they responded as follows:

1. "We always tell you when we are falling behind, but you don't seem to understand and are surprised when we need more time."

   "We remind you of the deadline; we ask you if a given date is still the deadline; we mention we are working overtime and even coming in at weekends; we send an unsolicited update that does not specifically state we are behind but shows where we are on the timeline (which is not where we need to be if we are still on schedule). We assume you Americans are reading these messages correctly (since you do not say you don't understand) and you have postponed the deadline. But you Americans just don't get it."

2. "You don't give us very much guidance, so we have to try to guess what you're looking for, and sometimes we guess wrong."

   "We can't tell you that we do not understand something you have explained because this could embarrass you by implying you did not give a very good explanation."

   "When you ask us the question, we probably would casually say 'yes' and then fully expect you to follow up, checking in regularly to see if we had any questions. When you do not follow up, in effect, taking 'yes' for an answer, we are forced to work on our own rather than approach you, which would embarrass you by asking for further explanations."

   "We would like you proactively to offer guidance and tell us what to do."

3. "We give honest feedback, but sometimes you don't listen."

   "We can't possibly say anything negative to you. What we can do is not say anything positive or not say anything at all. Just not saying anything doesn't mean we agree with you or approve of what you are saying."

Since the whole subject of culture and cultural differences had been taken off the agenda at the beginning of the offshore experiment, GBS had to find other, more conventional explanations for what was happening. In the case of the three complaints, the causes had to be located elsewhere, with one or more of the "usual suspects": the wrong skillset, incompetence, not enough experience, or, simply, individual staff members who were just "difficult".

And the solutions, likewise, had to fit these standard explanations: tighten up the job qualifications, improve the interview and selection protocols, do more targeted training, and replace difficult people. In the end, because GBS had turned a blind eye to culture, it never identified the true causes of the three problems, and its "solutions", of course, had little or no effect.

For two years, nothing happened – nothing, that is, except for growing frustration and discontent inside GBS with all things offshore, undermining the entire strategy and jeopardizing ambitious expansion plans. In the end, the impasse forced GBS to re-examine its "you-won't-notice any-difference" strategy and to engage the services of an outside cultural consultant who had worked with numerous American and Indian companies. The consultant was charged with determining whether cultural differences were disrupting the working relations between US and Indian colleagues. When the consultant found that cultural differences were at the heart of the three complaints described earlier, senior leadership at GBS was obliged to acknowledge that culture was an "issue" after all and devise a strategy to address its impact.

3 BACKGROUND KNOWLEDGE

3.1 The authors' points of reference

Craig Storti
"I am primarily a trainer in intercultural communications. I am also the author of several books in the field. I am a practitioner but not an academic. Most of my clients are American companies, American universities, and US government departments, although I have also done work in the UK, northern Europe and India. I have lived for extended periods of time in North Africa, Nepal, the UK and Sri Lanka, and I am the consultant mentioned in this case. I have every reason to believe that I possess an extremely Ameri-centric view of the world, and, to be even more precise, a Vermont-centric view. We New Englanders can be a tad provincial."

Peter Franklin
"I am a professor teaching on BA, MA and MBA programmes at the Hochschule Konstanz, a small university in south Germany. I research and write for academic and practitioner audiences on intercultural communication and intercultural management. In addition to my university work, since 1989 I have advised, trained and addressed numerous corporate and institutional clients on working, managing and leading across cultures. I believe cultural difference can be an enrichment and not merely a difficulty to be mastered. Born and bred on the coast of East Kent, UK, within sight of the European continent, I have spent all my working life based in Germany but have often worked for short periods in other European countries and in China. I now live on the banks of Lake Constance within sight of Switzerland."

3.2 Concepts, models, frameworks

3.2.1 Communicating across cultures

At the heart of the three complaints is the classic cultural dynamic wherein people from one culture (call it culture A) inevitably interpret the behaviour of people from another culture (call it culture B) from their own (culture A's) point of view. This is unavoidable, of course; what other point of view do people from culture A have? But if the people we are interacting with are not from our cultural background, then using the life experience learned in A to make sense of the behaviour of people from B is a questionable strategy.

This dynamic explains why the Americans and Indians working for GBS could look at the same three sets of behaviours – regarding deadlines, asking questions and giving feedback – and come up with completely different interpretations. Behaviour, in other words, does not have inherent or built-in meaning; it has whatever meaning people assign to it. And people from different cultures will often assign different meanings to the same behaviour.

When people communicate and cooperate in any setting, not just across cultures, they do not simply transfer meaning but they *co-construct* understanding and indeed sometimes more explicitly actually *negotiate* understanding. This is because it is impossible to express everything explicitly in the language code (and even if this were possible, it would frequently not be appropriate). They have to interpret, or give meaning to, a large part of what is said – alone or in a joint undertaking. They do this by using their proficiency in the language they are communicating in and their ability to interpret non-verbal signals, their knowledge of the world and the particular situation in which they find themselves, their knowledge of their interlocutor and, not least, of the culture and cultures of the people involved.

When people communicate across cultures, this co-construction of understanding can become particularly difficult, because people communicating draw on 1) different sets of cultural knowledge; 2) this is often unconscious to themselves but 3) sets the norm for behaviour in their own cultural setting (and often not for behaviour in the other culture). Consequently, communication can easily break down, become dysfunctional and lead to transactional and relational conflict. This in fact makes the explicit negotiation of meaning more necessary although for relational reasons (for example, the threat to face), it may not take place.

As Spencer-Oatey and Franklin (2014) report, research into international teams has regularly identified three strategies for handling culturally influenced misunderstanding: being flexible in the use of communication styles (e.g. Holmes et al. 2011); spending time sharing background information before focusing on task (e.g. DiStefano & Maznevski 2000); and double checking the meaning of key words (e.g. Jankowicz & Dobosz-Bourne 2003).

Not only do we have to pay special attention to the management of meaning in intercultural communication, the management of interpersonal relations also requires careful handling because of different notions of what is appropriately polite behaviour. Leech (1983/2005) suggests that politeness maxims or constraints (e.g. Tact, Generosity, Modesty, Agreement) influence people's behaviour, and that how important a given politeness maxim is can vary from culture to culture.

The concept of face is of central significance when it comes to behaving politely and handling and explaining relationships in intercultural interaction. Goffman (1967:5) defined face as "the public self-image that every member wants to claim for himself", and from this Brown and Levinson (1987) developed what has become a well-established theory of politeness. This theory highlights the notion of face, and how face can be damaged and impoliteness occur through what are known as face-threatening acts, particularly through speech acts such as requests. As Spencer-Oatey and Franklin (2014) point out, theorists differ on the question of how culture is related to face. Some linguists (e.g. Brown & Levinson 1987) believe that face sensitivities are universal whereas Ting-Toomey (1999), for example, suggests that individualists are mainly concerned about their own face, whereas collectivists are mainly concerned about other people's face.

3.2.2 The cultures of the USA and India compared

Key to an understanding of this case are insights into the different national cultures of the USA and India.

There follows an overview of the differences between the two cultures as ascertained in etic studies by Hofstede (1980/2001), and House et al. (2004), which should be consulted if the terms and concepts are unfamiliar.

Table 14.1 Overview of the differences between the two cultures

Cultural dimension	USA	India
Power distance (Hofstede): expectation and acceptance that power is distributed unequally	lower: 40/38	higher: 77/10–11
Power distance – practice (House et al.): expectation and acceptance that power is distributed unequally	Band B	Band A
Individualism (Hofstede): prime orientation to self	high: 91/1	lower: 48/21
Societal institutional collectivism – practice (House et al.): institutional practices encourage and reward collective action	4.20, Band B	4.38, Band B
Societal in-group collectivism – practices (House et al.): individuals express pride, loyalty and interdependence in their families	4.25, Band C	5.92, Band A
Performance orientation – practices (House et al.): innovation, performance and improvement are encouraged and rewarded	4.49, Band A	4.25, Band B
Assertiveness – practices (House et al): value assertive, tough and dominant behaviour for everyone	4.55, Band A	3.73, Band B
Humane orientation – practices (House et al.): encourages and rewards people for being fair, altruistic, friendly, generous, caring, and kind to others	4.17, Band C	4.57, Band B
Communication style (Hall & Hall 1989)	fairly low context communication	high context communication

Key: House et al: figures refer to scores for practices. Band A is high, Band C is low

Hofstede: first figure is score, second figure is rank

Two of the most often cited differences between US and Indian management styles are: (1) the American instinct to delegate authority vs the Indian instinct to centralize authority; and (2) the American tendency to minimize differences in rank vs. the Indian tendency to emphasize differences. With respect to the former, Americans believe that those who manage least manage best, that direct reports do their best work if they are given broad objectives and guidelines and then left alone to reach those objectives in the way that suits them best. For their part, Indian managers typically retain more control over the work of their staff (in part because they are also held more closely accountable for it), and staff expect close guidance and supervision.

With regard to rank, America is a famously egalitarian culture; people believe that no one is inherently superior to anyone else, regardless of their rank. Direct reports are very sensitive to any actions on the part of management which might suggest a superior/inferior dynamic. And managers are very careful not to "pull rank" (to act superior) and not to "wear their rank on their sleeve" (to draw attention to occupying a higher rank). It is not that Americans do not hold different ranks, but only that people should not be treated differently merely because of their rank.

Indians tend to be very aware of and sensitive to differences in rank; one treats one's superiors, one's peers, and one's inferiors (and Indians actually use these terms) in distinctly different ways. It is not appropriate to treat a peer the way one treats a superior or one's direct report. Rank determines how one gives feedback and how one questions or challenges dubious guidance or mistaken directions.

For further insights from emic publications on India and the USA, see the recommended reading (section 3.3).

3.2.3 Intercultural competence development

Trainers and consultants developing intercultural competence in others have a repertoire of approaches and methods at their disposal, many of which are briefly described in the following overviews. If you are unfamiliar with the literature, follow up the references and see the recommended reading.

In a seminal article in the first *Handbook of Intercultural Training* (Landis & Brislin 1983), Gudykunst and Hammer presented a "classification scheme for training techniques" (1983:126). They distinguish, firstly, between culture-general and culture-specific training and, secondly, between the "university model", or didactic/expository set of methods and the experiential/discovery set of methods. Gudykunst and Hammer placed these two sets of concepts on intersecting axes, thus forming taxonomic quadrants. Gudykunst, Guzley and Hammer (1996) elaborated on the original classification, providing the material for Figure 14.1.

Current best practice uses all these methods or elements of them, although they may be known by different names.

	Experiential/discovery				
	I. Experiential – culture-general		II. Experiential – culture-specific		
Culture-general	Human relations training	Intercultural communication workshop	Bicultural human relations training	Bicultural communication workshop	Culture-specifc
	Culture-general simulations (incl. culture contrast)	Self-confrontation	Culture-specific simulations	Culture-specific role-plays	
	Self-assessments				
	Academic courses in intercultural communication cultural anthropology & cross-cultural psychology	Kraemer's cultural self-awareness	Foreign language training	Area orientation briefings	
	Written material	Lecture/ discussion techniques	Culture-specific assimilators	Written material	
	Video material	Culture-general assimilators			
	III. Didactic – culture-general		IV. Didactic – culture-specific		
	Didactic/expository				

Based on Gudykunst & Hammer (1983:126–140) and Gudykunst, Guzley & Hammer (1996:66–72) and adapted from Spencer-Oatey & Franklin (2009:218)

Figure 14.1 Gudykunst and Hammer's classification scheme for training techniques

Fowler and Blohm (2004) have developed a taxonomy of methods listing practically all methods and techniques currently used. They use an elaborate set of criteria, which results in an effective tool for selecting methods for various development scenarios. The methods listed are described as "cognitive", "active" (although interactive may be a more appropriate term), "intercultural" or "other" and their outcomes are designated as supporting the development of knowledge, skills or attitudes:

Table 14.2 A classification of development methods and their expected outcomes

Nature of method	Method	Development outcome
Cognitive	Lecture, briefing	Knowledge
	Written material	Knowledge
	Computer-based training	Knowledge, skills
	Self-assessment	Knowledge
	Case studies	Knowledge, skills
Active	Simulations and games	Knowledge, skills, attitudes
	Role play	Skills, attitudes
	Exercises	Knowledge, skills
Intercultural	Contrast culture, contrast American	Attitudes
	Critical incidents	Knowledge, skills, attitudes
	Culture assimilator, intercultural sensitizer	Knowledge, skills, attitudes
	Culture analysis	Knowledge, skills
	Kraemer's cultural self-awareness, Storti's cross-cultural dialogues	Knowledge, attitudes
	Area studies	Knowledge
	Immersion	Knowledge, skills, attitudes
Other	Visual imagery	Knowledge, attitudes
	Art and culture	Knowledge, skills, attitudes

Source: adapted from Fowler and Blohm (2004) and Spencer-Oatey & Franklin (2009).

3.3 Recommended reading

Althen, G. with Bennett, J. (2011). ***American Ways: A Cultural Guide to the United States.*** **Boston: Intercultural Press.**

Degler, C. (1984). ***Out of Our Past: The Forces That Shaped Modern America.*** **New York: Harper & Row.**

Kakar, S. & Kakar, K. (2007). ***The Indians: Portrait of a People.*** **New Delhi: Viking Penguin.**
The authors are a psychoanalyst (Sudhir) and an anthropologist (Katharina) who bring the insights of their two professions to the topic. There is more anthropology than psychology in these pages (sample chapter titles include: The Inner Experience of Caste, Indian Women: Traditional and Modern, Religious and Spiritual Life, Health and Healing), but it is a very thoughtful and subtle examination of Indian culture.

McElroy, J. H. (1999). ***American Beliefs: What Keeps a Big Country and a Diverse People United.*** **Chicago: Ivan R. Dee.**

Spencer-Oatey, H. & Franklin, P. (2009). ***Intercultural Interaction: A Multidisciplinary Approach to Intercultural Communication.*** **Houndmills, Basingstoke: Palgrave.**
Chapters 4 and 5 are particularly relevant to Question 1 in this chapter, and Chapter 9 to Question 2. The book as a whole provides rapid access to current ideas and practice in intercultural communication. Drawing on concepts and findings from a range of different disciplines and using authentic examples of intercultural interaction to illustrate points, it offers a wealth of insights into the process. Part 1 explores conceptual issues: the nature of culture and intercultural interaction competence; the impact of language and culture on understanding, rapport and impression management; cultural and adaptation processes. Part 2 deals with practical applications: how competence in intercultural interaction can be assessed and developed. Part 3 focuses on research: topic areas that can be investigated and methods and approaches for doing so. Part 4 provides a rich list of resources for further study.

Storti, C. (2007). ***Speaking of India: Bridging the Communication Gap When Working with Indians.*** **Boston: Nicholas Brealey.**
This book is a comparative analysis of US and Indian culture, especially with reference to the workplace. It highlights key differences in management and communication styles, presents examples of how these differences affect everyday interaction, and suggests practical strategies for bridging the cultural gaps.

Storti, C. (2005). ***Americans At Work: A Guide to the Can-Do People.*** **Yarmouth, Maine: Intercultural Press.**

Varma, P. K. (2006). ***Being Indian.*** **London: Arrow Books.**
This book is a brilliant analysis of the Indian mindset, of how Indians think and why they think that way. It is indispensable for anyone who wants to understand Indians better.

4 QUESTIONS ON THE CASE

1. What could be possible cultural explanations for the three complaints? Why don't Indians tell Americans when they are falling behind? Why do Indians say they understand something when apparently they do not (and feel they have to guess what the Americans want)? Why do the Indians feel they give honest feedback, but the Americans insist they do not?
2. Suggest the elements of an intercultural competence development programme which a trainer/consultant could implement for the US and Indian employees of GBS.
3. What other measures could GBS take to improve the communication and cooperation between GBS USA and GBS India?
4. How should GBS introduce the subject of culture/cultural differences after it had been explicitly and very publicly downplayed?
5. What synergies can GBS expect to create by raising company-wide awareness of the cultural issue? What leverage can GBS gain by acknowledging the reality of cultural differences?

5 REFERENCES

Brown P. & Levinson S. C. (1987). *Politeness: Some Universals in Language Usage*. Cambridge: Cambridge University Press.

DiStefano, J. J. & Maznevski, M. L. (2000). "Creating value with diverse teams in global management". In: *Organizational Dynamics*, 29:1, 45–63.

Fowler S. & Blohm J. M. (2004). "An analysis of methods for intercultural training". In: Landis, D., Bennett, J. & Bennett, M. (Eds), *Handbook of Intercultural Training*, 37–84. 3rd ed. Thousand Oaks, CA: Sage.

Goffman (1967). *Interaction Ritual: Essays in Face to Face Behavior*. Chicago: Aldine.

Gudykunst, W. B., Guzley, R. M., & Hammer, M. R. (1996). "Designing Intercultural". In: Landis D. & Bhagat, R. S. (Eds), *Handbook of Intercultural Training*, 66–72. Thousand Oaks, CA: Sage.

Gudykunst, W. B. & Hammer, M. R. (1983). "Basic training design: Approaches to intercultural training". In: Landis, D. & Brislin, R. W. (Eds), *Handbook of Intercultural Training*, 1,126–140. New York: Pergamon Press.

Hall, E. T. & Hall, M. R. (1989). *Understanding Cultural Differences*. Yarmouth: Intercultural Press.

Hofstede, G. (1980/2001). *Culture's Consequences*. Thousand Oaks, CA: Sage.

Holmes, J., Marra, M. & Vine, B. (2011). *Leadership, Discourse, and Ethnicity*. New York: Oxford University Press.

House, R. J., Hanges, P. J., Javidan, M., Dorfman, P. W. & Gupta, V. (2004). *Culture, Leadership, and Organizations: The GLOBE Study of 62 Societies*. Thousand Oaks, CA: Sage.

Jankowicz, A. D. & Dobosz-Bourne, D. (2003). "How are meanings negotiated? Commonality, sociality and the travel of thoughts". In: Scheer, J. (Ed.), *Crossing Borders, Going Places*. Giessen: Fischer-Verlag.

Leech, G. (1983/2005). *The Pragmatics of Politeness*. New York: Oxford University Press.

Spencer-Oatey, H. & Franklin, P. (2014). "Intercultural interaction". In: Chapelle, C. A. (Ed.), *The Encyclopedia of Applied Linguistics*. Ely: Wiley. DOI:10.1002/9781405198431.wbeal1446

Spencer-Oatey, H. & Franklin, P. (2009). *Intercultural Interaction: A Multidisciplinary Approach to Intercultural Communication*. Houndmills, Basingstoke: Palgrave.

Spencer-Oatey, H. & Tang M. (2007). "Managing collaborative processes in international projects". In: *e-Learning Initiatives in China: Pedagogy, Policy and Culture*, 159-173. Hong Kong: Hong Kong University Press.

Statistics Brain (no date). Job outsourcing statistics. Retrieved on from www.statisticbrain.com/outsourcing-statistics-by-country/. 23.1.2016.

Ting-Toomey, S. (1999). *Communicating Across Cultures*. New York: Guilford.

Part 3

Achieving Complementarity and Synergy

15

Achieving Complementarity and Synergy: The Third Step to Leveraging Diversity in Intercultural Management

Christoph Barmeyer and Peter Franklin

1 THE ENRICHING NATURE OF INTERCULTURALITY

Despite processes of harmonization and standardization in society, culture and business, cultural otherness still exists, as is evidenced by decades of discussion about the convergence and divergence of values and practices (Adler 2008; Barmeyer & Mayrhofer 2008; d'Iribarne 2009; Hofstede 2001; Sorge 2004). Otherness can be neither denied nor suppressed. In this respect, interculturality, with its genesis in (cultural) otherness and in the resulting divergent interpretive repertoires, remains a central and relevant topic in the study and practice of international management.

As a result of the divergent expectations, norms, modes of interpretation and practices of those involved, intercultural work settings are often conflictual or at least involve frictional loss. This is illustrated in countless critical incidents which unnecessarily and unproductively eat up resources of energy, time and money in organizations. Owing to misunderstandings, interculturality can lead to targets and budgets not being met, as we exemplify in the first part of this book. However, intercultural management research and practice can explain misunderstandings and provide insights into how they may be reduced or even avoided. What is more, psychology and communication studies and, to a lesser extent, management studies and applied linguistics, offer insights as to the qualities and competencies which enable managers to handle the cultural interface effectively and appropriately and to deal with the dynamic and psychological results of the intercultural interaction, as we discuss and illustrate in the second part of the book.

In addition to the familiar approaches which focus, on the one hand, on the analysis of differences and difficulties and, on the other, on the competencies of the interculturally competent individual, there exists a further approach which views interculturality in a positive and productive light as a resource.

So far there has been little research and few publications devoted to this kind of constructive interculturality. Stahl and Tung (2015) also come to this conclusion. In their content analysis of nearly 250 articles which appeared over a period of almost 25 years in the *Journal of International Business Studies*, the internationally most significant periodical on international management research, they show the extent to which problematic and negative aspects of interculturality are emphasized and positive aspects largely neglected:

> While there are suggestions in the literature that cultural diversity can offer meaningful positive opportunities to individuals, groups, and organizations, we argue – and demonstrate empirically – that the problem-focused view of cultural diversity is by far predominant in research on culture in International Business. In other words, we know much less about the positive dynamics and outcomes associated with cultural differences than we know about the problems, obstacles, and conflicts caused by them. (Stahl & Tung 2015:393)

This "positive cross-cultural scholarship" approach assumes cultural differences can have effects which are not merely negative and conflictual but also complementary and thus enriching in nature. This proposition leads to the central concepts of cultural complementarity and intercultural synergy illustrated in the case studies of the third part of the book. In these concepts, interculturality is seen as a dynamic process of joint construction and negotiation of meaning and action.

2 THE CONCEPTUAL FRAMEWORK AND THE CASE STUDIES

2.1 Cultural complementarity

Cultural complementarity describes a state in which particular and seemingly contradictory, but in themselves equally valuable, value-based characteristics (such as attitudes, norms, behavioural patterns, practices) of individuals from different groups complement each other to form a whole. From an intercultural viewpoint, when individuals or groups come from different social systems and interact together, these properties can represent relative differences. Intercultural complementarity (Barmeyer 2007; Hampden-Turner 2000), employed consciously as a management approach, aims to combine these differences so that they lead to complementary (rather than contrasting and potentially conflictual) actions and behaviours. The benefit this creates is enhanced performance, in that the characteristics best suited to the context, task and individuals involved are employed. In contrast to intercultural synergy (see below) new, hitherto unknown but desirable benefits are not necessarily the result.

Complementarity is an idea long established in Asian philosophy and religion, for example in Taoism (Hansen 2000). In Western intellectual history, the notion of complementarity developed in the natural sciences, in particular physics, and gradually established itself in the social sciences and in cultural studies (Buchheim 1983; Otte 1990). Physicists such as Niels Bohr

(1885–1962), Werner Heisenberg (1901–1976) and also Carl Friedrich von Weizsäcker (1912–2007) use the term from the 1920s onwards, which until then was known mainly in connection with Goethe's complementary colours, to describe the complete and holistic description of properties of objects, research methods and philosophical approaches.

The state of complementarity displays systemic and holistic elements which interact together; as Crouch (2010:120) puts it: "A difference becomes a complementarity when it 'works'". Writing of institutional complementarity, Crouch (2010) goes on to find three different approaches to the subject in the literature:

- Complementarity is based on contrasts, differences and contradictions. By combining different individual elements and components it compensates for systemic deficits. This means that the individual elements need each other in order for themselves and the system to survive.
- Complementarity is based on commonalities and similarities. Systemic elements influence each other and reinforce certain effects.
- Complementarity is understood, from an economic point of view, as the complementation of elements as resources, such as factors of production.

Whether they are contrasts or commonalities, as in the first or second conceptualization above, elements lead to systemic stability in social systems, such as in organizations or the institutional relationships in a country:

> The idea of Wahlverwandtschaft (elective affinity) is often used to describe this process whereby institutions across many different parts of a society find some kind of intellectual fit together, mainly through cognitive processes and social learning. (Crouch 2010:122–123)

In order to achieve cultural complementarity in management interaction both at the organizational and also at the individual levels of the kind described above for institutions, certain cognitive, behavioural and affective competencies (knowledge, skills, attitudes, characteristics), as described and exemplified in the second part of this book, are required in individuals to support what Crouch above describes as a process of social learning. Three fundamental conditions need to be fulfilled for these competencies to be able to bring about the desired cultural complementarity:

- The individuals involved must possess a value-free openness to enable them ethno-relatively to recognize and value the characteristics and properties of other (cultural) groups. They must move from rejecting or merely tolerating cultural otherness towards accepting (Bennett 1986; Hawes & Kealey 1981; Kelley & Meyers 1993; Langer 1989; Wiseman et al. 1989) and valuing it (Bennett 1979; Cui & Van den Berg 1991). In this way, the characteristics and properties of other groups acquire the status of strengths. There are thus no polarities such as either/or or right/wrong but continua of both/and.
- The characteristics valued as qualities and strengths are consciously employed as resources.

- The characteristics are combined to correspond best to the situation to be managed in the given context.

The three kinds of complementarity and the three necessary conditions discussed above are illustrated to varying extents and in varying constellations in the case studies that follow. Two cases contrast not only differences in cultures and underline their complementarity, but take a holistic view of contextual factors.

"Future+: Intercultural Challenges and Success Factors in an International Virtual Project Team", conceived by Christoph Barmeyer and Ulrike Haupt, deals with a central concern for international virtual project teams: how to steer and manage the overall work process and how to motivate team members in a culturally sensitive way by alternating between social physical proximity and social virtual distance. Using the example of product development in the industry sector, the Franco-German case study illustrates the importance of contextual, cultural and personal factors that can lead to a complementary combination of diverse, geographically dispersed resources.

The case study "A Tough Day for a French Expatriate in Vietnam: The Management of a Large International Infrastructure Project", written by Sylvie Chevrier, reveals the importance of cultures in international projects, neither exaggerating nor denying the way they influence interactions at work. Among the many variables impacting the dynamics of working relationships – public–private organizations, foreign–domestic actors, customer–provider role, political–technical issues – differences in cultures also play a role both impeding and enhancing the dynamics of the project. While the case shows how cultural differences intervene in the management of a large project in Vietnam in the transportation industry, more significantly here the analysis underlines the complementarity of interactants from both the French and Vietnamese cultures and provides recommendations to improve the management of the local Vietnamese team by French expatriates.

2.2 Synergy and intercultural synergy

Synergy, and especially its plural, synergies, are terms which in recent years have acquired negative connotations thanks to their use to mean cost-savings resulting, for example, from combining functions and services of organizations involved in mergers and acquisitions. We use the term here in a very different sense. Intercultural synergy in the context of international management can be understood as the outputs which arise from the combination and interaction of individuals from different cultures and which are of higher quality than the sum of the individual actions (Barmeyer 2007). At the outset of the interaction these qualitatively superior outputs are unknown in nature (and in this respect different from cultural complementarity) but they are desirable and, thanks to the complementary perspectives and characteristics available, a benefit for social systems in general and for organizations in particular (Adler 1980). This benefit results not from merely establishing a complementary relationship among cultural othernesses with their respective perspectives and strengths (as in complementarity). Rather the benefit is generated by allowing and facilitating the creation of a synergistic relationship among cultural othernesses with the intention of developing creative and innovative outputs. Meanings and actions are co-constructed and negotiated in social interaction. As a result of the differing culturally influenced perspectives, values and practices of the interactants, these meanings and actions have at least the potential to be creative and innovative.

With origins in the natural sciences, in particular in physics[1], the notion of synergy became established in the social sciences thanks to those working in humanistic sociology in the USA in the middle of the 20th century. Fuller (1975:88) defines synergy as "the behavior of whole systems that cannot be predicted by the behavior of any parts taken separately." The organizational psychologist Abraham Maslow was responsible for spreading the term in the 1950s with reference to social and cultural systems and in so doing built on the unpublished manuscripts[2] of the cultural anthropologist Ruth Benedict (1887–1948):

> I shall call this gamut [of acts and skills] synergy, the old term used in medicine and theology to mean the combined action. In medicine it meant the combined action of nerve centers, muscles, mental activities, remedies which by combining produced a result greater than the run of their separate actions. (Maslow & Honigmann 1970:326)

Benedict developed a notion of synergy which is based on a holistic and systemic approach and which refers in particular to communities (Benedict 1934; Maslow 1964:153). On the basis of her consideration of autochthonous groups and communities, Benedict came to the conclusion that some social systems succeed in living together peacefully and harmoniously and in developing together – she calls these "high synergy" societies – and that other social systems are, on the other hand, marked by strife and conflicts and by the prevalence of "low synergy". These are extreme positions. Maslow assumes that modern societies display hybrid forms of both high and low synergy institutions.

These cultural patterns can also be found in organizations and companies (Adler 1980; Harris, 2004). Individuals and social systems can act synergistically if they can succeed in integrating and using (contrasting) values. As Maslow (1964:163) puts it: "High synergy from this point of view can represent a transcending of the dichotomizing, a fusion of the opposites into a single concept."

---

[1]There are many cases found in science where the sum of parts attains characteristics different from what can be assumed from the parts. For example, the metal alloy of chrome, nickel and steel is much stronger than any of those metals by themselves.

[2]It is assumed that Benedict deliberately did not publish her writings on synergy as she was concerned that they could be regarded as utopian, idealistic and unscientific by the scientific community.

The notion of intercultural synergy has been made known in theorizing and research into management and organizations by Adler (1980, 1983, 2008) as well as by Moran and Harris (1983). They see the interaction of people from different cultures as the cause of synergy when a number of people cooperate closely and transform risk into opportunity:

> Cultural synergy, as an approach to managing the impact of cultural diversity, involves a process in which managers form organizational strategies, structures, and practices based on, but not limited to, the cultural patterns of individual organization members and clients. Culturally synergistic organizations create new forms of management and organization that transcend the distinct culture of their members. This approach recognizes both the similarities and differences among the cultures that compose a global organization and suggests that we neither ignore nor minimize cultural diversity, but rather view it as a resource in designing and developing organizational systems. (Adler 2008:109)

Thus intercultural synergy represents the desired "positive" and constructive aspect of interculturality which tries to use cultural diversity as a resource and a potential for creativity. Synergy is understood as a creative synthesis and as a social process of human development (Maslow 1964).

Although intercultural synergy is the positive result of intercultural interaction, and although constructive intercultural management is plausible and desirable, the notion of intercultural synergy has remained little explored both on the theoretical and conceptional level and on the practical and empirical level. Conceptionally, the construct has been the subject of little research and has thus not been developed to any great extent. In many standard works on cross-cultural or intercultural management, synergy is not even mentioned. Neither in Hofstede's seminal work, *Culture's Consequences*, is there a discussion of synergy;[3] nor in Peterson and Sondergaard's (2008) four-volume *Foundations of Cross Cultural Management*, which brings together classic contributions from five decades of research, is there an article on synergy apart from Adler's (2008). The same goes for the *Blackwell Handbook of Cross-Cultural Management*, edited by Gannon and Newmann (2002). There is no article on synergy in the *Cambridge Handbook of Culture, Organizations, and Work* edited by Bhagat and Steers (2009), in Jack and Westwood's *International and Cross-Cultural Management Studies. A Postcolonial Reading* (2009) or in the collection of case studies *Cross-Cultural Management in Practice. Culture and Negotiated Meanings* (2011), edited by Primecz, Romani and Sackmann.

Even on the basis of this cursory survey of works on cross-cultural and intercultural management, the impression prevails that intercultural management research has preferred so far to take a somewhat one-sided, problem-oriented approach to interculturality. Perhaps this is connected with the strong

[3]Indeed, Hofstede, in a much-quoted interview, says "Culture is more often a source of conflict than of synergy".

influence of social psychology and communication studies, where the hundreds of studies of effectiveness in intercultural interaction seem to be driven more by an interest in reducing the potential for dysfunctionality than using the potential for benefit.

The literature seems to indicate that empirically, it is difficult to achieve intercultural synergy in international management practice. The few empirical studies refer mainly to small social entities such as work groups (Adler 2008; Gabriel & Griffiths 2008; Köppel 2007; Stumpf 2005; Stahl et al. 2009; Tjitra 2001; Zeutschel 1999), and only rarely to whole organizations, for example in mergers and acquisitions (Brock 2005). Even Adler (2008), for example, leaves undescribed and unillustrated the precise nature of the process she mentions, merely recommending to "create new alternatives based on, but not limited to, the cultures involved" as the action required. How to "do" intercultural synergy remains mysteriously vague, a deficit which, we believe, the case studies in this part of the book go some way to removing.

2.2.1 Framework conditions and interactants

In order to achieve cultural complementarity and intercultural synergy in work settings, it seems to be of fundamental importance that certain framework conditions are present and also that certain processes are applied, such as in the models and methods elaborated on by Adler (1980), Hampden-Turner (1990) or Maznewski and DiStefano (2000) and which are described in this section and illustrated in the cases. These framework conditions include – in addition to structural and strategic conditions – above all, the participation of individuals with their particular experience and competencies, among them an ethnorelative attitude, as discovered by Barmeyer and Davoine (2014) to be the case at the Franco-German television station ARTE. In particular, biculturals play a special role. Because some individuals – due to mobility and immigration (Heckmann & Schnapper 2003) – often internalize more than one linguistic and cultural reference system, they are considered as bicultural (Brannen & Thomas 2010; Mahadevan 2012). As a result of their insider/outsider status they can be described as polycentric, i.e. able to apply diverse meaning and action systems and to take up more neutral meta-positions than people who have been socialized in a single context. Bicultural staff may be found at the interface of different organizations and national cultures and may thus play a key role in creating synergy and indeed negotiating a new culture (see below). As "boundary-spanners" (Yagi & Kleinberg 2011) they make valuable contributions – often unconsciously – to the understanding and functioning of organizations.

They are similar in this respect to a growing group of intercultural and bicultural people (Brannen & Thomas 2010), such as:

- Third culture kids (TCKs) (Pollock & Van Reken 2001): children who were raised in a culture outside their parents' culture for a significant part of their socialization.
- Third culture individuals (TCIs) (Moore & Barker 2012): people who have spent a significant amount of time in cultures other than their own.

- Global nomads (Matthewman 2011): people who frequently move from one country to another working as expatriates or in jobs that are location-independent such as IT. They are often the children of parents of mixed nationalities who have experienced a socialization outside the cultures of origin of their parents.
- Cosmopolitans or cultural marginals (Bennett 1993; Fitzsimmons et al. 2013).

People can experience both the negative and positive effects of cultural marginality (Moore & Barker 2012). They have been described by Bennett (1993) as *encapsulated* marginals (who experience insecurity and alienation from their own cultural frames of reference) and *constructive* marginals (who experience security and an authentic relationship towards their own cultural frames of reference). Interestingly, the constructive and positive aspects were also identified in a meta-study on marginals (Fitzsimmons et al. 2013:592):

> Taken together, these studies suggest that some marginalised individuals may possess unique advantages in global and cross-cultural domains. Yet the myth that marginals consistently have the worst performance in personal and global work settings persists because there is no theoretical explanation for overturning the myth.

In the part of the book currently under review, two cases in particular deal with such framework conditions including the biculturality of individuals in organizations. In his case study "Japan Tobacco International: Managing and Leveraging Cultural Diversity", Yih-teen Lee offers a rich ground for discussing how multicultural diversity can be managed. The author asks how cultural differences may become an asset for MNCs and how they may be leveraged. The case shows how a company can embrace diversity and manage cultural integration with the help of proactive strategic management and culture-sensitive HR practices. The case also addresses the topic of the characteristics and competencies managers need. The global mindset and the way people manage their cultural identities may also play a role in determining how they approach cultural diversity. A framework of biculturalism/multiculturalism is presented in order to understand how one's identity configurations, at both the individual and organizational level, may be another success factor for international managers and MNCs in leveraging cultural diversity.

The case study by Jasmin Mahadevan "Leveraging the Benefits of Diversity and Biculturalism through Organizational Design" stresses as its starting point that cultures have become fluid and no longer only refer to societal cultures but also to multiple sub- and micro-cultures. This is why cultural differences are increasingly found "at home" and within the organizational working context. For bicultural individuals, this is linked to a life experience in the "in-between", which demands constant adaptation to different cultural meaning systems, depending on the context in which they are involved. By taking a resource-based view of multiculturalism, especially of bicultural individuals, the case study of a German technological company discusses how the benefits of diversity, especially biculturalism, can be utilized through organizational design. Bicultural individuals, especially, are highly valued core members of the organization whose competencies and qualities are leveraged through organizational design. The case shows that to achieve intercultural synergy in a holistic way, micro-individual, meso-organizational and macro-societal demands need to be aligned.

These two case studies make clear that in addition to contextual factors, framework conditions and person-related factors, the bi- and multiculturality of individuals, in particular, have a special significance: multicultural managers are significant interactants in multinational companies in that, as intercultural bridge-builders, they can take account of new societal contexts such as hybridization and multiple dynamic cultures (Fitzsimmons et al. 2011). In an increasingly globalized world economy still shaped by ethnocentric assumptions and strategies, interculturally competent managers represent an important resource for multinational companies in their personification of global thinking and acting. They act as interpreters or mediators between languages and cultural systems, as boundary spanners (Yagi & Kleinberg 2011), acting between the different cultures represented in the organization. In this way, they are significant bearers and implementers of intercultural synergy (Stahl & Brannen 2013).

2.2.2 Processes and methods

In addition to framework conditions, processes and immanent models are necessary to achieve cultural complementarity and intercultural synergy. These are constructed consciously or unconsciously as a result of the communicative actions of interactants from different cultural settings. They are co-constructed and/or negotiated (Brannen & Salk 2000; Primecz et al. 2011) as a result of cultural contact and two-way processes of interpretation, adaptation and learning in specific contexts (Sackmann & Phillips 2004). A process orientation, which regards interculturality above all as a process of exchange and development, and not as a mere confrontation of culture-specific properties, is one way to achieve intercultural synergy. As intercultural synergy in organizations – apparently – rarely emerges spontaneously, it requires the active support and facilitation of managers. Adler (1980) suggests various steps to facilitate the creation of intercultural synergy: (1) Situation Description, (2) Cultural Interpretation, (3) Cultural Creativity and (4) Cultural Synergy. In the absence of further elaboration, WorldWork Ltd., in their International Competency Framework (see Chapter 11 of this book), convincingly interprets this creation of new alternatives as "an approach to facilitating group and team work to ensure that different cultural perspectives are not suppressed, but are properly understood and used in the problem solving process" (www.worldwork.biz).

Another similar process is described and further developed by Hampden-Turner (1990) in his dilemma theory. A dilemma is a situation in which an interactant must choose among several options, each with various advantages and disadvantages, in order to achieve his/her goal. For social systems, bipolar values are generally regarded as suggestions for solving societal problems. However, these are not to be regarded as absolutes but as virtues which, systemically speaking, can be caused to have a harmonious relationship to one another. As every social system develops specific values to deal with its environment, the result in the intercultural context is an area of conflict between complementarity and synergy on the one hand and confrontation and crises on the other (Demorgon 1998; Hampden-Turner & Trompenaars 2000). Dilemma theory regards values as bipolar but, unlike the Hofstedian cultural dimensions, also, and in particular, as dynamic and circular. By integrating differences (reconciliation), the theory contributes to a dynamic development of cultural dimensions (Hampden-Turner 2000).

The process of reconciliation according to Hampden-Turner (2000) consists of the following steps: (1) Recognize cultural differences by describing the situation and the problem, (2) Respect cultural differences by identifying and analysing dilemmas, (3) Reconcile cultural differences by resolving intercultural dilemmas finally (4) Realize and root in order to install best practices and possible synergistic action. The application of dilemma theory as a process model for intercultural development is to be found in two of the case studies in this part of the book.

"Going Global versus Staying Local: The Performance Management Dilemma in the International Context" by Fons Trompenaars and Riana van den Bergh provides an illustration of the tensions that are often faced in the international human resource management context where head office tries to apply universal performance measures which may not necessarily be appropriate in local subsidiaries. Whilst globalization is almost synonymous with standardization, regional differences require different approaches. Thus, although traditional Western-based management principles, such as expectancy, equity and reinforcement theories suggest that a tight linkage between employee competence, performance and rewards should produce positive motivation, empirical findings may show opposite results in countries such as Japan and China, where the employee is not merely considered to be an instrument and a resource. The authors show that by identifying value differences between contrasting cultures, organizations can anticipate the impact of these differences and search for ways to reconcile the resulting conflicts.

The next case study, "A Parcel to Spain: Reconciling Cultural and Managerial Dilemmas Caused by the Implementation of Corporate Culture Instruments", by Christoph Barmeyer, Eric Davoine and Vincent Merk, focuses on the reception and application of corporate cultural instruments, namely value statements and codes of conduct, transferred from US headquarters to its German subsidiary. This reception process may also include the possibility of interpretations and violations of these codes and charters. Illustrated by a critical incident triggered by differing interpretations of the corporate culture, the case study shows, by using dilemma theory, which options exist to defuse an existing conflict or, more accurately, to achieve a synergistic solution which benefits both the interactants and the organization.

"Managing Glocally: Resolving Intercultural Challenges in the Management of Local Multicultural Teams in a Multinational Venture", Laurence Romani's case study, also focuses on intercultural processes. The MBI process model (M – mapping commonalities and differences, B – bridging differences and then I – integrating them) originally conceived by Maznewski und DiStefano (2000) is used to shape intercultural team processes. The case presents a frequently occurring situation in the service industry. A multinational company, organized around regions, cultivating a strong organizational culture and even adopting ethnocentric points of view, merges with another company. As a consequence, strong organizational and other cultures, e.g. gender, profession, generation, need to be renegotiated and multicultural teams need to be managed. The difficulty is to combine different expectations. The MBI model can help to identify diversity and manage it in a respectful way.

The interactants from different cultural settings involved in complementary and synergistic solutions are not only aware of their characteristics, shaped by their own culture and by other cultures, but they succeed in combining features synergistically and thereby in managing and developing complex systems such as organizations. This assumes a high degree of mutual acceptance and the willingness to value otherness, i.e. features of other cultures, as strengths. Thus a particular role is played by intercultural competence, as the second part of this book makes clear. Only few interactants, such as bi- and multicultural people, possess intercultural competencies to a high degree (Fitzsimmons et al. 2011) and are able to implement appropriate strategies in organizations through the use of systemic intercultural learning and development processes (Mahadevan 2012). Synergistic intercultural management is based on a complex combination of numerous influencing factors, processes and interactants.

This is made clear in "Strategic Alliances and Intercultural Organizational Change: The Renault–Nissan Case" by Christoph Barmeyer and Ulrike Mayrhofer. The Renault–Nissan alliance, associating interactants from two different national and corporate cultures, has become the most productive and longest-lasting intercultural alliance among major car manufacturers. Its success can be seen as a positive exception and a future role model in the field of intercultural management. Thanks to a multicultural leader applying intercultural leadership techniques, the companies went through a complex and broad process of organizational development and change that can be seen in many ways as synergistic best practices. Carlos Ghosn, CEO of Renault–Nissan, underlines his view: "Synergy is not only what exists in one company or the other. It is not just about transferring best practices. It's also about creating together something that neither one could have done alone" (Stahl & Brannen 2013:496).

REFERENCES

Adler, N. (1980). "Cultural synergy: The management of cross-cultural organizations". In: Burke, W. W. & Goodstein, L. D. (Eds), *Trends and Issues in OD: Current Theory and Practice*, 163–184. San Diego: Pfeiffer & Company.

Adler, N. (1983). "A typology of management studies involving culture". In: *Journal of International Business Studies*, 14:2, 29–47.

Adler, N. (2008). *International Dimensions of Organizational Behavior*. Cincinnati: South Western.

Barmeyer, C. (2007). *Management interculturel et styles d'apprentissage. Etudiants et dirigeants en France, en Allemagne et au Québec*. Québec: PUL.

Barmeyer, C. & Davoine, E. (2014). "Interkulturelle Synergie als 'ausgehandelte' Interkulturalität: Der deutsch-französische Fernsehsender ARTE". In: Moosmüller, A. & Möller-Kiero, J. (Eds), *Interkulturalität und kulturelle Diversität*, 155–181. Münster: Waxmann.

Barmeyer, C. & Mayrhofer, U. (2008). "The contribution of intercultural management to the success of international mergers and acquisitions: An analysis of the EADS group". In: *International Business Review*, 17:1, 28–38.

Benedict, R. (1934). *Patterns of Culture*. Boston: Houghton-Mifflin.

Bennett, J. M. (1993). "Cultural Marginality: Identity issues in intercultural training". In: Paige, R. M. (Ed.), *Education for the Intercultural* Experience, 109–135. Yarmouth: Intercultural Press Inc.

Bennett, M. J. (1979). "Overcoming the golden rule: Sympathy and empathy". In: Nimmo, D. (Ed.), *Communication Yearbook 3*, 407–422. New Brunswick, NJ: Transaction Book.

Bennett, M. J. (1986). "A developmental approach to training for intercultural sensitivity". In: *International Journal of Intercultural Relations*, 10, 179–186.

Bhagat, R. S. & Steer, R. M. (2009). *Cambridge Handbook of Culture, Organizations, and Work*. Cambridge: Cambridge University Press.

Brannen, M. Y. & Salk, J. (2000). "Partnering across borders: Negotiating organizational culture in a German-Japanese joint venture". In: *Human Relations*, 52:4, 451–487.

Brannen, M. Y. & Thomas, D. C. (2010). "Bicultural Individuals in Organizations: Implications and Opportunity". In: *International Journal of Cross Cultural Management*, 10:1, 5–16.

Brock, D. M. (2005). "Multinational acquisition integration: The role of national culture in creating synergies". In: *International Business Review*, 14, 269–288.

Buchheim, W. (1983). *Beiträge zur Komplementarität*. Berlin: Akademie-Verlag.

Crouch, C. (2010). "Complementarity". In: Morgan, G., Campbell, J., Crouch, C., Pedersen, O. K., & Whitley, R. (Eds), *Comparative Institutional Analysis*, 117–137. Oxford: Oxford University Press.

Crozier, M. & Friedberg, E. (1981). *L'acteur et le système: Les contraintes de l'action collective*. Paris: Le Seuil.

Cui G. & Van den Berg, S. (1991). "Testing the construct validity of intercultural effectiveness". In: *International Journal of Intercultural Relations*, 15, 227–241.

d'Iribarne, P. (2009). "National Cultures and Organizations in Search of a Theory: An Interpretative Approach". In: *International Journal of Cross Cultural Management*, 9:3, 309–332.

Demorgon, J. (1998). *Histoires interculturelles des sociétés*. Paris: Anthropos.

Fitzsimmons, S. R., Lee, Y. T. & Brannen, M. Y. (2013). "Demystifying the myth about marginals: Implications for global leadership". In: *European Journal of International Management*, 7:5, 587–603.

Fitzsimmons, S. R., Miska, C. & Stahl, G. (2011). "Multicultural employees: Global business' untapped resource". In: *Organizational Dynamics*, 40:3, 199–206.

Fuller, B. R. (1975). *Synergetics, Explorations in the Geometry of Thinking*. New York: Macmillan.

Gabriel, Y. & Griffiths, D. S. (2008). "International Learning Groups: Synergies and Dysfunctions". In: *Management Learning*, 39:5, 503–518.

Gannon, M. J. & Newmann, K. L. (2002). *The Blackwell Handbook of Cross-Cultural Management*. Oxford: Blackwell.

Giddens, A. (1984). *Constitution of Society: Outline of the Theory of Structuration*. Cambridge: Polity Press.

Hampden-Turner, C. (1990). *Charting the Corporate Mind*. London: Free Press.

Hampden-Turner, C. (2000). "What we know about cross-cultural management after thirty years". In: Lynch, D. & Pilbeam, A. (Eds), *Heritage and Progress. From the Past to the Future in Intercultural Understanding*, 17–27. Bath: LTS/SIETAR.

Hampden-Turner, C. & Trompenaars, F. (2006). "Cultural intelligence: Is such a capacity credible?". In: *Group & Organization Management*, 31:1, 56–63.

Hansen, C. D. (2000). *A Daoist Theory of Chinese Thought: A Philosophical Interpretation*. Oxford: Oxford University Press.

Harris, P. R. (2004). "European leadership in cultural synergy". In: *European Business Review*, 16:4, 358–380.

Hawes, F. & Kealey, D. J. (1981). "An empirical study of Canadian technical assistance". In: *International Journal of Intercultural Relations*, 5, 239–258.

Heckmann, F. & Schnapper, D. (2003). *The Integration of Immigrants in European Societies: National Differences and Trends of Convergence*. Stuttgart: Lucius et Lucius.

Hofstede, G. (2001). *Culture's Consequences: Comparing Values, Behaviors, Institutions and Organizations Across Nations*. Thousand Oaks, CA: Sage.

Jack, G. & Westwood, R. (2009). *International and Cross-Cultural Management Studies. A Postcolonial Reading*. London: Palgrave Macmillan.

Kelley, C. & Meyers, J. E. (1993). *The Cross-Cultural Adaptability Inventory*. Yarmouth, ME: Intercultural Press.

Kluckhohn, F. R. & Strodtbeck, F. L. (1961). *Variations in Value Orientations*. Westport, CT: Greenwood Press.

Köppel, P. (2007). *Konflikte und Synergien in multikulturellen Teams – Virtuelle und face to face Kooperation*. Wiesbaden: Deutscher Universitätsverlag.

Langer, E. J. (1989). *Mindfulness*. Cambridge, MA: Perseus Books.

Maddux, W., Leung, A. K., Chiu, C. & Galinsky, A. (2009). "Toward a more complete understanding of the link between multicultural experience and creativity". In: *American Psychologist*, 64:2, 156–158.

Mahadevan, J. (2012). "Utilizing identity-based resistance for diversity change – a narrative approach". In: *International Journal of Change Management*, 25:6, 819–834.

Maslow, A. (1954). *Motivation and Personality*. New York: Harper & Row.

Maslow, A. (1964). "Synergy in the society and in the individual". In: *Journal of Individual Psychology*, 20:2, 153–164.

Maslow, A. (1987). *Motivation and Personality*. New York: Harper & Row.

Maslow, A. H. & Honigmann, J. J. (1970). "Synergy: Some notes of Ruth Benedict". In: *American Anthropologist*, 72, 320–333.

Matthewman, J. (2011). *The Rise of the Global Nomad: How to Manage the New Professional in Order to Gain Recovery and Maximize Future Growth*. London: Kogan Page.

Maznevski, M. & DiStefano, J. (2000). "Global leaders are team players: Developing global leaders through membership on global teams". In: *Human Resource Management*, 39, 195–208.

Moore, A. M. & Barker, G. G. (2012). "Confused or multicultural: Third culture individuals' cultural identity". In: *International Journal of Intercultural Relations*, 36, 553–562.

Moran, R. & Harris, P. (1983). *Managing Cultural Synergy*. Houston, TX: Gulf Publishing Co. & München: Rainer Hampp Verlag.

Otte, M. (1990). "Komplementarität". In: Sandkühler, J. (Ed.), *Europäische Enzyklopädie zu Philosophie und Wissenschaften*, Vol. 2, 847–849. Hamburg: Felix Meiner Verlag.

Peterson M. F. & Sondergaard M. (2008). *Foundations of Cross Cultural Management*. Thousand Oaks, CA: Sage.

Pollock, D. C. & Van Reken, R. E. (2001). *Third Culture Kids: The Experience of Growing Up Among Worlds*. Boston: Intercultural Press.

Primecz, H., Romani, L. & Sackmann, S. (2011). *Cross-Cultural Management in Practice. Culture and Negotiated Meanings*. Cheltenham: Edward Elgar.

Sackmann, S. A. & Phillips, M. E. (2004). "Contextual influences on culture research: Shifting assumptions for new workplace realities". In: *International Journal of Cross-Cultural Management*, 4:3, 370–390.

Schirrmacher, T. (2005). "Die Entdeckung der Komplementarität, ihre Übertragung auf die Theologie und ihre Bedeutung für das biblische Denken". In: *Professorenforum-Journal*, 6:3, 3–11.

Sorge, A. (2004). "Cross-national differences in human resources and organizations". In: Harzing, A. W. & van Rysseveld, J. (Eds.), *International Human Resource Management*, 117–140. London: Sage.

Spencer-Oatey, H. & Franklin, P. (2009). *Intercultural Interaction*. London: Palgrave Macmillan.

Stahl, G. K. & Tung, R. L. (2015). "Towards a more balanced treatment of culture in international business studies: The need for positive cross-cultural scholarship." In: *Journal of International Business Studies*, 46:6, 391–414.

Stahl, G. K. & Brannen, M. Y. (2013). "Building cross-cultural leadership competence: An interview with Carlos Ghosn". In: *Academy of Management Learning & Education*, 12:3, 494–502.

Stahl, G. K, Maznevski, M. L., Voigt, A. & Jonsen, K. (2009). "Unravelling the effects of cultural diversity in teams: A meta-analysis of research on multicultural work groups". In: *Journal of International Business Studies*, 41, 690–709.

Stumpf, S. (2005). "Synergie in multikulturellen Arbeitsgruppen". In: Stahl, G., Mayrhofer, W. & Kühlmann, T. (Eds), *Internationales Personalmanagement. Neue Aufgaben, neue Lösungen*, 115–144. München: Rainer Hampp Verlag.

Tjitra, H. W. (2001). *Synergiepotenziale und interkulturelle Probleme: Chancen und Herausforderungen am Beispiel deutsch-indonesischer Arbeitsgruppen*. Wiesbaden: Gabler.

Wiseman, R. L., Hammer, M. R. & Nishida, H. (1989). "Predictors of intercultural communication competence". In: *International Journal of Intercultural Relations*, 13, 349–370.

WorldWork (no date). International Competency Framework. Retrieved on 29 October 2015 from http://www.worldwork.biz/legacy/www/docs3/competencies.html

Yagi, N. & Kleinberg, J. (2011). "Boundary work: An interpretive ethnographic perspective on negotiating and leveraging cross-cultural identity". In: *Journal of International Business Studies*, 42:5, 629–653.

Zeutschel, U. (1999). "Interkulturelle Synergie auf dem Weg: Erkenntnisse aus deutsch/US-amerikanischen Problemlösegruppen". In: *Gruppendynamik*, 30:2, 131–160.

16

Future+: Intercultural Challenges and Success Factors in an International Virtual Project Team

Christoph Barmeyer and Ulrike Haupt

1 INTRODUCTION

Since the 1990s virtual teams, or globally dispersed teams, as they are more transparently known, have become a common organizational form in multinational companies (Davison & Ward 1999). Especially in international project teams, e.g. those concerned with product development, the use of sophisticated information technology makes it possible to integrate a great variety of geographically dispersed but complementary resources and competencies (Maznevski & Chudoba 2000).

Thanks to their structure and composition, projects, as temporary systems, are usually more agile, flexible and goal-focused than teams embedded in a line organization. Bringing people together in one team who do not belong to the same organizational unit and organizational culture can even, in monocultural project teams, lead to different goals and divergent ideas being created. The multicultural composition of a team will make the cooperation more complex but also richer in perspectives, languages, solutions, etc. As a result of the cultural diversity of their team members, international project teams, with their different perspectives, and in particular their specific, complementary competencies, can develop a greater degree of creativity and productivity than purely monocultural teams (Chevrier 2003, 2011; Stahl et al. 2009).

A central concern for such international, virtual project teams is how to steer and manage the overall process of working together and how to motivate their members in a culturally sensitive way by alternating between social *physical proximity* – the team members meeting, interacting and working together in one place – and social *virtual distance* – the team members interacting in virtual space by using information technology – in order to achieve the required goals and milestones of the project (Duarte & Snyder 2001).

Experience shows that as a rule, in team projects, the available creative potential is not leveraged to the full – even when team members have good task and project management competencies and sufficient knowledge of the project's lingua franca, usually English. Only by taking into account the – frequently ignored – cultural level is it possible to trigger complementary and thus synergetic behaviour by the team members and in this way bring about the success of the project.

In this Franco-German case study of product development in the industry sector we illustrate the importance of contextual, cultural and personal factors that can lead to a complementary combination of diverse, geographically dispersed resources.

2 CASE DESCRIPTION

> "Either you successfully complete the Future+ development by the end of next year or the future of our business unit looks very black, as does the future of the French site. The product must be launched in eight months. I know you can do it."

The message contained in the telephone call from the R&D board member could not have been clearer. Sven Breitenbach, the German project leader, has been worried for weeks. The development of one of InterTech's key products, for which he is responsible, is making very slow progress.

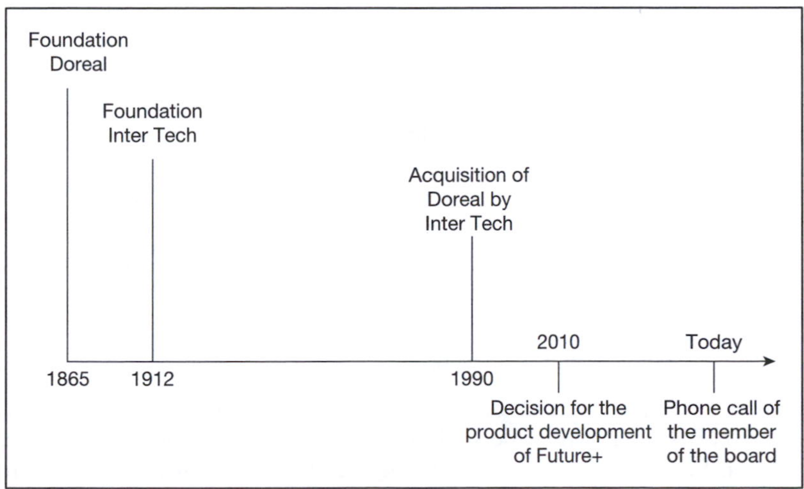

Figure 16.1 Timeline Doreal and InterTech

After many months of virtual cooperation between the German and French colleagues, their work is dogged by complications, setbacks and delays, which are not only costing money but are ruining the working atmosphere. The motivation of the virtual project team is at a low and the mood among the team members very poor. Pressure is increasing and, to make matters worse, the management board has intervened.

2.1 The situation: the Future+ Project

The Future+ Project is located in a German company – one of what are known as the hidden champions – which has foreign subsidiaries responsible for sales and, to a certain extent, also for R&D and production. Many years ago InterTech acquired a similarly medium-sized French company from Brittany, also operating internationally, by the name of Doreal, which had been working as an equal partner with InterTech for many years. Doreal has existed a number of decades longer than InterTech and is extremely well known in France. Some of the top French managers are on the German management board and supervisory board.

InterTech and Doreal complement each other: while the French company has a strong position and is well known in countries in southern Europe such as Italy, Spain and Portugal, and in Latin America, the German company is well represented in German-speaking and Scandinavian countries.

As far as organizational culture is concerned, in the last two years InterTech has worked hard on its corporate values in a process involving horizontally and vertically mixed groups. Its values are openness, professionalism, perfection, the ability to give and receive criticism, continuity and diversity. There hasn't been a similar process at Doreal. The marketing brochures repeatedly use such terms as customer orientation, flexibility and innovation leadership. The workforce has been in place for a long time, staff turnover is low and a good working atmosphere prevails.

The management board decides that engineers from the French site working with engineers from Germany should bring the Future+ innovation project to market within three years.

The Future+ Project has high strategic significance for the company. Through technological innovation the intention is to create a product to lead the market, which should not only increase turnover in the coming years but also open up a new customer target group.

2.2 The challenge: difficult team work

The project is made even more complex by organizational structures and processes partly unknown to the staff, the geographical distance between the two sites in France and Germany and language barriers (low competence in French and German, average proficiency in English). Misunderstandings and problems repeatedly occur in the project team.

What the German team members are thinking and saying...

At a meeting, the members of the German project team talk about their experiences so far of working with the French:

"The French have yet again not replied to our email. They don't seem to be able to work very reliably and effectively. But we are under such time pressure. And we can't continue without this milestone."

"It's so difficult in English. I can't express myself as precisely as I would like to. The English of our French colleagues doesn't seem to be much better than ours."

"I am amazed how vague the French are. All my detailed questions are answered with a single, very general reply. I am really beginning to wonder if they know what they are doing."

"I think they see products differently from the way we do. They believe the product must meet client wishes entirely. And so they replace their products every few years. Where's the continuity?"

"They call it 'leading-edge technology'. But that is absolutely not the way to build a reputation and a brand. Our degree of brand awareness is simply amazing in German-speaking countries and northern Europe."

What the French team members are thinking and saying ...

At the same time the French team members are meeting.

"Really – now they are talking about 'good collaboration'. For us collaboration is nothing we can regard positively. The *collaborateurs* were the French who worked with the Nazis in the Second World War."

"Why don't they just ring up? You can discuss many things so much more clearly and quickly on the phone."

"I have the feeling that the German company is grabbing a lot of power and influence. And now it seems they want to take over our sales operation. But our brand awareness is so high in southern Europe and Latin America. And we have extensive and stable networks in France. That is absolutely invaluable."

"This matrix structure that has been introduced is just causing confusion and chaos. Who is now responsible for making decisions?"

"Their brand is completely unknown here. Even if it is known, the German products are too expensive."

"It would be helpful if we could actually meet. Many of the colleagues are completely unknown to us. How are we supposed to form trusting relationships with them on the internet? It can't work having two sites."

"I find it amazing how specific the German colleagues are. I continually get detailed questions I can't answer. Everything is presented in such detail. What is the point? Do I have to know all that? I wonder where they get the time from ..."

"I just wonder if they see the products in the same way. Recently I asked my German colleague what he actually meant by quality. He answered along the lines of 'Meeting customer requirements with a minimum of errors and a good appearance'."

The two team leaders The team is headed up by a German team leader in Germany and by a French team leader in France. The team leaders are also both engineers. They both went on to higher education in the other's country and they both speak the other's language. They can communicate not only in French and German but also in English. And, what's more, they like the other's country and are familiar with it.

Sven Breitenbach's CV

Dr Sven Breitenbach, Dipl.-Ing., is aged 37 and comes from Hamburg. After spending a year at a school in Hamburg's twin town of Marseille he qualified for university entrance but did an apprenticeship as an electrician. After doing a trip around the world at his own expense, he studied electronic engineering in the German city of Karlsruhe, spending one semester in Paris. As a member of the research staff he did his doctorate on new materials at the renowned technical university in Aachen. At the age of 31 he joined InterTech. As a result of his excellent knowledge of French and France he was chosen to head up the Future+ Project.

Luc Clapier's CV

Luc Clapier was born in Brest, in Britanny. He is 32 years old. Like many French youngsters, he acquired his university entrance qualification at the age of 17, did a two-year preparatory course ("Classe préparatoire") and, thanks to his excellent grades, gained a place at a renowned *Grande Ecole* for engineers in Lyon, the *Ecole Centrale*, where he studied engineering, specializing in materials science. As he had always been interested in Germany and wanted to use the German that he had improved in his preparatory class, he spent a year at Munich University. After starting his career at the age of 24 with Renault Trucks in Lyon, he headed various development projects there before going on to work for Peugeot-Citroën (PSA) in Sochaux. For personal reasons, he subsequently took on a position of responsibility in a medium-sized company in his hometown, which had just been acquired by the German company InterTech.

The team leaders see lots of opportunities As a result of the disconcerting phone call from the management board member, Sven Breitenbach decides to set up a meeting in Paris with his French opposite number, Luc Clapier, to talk about the project and the problems which had arisen.

SB: Do you recall, Luc, how euphoric we were when we started the project a year ago? We were really pleased about this important and fascinating project. The budget and the support of the management board were really good.

LC: And now trouble is on the way. We haven't achieved important milestones and we are slipping further and further behind.

SB: How could all this happen?

LC: Well, my French colleagues and also our colleagues in the team are not very motivated. They are afraid …

SB: What do you mean?

LC: Perhaps you don't notice it at the big site in Germany but we are sensing that functions such as sales and marketing are slowly moving away from France to you. We are not only losing influence but perhaps we are also going to lose jobs.

SB: But you know, too, that we have to centralize certain functions. Otherwise there is so much senseless duplication of work. And it all costs so much. After all, we are a single company.

LC: Rationally I can understand all that. But emotionally it is a different matter. Rumour has it that our project is likely to be one of the last in which R&D are carried out in the French site.

SB: But that is just rumour. You French are very innovative and the whole group profits from that. And that is another reason why our Franco-German product development will be a success.

LC: And what about the announcement that the French company's name is to be retained only for a number of products? That will mean that the name of our well-known and long-established company just becomes a brand.

SB: Luc, you know that I can't solve these problems. These are strategic decisions made by the board of management. And there are French representatives on the board, too …

LC: … who have to defend themselves against a majority of German-speaking colleagues. No, structures and processes are not as transparent as we would wish.

SB: We also don't understand how decisions are made in France. But let's talk about our project. That at least is something we can influence.

LC: Let's speak about our team. That is our most valuable asset. I think they find the cooperation difficult. They all have little international experience. They also don't speak foreign languages except for English.

SB: Yes. It is unusual that you and I can communicate in three languages.

LC: We had the good fortune to be able to study in each other's country and to do an internship there. We are a little familiar with the culture and also appreciate it.

SB: We have a real advantage.

LC: Our team colleagues know so little about the other culture. I think that is why so many misunderstandings occur.

SB: But fortunately we can rely on the competencies of our colleagues. Time and time again I notice how good your people and mine are at their job. They are highly specialized engineers and techies.

LC: We have a lot in common there. Technical understanding, the terminology, the approaches. But I notice again and again how detailed and precise you Germans are. You have to admit you are more specialized than we are. We like to see the big picture.

SB: And that is a real strength you have. We Germans get lost in the details and can't see the wood for the trees.

LC: Instead you think of everything that could possibly happen. That is a strength of our bicultural team. If only we could manage to combine these differences.

SB: That is what I see as our main task. We have to guide, coordinate …

LC: … and combine the strengths of our team members.

SB: What exactly are our strengths?

LC: Well, if we take a look at processes, I think you have formalized and reliable processes and procedures. You have long-term planning and detailed cost calculation and accounting.

SB: Thank you for your compliments! When I look at your people, I'm fascinated by how quickly your new product developments move ahead and how flexible your processes are. You are much quicker than we are.

LC: Because we don't take everything into account. You have tried and tested technology. A high degree of precision. And enormous durability and solidity come from the high-quality material you are able to use.

SB: Which costs us a great deal of money. You somehow manage to have low development and production costs.

LC: That is where our ability to create something new from what already exists comes in. Understanding the big picture is useful.

SB: Also, I think that you are very good at innovation. I just need to think of the energy-efficient technologies you have developed. Your products are also very light and compact.

LC: On the other hand, you have the specific know-how for larger and high-end machines with a high mark-up.

3 BACKGROUND KNOWLEDGE

3.1 The authors' point of reference

The authors, Christoph Barmeyer and Ulrike Haupt, are specialists in intercultural management, especially Franco-German cooperation. They have a systemic–integrative mindset, which takes account of the importance of context (e.g. corporate biography, structures, processes etc.) and relationships, and applies an in-depth comparative–intercultural approach, which incorporates culture-specific elements. They believe that cultural differences are not a problem, but a resource that can be used in complementary and synergetic ways by detecting, accepting and combining strengths. More information about their approaches (and some articles) can be found on their websites: www.uni-passau.de/barmeyer, www.culturebridge.de.

3.2 Concepts, models, frameworks

The overall view of the project: the three-factor model Intercultural team and project work, which typically takes place in interpersonal interactions, is influenced by various factors. Thus these situations cannot be analysed and explained in exclusively cultural terms. The analysis of the situation should rather be extended to include influencing factors such as the persons involved and the context (Barmeyer & Haupt 2007; Hammerschmidt 2010:227).

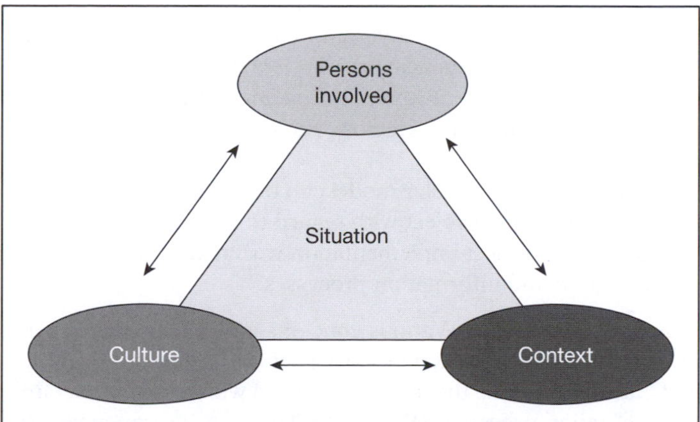

Figure 16.2 The three-factor model

Components of the three-factor model

Table 16.1 Components of the three-factor model

Influencing factors	Components
Context Difficult to shape or influence	• Place • Socioeconomic environment (market, politics, competition) • Background, history, organizational structure • Organizational processes • Power relationships • Nature of project
Culture Can be shaped and influenced to some extent	• Expectations and ideas • Perceptions and stereotypes • Meanings and sense (symbols) • Communication and language • Practices and artifacts • Values and norms • Organizational culture • Professional culture
People Can be influenced to some extent	• Personality • Interests • Experience • Education • Qualities, attitudes • Position and function • Competencies (task-related, intercultural, linguistic, management)

This three-factor model makes possible an analysis of the situation on a meta-level from three different perspectives and can be used to clarify the significance of the three factors influencing the project. Using the model thus makes it easier to discover whether in intercultural interactions "culture" plays an influential role or whether other factors such as those related to context or person do so.

For practitioners this triangular model can be used as an orientation instrument at the beginning of a project with regard to the selection of project team members and during project implementation with regard to project operations and communication and information processes.

Intercultural complementarity Various concepts and forms of constructive and productive intercultural interaction exist such as interculture, third culture, negotiated culture, dilemma theory or synergy, in which the interactants engage in various adaptation processes (Hampden-Turner & Trompenaars 2000).

Another similar concept is that of intercultural complementarity. This concept describes specific, apparently contradictory but in fact complementary properties, of people or groups. These properties may be characteristics and features, ways of thinking and behaving which represent qualities and are motivated by values and oriented towards norms. Regarded interculturally – when people and groups come from different social systems and interact – these properties may represent relative differences. An approach based on intercultural complementarity now tries to combine them and to allow them to interact so that they complement each other.

Various states and actions help to achieve intercultural complementarity:

- The basis is formed by an open, neutral and, in that sense, value-free fundamental attitude and ability to recognize ethno-relatively, and also value, the particular characteristics and properties of other cultural groups such that they take on the form of qualities and strengths. Thus there are no polarities such as "either/or" or "right/wrong" but a continuum of "both/and".
- The properties are consciously regarded as qualities and strengths.
- The properties are applied and combined in accordance with the particular situation.

The development model depicted in Figure 16.3 makes clear how particular goals may be achieved in a particular process, for example in a project team or an organization. The goal is the achievement of performance and productivity. This goal can be achieved by applying various approaches, which as a rule are marked by certain culturally influenced values and generally take the form of differences. On the one hand, some people and groups achieve the goal through "planning and organization"; on the other, some people achieve the goal through "improvization and flexibility".

Each approach can lead to the goal; each has strengths and weaknesses. If a strength is applied intensively, this may mean it becomes a weakness. Large amounts of improvization and flexibility may lead – not merely subjectively but quite objectively – to disorderly and heterogeneous processes, which in turn may be susceptible to error and lead at worst to chaos. Large amounts of planning and organization, on the other hand, may lead to rigidity and bureaucracy and allow no room for sensible adjustment.

Intercultural complementarity focuses on strengths and is implemented by combining differences, which complement each other. In this example, intercultural complementarity means that in a circular and often temporary process it is possible to combine the respective strengths of those involved, for example when in particular phases of a project, planning has a great significance, whereas in others improvization is important. So, at the beginning of a project a high degree of improvization can generate many and unexpected ideas; in another phase planning may be important to give structure and order. Particularly important is the intercultural space between the two properties, which represents the combination of these properties.

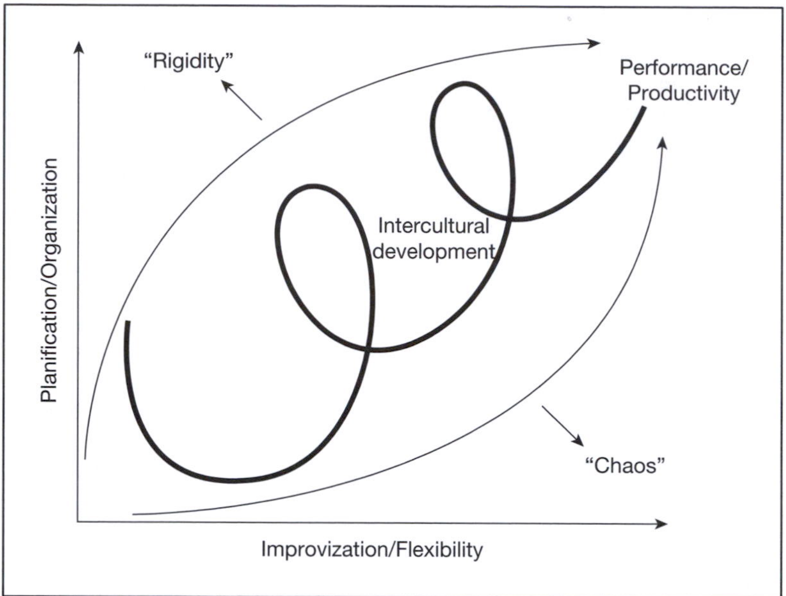

Figure 16.3 Goal achievement through intercultural complementarity

Intercultural interaction is here seen as a reciprocal – if possible, equitable – communication and cooperation process of negotiation in dialogue form in which adaptation, learning and development processes take place which contribute to goal achievement.

3.3 Recommended reading

Chevrier, S. (2003). "Cross-cultural management in multinational project groups". In: *Journal of World Business,* 38, 1–9.
This article contributes to a better understanding of the dynamics of international project groups by describing the strategies project leaders have implemented to cope with cultural diversity. Three kinds of cross-cultural practices emerged from the comparative study of European project groups: (1) to draw upon individual tolerance and self-control, (2) to enter into a trial-and-error process coupled with relationship development and (3) to capitalize on transnational corporate or professional cultures. The article points to the necessarily culture-specific approaches of intercultural management in transnational project groups.

Hampden-Turner, C. & Trompenaars, F. (2000). *Building Cross-Cultural Competence.* West Sussex: Wiley.
A book on the reconciliation of dilemmas and the creation of intercultural complementarity and synergy. The central idea is that other cultures are not randomly different from one another but inversions of one another's values, reversals of the order and sequence of looking and learning. The reconciliation

of dilemmas – which brings together value or other differences – is illustrated with many practical cases.

Maznevski, M. L. & Chudoba, K. M. (2000). "Bridging space over time: Global virtual team dynamics and effectiveness". In: *Organization Science,* 11, 473–492.
This article built a grounded theory of global virtual team processes and performance over time (21 months). First, it proposes that effective global virtual team interaction comprises a series of communication incidents, each configured by aspects of the team's structural and process elements. Effective outcomes are associated with a fit among an interaction incident's form, decision process, and complexity. Second, effective global virtual teams sequence these incidents to generate a deep rhythm of regular face-to-face incidents interspersed with less intensive, shorter incidents using various media.

Stahl, G. K., Maznevski, M. L., Voigt, A. & Jonsen, K. (2009). "Unraveling the effects of cultural diversity in teams: A meta-analysis of research on multicultural work groups". In: *Journal of International Business Studies,* 41, 690–709.
The article examines – on the basis of increased divergence and decreased convergence – whether the level (surface level vs. deep level) and type (cross-national vs. intra-national) of cultural diversity affect team processes differently. It hypothesizes that task complexity and structural aspects of the team, such as team size, team tenure and team dispersion, moderate the effects of cultural diversity on teams. The hypothesis is tested with a meta-analysis of empirical studies of processes and performance in 10,632 teams. Results suggest that cultural diversity leads to process losses through task conflict and decreased social integration, but to process gains through increased creativity and satisfaction. The effects are almost identical for both levels and types of cultural diversity.

4 QUESTIONS ON THE CASE

1. Assess what are the main factors influencing the project and assign them to the three-factor model. What are the main problems and intercultural challenges?

Influencing factors	Challenges
Context	
Culture	
People	

2. Assess the current success factors in the project and other possible future success factors, using your own ideas and the recommended reading. Assign them to the table. If you have read the recommended article by Maznewski and Chudoba (2000), consider the "intercultural heartbeat". What further measures can be taken to ensure the success of the project? What solutions do you suggest?

Influencing factors	Existing and potential future success factors
Context	
Culture	
People	

3. To what extent are the differences which exist also opportunities from which synergies could result? List the strengths (for example of the project members, products and processes). How could these be connected to produce complementarity?

French strengths/advantages E.g. marked customer orientation: product is adapted to customer's needs.	**German strengths/advantages** E.g. marked product orientation: product is recommended to the customer.
Looking inwards *Project members:*	**Looking inwards** *Project members:*
Product:	*Product:*
Process:	*Process:*
Looking outwards: market *Product:*	**Looking outwards: market** *Product:*
Process:	*Process:*

5 REFERENCES

Barmeyer, C. & Haupt, U. (2007). "Der Brückenschlag. Zielorientierte Situationsanalyse aus drei Perspektiven". In: Rauen, Christopher (Ed.), *Coaching Tools 2*, 133–139. Bonn: ManagerSeminare.

Chevrier, S. (2003). "Cross-cultural management in multinational project groups". In: *Journal of World Business*, 38, 1–9.

Chevrier, S. (2011). "Exploring the cultural context of Franco-Vietnamese development projects: Using an interpretative approach to improve the cooperation process". In: Primecz, H. Romani, L. & Sackmann, S. (Eds), *Cross-Cultural Management in Practice: Culture and Negotiated Meanings*, 41–52. Cheltenham: Edward Elgar Publishing.

Davison, S. C. & Ward, K. (1999). *Leading International Teams*. London: McGraw Hill.

Duarte, D. & Snyder, N. (2001). *Mastering Virtual Teams*. San Francisco: Jossey-Bass.

Hammerschmidt, A. (2010). "Sic! Ein Diagnoseinstrument zur Orientierung in der transkulturellen Unübersichtlichkeit". In: Barmeyer, C. I. & Bolten, J. (Eds), *Interkulturelle Personal- und Organisationsentwicklung*, 217–232. Sternenfels/Berlin: Wissenschaft & Praxis.

Hampden-Turner, C. & Trompenaars, F. (2000). *Building Cross-Cultural Competence*. West Sussex: Wiley.

Maznevski, M. L. & Chudoba, K. M. (2000). "Bridging space over time: Global virtual team dynamics and effectiveness". In: *Organization Science*, 11, 473–492.

Stahl, G. K., Maznevski, M. L., Voigt, A. & Jonsen, K. (2009): "Unraveling the effects of cultural diversity in teams: A meta-analysis of research on multicultural work groups". In: *Journal of International Business Studies*, 41, 690–709.

17

A Tough Day for a French Expatriate in Vietnam: The Management of a Large International Infrastructure Project

Sylvie Chevrier

1 INTRODUCTION

Large infrastructure projects, such as the construction of power plants, motorways, stadiums, etc. are generally conducted by highly complex organizations involving many partners. A contracting authority commissions a company with the task of project management. This company, in turn, is assisted by engineering consultants and technical service providers.

In emerging countries, such organizations are often international and include local authorities, international and domestic lenders to fund the project, foreign and national technical partners and local subcontractors.

Managing these projects requires the ability to handle their inherent financial, technical and organizational complexity. Managers have to deal with challenging technical issues while controlling costs and deadlines for delivery. In large international projects the challenges are further increased by intercultural issues pervading the work relations between partners (Shore & Cross 2005; Winch et al. 2000).

However, these intercultural issues are rarely dealt with thoroughly. Partners under high pressure often disregard them in favour of the core, more obvious problems they are dealing with. In contrast, some managers use negative stereotypes to explain major difficulties resulting from inappropriate behaviour by other nationals. The way in which culture's mental representations and its thus "invisible" features impact work is not easy to unravel for managers with their head down in daily action.

The point of this case is to reveal the importance of cultures in international projects, neither exaggerating nor denying the way they influence interactions at work. Among the many variables impacting the dynamics of working relationships – public/private organizations, foreign/domestic actors, customer/provider roles, political/technical issues – differences in cultures also play a role in both impeding and enhancing the dynamics of the project.

This case will show how cultural differences affect the management of a large project in Vietnam in the transportation industry. This analysis underlines the complementarity of actors from both the French and Vietnamese cultures and provides recommendations to improve the management of the local Vietnamese team by French expatriates.

2 CASE DESCRIPTION

2.1 The situation: company background

The severe traffic congestion of Hanoï led the authorities to launch new public transportation projects. A few months ago, a French company, Ingenirik, won a competitive bidding process for the first phase of this strategic project for Hanoï City. This company has internationally acknowledged expertise in developing sustainable mass public transport. It has received many quality marks and professional distinctions. The company prides itself on proposing innovative, tailored and appropriate solutions to its customers.

For the first phase, Ingenirik is in charge of carrying out all design studies for the project, preparing tender documents including assisting with reviewing bids, and awarding contracts. Ingenirik also assists the public client with financial management of the project and will be responsible for supervising work during the construction and installation phase.

To prepare the bid, Ingenirik set up a project office in Hanoï. When it was awarded the contract, the project office tripled in size with the arrival of nine additional French expatriates and the massive recruitment of local people with various backgrounds: civil engineers, management graduates, environment specialists, etc. These young professionals had received good education and training in their field in Vietnam and most of them had some brief professional experience. Few of them had already worked for a foreign company. The local office had difficulties finding highly qualified transportation specialists, so most of the transportation system design team is composed of expatriates.

However, the company recruited Le Thi Thai, an experienced engineer from Vietnam who used to work for a governmental transportation agency. She has over 15 years of experience and a good network of knowledgeable and powerful people in the public transportation authorities. Bruno, the French project director, has appointed Le Thi Thai as his local counterpart to manage the project. The team includes about 30 people, half of them French, half of them Vietnamese.

The team is in charge of all aspects of the project: coordination with the customer and the authorities, managing the design phase, drawing up and revising technical documents as well as translations.

Bruno worked at Ingenirik head office to prepare the project and travelled several times to Hanoï. After Ingenirik won the competition for the engineering of the project, Bruno was excited to move to Hanoï. He feels quite enthusiastic about the project. This is his second experience as an expatriate project director. He was chosen after the success of his first project in Latin America. He previously worked as an engineer and a project assistant and has developed good technical expertise in transportation systems, which has fostered his steep career path.

2.2 The challenge: the meeting with the national authorities

Today, Bruno thinks, will be an important day because of a meeting with the authorities. Engineers in coordination with the local authorities have worked hard to define the most appropriate track layout for the transportation line. The experience of the French expatriates in previous projects was very useful to anticipate the pitfalls inherent in this type of project. Thanks to Thai's good relations with the city authorities and many meetings, they have come to an agreement on the route, which has to be validated by the Ministry of Transportation. Bruno has repeatedly asked the Ministry for an appointment for this validation but has not managed to set one up, though his contact seemed to understand how strategic the project was for the city. After three weeks of vain attempts to get an appointment Thai stepped in and eventually set up this meeting for Bruno and herself. They prepared carefully to make the case for the project. All details had been checked with the team and the presentation of the project was ready.

At 9 a.m. sharp Bruno and Thai enter the large office of the Minister's most senior official, a small man in his 60s. He is assisted by five other officials who very briefly introduce themselves. Bruno holds the presentation in English and an interpreter translates for the Vietnamese officials. From time to time Le Thi Thai adds a few details in Vietnamese but Bruno thinks she is unexpectedly quiet during this meeting. The senior official hosting the meeting frowns at the layout proposal. He insists that Hanoï has swampy land and that further investigations have to be undertaken to ensure the right route has been selected. Bruno repeats again and again that engineers have taken the wet underground into account when they determined the best route layout. Their first concerns were traffic safety and technical feasibility but they also tried to limit the compulsory purchase of property because of impacts on the environment and on the public good. He insists that the local authorities are aware of these technical constraints and have approved the layout. The senior official does not seem to be convinced and asks for more investigations. Bruno is about to reply when Thai says that she perfectly understands the reluctance of the Minister's top aide and that additional studies have to be made; they will ask for a new appointment after this new investigation has been conducted.

Bruno is very angry and feels completely betrayed by Thai: they have done so much work together and until yesterday she definitely supported the decisions! Furthermore, useless additional studies will delay the project and will unavoidably increase costs.

Back to the office Back in the car, Bruno cannot keep calm. He yells at Thai: "Why did you accept new investigations? You know perfectly well that none of his arguments was sensible! We know about the wet underground and our solution takes that into account. You did not support me. You could have translated what I said into Vietnamese to be sure that they properly understood but you did not; even worse, you said you agreed with him!" Thai patiently waits for a pause in Bruno's rant and insists that she still fully agrees with Bruno on technical issues. As Bruno is completely puzzled, she adds that she could not express her true opinion. She could not contradict the senior official, especially in front of the other officials because of his social status. Bruno has trouble in accepting what seems to him so hypocritical and cowardly. He asks: "What are we going to do now?" Thai says that she guesses that the senior official was not satisfied with the solution: the swamp issue was a pretext but probably not the real problem. She has to use her network and ask someone she knows at the Ministry to find out informally what is making him so upset. If they understand that, they will be better able to convince him next time.

While he is driving back in the dense traffic, Bruno realizes yet again that their project will fulfil a genuine need and he is determined to work hard for its success. Since he arrived a few months ago, the project has progressed quite well. The local engineers are eager to learn from their French counterparts and he is impressed by the speed with which the tasks are performed by the Vietnamese team. He has learnt from his Latin American experience to give detailed instructions to get the work done on time and to cultivate close relationships and a friendly atmosphere in his dealings with his staff and colleagues. Every Monday he organizes a staff meeting to review the progress of projects. Much to his regret, Le Thi Thai and he are the only ones to contribute freely to the discussions. The young engineers do not speak unless they are invited to do so and they never mention their problems. Despite these regular meetings, for instance, Bruno learnt lately about one important technical problem the Vietnamese engineers had been struggling with for several weeks. Bruno was only informed when another French expatriate, Francis, discovered it. To get to know the young engineers better and to follow their progress, Bruno decided to set up one-to-one interviews with his team. During the most recent Monday meeting he announced the first round of interviews for next week and now he has to prepare for these interviews.

The resignation Bruno obtained a copy of the formal guidelines for individual interviews from the Ingenirik head office in Paris, and he is looking at them when Le Thi Thai enters his room. She looks uncomfortable and Bruno thinks it may be due to their previous meeting. Thai talks about the programme for the afternoon and incidentally tells him that Nguyen Minh Anh has just resigned. Bruno is astounded to hear about this resignation. Anh is a young civil engineer they recruited a few months ago and with whom they were very satisfied. He was under pressure like the rest of the team because of short deadlines but the recent main technical obstacle was solved thanks to the help of Francis and the project was again progressing quickly. Nguyen Minh Anh had shown no sign of dissatisfaction that might have warned Bruno. Thai says she does not know the reasons why Anh resigned. As the conversation moves on, Thai asks Bruno about the one-to-one interviews and suggests taking more time to think about the best way to conduct them before starting the procedure. Bruno is getting used to Thai's indirect messages. He understands that she is asking him not to go ahead with the interviews. Bruno thought it was a good initiative. Nobody spoke out against them when he announced them. He thought they could help to show recognition of the work that is done by the young recruits and increase their professionalism. Such interviews could help to anticipate problems and plan training sessions that the young engineers seem to be very fond of. Bruno is quite confused.

The ultimate disappointment Bruno, followed by Thai, is going out of his room to meet the team and learn more about Anh's resignation when he hears a lively discussion between two young employees. The Vietnamese engineer is explaining to Marc, his French colleague, that the supplier who provided a quote is no longer committed to the previous prices since raw material prices have increased. Marc wonders how he is supposed to make forecasts in a country where commitments are so unreliable! Marc exclaims: "The supplier increases prices by 15% within three weeks! They don't know how to calculate costs!" Responsible for the commercial side, Marc is worried about his ability to handle such uncertainties. Bruno calms Marc down. Thai says she will contact the supplier and try to negotiate reduced prices.

Bruno, quite upset after this tough day, says to himself: "This dual project management is really valuable! Thai and I couldn't handle things so well without our profiles complementing each other in this way."

3 BACKGROUND KNOWLEDGE

3.1 The author's point of reference

The author, Sylvie Chevrier, has been conducting research on cross-cultural work teams for over 20 years in collaboration with the "Gestion & Société" (Management and Society) team founded by Philippe d'Iribarne. The purpose of this research group is to understand how cultural contexts shape the dynamics of organizations and how cross-cultural issues should be taken into account when taking managerial action in a globalized world. Drawing upon the work of d'Iribarne (1989, 2012), the research team considers culture as a shared framework of meaning associated with a particular vision of the proper way of living together. In cross-cultural situations, the point is to find agreements on practices which still make – different – sense to the actors and to value differences for the complementarity of the partners' actions.

This case study draws upon several surveys and action research carried out in Vietnam by the "Gestion & Société" team (Chevrier 2011; Segal 2011).

3.2 Concepts, models, frameworks

The theoretical background first introduces the interpretative definition of culture that will be used in this case study. It also provides theoretical references concerning different views of ethics, the transfer of management practices across cultures and the building of intercultural synergies.

The interpretative approach to culture The dominant approach to cultures is based on the average of values in a society captured through dimensions (for example, Hofstede 1980/2001). In this case, we invite the reader to use an interpretative approach which focuses on understanding meaning from an insider's point of view. As Primecz et al. (2011) state, cultural dimensions may be used for comparisons but are less useful for the study of interactions and the building of synergies.

However, the interpretative approach does not assert that people from a given culture would all give the same meanings to the same things. Obviously in modern societies opinions vary dramatically not only between social groups but also between individuals. Rather, cultures are characterized by a shared framework of meaning: "a certain vision of what constitutes a proper way of living together" (d'Iribarne 2012:108). This frame of meaning relates to views of authority, freedom, dignity, duty and negotiating conflicting points of view:

> It is by referring to this vision that actors can give meaning to what they experience. Each society's ideal vision of harmonious co-existence is incessantly present in the background when people talk about their experiences, whether they are positive or negative. [...] this is not to say that actors are conscious of this vision or that they are able to explain it in clear terms. It remains in some way implicitly self-evident. It is up to the researcher to make out its contours. (d'Iribarne 2012:108)

For d'Iribarne (2009) cultural worldviews are rooted in the opposition between a fundamental concern shared by the members of a society and a means of enabling them to avoid this anxiety. The presence of a fundamental concern does not prevent other sources of anxiety but these do not necessarily affect the functioning of the society so deeply.

For instance, in French society, the fundamental concern is the fear of accommodating, or giving in to, a powerful person out of fear or self-interest. Acting this way evokes servility and loss of dignity. Quite a lot of French vocabulary is associated with this most feared experience (*plier, céder, se soumettre, s'abaisser, ramper, se compromettre,* etc.). In contrast, the courage to resist, to face and stand up to more powerful actors is much more desirable. Even if one is defeated, resistance appears heroic. Many French myths from Vercingetorix to Jean Moulin glorify such resistance.

In France, the fundamental concern can be avoided if an individual is treated with the appropriate consideration due to his/her social position. In the world of work, social rank is determined by one's profession (*métier*). A profession is, partly implicitly, associated with rights and duties that are to be respected (d'Iribarne 2012). Interacting in conformity with these social obligations allows professionals to maintain their dignity.

Ethics of loyalty, ethics of purity Among the various aspects of proper ways of living together constituting a culture, ethics regulating relationships with others play an important role. D'Iribarne & Henry (2007) distinguish between two ideal types of ethics.

The ethics of purity refer to the ideal good man. They consider that the good man should respect the requirements of a transcendent ideal. This means that the right behaviour in relations with others does not depend upon the kind of relationships we have with others: "duty binds us to others irrespective of the relationship we have with them, to man in general, to strangers, to enemies even" (d'Iribarne & Henry 2007:179). The transcendent ideal or authority might vary according to cultures: God, rules, reason. However its prescription applies to all circumstances. A sense of duty related to these general and abstract principles pervades people and should guide their behaviour. This does not mean that in a culture dominated by the ethics of purity, everyone acts ethically and never transgresses the principles. It means that the principles constitute a strong criterion to judge the legitimacy of actions. For instance, if telling the truth is a guiding principle, people may tell lies but feel guilty about it or consider they have good reasons to tell such a lie that excuse their violation of the rule.

The ethics of loyalty, on the other hand, refer to specific people. "The prime concern is loyalty to the groups one belongs to, be it a family, clan, brotherhood or network of interests" (d'Iribarne & Henry 2007:179). The duty towards others depends on the kind of relationship we have with them. Demonstrations of extreme commitment should be given to members of the group (e.g. giving help, time, possessions) while not much is due to strangers. "If an individual neglects his duty, the risk is not that he will feel unworthy in the presence of a transcendent authority, but that he will suffer the vengeance of the group he has betrayed. This group will not fail to use means of control and retaliation" (d'Iribarne & Henry 2007:179). Here again, it does not mean that everyone is loyal and never betrays their relatives or group. It means that by doing this, people are exposed to social exclusion and losing face rather than feeling guilty. In a similar way, Fons Trompenaars (1993) contrasts universalist and particularist ethics. In Northern Europe, ethics mostly refer to the respect of principle while in Asian countries the ethics of loyalty is dominant.

Transfer of management practices across cultures Management practices are developed in a given cultural and organizational context to fulfil needs or improve existing methods. They are not merely technical devices but are embedded in the social context where they originated. For instance, a reporting system cannot just be seen as an objective universal tool. It conveys implicit representations of who should report to whom, on what issues, to what extent and how often. Behind such a tool is a conception of control and authority.

When a management practice is transferred from one country to another, it brings with it the invisible underlying cultural assumptions of its creators. In some cases, the practice is favourably reinterpreted in the receiving country. Cultural resources allow employees to give positive meaning to this practice. It may even be implemented with greater success than in the country of origin (d'Iribarne & Henry 2007). In other cases, the reinterpretation process does not lead to an acceptable practice but, for example, to the bending of rules, to ostensible adoption without effective implementation or even to the rejection of the unwelcome tool (Barmeyer & Davoine 2011; Dalton & Druker 2012).

Cultural analysis focuses on unveiling hidden cultural assumptions underlying management practices and revealing the cultural re-interpretations of the new users. Understanding these meanings enables us to account for the behaviours of employees facing the new practices.

Intercultural synergy Differences in cultures may hinder cooperation because of misunderstandings but it may also enrich the shared work. Synergies may stem from two processes: building common ground and valuing specific strengths separately. Building common ground sometimes happens by chance without a clear awareness of the decisive elements that made it work (d'Iribarne & Henry 2007). But most often, leaving things to chance or intuition results in more irritation than synergy. A more systematic process may improve the results and, most importantly, may help actors understand in which circumstances they may replicate innovative solutions they have come up with (Chevrier 2011).

The first step consists in understanding others' sense-making system by evidencing cultural interpretations of problematic work issues. This cultural knowledge enables partners to give meaning to what seemed at best incomprehensible and at worst, unacceptable (Chevrier et al. 2013). It helps people to refrain from negative judgements and to move towards mutual understanding.

The second step is to turn this cognitive shift into appropriate action. When they work together, partners have to define common procedures, rules and ways of managing a meeting, making decisions, monitoring work, solving conflicts, etc. Once they have understood as a result of taking step one what people are really committed to and what is more negotiable, they may develop shared practices. This does not mean that partners give up their original cultural frames of meaning. The point is to identify practices that take on a positive meaning in both cultural worldviews, even if these meanings remain different. In other words, people may change their ways of doing things as long as they are legitimate in their prevalent cultural world (Chevrier 2011). Depending on cultural differences, common ground may be more or less difficult to find. Adopting the other person's way of doing things, making compromises or inventing ad hoc new management practices are the main options.

Working together may also leave space for different practices. For instance, the management styles of two managers may not be the same and both may be effective. The split of responsibilities may allow people to value their specificities in their scope of action. In this case, synergy does not derive from common ground but from the co-existence of complementary skills to perform different tasks. Cultural differences are then valued as distinctive abilities in a work team composed of specialists from various disciplines.

3.3 Recommended reading

Barmeyer, C. & Davoine, E. (2011). "The intercultural challenges in the transfer of code of conduct from the US to Europe". In: Primecz, H. Romani, L. & Sackmann, S. (Eds), *Cross-Cultural Management in Practice: Culture and Negotiated Meanings*, 53–63. Cheltenham: Edward Elgar Publishing.
This chapter studies the implementation of a code of conduct in two European subsidiaries of a US-based multinational company. It shows the reasons for resistance towards this practice which originated in the USA. This case illustrates the challenges of transferring management tools to foreign units.

Chevrier, S. (2011). "Exploring the cultural context of Franco-Vietnamese development projects: Using an interpretative approach to improve the cooperation process". In: Primecz, H. Romani, L. & Sackmann, S. (Eds), *Cross-Cultural Management in Practice: Culture and Negotiated Meanings*, 41–63. Cheltenham: Edward Elgar Publishing.
This chapter deals with collaboration between French and Vietnamese partners in development projects. The chapter reveals the mutual perceptions of partners and shows the different views of individual autonomy, empowerment and work ethics that explain them. It also gives insights which can help to encourage smoother cooperation and build on this cultural diversity.

Dalton, K. & Druker, J. (2012). "Transferring HR concepts and practices within multinational corporations in Romania: The management experience". In: *European Management Journal*, 30:6, 588–602.
The article examines the transfer of human resource management (HRM) concepts and practices within a sample of multinational enterprises in Romania. It looks at the relative importance of "country of origin" and "host country" influences in shaping the cross-cultural transfer of HRM. The legacy of history and national culture, especially the legacy of communism, are highlighted.

d'Iribarne, P. (2009). "National cultures and organizations in search of a theory: An interpretative approach". In: *International Journal of Cross-Cultural Management*, 9, 309–321.
This article defines national culture by applying an interpretative approach. It presents a theory of cultures, each built upon a core concern which is at the heart of social life. This basic concern can be related to major concepts or frames of reference which shape people's interpretations.

d'Iribarne, P. (2012). ***Managing Corporate Values in Diverse National Cultures. The Challenge of Differences.*** **London: Routledge.**

This book studies how Western companies manage their corporate values across countries. While people's expectations might be similar, companies should adjust the diffusion of their corporate values if they are to meet them. If some corporate values largely make sense, others appear to be culturally specific and should be adjusted to specific contexts.

d'Iribarne, P. (2014). ***Theorising National Cultures, AFD.***

www.afd.fr/webdav/site/afd/shared/PUBLICATIONS/RECHERCHE/Scientifiques/Co-editions/Theorising_National_Cultures.pdf

This book contributes to the debate over the notion of culture and provides a definition of national culture based upon a series of field research work conducted in both countries in the North (France, USA, Germany, etc.) and South (Mexico, Morocco, India, China, Cameroon, etc.). It highlights the way in which the social life of each people is haunted by its own specific core concern.

Primecz, H., Sackmann, S., & Romani, L. (Eds) (2011). ***Cross-Cultural Management in Practice. Culture and Negotiated Meanings.*** **Cheltenham: Edward Elgar.**

The first chapter of this book elaborates on the advantage of using an interpretive approach to understanding actors' perspectives in cross-cultural interactions. The chapters that follow provide examples of cross-cultural interactions across many different countries, analysed from an interpretive perspective.

Shore, B. & Cross, B .J. (2005). "Exploring the role of national culture in the management of large-scale international science projects". In: ***International Journal of Project Management*****, 23:1, 55–64.**

Using evidence from two case studies, this paper explores the role of national culture in the management of large-scale science projects. It raises questions about the relevance of this topic and proposes a method for studying the role of culture in the management process. Even if this paper relies on the dominant approach to cultures (Hofstede's cultural dimensions) that we do not use in this case, it shows that taking account of cultural issues in international projects is quite relevant.

Segal, J. (2011, 4 November). ***Le management international au Vietnam. L'apprentissage des méthodes internationales de management dans le contexte socioculturel vietnamien.*** **Conference, Hanoï.**

This paper presents a study of the transfer of management practices in several Vietnamese companies including management by objectives and key performance indicators. It shows how practices are reinterpreted within the local cultural framework and how local personnel use them or have trouble adapting to them.

Trompenaars, F. (1993). ***Riding the Wave of Culture. Understanding Cultural Diversity in Business.*** **London: Nicholas Brealey Publishing.**

This classic book on national and organizational cultures presents several variables differentiating national cultures – including universalist and particularist cultures – and a taxonomy of five organizational cultures. It eventually draws links between organizational and national cultures.

Winch, G. M., Clifton, N. & Millar, C. (2000). "Organization and management in an Anglo-French consortium: The case of Transmanche-Link". In: *Journal of Management Studies*, 37:5, 663–685.
This paper presents the results of a comparative organizational assessment of the behaviour and organization of the British and French managers who constructed the Channel Tunnel. Despite the common adhocratic organization, the British and French respondents differentiate on five dimensions: fonceur/procedural; competitive/collegial; involved/distanced; individualistic/supportive; and stress. The authors propose a preliminary explanation of the results in terms of a configurational analysis of the differences between the British and French managers.

4 QUESTIONS ON THE CASE

1. What cultural framework may help to understand the behaviour of Le Thi Thai during the meeting with the governmental authorities?
2. What hypothesis can be formulated to explain the unexpected resignation of Nguyen Minh Anh just before his interview with Bruno?
3. To what extent are Bruno and Thai complementary? What are their respective roles and strengths in the management of the project? How could their complementarity be enhanced?

5 REFERENCES

Barmeyer, C. & Davoine, E. (2011). "The intercultural challenges in the transfer of code of conduct from the US to Europe". In: Primecz, H., Romani, L. & Sackmann, S. (Eds), *Cross-Cultural Management in Practice: Culture and Negotiated Meanings*, 53–63. Cheltenham: Edward Elgar Publishing.

Chevrier, S. (2011). "Exploring the cultural context of Franco-Vietnamese development projects: Using an interpretative approach to improve the cooperation process". In: Primecz, H., Romani, L. & Sackmann, S. (Eds), *Cross-Cultural Management in Practice: Culture and Negotiated Meanings*, 41–52. Cheltenham: Edward Elgar Publishing.

Chevrier, S. & Viegas Pires, M. (2013). "Delegating effectively across cultures". In: *Journal of World Business*, 48:3, 431–439.

Dalton, K. & Druker, J. (2012). "Transferring HR concepts and practices within multinational corporations in Romania: The management experience". In: *European Management Journal*, 30:6, 588–602.

d'Iribarne P. (1987). *La Logique de l'honneur. 1st ed.* Paris. Le Seuil.

d'Iribarne, P. (2009). "National cultures and organizations in search of a theory: An interpretative approach". In: *International Journal of Cross-cultural Management*, 9, 309–321.

d'Iribarne, P. (2012). *Managing Corporate Values in Diverse National Cultures. The Challenge of Differences.* London: Routledge.

d'Iribarne, P. (2014). *Theorising National Cultures.* AFD.

d'Iribarne, P. & Henry, A. (2007). "Successful companies in the developing world, managing in synergy with cultures, notes and documents". In: *Agence Française de Développement*, 36.

Hofstede, G. (1980/2001). *Culture's Consequences: Comparing Values, Behaviors, Institutions and Organizations Across Nations.* Thousand Oaks, CA: Sage

Primecz, H., Sackmann, S. & Romani, L. (Eds) (2011). *Cross-Cultural Management in Practice. Culture and Negotiated Meanings.* Cheltenham: Edward Elgar.

Shore, B. & Cross, B. J. (2005). "Exploring the role of national culture in the management of large-scale international science projects". In: *International Journal of Project Management*, 23:1, 55–64.

Segal, J. (2011, November). *Le management international au Vietnam. L'apprentissage des méthodes internationales de management dans le contexte socioculturel vietnamien.* Conference, Hanoï.

Trompenaars, F. (1993). *Riding the Wave of Culture. Understanding Cultural Diversity in Business.* London: Nicholas Brealey Publishing.

Winch, G. M., Clifton, N. & Millar, C. (2000). "Organization and management in an Anglo-French consortium: The case of Transmanche-Link". In: *Journal of Management Studies*, 37:5, 663–685.

18

Japan Tobacco International: Managing and Leveraging Cultural Diversity

Yih-teen Lee

1 INTRODUCTION

Research has shown how culture – national, organizational or associated with other categories – shapes one's values and ways of making sense of events. This in turn has serious consequences for how people behave and perform at work. One challenge for multinational companies (MNCs) is to handle multiple cultural diversities. In other words, MNCs need not only to manage cultural differences between two countries (often between their countries of origin and another country), but also to establish a consistent system that unifies its international operations across multiple cultures. A classic tension exists between whether to maintain a more centralized global culture or to be more responsive to local culture and allow for more flexibility.

The case of Japan Tobacco International (JTI) offers a rich ground for discussing how such multicultural diversity can be managed. As suggested by its very name, JTI seems to indicate an interesting paradox in terms of cultural diversity. First, the word Japan brings an unequivocal connotation of a connection with Japanese culture. Yet at the same time, the word international also suggests a clear global orientation. This case includes learning insights for several aspects of international management.

First, it can open a classical debate on the pros and cons of cultural diversity. Although research has indicated that diversity per se does not necessarily relate to outcomes such as performance, and that what matters is how diversity is managed, this debate may still be useful in order to summarize key findings in this field. In particular, the question can be put in a somewhat different way: do cultural differences always matter?[1] When may cultural differences become irrelevant, or even an asset for MNCs?

---

[1]Cf. Hofstede's seminal work on culture's consequences (1980/2001).

The case also touches upon issues of international human resource management (IHRM), with insights and concrete examples about how HR practices may contribute (or not) to the creation of an organizational culture that embraces diversity. Furthermore, the case may offer insight on how JTI managed the cultural integration of its acquisition, Gallaher, whose corporate culture was very different from that of JTI. The case can be used to discuss how JTI simultaneously managed national and organizational cultural diversity.

One pertinent question this case tries to raise is how to leverage cultural diversity effectively. It is not sufficient simply to reduce diversity and in this way overcome the potential shortcomings diversity may produce. In fact, international companies and managers alike need to think proactively about how best to leverage cultural diversity and turn such potential threat into their benefits. One challenge JTI was facing, as described in the case, was that it did not innovate enough. The case can be used to stimulate reflection and discussion on how managers and companies can better leverage multiple diversities to achieve desirable outcomes, such as innovation.

Finally, this case can also be used to address the topic of the characteristics and competences managers need for managing cultural diversity effectively. In addition to frameworks of Cultural Intelligence, cross-cultural competences, and global mindset, the way people manage their cultural identities may also play a role in determining how they may approach cultural diversity. I suggest particularly that the framework of biculturalism/multiculturalism is highly relevant to understanding how one's identity configurations, at both individual and organizational levels, may be another critical factor for international managers and MNCs to successfully leverage cultural diversity.

2 CASE DESCRIPTION

2.1 The situation: company background[2]

Four years after the acquisition of Gallaher by JTI, the integration is considered successful. The total headcount of JTI increased from 12,928 in 2007 to 25,000 in 2011. The level of diversity in JTI has increased further. However, top management of JTI is wondering whether diversity has been fully leveraged, and how JTI can unleash the innovative potential of its people in order to face new challenges.

Japan Tobacco International (JTI) is the international tobacco division of Japan Tobacco Inc. (JT), and is currently the world's third largest tobacco company with a global market share of 11% and market capitalization of

---

[2]A slightly different version of the case has been published by IESE Publishing. The author would like to thank Dr. Steven Poelmans, who contributed to the preparation of the original version of the case. Note that the job title of the managers reflects only their job function at the time of the interview (in 2011) and is subject to change.

approximately $32 billion. The headquarters of JTI are based in Geneva, Switzerland. The company was formed in 1999 when Japan Tobacco Inc. acquired for $7.8 billion the international tobacco operations of the US multinational R. J. Reynolds (RJR).

From the very beginning, the objective was to create JTI as an international company. As Bill Schulz, Senior Vice President of Global Supply Chain, said:

> "I do remember in the very, very early days of the integration, the CEO of JT, at that time Honda-san, came into our big factory in Trier, Germany. He spent time with the people that night. We went out for dinner and had a few beers. He was quite vocal that he didn't want to create a Japanese company. He wanted to create an international company."

Currently, the Executive Committee consists of 17 members, of 12 nationalities. JTI considers itself a truly international and multicultural business.

JT fundamentally shaped the culture of JTI with long-term thinking. While the former RJR culture focused very much on short-term quarterly earnings with high pressure on immediate delivery, JTI focused from the beginning on long-term results with an emphasis on investment in people and infrastructure that will bring benefits in five to ten years. Now, people are starting to see the fruit of such long-term thinking. "If I look back at what JT said they would do, they really did it", commented Heinz Von Allmen, responsible for Corporate Training & Development, "and today we are the fastest growing tobacco company in the world".

Certain managers observed the influence of Japanese culture on JTI. For example, people often attribute the long-term vision and the notion of quality to the Japanese heritage. Moreover, decision making in JTI may also be subject to such influence, in that there tends to be a kind of consensus-seeking process – people really bring everybody on board and look at issues from different angles, making sure that everyone is more or less aligned before making a final decision. However, instead of being a typical Japanese company, JTI embraces many other cultural elements in the company and remains highly international.

2.2 The challenge: the acquisition of Gallaher and its integration

In 2007, JTI acquired Gallaher, a FTSE 100 business, for £9.4 billion, and further consolidated its position as the third largest cigarette manufacturer in the world. However, to integrate two business entities of such size is not an easy task. One of the key challenges for JTI was to handle the huge differences between JTI and Gallaher. For example, people of the leaf function (growing, grading, blending and trading tobacco leaves) at Gallaher "are entrepreneurs, and they're quite flexible", said Paul Neumann, Senior Vice President of Global Leaf. "When former employees of Gallaher took a look at JTI, we had this reputation of being very structured, very slow to change, very bureaucratic. And how do you convince this function and these individuals to move into this organization?" JTI needed to address such differences and convince former Gallaher people that "living in a structure is not bad", in the words of Paul Neumann. Also, the two companies had very different business models. Whereas JTI developed clear business standards and processes, and strived for long-term and high-quality results, the Gallaher model tended to be "very optimistic and seek aggressive cash flow benefits, at the expense of maybe a longer-term view" said Bill Schulz. Furthermore, the structure and composition of the two companies differed significantly. For example, Heinz Von Allmen found that Gallaher's European Works' Council was mainly UK-based and dominated by the British background and style. JTI's European Works' Council, however, was multi-country and rather dominated by Germans. Hence JTI also needed to address such differences of mindset in its structure.

Another related challenge was to retain Gallaher's key talent. Facing radical changes in work style and culture, certain Gallaher people considered leaving the company. JTI managers sensed that some of the good things at Gallaher (e.g. speed-to-market, entrepreneurial skills) seemed to have been lost after the integration. The JTI integration team had to treat people with respect and avoid causing talented people to leave. Finally, because the operations of JTI and Gallaher were not totally complementary (i.e., in some countries both had plants or operations but only one would be needed after the acquisition), JTI also needed to deal with emotional issues of job loss and let certain people go with dignity.

Despite these challenges, the acquisition was regarded as successful not only because of its financial results but because of what it achieved in terms of integration. The main success factors were:

1. **Very careful preparation before the acquisition.** JTI leveraged the knowledge and experiences obtained from its acquisition of RJR in 1999 in preparing the integration with Gallaher. An integration handbook had been compiled even before the deal. Heinz Von Allmen explained: "If we want to address the key questions of integration, we're going to have to be prepared beforehand. So we addressed all these questions in the handbook: how would a compensation package look? How do we design an organization?"
2. **Utilization of JTI processes.** As JTI was quite successful with the tools and processes it had, it was decided that JTI processes would be the main framework for the new company after integration. However, the JTI team also stayed humble and granted freedom to adjust to local circumstances.
3. **Speed of integration planning and implementation.** JTI decided to move very fast and used the 80/20 rule to focus its energy and attention in the integration process. As Bill Schulz said: "We weren't going to dig for the last detail. We tried to move as fast as we could, and we communicate and even over-communicate with our teams".

4. **Integrating diversity and treating all employees fairly.** According to Guergana Andreeva, Regional HR for CIS+ (the Commonwealth of Independent States (plus Balkan countries):

   "[O]ur objective was to make the maximum out of integration, which meant we needed to integrate also the diversity, and take the best of both companies [...] so in every market, we have actually imposed rules that we cannot have a management team that was formed only by the representative of one of the companies. And by doing that, we've actually brought the perspective of both companies to each marketplace."

   People were treated with respect and fairness.

A post-implementation audit was conducted after the acquisition, and a book called *Deal and Integration Summary* was published. This book not only presents detailed milestones of the acquisition, but also offers deep reflections on the success drivers and items with potential for improvement across all the stages of the integration process.

Diversity within JTI

One of the key values of JTI is to create synergy through diversity (HR Integration Handbook). "In the company we have 104 nationalities, 31 different languages. So it's good that we all speak NVG (not very good) English as a common language. In headquarters alone, we have 55 nationalities", Heinz Von Allmen explained. In fact, diversity is an inherent part of JTI since its creation resulted from the JT purchase of RJR, where East meets West. The acquisition of Gallaher further enriched the diversity within JTI. See Figures 18.1 and 18.2 for the distribution of JTI's offices and plants around the world.

JTI experiences the benefits of diversity in the following ways. First, diversity brings different skills and perspectives. Paul Neumann observed that each of the different cultural backgrounds has different skillsets. And these all have their strengths and their weaknesses. Also, in analysing a problem, people from different cultures coming together somehow bring different ways of looking at solutions. Second, diversity offers opportunities for personal development. By being open to different opinions and accepting disagreement, discussions and exchanges of ideas help people to develop and grow, as Takehiko Tsutsui, Vice President of Corporate Strategy, commented: "It's not only me doing things, but I can learn things every day through my colleagues. Of course, I have my core skillset that I rely on day-to-day, but at the same time I can feel myself strengthening as I walk around the corridor of JTI." People become more adaptive and do not stick to their own way of doing things. Paul Neumann shared this observation: "Over a period of time you'll find that the Japanese will take more risks and be more open, while you'll find that the Anglos will be a little less aggressive and you'll think, 'Hmm, maybe I should think twice about this decision.'"

Such experiences also make people more international, and somehow transform them to go beyond their own cultural origin and develop a new level of global identity. "I could never, ever go back to England and work in a company

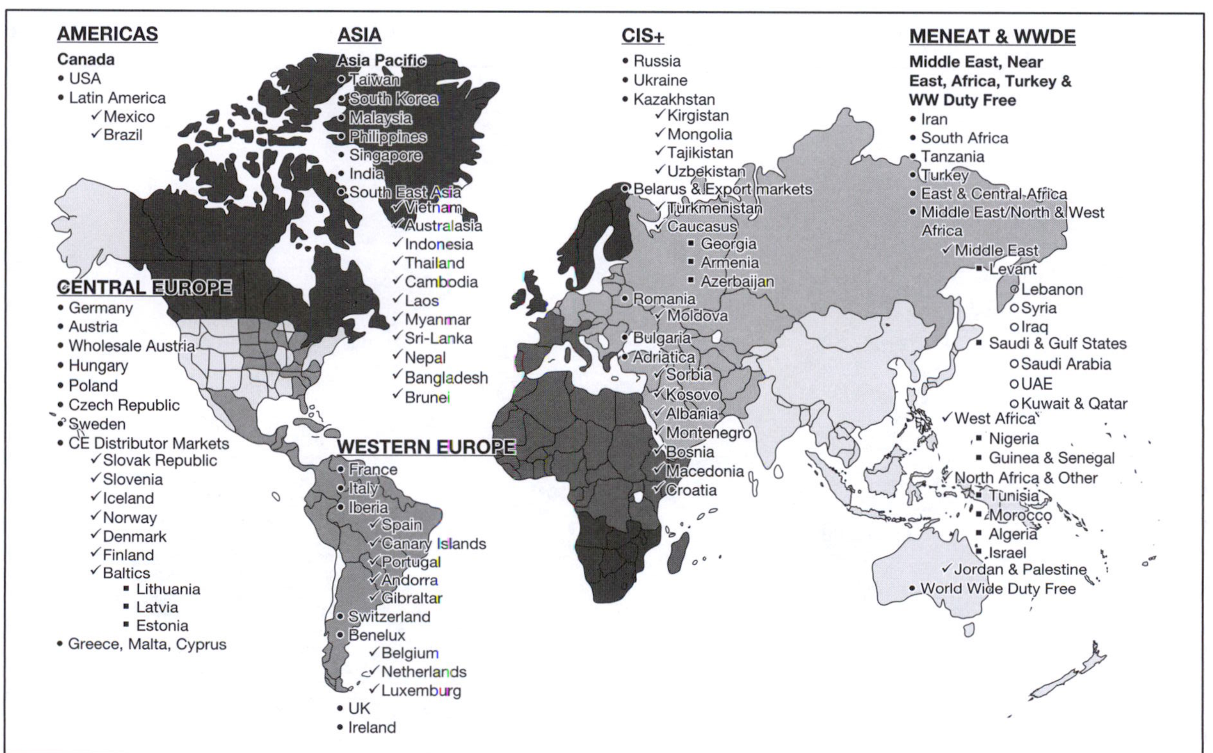

Figure 18.1 JTI's six regions and markets

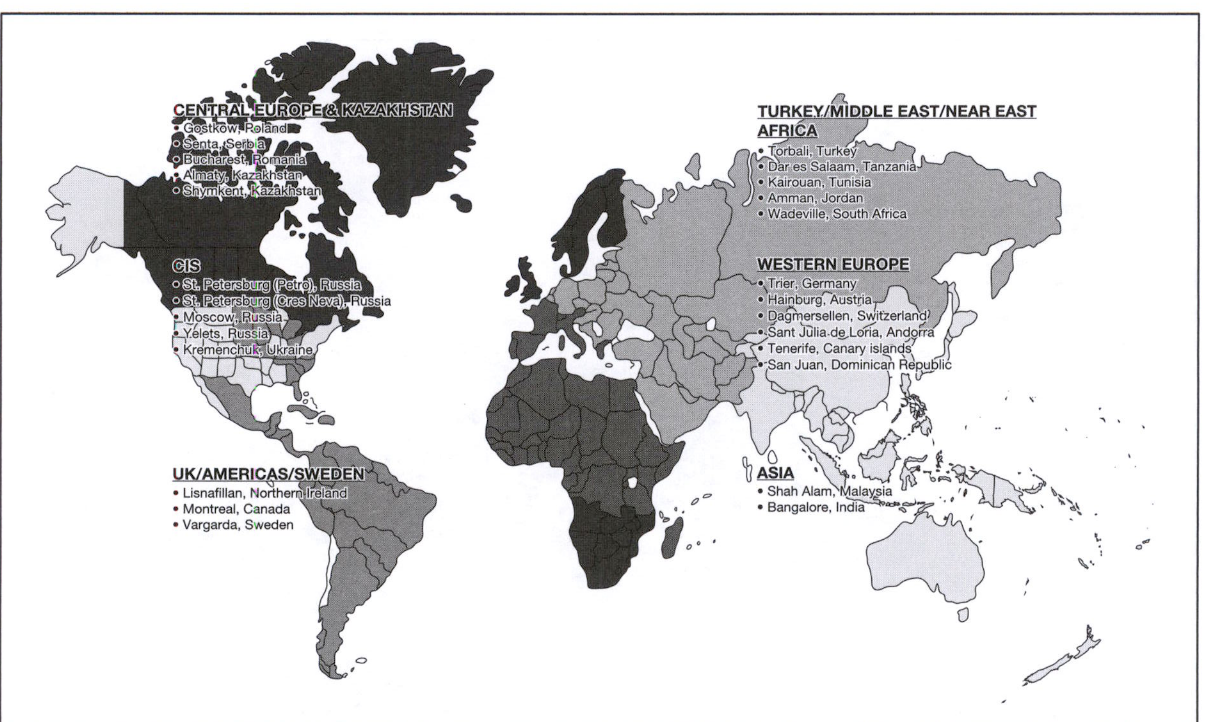

Figure 18.2 JTI's six global supply chain manufacturing areas and factories

full of English people. I think I'd go crazy," said Andrew Pendrill, Functional HR for Global Supply Chain and Global Leaf. "I think many people here from different nationalities would tell you the same thing. Sometimes I find that you have more in common with your colleagues who are from different countries but work in this multinational environment than your old friends and colleagues back home." Several JTI managers also indicate that it is more fun to work in such a diverse environment.

The drawback of such diversity was felt in communication. First, as diverse people tend to have different perspectives and opinions, if they are in a context where they are allowed to talk freely it takes a somewhat longer time for solutions to come up. Second, English is JTI's working language, but it is not the mother tongue of most of the JTI employees. Hence JTI spends more time in language training and people may still use "not very good English". Fortunately, "people are very forgiving", said Bill Schulz, "and accept strong accents, and less than perfect English". In the end, JTI sees that the benefits of diversity far outweigh its costs and feels that it's worth it.

In terms of gender, JTI remains a rather male-dominated company. For example, the executive committee doesn't have any women. Nevertheless, the fact that three of the 26 JTI factories are managed by females is considered a step towards more gender diversity. "I can assure you we're not thinking about females/non-females when we're doing our succession planning", Bill Schulz commented, "but this is an area the company should try and make progress in".

Embracing diversity: HR system, culture, and leadership "Diversity itself does not create a lot of value", commented Takehiko Tsutsui, "but the infrastructure you have within the organization which allows diversity creates a lot of value in my view". Surprisingly, there is no formal diversity policy within JTI. As Heinz Von Allmen said: "We don't have a diversity policy. I was asked several times, 'What does your diversity policy look like?' and I said, 'Never seen it'. We don't have it." There is not even formal training for people's international transition. Lacking a formal policy, however, JTI embraces diversity through its HR system, culture, and leadership.

Various aspects of its HR practices contribute to the value of diversity in JTI.

1. **Recruitment and selection.** "Hire for attitude, train for skills" is a well-known slogan in JTI because managers believe that while skills can be added or improved through training, attitude is very difficult to change. Hence, it is important to get the hiring right. Important attitudes include being open to new ideas, honesty in relationships, and belief in long-term vision and quality. In fact, Heinz Von Allmen suggested that "the willingness and the capability to work with people from different areas of the world, from different backgrounds, to accept differences are critical for JTI hires".
2. **Performance appraisal.** "We rate performance and decide on salary increases based on two factors: achieving your business objectives and what behaviour you have demonstrated", Guergana Andreeva explained, "and

those two factors (results and attitude) have equal weight in the overall performance rating". Such an appraisal system reinforces the importance of the right attitude in JTI. Recently, the chief financial officer (CFO) of one of the markets was asked to leave JTI in spite of his outstanding professional performance. The reason for this separation was that, despite being one of the best financial people technically, he did not demonstrate the attitude JTI emphasizes, particularly in his relationship with his peers. This was a very tough decision for JTI, and it took almost two years and lots of deliberations for the company to reach this conclusion.

3. **Promotion criteria.** In addition to proving oneself in delivering results and demonstrating the four core competencies of JTI (think the business, maximize your contribution, energize people and drive results), international mobility and experience play an important role in promotion decisions in JTI. All the managers of Work Group 1[3] had worked in one other country at least once. One's career may be jeopardized if one constantly refuses to move internationally. Sometimes, the recognition of the benefits of international experience and exposure goes all the way through JTI. For example, Senior Vice President of Global Leaf, Paul Neumann, said: "My assistant is Italian. She has an Italian passport but basically spent all of her life in Switzerland. And it helps because then she might speak three or four languages but she grew up in an Italian type of culture in Switzerland. So I think it helps all the way through."

Diversity seems to be part of JTI's DNA. In recruitment, in succession planning meetings, in all kinds of managerial decisions, people's nationality and passport are rarely mentioned, if ever. Rather, people are thinking about who is best for the job and nationality is not a consideration. Diversity just happens like that, and is part of the culture of the organization. According to Paul Neumann, "once you get that company culture, you don't even think about diversity. We don't have to push diversity. It's irrelevant to the way we run our business. Because you don't ... it just becomes a way of life".

Leadership, particularly that of CEO Pierre de Labouchere, was also instrumental in the development of JTI's culture of diversity. The CEO is known for walking the talk. In addition, "Pierre de Labouchere has been in his chair since 1995," Heinz Von Allmen explained. "Almost all the Executive Committee was appointed by the CEO. There's not a single tool or process... and particularly in the HR area, that was not signed off on by the CEO. It's the CEO's handwriting."

Keeping up with excellence: future challenges for JTI

Despite JTI's fast growth and its success in achieving excellence with a culture of diversity, managers sensed certain challenges that the company may need to face in the future.

One challenge is recruitment. Since tobacco companies normally do not have a very positive image, JTI puts more effort into employer branding so as

[3] There are four Work Groups in JTI: WG1, WG2, WG3, and WG4. WG1 includes managers at the highest levels such as CEO and VPs.

to attract and keep passionate and qualified professionals. The current branding of JTI is built around its strengths, like diversity, excellence, and long-term vision. These elements may distinguish JTI from other companies in competing for talent.

Also, JTI has to create a learning culture to help its managers develop. "We need to put more effort into educating managers on how to be better managers and how to develop people underneath", Guergana Andreeva said:

> "In the coming year, we will be focusing on 'the manager as a developer' in order to ensure that we have a healthy internal pipeline of talents. Another reason for focusing on this topic is that managers at all levels in the organization are key to the development of internal talent and to the creation of a learning culture. We have identified through a number of assessments that this is probably the weakest side we have in the organization."

Some managers are worried that JTI is "not innovative enough", an issue commonly raised in the Executive Committee, as Bill Schulz stated explicitly:

> "We talk about [innovation] as one of our values. And we need to improve. We talk about it deliberately. We have teams set up for it. We have task forces, but I don't think we're innovative enough somehow. How does this company unleash innovation? There are so many good ideas. There are so many good things going on. But then how do we bring those to a project that we can really get involved in and deliver?"

Guergana Andreeva also commented: "Yes, we are diversified, and we have a lot of ideas. But how do we put the ideas into practice? Do we leverage the diversity to the maximum degree? How can JTI unleash innovation?"

Furthermore, as JTI becomes larger over the course of time, it also faces the challenges of being slower. How can JTI energize the organization when it comes to a stage where things get more stable? As Guergana Andreeva described it:

> "It's easy to bring people in a room and give them a good talk; and people are very intelligent, instantly understand what needs to be done. The challenge is how to put it in practice while you run your business; while you're in charge of delivering numbers, do you have enough time to engage every single person in your organization?"

Yet this is a key to being able to thrive on diversity and ensure the long-term success of the company. For Bill Schulz, it is a question about how to get employees engaged:

> "We have task forces, we have succession programmes. We have all sorts of techniques to make sure that when somebody comes in, when they punch in, and they go to their job, that they're not punching their brains out. We want to make sure that their brains are engaged, and they're looking for better ways to do things. This is not a new challenge. All companies are trying to get their grip on this. I know what we're doing… I know all the steps we're taking. We're working hard on it, but I'm not satisfied."

3 BACKGROUND KNOWLEDGE

3.1 The author's point of reference

The author, Yih-teen Lee, is especially interested in leadership, cultural competences, and the interplay of multiple cultural identities in cross-cultural collaboration. He contends that, for both individuals and organizations, the way one manages one's cultural identities may have significant effects on one's intercultural effectiveness (Lee 2010). Building on the work of cross-cultural psychology on biculturalism and acculturation strategies, he suggests that sometimes not strongly identifying with any culture (i.e., a kind of cultural "homelessness") can create cognitive and affective advantages for managers and organizations in overcoming the challenges of diversity, complexity and uncertainty embedded in global business activities (Fitzsimmons, Lee, & Brannen 2013).

3.2 Concepts, models, frameworks

3.2.1 Cultural differences and their consequences at work

Since the publication of Hofstede's seminal work *Culture's Consequences* (1980/2001), scholars have started to recognize how culture shapes one's way of making sense of events, which may have serious consequences in terms of how people of different cultural backgrounds perform their work. For example, it has been shown that cultural differences will influence how people communicate, express emotions, develop trust, form social networks, negotiate and lead.

Very often, cultural differences are presented, rightfully, as challenges and problems for international managers to handle. Frameworks such as Cultural Intelligence (Earley & Ang 2003), cross-cultural competences (Lee et al. 2007), global mindset (Javidan et al. 2007), and global leadership (Mendenhall et al. 2012) all emphasize the importance of being aware of and understanding cultural differences.

However, do cultural differences always create difficulties and trouble? When will differences become neutral or even a positive asset for companies? Recent research on diversity seems to suggest interesting insights in this regard. Whereas cultural differences can potentially hinder mutual understanding and collaboration among workers from different cultures, such cultural diversity may also add value to teams and companies (e.g., Roberge & Dick 2010; Stahl et al. 2009). It depends on how the diversity is managed.

Shore, Randel, Chung, Dean, Ehrhart and Singh (2011) offer a useful framework to consider when and how cultural differences matter. They present a 2×2 framework which suggests that uniqueness and belongingness work together to create feelings of inclusion (see Figure 18.3). When a unique individual is an accepted member of the group and the group values their particular unique characteristics, inclusion occurs. Normally cultural differences will not only be present but also cherished as sources of unique insights. On the other hand, it is also possible that organizations and teams create a culture where the individual is not treated as an organizational insider with unique value in the work group, but other employees or groups are considered insiders. Within the framework, this is "exclusion". Normally, harmful cognitive, emotional, and health outcomes can occur in such situations.

When there is high belongingness and low value in uniqueness, the situation is such that an individual who is unique is treated as an insider but he or she conforms to the dominant norms of the culture. This is the case known as "assimilation". Finally, those who are low on belongingness but highly valued for their uniqueness are in the situation of "differentiation".

Such a framework is useful in discussing organizational policies or cultures aiming towards diversity, and cultural differences in groups or companies. When companies attach little value to uniqueness, there may be two possible effects: (1) cultural differences are downplayed – people simply focus on the common cultural denominator. However, people may still feel cherished and united (i.e. assimilation); (2) cultural differences are ignored and people do not feel a common sense of belonging (i.e. exclusion). It would be interesting to discuss how companies can consciously use these strategies to leverage cultural differences.

	Low Belongingness	High Belongingness
Low Value in Uniqueness	**Exclusion** Individual is not treated as an organizational insider with unique value in the work group but there are other employees or groups who are insiders.	**Assimilation** Individual is treated as an insider in the work group when they conform to organizational/dominant culture norms and downplay uniqueness.
High Value in Uniqueness	**Differentiation** Individual is not treated as an organizational insider in the work group but their unique characteristics are seen as valuable and required for group/organization success.	**Inclusion** Individual is treated as an insider and also allowed/encouraged to retain uniqueness within the work group.

Figure 18.3 Inclusion framework

Source: Shore et al. (2011). Reproduced with permission.

3.2.2 Multicultural identities and global mindset

Identity provides an individual with a systematic means of defining others as well as defining oneself. Consequently, identity functions as a self-regulatory social-psychological structure in that it directs attention, processes information, determines attitudes and orients behaviours (Hogg & Terry 2000). Cultural identities play a crucial role in the dynamics of intercultural interaction in the following ways. First, cultural identities may facilitate the processing of certain information so that specific cultural knowledge is cognitively accessible (Hong et al. 2003; Verkuyten & Pouliasi 2006). Second, cultural identities may also lead individuals to adopt or endorse certain cultural values, which can provide grounds for cultural understanding and attitudinal outcomes in intercultural encounters (Brown 2000). Furthermore, because cultural identities are often maintained by inter-group comparison, and because cultural or social groups usually seek positive differences between themselves and reference groups as a result of the desire to enhance self-esteem, individuals tend to develop favourable images of the in-groups and share pejorative perceptions of out-groups. In sum, cultural identities play a far-reaching role in determining one's cognitive, affective and behavioural responses to cultural stimuli in intercultural encounters (Toh & DeNisi 2007).

Berry's (1990) framework on acculturation strategies (Figure 18.4) serves as a useful framework for understanding how cultural diversity can be managed. In general, when people adopt the integration strategy in acculturation, they tend to embrace both (or multiple) cultural systems and can connect well with people from these cultural backgrounds. Cultural differences may not represent a challenge for such individuals as they somehow have internalized multiple cultural value systems and norms and hence can easily switch codes and bridge differences. When people hold one-sided identity configurations (i.e. identity assimilation and separation), they would have more difficulty accepting or handling diversity. The either/or identification approach may force them to side with one particular culture and prevent them from appreciating positive elements in other culture and, as a result, from embracing diversity.

The most interesting, and also most ambiguous, case is of those who belong in the category of marginalization. In bicultural research, marginalized people are generally considered as suffering most from isolation and stress. They tend to be cut off from various cultural groups and cannot find an adequate place in cross-cultural settings. However, recent research is starting to reveal the hidden potential of such individuals, suggesting that they may possess a higher level of cognitive complexity, and capabilities for handling uncertainty and embracing diversity (Fitzsimmons et al 2013; Lee 2010). Sometimes not strongly identifying oneself with any culture may offer individuals a special position of neutrality that reduces potential identity threat and the pressure to conform to specific cultural norms.

When companies can develop mechanisms to encourage their people to adopt either the integration or marginalization acculturation strategies, cultural diversity can be better managed and appreciated. Although cultural identities can be dynamic and may be activated and made salient by specific context and event, it is possible for individuals and companies to consciously develop some desirable identity pattern.[4]

[4]Note that the word "assimilation" is used in both models yet in very different contexts and also with very different meanings. To avoid unnecessary confusion, I suggest to instructors not to use Berry's full model, but simply refer to the modes where individuals can embrace both (or multiple) identities (i.e., bicultural integration) and where they keep a distance from all cultural identities (i.e., marginalization).

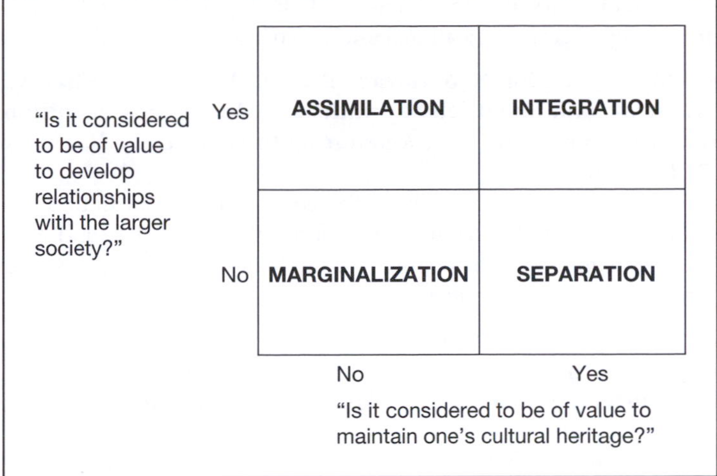

Figure 18.4 Berry's acculturation model (1997)

Source: Berry (1990). Reproduced with permission.

3.3 Recommended reading

Berry, J. (1990). "Psychology of acculturation: Understanding individuals moving between cultures". In: Brislin, R. (Ed.), *Applied Cross-Cultural Psychology*, 232–253. Newbury Park, Sage.
This article presents central elements of adaptation and acculturation processes and the questions of "cultural maintenance" (can the individual/collective retain their own cultural origin – minority – identity?) and "contact and participation" (can the individual/collective make positive intercultural contact with the dominant – majority – society?) It exposes and discusses a model of acculturation strategies linked to the individual and society.

Fitzsimmons, S. R., Lee, Y. T. & Brannen, M. Y. (2013). "Demystifying the myth about marginals: Implications for global leadership". In: *European Journal of International Management.* 7:5, 587–603.
This article suggests that marginals, a type of bicultural (or multicultural) individual who has internalized more than one culture yet does not identify strongly with either or any of them, may possess specific advantages in overcoming challenges in terms of diversity, complexity and uncertainty in a global context. It offers an interesting perspective on how individuals and organizations can manage their cultural identities to reduce identity threats of members of different cultural groups and to leverage the benefits of diversity.

Kusstatscher, V. & Cooper, C. L. (2005). *Managing Emotions in Mergers and Acquisitions.* Cheltenham: Edward Elgar Publishing.
This book addresses the issues of emotion that may occur in the process of mergers and acquisitions, and underlines the importance of managing these tough "soft factors" in such processes. It also offers useful theoretical

frameworks for better understanding emotion and identity in M&A and how to manage them via proper communicational and behavioural strategies.

Levy, O., Beechler, S., Taylor, S. & Boyacigiller, N. A. (2007). "What we talk about when we talk about 'global mindset': Managerial cognition in multinational corporations". In: *Journal of International Business Studies,* 38:2, 231–258.
This article provides an in-depth review of the concept of global mindset at various levels of analysis. It clarifies the meaning of global mindset and how it can contribute a higher level of cognitive complexity for individuals and companies handling cultural diversities.

Shore, L. M., Randel, A. E., Chung, B. G., Dean, M. A., Ehrhart, K. H. & Singh, G. (2011). "Inclusion and diversity in work groups: A review and model for future research". In: *Journal of Management*, 37:4, 1262–1289.
This article offers useful insights on the management of diversity with the inclusion framework, which combines the values of uniqueness and a sense of belonging to form a 2x2 matrix for different situations which might contribute towards cultural diversity.

Stahl, G. K., Maznevski, M. L., Voigt, A. & Jonsen, K. (2009). "Unraveling the effects of cultural diversity in teams: A meta-analysis of research on multicultural work groups". In: *Journal of International Business Studies*, 41, 690–709.
This meta-analytical study examines the effects of cultural diversity on various team processes and outcomes, with an attempt to shed light on the often ambiguous and inconclusive results regarding the effect of diversity on performance. It found that diversity can be associated with *both* process gains and process losses, hence it is important to capture the more complex picture about the level and type of diversity involved and how diversity is managed to understand its relationship with performance outcomes.

4 QUESTIONS ON THE CASE

1. Assess the degree of cultural diversity within JTI. What are the potential benefits and challenges related to such diversity?
2. How does JTI manage cultural diversity in the company? Why have cultural differences within JTI not created obvious obstacles to cross-cultural collaboration?
3. How can JTI better leverage the diversity within the company to foster innovation?

5 REFERENCES

Berry, J. (1990). "Psychology of acculturation: Understanding individuals moving between cultures". In: Brislin, R. (Ed.), *Applied Cross-Cultural Psychology*, 232–253. Newbury Park: Sage.

Berry, J. W. (1997). "Immigration, acculturation and adaptation". In: *Applied Psychology: An International Review*, 46:1, 5–34.

Brown, R. (2000). "Social identity theory: Past achievements, current problems and future challenges". In: *European Journal of Social Psychology*, 30:6, 745–778.

Earley, P. C. & Ang, S. A. (2003). *Cultural Intelligence: Individual Interactions Across Cultures*. Stanford: Stanford University Press.

Fitzsimmons, S. R., Lee, Y. T. & Brannen, M. Y. (2013). "Demystifying the myth about marginals: Implications for global leadership". In: *European Journal of International Management*, 7:5, 587–603.

Hofstede, G. (1980/2001). *Culture's Consequences: International Differences in Work-Related Values*. Beverly Hills, CA: Sage.

Hogg, M. A. & Terry, D. I. (2000). "Social identity and self-categorization processes in organizational contexts". In: *Academy of Management Review*, 25:1, 121–140.

Hong, Y. Y., Benet-Martínez, V., Chiu, C. Y. & Morris, M. W. (2003). "Boundaries of cultural influence: Construct activation as a mechanism for cultural differences in social perception". In: *Journal of Cross-Cultural Psychology*, 34:4, 453–464.

Javidan, M., Steers, R. M. & Hitt, M. A. (2007). *The Global Mindset*. Oxford, UK: Elsevier JAI.

Lee, Y. T. (2010). "Home versus host – Identifying with either, both, or neither? The relationship between dual cultural identities and intercultural effectiveness". In: *International Journal of Cross Cultural Management*, 10:1, 55–76.

Lee, Y. T., Calvez, V. & Guénette, A. M. (2007). *La Compétence culturelle: S'équiper pour les défis du management international*. Paris: L'Harmattan.

Mendenhall, M. E., Oddou, G. R., Osland, J. S., Bird, A. & Maznevski, M. L. (Eds) (2012). *Global Leadership: Research, Practice, and Development*. London: Routledge.

Roberge, M. É. & van Dick, R. (2010). "Recognizing the benefits of diversity: When and how does diversity increase group performance?" In: *Human Resource Management Review*, 20:4, 295–308.

Shore, L. M., Randel, A. E., Chung, B. G., Dean, M. A., Ehrhart, K. H. & Singh, G. (2011). "Inclusion and diversity in work groups: A review and model for future research". In: *Journal of Management*, 37:4, 1262–1289.

Stahl, G. K., Maznevski, M. L., Voigt, A. & Jonsen, K. (2009). "Unraveling the effects of cultural diversity in teams: A meta-analysis of research on multicultural work groups". In: *Journal of International Business Studies*, 41, 690–709.

Toh, S. M. & DeNisi, A. S. (2007). "Host country nationals as socializing agents: A social identity approach". In: *Journal of Organizational Behavior*, 28:3, 281–301.

Verkuyten, M. & Pouliasi, K. (2006). "Biculturalism and group identification: The mediating role of identification in cultural frame switching". In: *Journal of Cross-Cultural Psychology*, 37:3, 312–326.

19

Leveraging the Benefits of Diversity and Biculturalism through Organizational Design

Jasmin Mahadevan

1 INTRODUCTION

In today's globalized world, intercultural organizational fields have become increasingly complex (Mahadevan et al. 2011). Globalization also goes hand in hand with increasing mobility and migration (Urry 2000). Hence, in many European countries, the number of individuals whose ancestors immigrated or who immigrated themselves has increased (Heckmann & Schnapper 2003). These individuals often have internalized more than one cultural scheme and can therefore be considered bicultural (Brannen & Thomas 2010). As a result, the borders between cultures do not only refer to societal cultures anymore, but also to societal sub- and micro-cultures (Mahadevan et al. 2011). Due to increasing mobility and migration, the boundaries between cultures have become fluid, a process which is linked to increased individualization (Urry 2000). Hence, perceived cultural difference is not only to be found "abroad" but "at home" and within the everyday context of one's work and personal life (Prasad et al. 2006). For bicultural individuals, this is linked to a life experience in the "in-between" which requires constant adaptation to different cultural meaning systems, depending on the context in which one is engaged (Brannen & Thomas, 2010).

At the same time, the issue of organizational design has been raised with renewed interest in the field of management and organization studies. The 2012 annual colloquium of the European Group for Organizational Studies (EGOS), for example, has been exclusively dedicated to this theme (see www.egosnet.org). Through design, organizations try to shape their structures, processes and practices in such a way that they meet both inner- and extra-organizational demands and changes (Cunliffe 2008:25–42). From an intercultural perspective, this implies that micro-individual, meso-organizational and macro-societal demands need to be aligned (Mahadevan et al. 2011).

When facing increased workface diversity, organizations specifically need to design inclusive structures and policies that provide equal opportunities for each member (Wilton 2010:309–336) and to align these policies with larger socio-political frameworks of immigration policies, laws and procedures (Heckmann & Schnapper 2003) in the best possible manner. Only then will they be able to manage their talents in the best possible manner (Al Ariss et al. 2014). Diversity research focuses on how to include these minorities (Prasad et al. 2006). Yet, in many organizations, especially those which experience increasing workforce diversity for the first time, current organizational design and micro-cultural sense-making often hinders diversity change and prevents the inclusion of minority groups (Mahadevan 2012). As a result, diversity change is hard to implement (ibid.). So far, interpretative intercultural management research has explored micro-cultural sense-making in intercultural interactions (e.g. Mahadevan et al. 2011). Yet it has not been acknowledged how organizational design could facilitate inclusive practices. Often, those who are part of a cultural minority group are perceived as an inconvenience; their potential to bring new and previously unacknowledged strategies, ideas and practices to an organization remains unseen (Mahadevan 2012).

This case takes a resource-based view (see Wilton 2010) on multiculturalism, especially on bicultural individuals, and discusses how the benefits of diversity, especially biculturalism, can be utilized through inclusive organizational design. It refers to a German technological company which – accidentally – designed its organization in such a way that the requirements for being a successful employee are virtually identical to the abilities of bicultural individuals. These individuals are not seen as organizational obstacles but as highly valued core members who are enabled and included through organizational design. At the same time, socio-political demands in Germany, such as calls for improved integration of immigrants in high-performance industries, are met. In summary, this case does not present a cultural problem to be solved but an accidental solution to it which is reflected upon with the help of theory and brought to the conscious strategic level of organizational design.

2 CASE DESCRIPTION

This case refers to a German software company, to be called The Relationship Company in this study. The following case description is based on information on the corporate website and several interviews which were conducted with members of the core organizational unit between 2011 and 2012 (Heyer 2012).[1] For several purposes, including the need

[1]Many thanks go to Katrin Heyer, BSc, former student of the International Business Administration and Engineering programme and student assistant at Pforzheim University, for her contribution in preparing this case study. This case benefited greatly from her practical research in The Relationship Company and her initial theoretical analysis of the field.

for strict confidentiality, some adaptations have been made to this case by the author.

Currently, The Relationship Company employs approximately 500 employees; it is active in the area of customer relationship management (CRM) tools. During the last five years, The Relationship Company has experienced considerable growth and has employed a large number of highly qualified individuals. However, The Relationship Company does not monitor the profile of its employees; the corporate HR department does not gather any specific information on employees.

The Relationship Company develops IT tools which help companies to manage their customer relations in the best way possible. In order to meet customer requirements, the CRM tools which are offered by The Relationship Company need to be constantly innovated, developed and customized for the demands of the specific clients and various stakeholders. These stakeholders include companies, public media, society, end customers and many more. The company is currently one of the leading companies in the area of CRM tools in Germany. In order to meet the demand for constant innovation, The Relationship Company initiated a radical organizational redesign a few years ago. A key part of this strategy was a change from a previous matrix design towards a network organization comprised of several independent entities, to be called Relationship Companies. These Relationship Companies share resources from a core organizational unit, to be called The Relationship Engine. "A Relationship Company for every customer" became the slogan, which emphasized the underlying motivation for this change in organizational design, namely a high customer orientation with regard to innovative CRM solutions. It verbalized the overall strategic aim to place CRM at the centre of organizational strategy.

Every Relationship Company is free to pursue its own strategy in order to develop new, innovative and customer-oriented solutions and tools. Furthermore, every employee is allowed to found their own Relationship Company if they have an innovative new service or potential new product and if their proposal is evaluated positively by higher management. Core services which are provided by The Relationship Engine include finance, human resources, information technology and research, development, marketing and customer service.

Organizational design A key strategic task of The Relationship Company lies in developing solutions which prepare the company for future challenges in the IT business. Therefore, The Relationship Engine also includes an innovation team which is active in writing research proposals and applying for national and international research funds in close cooperation with research institutes and universities. The Innovation Team is located in the inner circle of The Relationship Engine and consists of six team members who provide the core service "research" to all Relationship Companies. The team acts as an interface between various external stakeholders and the different Relationship

Companies for all matters concerning research and development. The original presentation of data on this team can be found in Heyer (2012). The Innovation Team's working conditions and their individual profiles can be considered typical for those working at The Relationship Company and will be used to exemplify this business case.

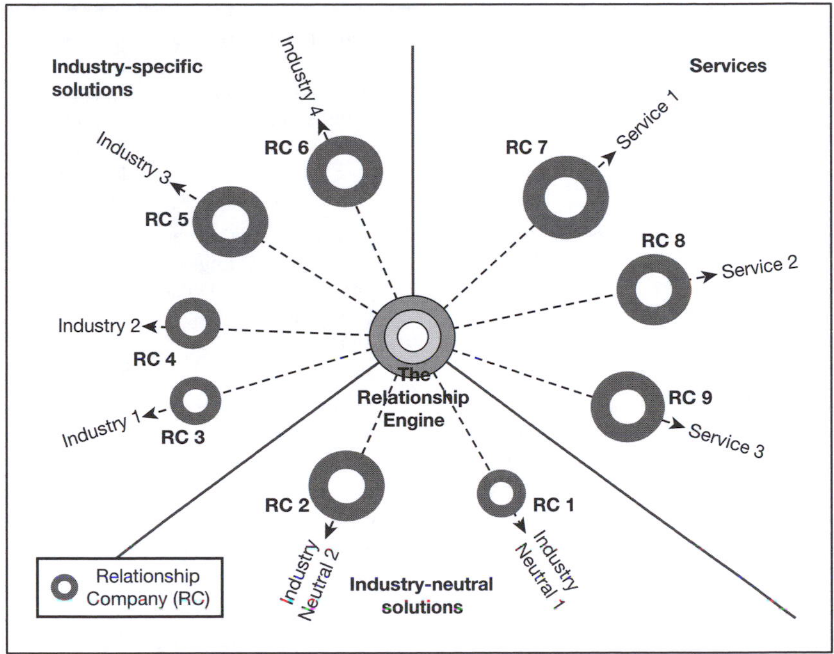

Figure 19.1 The Relationship Company's organizational design
Source: Based on corporate website (2013).

The innovation team is comprised of six team members who are supported by two administrative employees. Each of them acts as project leader in numerous research projects. At the time of research, two of the six project leaders were employed only part time, pursuing their master's degree or doctoral degree during the other days of the week. The other four project leaders worked full time, one of them also part of the board of managers, one of them part of the strategic team of the company and two responsible for internal innovation, working in close cooperation with the Relationship Companies. Hence, in terms of organizational hierarchy, professional experience and academic qualification, the Innovation Team itself is internally diverse. Also with regard to their professional backgrounds and personal life stories, the project leaders are very diverse. According to top management, this diversity of corporate employees is part of a purposeful strategy which aims at facilitating innovation through diverse perspectives.

Table 19.1 gives an overview on the personal profile of the six project leaders (PL).

Table 19.1 The members of the Innovation Team

Person	Age	Gender	Educational background	Country of birth	International experience	Language skills	Remarks
PL 1	29	m	Degree in Business Administration	GER	Some months in GB, spends six months per year in Japan	German, English, Japanese	Spouse lives in Japan; works part time, pursuing doctoral degree
PL 2	27	m	Bachelor degree in Intercultural Management	CHN	Grew up in China, returned to Shanghai, China for his studies	German, English, Chinese	Works part time, pursuing MSc in Information Science
PL 3	35	m	Degree in Industrial Eng., Doctoral degree in Computer Eng.	GER	Three months in England	German, English, French	
PL 4	29	f	Bachelor and master's degree in International Management	RUS	Six months in the United States	German, English, Russian	Spouse lives in Canada
PL 5	45	m	Doctoral degree in Industrial Engineering	GER	Several months in the United States	German, English	High German as second language
PL 6	46	m	Degree in Computer Science; Doctoral degree in Industrial Eng.	GRE	Grew up in Greece; returned there after studies for some time	German, English, Greek	

Sources: Based on Heyer (2012:12).

Work practice in the projects The team of six project leaders and two administrative employees meet once a week to discuss projects, to distribute incoming projects and to exchange their experiences within their respective projects. Each project leader is in charge of four to six different projects, a role which is carried out to different degrees of involvement. Projects take place on a local, national or international level; they are carried out mainly in Europe, with some exceptions. This kind of project work requires many business trips and travelling to attend international meetings all across Germany and Europe. As a result, the project leaders do not have the opportunity to meet in person every day; sometimes, they do not see each other for weeks. Hence, a lot of communication takes place electronically, via email or online calls. Often, data and joint work-in-progress – not only within the team, but also while interacting with the respective Relationship Companies – is stored, shared or exchanged virtually.

The allocation of the research projects is prepared by the group leader. He or she does this by considering the individual skills and interests of the project leaders. Each project allocation is discussed within the group and a joint decision is made on who will lead which project. As a result, every project leader will be responsible for projects he or she has a certain connection to or interest in, and which fit his or her abilities and experience. In the process of carrying out the project, it is not important how the work is done but that the work is completed and that output is generated. This gives the project leaders a high degree of freedom and self-management when dealing with their work.

After the projects have been allocated to the project leaders in this manner, the largest amount of the actual project work is done outside the group of project leaders and within the different Relationship Companies. The core project work which remains within the Innovation Team lies in acquiring new projects, in exchanging experiences and in discussing ongoing projects and their progress.

The project leaders' work process can be roughly divided into the phases "prior to a project", "during a project" and "after a project". Prior to a project, the project leader has to have an innovative idea and align it with the company's strategy in order to check the potential benefit this innovative idea could have. Next, the project leader has to search for a research tender from suitable institutions such as the European Union, German ministries or specific regional ministries or institutions. Besides this, the project leader has to find suitable project partners, either nationally or internationally, in order to form a consortium. Then, she or he has to write a project proposal and to submit it to the institution tendering the research project. This might consist of up to 150 pages.

When the application is accepted, the project commences. The project leader now assumes the role of project coordinator, and the actual project work begins, she or he being either the leader of the whole project or its coordinator and communicator within the organization and towards external partners. During this time, numerous meetings need to be organized, the progress of the project needs to be monitored and reports for the funding organization have to be written in order.

After the project is finished, the project leader will need to present the outcome of the project to the tendering institution as well as to their own organization and to show how the research solutions can be used within the organization. A final report needs to be written and – in most cases – to be published in English and/or German.

Together, the specific organizational design of The Relationship Company, its purpose of developing pioneering and tailor-made technological relationship solutions for a number of stakeholders and its complex project work requirements can be summarized as a very innovative, open environment for new ideas and solutions. Such an environment places certain demands on those working within it. These demands can be summarized as follows:

Competencies required Firstly, project leaders need to have excellent communication and social skills as well as high levels of empathy. This involves being able to present and discuss ideas and to express leadership in interaction with different target groups and in different organizational, national and cultural environments (with the ability to switch between different social and cultural codes).

Second, project leaders need to be flexible and be able to adapt themselves to changing conditions and different teams. This involves being mobile and internationally minded, because of the need to meet with partners and stakeholders in several locations and to travel constantly.

Third, project leaders need to be constantly innovative in order to write applications for new research projects and report on the implemented innovations and their contribution, while always being creative.

Fourth, due to the changing boundary conditions and the singular nature of each project, project leaders need to constantly acquire new knowledge and to apply this knowledge socially. To do so, they need to have the ability to tolerate ambiguity and uncertainty. This is a frequently occurring element in many measurements of intercultural competence. Furthermore, they need to be comfortable with bearing responsibility but also with sharing questions, thoughts and decisions collaboratively (collaborative leadership style).

In summary, the organizational environment created by The Relationship Company provides a lot of individual freedom and the opportunity for self-directed management. It demands high flexibility as well as adaptability and the courage to have innovative ideas or to bring innovative ideas to the fore. Moreover, the project leaders are often confronted with different views and opinions which they have to process and handle during their daily work in projects or within the organization. Contrary to what one might expect as an outsider, this working environment is not felt as a pressure or even as something exceptional in the Innovation Team; rather this is seen as "how work should be" or a "normal working environment". The Innovation Team is praised by top management as a very successful unit of the company. However, when asked why this might be so, no specific answer is given besides "there are just very intelligent people in this team". Top management is aware that organizational design facilitates innovative thinking; however, it is of the opinion that "less intelligent employees" might not be able to leverage their innovative potential in a similar fashion.

When The Relationship Company's organizational design is compared with most organizational environments in the German context one recognizes that it does not display "normal" German organizational structure, which tends to be rule-oriented and slow to change. Furthermore, based on cross-cultural theory such as cultural dimensions and standards, Germany has been characterized as a societal context wherein individuals wish for stability, tend to be rule-oriented, are eager to avoid uncertainty through meticulous planning and might not be very used to tolerating ambiguity. Even German IT organizations, when compared to their counterparts in the Silicon Valley or the Indian IT capital of Bangalore, tend to be more "conservative" in this manner than their competitors from a different societal cultural context.

Therefore, when compared to other similar organizational contexts in Germany, both the radical innovative network design of The Relationship Company and how this structure is interpreted by those working within it stand out. Yet this is not how those within the organization feel; rather, those performing well perceive their capabilities as "normal" and do not have the feeling that they might have special capabilities. From their perspective, they are just doing a normal job which is challenging but which is manageable in a comfortable manner. If any reason for high performance is given at all, it is a notion of "being clever" or "a capable employee". Otherwise, no special and shared characteristics of the members of the Innovation Team are mentioned. The project leaders perceive themselves and are perceived by others as being very diverse in terms of age, gender, cultural background, professional experience, academic qualification and personal life story. Therefore, no common traits are identified that those within the group might share.

In the next section, this view on "individual cleverness" as being the sole reason for high performance is challenged with the help of theories on biculturalism. This insight is applied to the question of how organizational design could utilize biculturalism as an organizational resource for high performance. Prior to this and based on the assumption that any individual perspective can only be a subjective interpretation of the social world, the theoretical perspective of the author is highlighted.

3 BACKGROUND KNOWLEDGE

3.1 The author's point of reference

Jasmin Mahadevan views culture and identities from a social constructivist perspective, namely as a process through which individuals give meaning to themselves in relation to others and to the social world surrounding them. She is intrigued by complex organizational fields in which these social and cultural identities need to be constantly negotiated and interpreted in numerous contexts. From her viewpoint, diversity, mobility, the experience of cultural and social difference, and the constant creation of new and shared meanings are normal phenomena in these fields. She therefore tries to uncover how individuals experience diversity and which cultural and social categories are meaningful to them in which context. Her work pays special attention to the hidden dimensions of diversity, i.e. bicultural individuals in organizations. Jasmin Mahadevan is native German with a family history and a personal life experience of biculturality, migration and mobility.

3.2 Concepts, models, frameworks

Organization theory has formulated the axiom that organizational environments should not be shaped by accident, chance or sheer luck. Rather, organizational structure should be based on conscious decisions, and in this way structure should follow strategy (Cunliffe 2008). This axiom is true for all types of organizations, whether based on dynamic organizational design principles, such as network organizations or learning organizations, or more stable and long-term orientated, with a formal hierarchy (e.g. a line or matrix organization). Likewise, from a theoretical perspective, the organizational structure chosen should enable employees to perform in the best possible way as defined by corporate strategy. Ideally, employees perform based on intrinsic motivation and without perceiving gaps or contradictions between individual and organizational goals (Wilton 2010). In this way, (1) organizational strategy, (2) organizational structure and practices and (3) organizational members' interpretations of this organizational environment and their identification with it are aligned. From an interpretative cultural perspective, it is the meaning which employees give to their corporate environment – i.e. the interpretation of structural boundary conditions – which make an organizational culture successful or not (Mahadevan 2012).

In The Relationship Company, the organizational design chosen – a network organization – is meant to enable corporate entrepreneurship and innovation. From a theoretical perspective, a network organization increases communicative possibilities, it reduces formal hierarchy and it lends itself to flexible, project-based collaboration. In Section 3.2.1, the background to organizational design and innovation, as well as to high-commitment HRM and to biculturalism, will be highlighted for the discussion of this case.

3.2.1 Network design and technology

The success of a network organization depends on both hard and soft features, especially if organizational structure is created in order to facilitate innovation. A hard feature of organizational design is, for example, a suitable technological environment; a soft feature is organizational culture. In this section, the hard feature "technology" will be introduced. According to Cunliffe (2008:51), a successful network organization is based on a technological environment which:

- reduces the need for physical proximity of organizations to and between their internal and external stakeholders (partners, customers, employees, managers);
- reduces the need for hierarchical controls;
- replaces direct integrating mechanisms such as supervision, face-to-face task groups and meetings, etc., with electronic linking and facilitates decentralization of decision making by making information available more freely to all levels of employees;
- supports flatter organizations (i.e. wider control combined with lesser hierarchy) by supporting managerial functions through information technology;

- Promotes an organic organizational structure which is highly able to deal with unexpected, complex and unprogrammed problems.

3.2.2 A resource-based view (RBV) of the firm

In addition to having a suitable technological infrastructure, a successful organizational design also utilizes organizational human resources in the best possible way. The ability to do so and to support this utilization of human resources and capabilities can be understood as a soft feature of organizational design which complements the hard feature of technology. Over the last few decades, human resource management (HRM) strategy has developed considerably (Lengnick-Hall et al. 2009). Rather than viewing individuals solely as a "resource" to be controlled, administrated and regulated in the most efficient way, modern HRM views human beings as intrinsically motivated, wishing for purposeful work and striving for self-actualization through work. Therefore, it becomes the key goal of HRM strategy to utilize this intrinsic motivation by making the work environment fit individual capabilities as well as possible and by utilizing individuals' intrinsic wishes to learn and develop themselves. Such an approach applies the resource-based view (RBV) to human resources (Colbert 2004; Wilton 2010:72–75), with the intention of linking individual motivations to corporate strategy and operations in the best way it can. If a company utilizes employees' intrinsic motivation, they will display "high commitment". Hence, the RBV of the firm has also been called "high-commitment HRM" (Wilton 2010).

The RBV of the firm is linked to the understanding that HRM strategy needs to be more than mere personnel administration. Rather, it should focus on providing constant learning opportunities for individuals and on enabling lifelong learning, thereby laying the foundation for a "learning organization" which is highly adaptive to changes and retains its innovative edge. In this way, HRM strategy directly influences organizational performance (Wilton 2010:76–83).

A high level of employee commitment – which is a key requirement for a successful network organization – can only be implemented if employees do not perceive the "rhetorics of HRM" and the actual practice and strategy of HRM as being a mismatch (Wilton 2010:3–21). Employees will only be highly committed if they perceive their implicit and explicit contract with the organization as fair, just, in their best interests and as enabling them to grow personally on the job. This understanding that the employee–employer relationship is more than just a formal contract is summarized as the "psychological contract" which individuals deem themselves to have with their employer (Wilton 2010:36–40). If the – mostly implicit and tacit – agreements of the psychological contract are violated, this will result in decreased individual work performance which is understood as a function of ability, motivation and opportunity (Wilton 2010:48–52). In summary, the challenge of high-commitment HRM, based on a resource-based view of the firm, lies in allocating a job to an individual with the right abilities, in motivating individuals, and in giving them the opportunity to perform (Wilton 2010:48–52).

3.2.3 Biculturalism as a focal point for successful high-commitment HRM

In a globalized and increasingly mobile world (Urry 2000), many individuals work and live across societal cultures or have a personal family history or life experience in the "in-between" (Mahadevan 2012). They experience difference and the need to include others in diverse work and life environments (Prasad et al. 2006). Interpretative cultural research focuses on how individuals make sense of themselves in relation to others in such diverse environments (Mahadevan et al. 2011).

From an interpretative perspective, culture is not considered on a macro-societal level and as an objective fact but rather as processes of identification (Lawler 2008) through which micro-cultures – also called "collective identities" – are created (Mahadevan et al. 2011). In a globalized and mobile world, individuals can be considered as members of many collective identities; depending on focus and individual strategy, different collective identities or cultural identifications will become salient in specific contexts (ibid.). A specific stream of research focuses on those individuals who are across, beyond or between societal cultures, so-called bicultural individuals.

As Brannen and Thomas put it (2010:6), "bicultural individuals identify with two (or more) distinct cultures because of having internalized more than one set of cultural schemas." According to Brannen and Thomas (2010:6), culturally mixed individuals will form the largest ethnic group in the United States by 2020. However, in contrast to common understanding, bicultural individuals are not only those who are born to parents from two different ethnic backgrounds or nationalities (Brannen & Thomas 2010). Biculturalism can also be acquired through expatriation, frequent travels, an intercultural marriage or simple exposure to another cultural environment which can be located in the next neighbourhood. Rather than focusing on the acculturation process of bicultural individuals, it is necessary to analyse how they perceive the relationship between those cultural schemes which they have internalized (Brannen & Thomas 2010:7). To do so, Brannen and Thomas (2010:8) propose a focus on Bicultural Identity Integration (BII). According to BII research, those bicultural individuals who perceive their different identities as being largely complementary and compatible (high BII) often perceive themselves as more competent and are more satisfied with their life than those who perceive their different identities as being mutually exclusive and conflicting (low BII). On the other hand, a perceived conflict between two identities could also lead to a higher cultural awareness. Based on this research, it is suggested that organizations shape work environments so that bicultural individuals do not need to split their identity into different parts in order to "fit" while at the same time these organizations enable them to reflect upon their cultural competencies. For example, for a person with Spanish ancestry in a German company, a high BII will be facilitated if this person is given a job where she or he can interact with Spanish partners or speak Spanish. For doing so, she or he would also need a good reflexive awareness of her or his cultural competencies in order to use them in the best possible way. However, this recommendation is only valid if this person has not yet split her or his identity into two halves in order to "integrate" well. By doing this, the potentially bicultural individual would marginalize her or his "other" cultural identity in a German environment and could not, therefore, access the Spanish cultural schema any more.

As Brannen and Thomas describe (2010), biculturalism is not only about the cultural schemes that can be accessed. It also refers to the special capabilities which can be developed through a high BII. They present six characteristics of bicultural individuals, individuals that can access more than one set of cultural schemas (high BII). These are:

1. Access to multiple cultural knowledge systems
2. Possession of cultural information which is highly self-relevant and hence highly accessible in memory
3. Shift between frame of reference, also called cultural frame switching
4. Greater empathy
5. Flexibility
6. Ability to integrate ideas in potentially novel and more creative ways.

These characteristics can be understood as additional benefits of diversity through lived biculturalism. Due to increasing mobility and migration, the number of potentially bicultural individuals has increased tremendously in virtually all (post-)industrialized countries. However, as the concept of BII shows, not all of these individuals leverage their potential because they perceive the different cultural schemas to which they might have access as mutually exclusive or even conflicting. This is especially true in situations where there is a minority and majority cultural identity (Brannen & Thomas 2010). In these situations, most potentially bicultural individuals tend to split off the minority part of their identity in order to fully fit into the majority cultural identity. However, they pay the price of a low BII and lose access to an alternative cultural schema. As a result, they cannot develop the specific characteristics of bicultural individuals with a high BII. From a RBV, it is therefore essential for successful high-commitment HRM to provide the boundary conditions for a high BII for potentially bicultural individuals to utilize their specific bicultural competencies (Fitzsimmons et al. 2011). Otherwise, the benefits of diversity and biculturalism will not be leveraged.

3.3 Recommended reading

Al Ariss, A., Cascio, W. F. & Paauwe, J. (2014). "Talent management: Current theories and future research directions". In: *Journal of World Business* 49:2, 173–179.

This article gives an introduction to a critical and holistic view of global talent management which acknowledges interrelations across micro-, meso- and macro-level. It highlights that fact that HRM needs to look beyond the individual (micro-) and the organizational (meso-) level in order to truly recognize high potential.

Brannen, M. Y. & Thomas, D. C. (2010). "Bicultural individuals in organizations". In: *International Journal of Cross Cultural Management*, 10:1, 5–16.
This editorial to a special issue provides an introduction to the concept of biculturality. It focuses on the question of how biculturality develops and on which factors actually support the development of bicultural competency. As a major finding, it is assumed that so-called "bicultural identity integration", i.e. perceiving dual cultural identities as non-conflicting and mutually beneficial, is not reached by all individuals who are familiar with two or more cultures but rather has certain requirements. HRM can support these requirements.

Cunliffe, A. (2008). *Organization Theory*. London: Sage.
This book provides a good overview and a concise introduction to organization theory. Organization theory asks the question of how an organization's structure, strategy and practice should be designed in order to deliver the best possible outcome; for example the best possible performance of an organization's employees. Details on organizational design can be found on pp. 25–43.

Lengnick-Hall, M. L., Lengnick-Hall, C. A., Andrade, L. S. & Drake, B. (2009). "Strategic human resource management: The evolution of the field". In: *Human Resource Management Review*, 19:2, 64–85.
This article gives a concise overview of the development of strategic HRM. Strategic HRM can be considered different from operative HRM which often concerns itself with mere personal administration. Strategic HRM is based on the assumption that human resources are the most important corporate assets for competitive advantage and need to be developed strategically and in synch with individual needs, organizational culture and operations, and corporate strategy.

Mahadevan, J. (2012). "Utilizing identity-based resistance for diversity change – a narrative approach". In: *International Journal of Change Management*, 25:6, 819–834.
This article provides an example of how organizational employees might react to increasing workforce diversity. It also discusses key concepts, such as identity and cultural change with regard to diversity. From an HRM perspective, it shows how an organization might transform employees' reactions – even resistance – to increasing diversity into a positive outcome based on the resource-based view in HRM.

Mahadevan, J., Weißert, S. & Müller, F. (2011). "From given cross-cultural difference to a new interculture: A Sino-German example". In: *Interculture Journal*, 14, 55–76.
This article introduces different approaches to cross-cultural theory and to managing cultural difference in organizations. Broadly speaking, it differentiates between the assumption that cultural difference is a given fact on a societal level which cannot be overcome (given culture) and the belief that individuals who interact have the potential to create new shared intercultures (cultural creation). Based on these theoretical assumptions, it is the task of

HRM to overcome initial cultural differences between corporate employees and to shape a corporate "interculture". The article gives an example of how such a development might take place.

Rousseau, D. M. (1995). ***Psychological Contracts in Organizations: Understanding Written and Unwritten Agreements.*** **Thousand Oaks, CA: Sage.**
The psychological contract is an important aspect of employer–employee relations. Broadly speaking, it refers to all aspects which are essential to the work agreement from the employee's perspective. These aspects go beyond the written contract (explicit contract) and verbal agreements and understandings (implicit contract). They refer to the overall understanding an individual has of their tasks and responsibilities. In modern HRM, it is understood that employees will cease to deliver outstanding performances or display high commitment if they have the feeling that the psychological contract has been violated by the employer.

Rousseau, D. M. (2004). "Psychological contracts in the workplace: Understanding the ties that motivate". In: ***Academy of Management Executive*** **18:1, 120–127.**
This article provides more background to the concept of psychological contracts (see Rousseau 1995).

Understanding the complexities of nomadic identities. Special issue of ***Equality, Diversity and Inclusion – an International Journal*** **(2015), 34:4, guest editor: Jasmin Mahadevan.**
This special issue provides an overview on current research and practice. Key findings on bicultural and mobile identities are presented and reflected upon. Suggestions for suitable research design are made. It is available at: www.emeraldinsight.com/toc/edi/34/4

4 QUESTIONS ON THE CASE

In this section, you will familiarize yourself with the three influencing factors organizational design, technological environment and HRM. These shape the organizational environment for utilizing the benefits of biculturalism. Please consider Tasks 1–3 to be preparatory tasks for the fourth question which focuses on synergistic interculturality through biculturalism.

Task 1: Organizational design The Relationship Company has given itself a network design. Please imagine you are the CEO of a company and need to make a decision on which organizational design to choose for your company. Now, look back on the case description and perform a general and a specific SWOT analysis on the organizational design of The Relationship Company with the help of theory. A SWOT analysis links internal strengths (S) and weaknesses (W) with external, e.g. market, opportunities (O) and threats (T). By doing so, it lays the foundation for strategic decision making in organizations.

The questions to be answered from your SWOT analysis of The Relationship Company's organizational design are:

1. Where do you see internal strengths and weaknesses of a network design (a) in general and (b) in the specific case of The Relationship Company?
2. Where do you perceive external opportunities and threats to a network design (a) in general and (b) to The Relationship Company specifically?

Task 2: Technology In order to be implemented successfully, network organizations need to be supported by the right kind of technological environment. Please look back on the case and the requirements of a suitable technological environment for a network organization. Now, identify the core elements of a suitable technological environment for an innovative network organization which also takes into account high workforce diversity on a cultural and a social level.

Task 3: HRM In addition to a supporting technological environment, successful network organizations need the right kind of people on board. Please consider the link between high-commitment HRM, the resource-based view of the firm and the need to constantly link individual motivation, ability and opportunity for high performance. Now, please look back upon the case and ask yourself: What kind of individuals does a company such as The Relationship Company need and how can it constantly ensure their performance? Please consider the constant need for innovation as a core aspect of The Relationship Company. Next, please link this analysis to a company which you might know from your own work experience. Did you have the feeling that your motivation and abilities were utilized in the best way possible and that you were given sufficient opportunities to perform at your best? If not, what would you have wished for?

Task 4: Biculturalism In The Relationship Company, it remains a mystery why the Innovation Team performs as well as it does. In summary, team members are perceived and perceive themselves simply as capable and "clever" individuals. Due to their high diversity, they are not perceived as having something in common. However, if the theory of biculturalism is considered, most of them might be perceived as being potentially "bicultural". Based on this observation:

1. Please look at the individual profile of each team member and identify influencing factors which might be considered as a disposition towards biculturalism. When doing so, please make sure to follow the broad definition of biculturalism in this chapter.
2. Now, please look back on your findings on organizational design, technology and HRM (Tasks 1–3) and try to summarize those factors which enable potentially bicultural team leaders to achieve a high Bicultural Identity Integration (BII) at work. How does The Relationship Company make its design, technology and HRM fit the specific requirements of bicultural individuals?

5 REFERENCES

Al Ariss, A., Cascio, W. F. & Paauwe, J. (2014). "Talent management: Current theories and future research directions". In: *Journal of World Business*, 49:2, 173–179.

Brannen, M. Y. & Thomas, D. C. (2010). "Bicultural individuals in organizations". In: *International Journal of Cross Cultural Management*, 10:1, 5–16.

Colbert, B. A. (2004). "The complex resource-based view: Implications for theory and practice in strategic human resource management". In: *Academy of Management Review*, 29:3, 341–358.

Cunliffe, A. (2008). *Organization Theory*. London: Sage.

Fitzsimmons, S. R., Miska, C. & Stahl, G. (2011). "Multicultural employees: Global business‘ untapped resource". *Organizational Dynamics* 40:3, 199–206.

Heckmann, F. & Schnapper, D. (2003). *The Integration of Immigrants in European Societies: National Differences and Trends of Convergence.* Stuttgart: Lucius et Lucius.

Heyer, K. (2012, May). *Hidden Dimensions of Diversity – Bicultural Competence among Migrant Elites and their Contribution to Successful Teamwork in Technical Companies*. Unpublished bachelor thesis, Pforzheim University, Germany.

Lawler, S. (2008). "Introduction: Identity as a question". In: *Identity: Sociological Perspectives*, 1–9. Cambridge: Polity.

Lengnick-Hall, M. L., Lengnick-Hall, C. A., Andrade, L. S. & Drake, B. (2009). "Strategic human resource management: The evolution of the field". In: *Human Resource Management Review*, 19:2, 64–85.

Mahadevan, J. (2012). "Utilizing identity-based resistance for diversity change – a narrative approach". In: *International Journal of Change Management*, 25:6, 819–834.

Mahadevan, J., Weißert, S. & Müller, F. (2011). "From given cross-cultural difference to a new interculture: A Sino-German example". In: *Interculture Journal*, 14, 55–76.

Prasad, P., Pringle, J. K. & Konrad, A. M. (2006). "Examining the contours of workplace diversity – concepts, contexts and challenges". In: Prasad, P., Pringle, J. K. & Konrad, A. M. (Eds), *Handbook of Workplace Diversity*, 1–22, London: Sage.

Urry, J. (2000). *Sociology beyond Societies*. London: Routledge. Wilton, N. (2010). *Introduction to Human Resource Management*. London: Sage.

20

Going Global Versus Staying Local: The Performance Management Dilemma in the International Context

Fons Trompenaars and Riana van den Bergh

1 INTRODUCTION

The drive towards internationalization and the need to become successful across borders was recognized at an early stage by Perlmutter (1969) in his seminal work on the evolution of companies from ethnocentric to polycentric. However, over the last few decades, management theory has been dominated by an American bias with "one size fits all" solutions (Newman & Nollen 1996:753) and very little empirical research has focused on developing management systems which account for cultural differences (Jackson 2002; Pollitt & Bouckaert 2005). Furthermore, management fads have been swinging from one end of the spectrum to the other, with little or no attempt to integrate the best of both worlds (Trompenaars & Hampden-Turner 2012).

Jackson (2002) is of the opinion that people are valued differently across cultures, with specific reference to work situations. Therefore, "multinational enterprises need to adapt their management practices to the national cultures" to incorporate both a humanistic and an instrumental view of human resources in order to achieve high business performance (Jackson 2002:754). The differentiation between a humanistic and instrumental view of employees can be closely related to the differentiation in cultural values underpinning management practices in the East and the West. For example, strict rules, standard procedures, pay-for-performance and individual rewards are generally characteristic of the Western approach to employees as human resources that should be managed effectively. Countries like the USA tend to value consistency and clarity with little room for flexibility or exceptions in implementation. At the other end of the continuum, countries like Japan, China and Italy follow a more humanistic approach where employees are seen as people who should be developed and mentored. In these countries, a more flexible approach is valued where one can adapt or interpret rules and change standards according to particular circumstances.

The following case study provides an illustration of the tensions that are often faced within the international human resource management context in which head office tries to apply universal performance measures which may not necessarily be appropriate in local subsidiaries.

2 CASE DESCRIPTION

2.1 The situation: company background

"I feel like I'm in a tug-of-war, and I'm the tugging rope." When she started her job at Qwenchy five years ago, Ms. Janet Jones could never have imagined that the small start-up run by two MBA students would grow into the global group it is today. She has seen the company grow and expand and her own position has grown with it. Today, she is heading up a meeting with all the country HR leaders in the Qwenchy Group, at the request of the CEO, Mr. J. A. Daniels. Mr. Daniels has a vision of introducing a new staff appraisal and reward system that is acceptable to the different countries in which Qwenchy operates. "Now is the time when we begin to exert influence over the manner in which we define, measure and reward performance in all parts of the organization," he had announced to the senior management staff at a quarterly meeting. "I would like each of you to send the people managing your human resource function to a meeting next month here at headquarters."

In a phone call before the meeting, he emphasized the importance of this project to Ms. Jones:

> "I want us to build a business case that demonstrates the importance and benefits of cultural diversity. This is a message we should communicate clearly to all those who attend. In order to leverage the diversity in Qwenchy, we need standard structures for measuring performance. I expect you, as an HR professional who has seen our company grow, to facilitate this meeting and ensure the buy-in of all our HR country leaders, Ms. Jones."

At the time, this seemed like a fairly reasonable request to Ms. Jones. But now, after four hours of back-and-forth discussions, she feels like all the country leaders are pulling at her in opposite directions. Right now she does not think that they are ever going to find agreement on an appropriate performance management system.

Email from Mr. J. H. Daniels to HR country directors of Qwenchy:

Qwenchy International

To:	National Human Resource Directors	
	Mr Yakomoto	Qwenchy International Japan

	Mr. Mantovani	Qwenchy International Italy
	Mr. Klaus	Qwenchy International Germany
	Mr. Khasmi	Qwenchy International UAE– Dubai
	Ms. Jones	Qwenchy International USA
From:	J. A. Daniels	
Date:	29 June 2014	
Subject:	Meeting Intro ASAS (Advanced Staff Appraisal and Reward System) 15 July 2014, 9.00 a.m. US Headquarters	
Attachment(s):	"Ten wise lessons for staff appraisal"	

Dear Country HR Directors,

I am happy to invite you to a "brainstorming meeting" on the introduction of our new Advanced Staff Appraisal and Reward System (ASAS). Until recently, staff appraisal and rewards have been a relatively underappreciated element within our organization. But times have changed. Motivated employees are in danger of being lost due to growing competition for top talent. Increasingly we realize that staff appraisal and competitive rewards should be the cornerstone of our company's human resources policy. Indeed, employee engagement can best be attained by increasing employee motivation and by rewarding results and contributions appropriately. One of the strongest motivational forces is the linkage between individual performance and rewards. Therefore, one of the main principles built into our new ASAS should be pay-for-performance. It is my belief that this is vital to guarantee the continuing existence of our company. We must recognize that how effectively, competitively and appropriately we define, measure and reward performance will impact on the quality of our workforce and our success. What I consider to be an ideal Staff Appraisal and Reward System for Qwenchy International comprises the following elements:

I Values

Entrepreneurship within Qwenchy International means recognizing that our performance relies on the motivation, commitment and expertise of our employees. People are a vital factor in Qwenchy's business, and people management is crucial to our success. Therefore, ASAS is to become management's primary instrument for guiding and steering our employees.

II Clear goals

The main purpose of the appraisal process is to improve performance. The main purpose of introducing pay-for-performance is to motivate staff.

III Clear criteria for what is being appraised

Individual targets should be set at the start of the appraisal period and performance should be reviewed regularly against fixed criteria such as key results achieved, effectiveness in reaching targets and contribution to business plans. Criteria should be established that will be used to measure competencies, such as performance under pressure, influencing others, safety awareness, effective planning, ability to defend opinions firmly and sense of reality.

IV Clear and consistent guidelines for the appraisal process:

- Scheduling of appraisal meetings.
- Preparation and procedures for appraisal meetings.
- Documenting the outcome of appraisal meetings using the Staff Appraisal Form.

V ASAS should be strongly linked to procedures for promotion and rewards

I feel strongly about introducing an individualized system of pay-for-performance, i.e. I want financial rewards to be dependent on individual contribution to business results. I believe this type of reward system is one of the strongest motivating forces imaginable. Obviously the recent financial crisis has shown we should not base rewards solely on short-term financial results that employees cannot influence, but this does not mean we should not sharply differentiate between high and low performers.

It is my intention to introduce ASAS in exactly the same way in all countries in which Qwenchy operates. I believe that we need a centralized and standardized approach to staff appraisal to ensure consistency and flexibility in terms of moving people around. Hence we will use only one standard Staff Appraisal Form worldwide. The primary objective of having your group discuss the process is for the process to be the same in all the countries we operate and work well in every country.

At the end of the meeting, I expect to have an outline of an ASAS which is feasible and acceptable to all of us. Ms. Jones will be at your meeting to represent my views and to feed your views back to me. I welcome as many recommendations and suggestions as possible.

I enclose a list of "Ten wise lessons for staff appraisal" that I, personally, have always found useful.

I look forward to your conclusions.

J. A. Daniels

Attachment: Ten wise lessons for an effective staff appraisal meeting (By: J. A. Daniels)

Please find below a number of tips we could use as part of the instructions that will be sent to all appraisers of Qwenchy's local operating companies for the next staff appraisal round.

1. ASAS should focus on appraising **specific results** as output, and **function-specific behaviour** as input.

2. Base your judgements on **performance and business results**: do not be misled by any kind of personal preference; do not be biased by prejudices, and leave "the person" out of consideration.
3. Evaluate each appraisal criterion in **isolation**. Do not let strong or weak points of the appraisee influence your evaluation of other criteria.
4. Don't be influenced by previous experiences you have had with the appraisee (a recent success or blunder should not bias the actual appraisal).
5. Evaluate on the basis of **this year only**. Past performances should not be taken into account.
6. Base judgements on **concrete facts**, not on notions or assumptions. The appraisal must be as **objective** as possible.
7. Don't be afraid of giving low ratings if necessary. A boss who always tries to stay in the safe middle is doing injustice to other well-performing employees.
8. Evaluate on the basis of **fair company norms**, even if the requirements of the job are not well defined and performance is difficult to measure.
9. **Be honest, open, frank and direct**. Don't be afraid of confrontations.
10. Make sure that ranking procedures for rewards are **consistent** with the actual appraisal. The Staff Appraisal Form should justify the salary increases.

2.2 The challenge

Earlier that day ...
Ms. Jones opened the meeting and welcomed all regional HR representatives. She started by saying:

> "Obviously, I'm very happy with Mr. Daniels' proposal. I want the group to agree, but I'm absolutely sure that Mr. Daniels has outlined an ideal ASAS here. So I would be quite disappointed if you rejected his idea of a universal and standardized ASAS. This works so well in the US; I don't see any reason why it wouldn't work in other countries too. I will be open to compromise, of course, if you can come up with a reasonable argument. I hereby open the meeting with the hope that our discussions are useful and by asking if you have any questions."

The Italian representative Mr. Mantovani was flabbergasted. He is against the idea of introducing ASAS worldwide in a standardized form. He reacted:

> "Ms. Jones, with all due respect for the professionalism of yourself and Mr. Daniels, I think that the cookie cutter approach might work well on pizzas but not on humans. In Italy we are concerned about a humane approach that respects each employee, and does not treat them as robots."

"Yes," Mr. Khasmi added, and continued:

> "Although we are not against having standardized, worldwide ASAS, I think it is wise to attune some aspects to the traditions and values of local operating companies. We need to respect our religious environment as well as our local cultures. Can we create some room for local adaptation?"

Ms. Jones responded by saying that some adaptations were likely around Mr. Daniels' outline. As long as the main philosophy was untouched, some local adaptations were permitted.

Mr. Klaus from Germany made it clear that he was particularly serious about one issue: the appraisee should also be evaluated on his/her compliance with the rules, procedures and regulations stipulated by the organization. "As long as we see clarity in the procedures and the way we need to apply the system at home, I don't see any problems."

The Japanese representative Mr. Yakomoto didn't think it was feasible to standardize ASAS worldwide. He expressed himself clearly and with diplomacy:

> "Each culture is different and has different ways of solving problems. For example, the so-called ten wise lessons would be totally counterproductive when applied to our country. How can you isolate a person from his/her job? How can you evaluate on the basis of this year only? Should you not take efforts and progress into account? What are concrete facts? Do they exist? How can they expect us to be direct and confrontational? Let's take these aspects into consideration as well."

"We in Italy would like to discuss some of those values and the ten wise lessons, which are not seen as very wise in Milano", added Mr. Mantovani.

"Mr. Mantovani, I fully agree with you" responded Mr. Yakomoto, and went on:

> "There are so many assumptions in Mr. Daniels' ten 'wise' lessons. Let's take the first where he suggests that ASAS should focus on appraising specific results of the individual as output, and individual function-specific behaviour as input. We would have a lot of problems with that in Japan".

"Wait a second," interjected Ms. Jones, "it is individuals who can perform and behave – teams cannot. That's why we chose this approach".

Mr. Klaus nodded his head to show agreement. He was very happy with the introduction of an individualized system of pay-for-performance; this can be a very strong motivational force. And he also added that the final responsibility should remain in the hands of the individual, otherwise the risk is that too many individuals will hide behind the backs of the others. "What we need as Qwenchy are entrepreneurs who take their own initiative and take their own responsibility".

Mr. Yakomoto was taken aback but responded:

> "I am not sure I agree with you, Mr. Klaus. Although pay-for-performance can indeed be a very strong motivational tool, I think an individualized system diminishes teamwork. Furthermore, I believe it is a shared responsibility of both appraiser and appraisee to improve performance. Evaluating

> performance is not sufficient. The appraiser should not act only as a judge. It is his/her responsibility to support and lead the appraisee to even better performance by practising mentorship, making development/training plans etc. We should not only evaluate people based on what they have achieved, but also on how they have achieved it, rewarding creativity, teamwork and personal development. Therefore, I find it necessary that the ASAS stresses this."

Mr. Khasmi agreed and said:

> "I do not believe in the principles of individual pay-for-performance as favoured by Daniels. I believe it is unfair to reward individuals at the cost of the team. Mr. Yakomoto and I think it is more motivating to reward a group (or department or division) than individual persons. If the group is motivated to work hard and receives a salary increase, every single individual will benefit from that. But it does not work the other way around. On the contrary, if an individual is rewarded extra for outstanding results, it might even demotivate the group (why are we all working so hard if we are not allowed to share in the profit?) Hence, the competitive aspect of individual pay-for-performance can have a disruptive aspect on the functioning of a team. Furthermore, the unstable business environment in Iran leads to continuously changing market conditions. It would be unfair to only evaluate the last year's performance when conditions out of an employee's control may affect performance!"

The meeting went quiet for a moment. "Perhaps we should take a break for lunch and then try to look at our different perspectives with fresh eyes after a break," suggested Ms. Jones.

During the lunch break, Ms. Jones retreated to her office for a quiet think:

> "Everyone wants something different and everyone seems to want the opposite of what everyone else wants – in any case, the opposite of what Mr. Daniels wants. Perhaps all these diverse viewpoints are more trouble than they're worth!"

3 BACKGROUND KNOWLEDGE

3.1 The authors' point of reference

Fons Trompenaars is known all over the world for his work as consultant, trainer, motivational speaker and author of many books on the subject of culture and business. Riana van den Bergh is a specialist in intercultural management and works as consultant and trainer with managers in multinational corporations. The authors focus their efforts on helping leaders and professionals manage and solve their business and cultural dilemmas through moving beyond traditional linear models of problem solving. Through translating business challenges into strategic dilemmas, organizations are better able to leverage and benefit from diversity arising from value differences by developing win–win solutions that integrate the best of both worlds.

3.2 Concepts, models, frameworks

Cultural differences and their consequences at work Cultural differences within the workforce raise critical management issues. Concepts such as conducting formal performance appraisals and basing rewards on individual performance have proven difficult to implement and to make work effectively in some parts of the world (Pollitt & Bouckaert 2005). Although it may seem logical that communitarian cultures may require performance appraisal measures which are different from those of individualistic cultures, globalization poses a critical dilemma to international HRM departments: While globalization is almost synonymous with standardization (Newman & Nollen 1996), regional differences require different approaches. However, as labour mobility also increases, the need for equitable rewards become more prominent as employees within the same organization seek equitable rewards across national borders. Thus, whilst traditional, Western-based management principles may not meet the needs of their Asian counterparts, all employees in the organization should be served by the reward system. The behavioural theories that have withstood research scrutiny in the "Western world" (e.g. expectancy, equity and reinforcement theories) suggest that a tight linkage between employee competence, performance and rewards should produce positive motivation (Jackson 2002). However, empirical findings have shown opposite results in countries like Japan and China, where the employee is not merely considered to be an instrument and a resource (Jackson 2002).

Trompenaars and others have conducted research on the dimensions of culture and have found that there is great variation across countries (Hofstede 1991; Trompenaars & Hampden-Turner 2004). In order to successfully build a performance management system that accounts for diverse value differences, it is important to understand the basic assumptions underlying different cultural orientations. Table 20.1 provides a reference framework for understanding these differences at a meta-level. In using this table, it is important to realize that no single culture fits the profile exactly and the framework is merely a simplification of reality to aid in the process of positioning cultures.

Contrasting cultural profiles

Table 20.1 Contrasting cultural profiles

Eastern/Southern cultures	Western/Northern cultures
Characteristics of cultures:	Characteristics of cultures:
Collectivist; hierarchical; particularistic; ascribed status; person-focused; external control; intuitive/holistic; high power difference	Individualistic; egalitarian; universalistic; achieved status; task-focused; internal control; analytical/reductionist; low power difference
Countries with cultures that favour this profile:	Countries with cultures that favour this profile:
Japan; China; Egypt; Indonesia; Turkey; Brazil; Venezuela; S. Korea; France; Greece; Italy; Spain	United States; United Kingdom; Canada; Australia

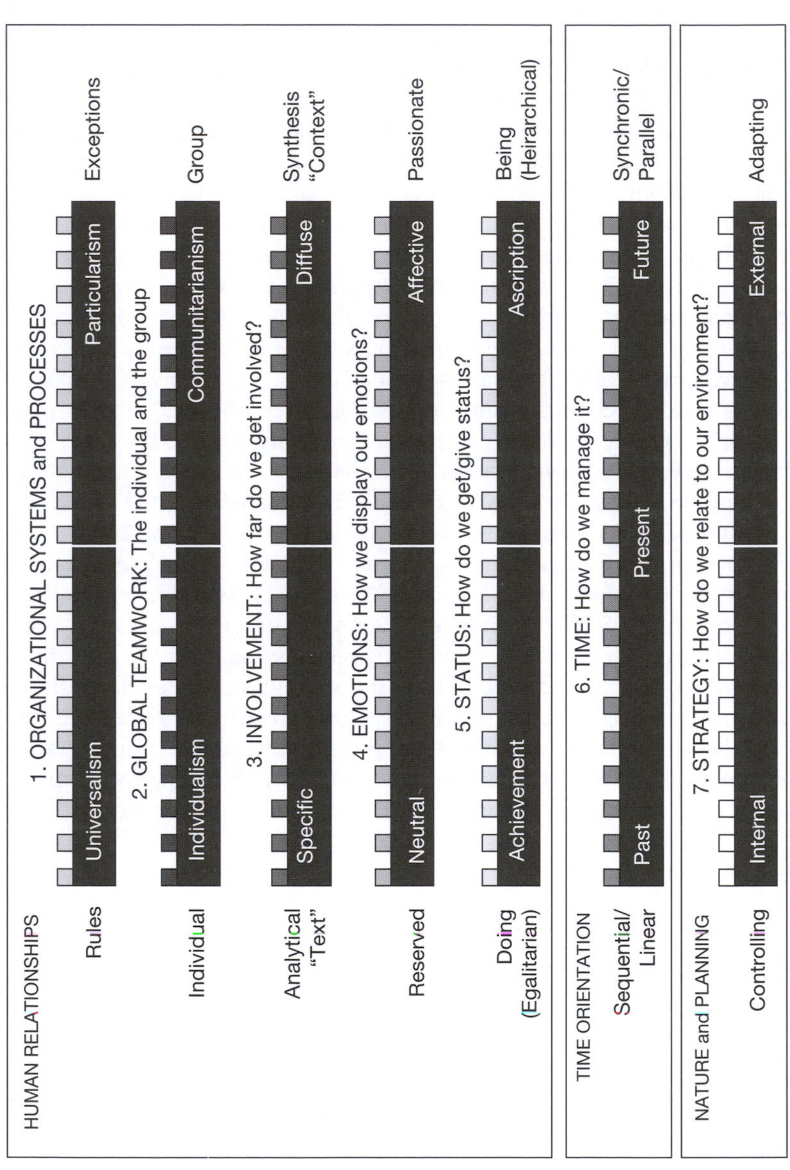

Figure 20.1 The seven dimensions of culture

The characteristics represented in Table 20.1 are based on cultural research by Hall (1976), Hofstede (1991), and Trompenaars & Hampden-Turner (2004) and can be summarized according to seven dimensions (Figure 20.1 and Table 20.2). These dimensions can be translated into strategic tensions that could potentially affect the development of performance measures in the international context (Trompenaars & Hampden-Turner 2012). They provide a critical framework for understanding the shaping role of culture (both at national level and between different functions, departments and groups) in determining the locus of human value ascribed to employees within an organization (Jackson 2002).

Table 20.2 The seven dimensions of culture

1. Universalism Rules, codes, laws, and generalizations	**Particularism** Exceptions, special circumstances, unique relations
2. Individualism Personal freedom, human rights, competitiveness	**Communitarianism** Social responsibility, harmonious relations, cooperation
3. Specificity Atomistic, reductive, analytic, objective	**Diffusion** Holistic, elaborative, synthetic, relational
4. Neutral Dispassionate, controlled, detached	**Affective** Enthusiastic, responsive, passionate
5. Achieved status What you've done, your track record	**Ascribed status** Who you are, your potential, connections
6. Inner direction Conscience and convictions are located inside	**Outer direction** Exemplars and influences are located outside
7. Sequential time Time is a race along a set course	**Synchronous time** Time is a dance of fine coordination

Cultural assumptions have a significant impact on the way people behave and interact with each other and consequently also affect the performance of an organization. Through identifying basic assumptions and recognizing their impact in a particular context, managers are able to frame their experiences and translate these meta-level dilemmas into real-life issues that can then be reconciled.

Reconciling seemingly opposing tensions It is important to identify differences between contrasting cultures, so that organizations can anticipate the impact of these differences and search for ways to reconcile the resulting conflicts. However, the danger of using a framework such as the seven dimensions model for understanding cultural differences is that one may view its value orientations as polar opposites, reinforcing existing stereotypes. In order to leverage effectively the strengths underlying each of these values, it is necessary not only to define these opposites, but also to recognize the values associated with each and to determine how the differences can be reconciled. By moving beyond traditional linear thinking patterns, the successful international manager is able to deal with complexity through the ability to deal effectively with paradox. For example:

> "How can we ensure recognition of the group's performance through identifying individual contributions... and then, how can we recognize individual contributions through the group and the group's performance?"

Table 20.3 (based on Jackson 2002:457) provides a framework for understanding the role of cultural values in performance management:

Table 20.3 The role of cultural values in performance management

Locus of human value	**Instrumentalism**	**Humanism**
	Seeing people as a means to an end	Seeing people as an end in themselves
View of people	Human resource management: People are a resource of the organization	People development: The organization should serve the ends of its people
Cultural factors	Individualism Control orientation Achievement orientation Egalitarian commitment	Communitarianism People orientation Relations orientation Loyal commitment
Orientation of performance management system	Job measurement Pay-for-performance Job descriptions Competencies	Worker participation Developing the person Social welfare Job commitment

Source: Based on Jackson (2002:457).

In the global organization, there is a continuous tension between the need for standards (a universal performance management system) and multiple reward systems that are tailored to local circumstances. However, performance and rewards management are inextricably woven together. The secret to successful management is to integrate and reconcile the tension between universal, globalized reward systems and particular, localized and customized performance measures.

3.3 Recommended reading

Jackson, T. (2002). "The management of people across cultures: Valuing people differently". In: *Human Resource Management*, 41, 455–475.
This article provides a better understanding of the way in which underlying values determine the way in which individuals are valued across cultures and workplaces. A conceptual framework for understanding the locus of human value provides insights into the key tensions between human resource management (instrumentalism) and people development (humanism). Treating employees from humanistic cultures from an instrumental perspective may lead to offence, alienation and/or lack of commitment.

Robert, J. G. (2011). ***Rewarding Performance: Guiding Principles; Custom Strategies*****. New York: Routledge.**
This book provides key insights into the principles guiding effective performance and rewards management, with guidelines and principles that can be incorporated into developing performance and reward strategies.

Perlmutter, H. V. (1969). "The tortuous evolution of the multinational corporation". In: ***Colombia Journal of World Business*****, January–February, 9–18.**
This article describes the evolution of companies from ethnocentric with a local focus to geocentric multinationals and will provide the student with a framework for understanding the evolution of Qwenchy from a local holding to a multinational business and the potential issues that may currently prevail within the organization.

Trompenaars, F. & Hampden-Turner, C. (2012). ***Riding the Waves of Culture*****. 3rd ed. London: Wiley.**
The seminal work by Fons Trompenaars and Charles Hampden-Turner addresses the impact of culture on business through case studies and findings from the largest database of managers around the world. Through illustrating the tensions between value dimensions and translating them to the business world, the book challenges the reader to think beyond linear either/or solutions to business dilemmas.

4 QUESTIONS ON THE CASE

1. There are tensions and opposing interests at various levels in this case study. Analyse the various interests and guidelines for the proposed ASAS system, utilizing the theory of locus of human value and the seven dimensions of culture model. Map out the following aspects:
   a) The locus of human value of Mr. Daniels, Ms. Jones, Mr. Mantovani, Mr. Yakomoto, Mr. Klaus and Mr. Khasmi.
   b) Compare the key guidelines suggested for the ASAS system with the guidelines that each of the HR country directors responds with or the reservations that they hold and try to identify the conflicting guidelines.
   c) Identify the cultural value dimension underlying each of the guidelines you have identified in b.

Please use the following worksheet for your analysis:

Locus of human value	**Instrumentalism**	**Humanism**
Who holds this locus?		
Requirement for measuring performance		
Cultural value dimension		

(*Continued*)

Requirement for measuring performance

Cultural value dimension

Requirement for measuring performance

Cultural value dimension

Requirement for measuring performance

Cultural value dimension

Requirement for measuring performance

Cultural value dimension

Requirement for measuring performance

Cultural value dimension

---

2. Identify the main conflicts from your analysis above and translate them into potential strategic dilemmas that Qwenchy has to reconcile when implementing a global performance management system. Propose a best-of-both worlds resolution for each of these dilemmas.

5 REFERENCES

Hall, E. T. (1976). *Beyond Culture.* New York: Anchor Books.

Hofstede (1991). *Cultures and Organizations: Software of the Mind.* London: McGraw-Hill UK.

Jackson, T. (2002). "The management of people across cultures: Valuing people differently". In: *Human Resource Management*, 41, 455–475.

Newman, K. L. & Nollen, S. D. (1996). "Culture and congruence: The fit between management practices and national culture". In: *Journal of International Business Studies,* 27, 753–779.

Perlmutter, H. V. (1969). "The tortuous evolution of the multinational corporation". In: *Colombia Journal of World Business,* January–February, 9–18.

Pollitt, C. & Bouckaert, G. (2005). *Public Management Reform: A Comparative Analysis – New Public Management, Governance, and the Neo-Weberian State.* New York: Oxford University Press.

Trompenaars, F. & Hampden-Turner, C. (2004). *Managing People Across Culture.* London: Wiley.

Trompenaars, F. & Hampden-Turner, C. (2012). *Riding the Waves of Culture.* 3rd ed. London: Wiley.

21

A Parcel to Spain: Reconciling Cultural and Managerial Dilemmas Caused by the Implementation of Corporate Culture Instruments

Christoph Barmeyer, Eric Davoine and Vincent Merk

1 INTRODUCTION

Corporate culture is a crucial part of organizations: it constitutes a shared identity for members of the organization, aids orientation and decision making and shapes the actions of employees. It can thus have a coordinating, integrating and motivational role (Brown 1998). Management can, however, also deploy corporate culture as a controlling or sanctioning instrument, as will be demonstrated in this chapter.

It is important to differentiate between two types of corporate culture. One type is a culture which has grown organically and is mostly *implicit* so that, while influencing the actual conduct of members of the organization, it is not necessarily found in any written form. The other type of corporate culture is one which is communicated and codified in an *explicit* form by way of documents as a management instrument (Barmeyer & Davoine 2011; Blazejevski 2006; d'Iribarne 2012; Palazzo 2002). However, it does not necessarily correspond with the actual culture that is in place.

In terms of management processes, corporate culture can be understood as a *resource*, which enhances value creation within the company. A "strong" corporate culture brings benefits here because there is a high level of consistency in shared patterns of action. Strong cultures can be distinguished by their wide acceptance and high degree of uniformity in planning and implementation. When it comes to implementing a strong corporate culture – and establishing and enforcing ethical conduct – instruments of corporate culture such as mission statements, corporate image, corporate principles, corporate values and codes of conduct are used (d'Iribarne 2012; Palazzo, 2002). These provide guidance to all parties involved in clarifying the company's overarching corporate objectives (Brown 1998). In this case we will focus on *corporate values* and *codes of conduct*.

In the process of internationalization, multinational companies (MNCs) are confronted with the challenge of harmonizing corporate culture throughout their subsidiaries, following the widely held idea that a strong global corporate culture will strengthen the company's identity and image and reduce transaction costs within the MNC. Since the 1980s, many MNCs have been attempting to create a coherent global corporate culture, a concept that has been developed in the US. There are two main objectives behind this.

Firstly, from a *business management* perspective, corporate culture is intended to help reduce complexity and improve cost efficiency by standardizing organizational structures and processes (planning, information/management and control systems). Corporate culture thereby fulfils the function of a global instrument, connecting systems of management, coordination and control. Here, corporate culture does not govern which tasks employees must carry out, but rather *the way* in which they are to perform them. The successful implementation and ability of these systems to function depends on the commitment of the agents, managers, employees and other stakeholders involved.

Secondly, from a *human resources* perspective, corporate culture helps stabilize the organization's identity and boost employee identification (Schein 1986). This identification with the company can bring about a high degree of motivation with regard to strategies, objectives, responsibilities and tasks and, among other factors, generate loyalty to the company.

Based on the US model, more and more European companies, particularly subsidiaries, are being affected by the introduction of global corporate cultures (Tempel et al. 2006), as instruments of corporate culture are transferred from the parent company to subsidiaries. Corporate values and especially codes of conduct can be defined as instruments to implement a normative "global organizational culture", proposing orientations for action in order to control and to regulate the employees' behaviours and practices in every subsidiary. This process can be described as *international transfer* (Barmeyer & Davoine 2011; Blazejevski 2006; Edwards et al. 2007). As a result, subsidiaries facing this kind of homogenization encounter conflicting dilemmas, namely the need for a global, uniform, corporate culture on the one hand, and the desire to respect and preserve local or country-specific characteristics on the other. Defining universally applicable rules of conduct and reaching employees who regard these rules as incompatible with their own culture also are a challenge. Previous studies have underlined the US-American tradition of codes of conduct and demonstrated a certain resistance in Europe towards this kind of normative instrument

(Barmeyer & Davoine 2011; d'Iribarne 2002; Helin & Sandström 2008; Talaulicar 2009).

This case focuses on the reception and application of corporate cultural instruments, namely value statements and codes of conduct transferred from the US headquarters to the German subsidiary (Palazzo 2002). This reception process may also include the possibility of violations of these codes and charters.

2 CASE DESCRIPTION

2.1 The Pharmatix Company

Pharmatix (the company name has been changed to preserve confidentiality) is an MNC in the pharmaceuticals industry with approximately 30,000 employees worldwide. Pharmatix is among the five largest companies in the world in its market sector, and is known for its innovative products and dedication to quality. The headquarters are in the US Midwest with subsidiaries in more than 20 countries, including Switzerland, Germany and France. The company was founded at the beginning of the 20th century in the United States and has developed a strong corporate culture based on fundamental values and norms. It grew in the 1990s through mergers and acquisitions. The German subsidiary came into being through a takeover.

Pharmatix sees itself as a community, resembling a family, in which interactions are based on trust. Control is not considered necessary, and is not often emphasized. The individual is responsible for the company. This is why self-responsibility concerning the achievement of objectives, working style and decisions regarding working hours are given to the employees and managers. Social responsibility, an ethical behaviour, is the central topic for the company, and is not only linked to suppliers and other stakeholders outside the company, but is also important internally. The regulation of the "community" and "ethical behaviour" is drawn from a worldwide code of conduct, and four corporate values, which are used, like in many other North-American companies, as managerial instruments (Palazzo 2002).

Normative instruments of the corporate culture of Pharmatix

Corporate values

The first element of the global corporate culture of Pharmatix consists of corporate values. Corporate values form the basis of a clearly defined, global corporate culture. Management research assumes that a high level of organizational consistency in the corporate culture – that is, relating to the strategic, planning, decision-making, work, management and control processes – can be achieved in particular by clearly communicating values and putting them into practice (Schein 1986).

Values can be defined as subjective, desirable general principles and decision-making rules within a group or company that govern conduct and relate to instruments or conditions. As benchmarks and preferences, they influence and organize individuals' ideas, feelings and behaviour, including that of employees and managers. Just as national cultural values are generally regarded as guiding individual conduct, *corporate cultural* values likewise provide decision-making tools and guidance regarding conduct in everyday business situations, particularly those involving ethical issues. Corporate values thereby provide a system of reference and orientation for employees in their day-to-day dealings with colleagues and stakeholders (Blasco & Zølner 2010).

Mercier (2001) examined the occurrence of certain corporate values across multiple sectors in 40 large French companies. He found that companies from different sectors often have the same corporate values.

Table 21.1 Occurrence of values in large French companies

Formalized corporate value	Occurrence in %
Respect for other people	55
Respect for customers	55
Trust	40
Value creation	35
Responsibility	30
Teamwork	27
Protecting the environment	27
Integrity	25
Professionalism	25
Innovation	22
Excellence	22
Quality	22
Commitment	22

Source: Mercier (2001:67), translation.

What values are supposed to characterize the company Pharmatix? Figure 21.1 sets out its corporate values.

Code of conduct

The second element of the global corporate culture of Pharmatix consists of the code of conduct. A code of conduct is based on corporate values and/or basic ethical ideas, generally drawn up by the parent company and issued to all employees in document form (Kaptein 2004). The code of conduct regulates the company's rights and responsibilities, particularly relationships between employees and stakeholders such as colleagues, customers, suppliers,

Integrity that embraces the very highest standards of honesty and ethical behaviour. We believe in operating with integrity in all our business dealings. We conduct ourselves in a responsible fashion as outlined in our Worldwide Code of Conduct.

Excellence that is reflected in our unsurpassed focus on quality and a continuous search for new ways to improve everything we do.

Respect for people that includes our concern for the interests of all people who touch – or are touched by – our company: customers, employees, shareholders, partners, suppliers and communities.

Trust and transparency: At the core of all ethical business dealings, there must be trust. Trust that others will do as they say, and trust that we will live up to our commitments. To accomplish this, we must also be transparent in the way we communicate with others, providing timely and accurate information.

Figure 21.1 Corporate values of Pharmatix

families and public institutions. The key issues dealt with are the handling of conflicts of interest, corruption, confidential information, health and safety, the environment, etc., as well as human rights and socially responsible working relationships in terms of corporate social responsibility (CSR) (Blasco & Zølner 2010).

In sum, the code of conduct serves as the basis for the decision-making process and guides the behaviour of managers and employees; it is a sort of guideline consisting of internal rules and regulations. Within the context of international management it is significant that US companies also transfer their codes of conduct to their foreign subsidiaries. One *legal* reason for this transfer is an American law (Foreign Corrupt Practices Act 1977), which stipulates that US companies can be held liable not only for the actions of US employees but also employees of foreign subsidiaries. This regulation was reinforced by the Sarbanes–Oxley Act (SOX) in 2002 that requires that all US multinationals and all multinationals listed on the New York Stock Exchange have a single, unique code of conduct that is distributed to all of the subsidiaries. This leads to a situation in which an international company adopts an institutional role in this context as a "non-state legislator".

Pharmatix's code of conduct is based on the four fundamental corporate values (Figure 21.1) and is considered by the management as a tool for developing a shared corporate culture with identical standards of conduct in all of the company's subsidiaries. Since the 1990s, the code of conduct has been added to and updated several times, translated into 15 languages and currently is 32 pages long. It is provided to all employees in the form of a booklet, which has to be signed on the last page by all employees upon recruitment. It starts with a letter from the CEO and then outlines various aspects of ethical behaviour (including social responsibility). In this way, it exemplifies the stated corporate values.

The Code of Business Conduct provides standards for conducting business consistently with the company's legal obligations, global policies, and core values.

At Pharmatix we have always understood that our success is possible because of our values, which include integrity, excellence, respect for people and trust and transparency.

The Code requires that we exercise the highest degree of ethical conduct in all our dealings with or on behalf of Pharmatix.

Compliance with the Code is essential to preserving and enhancing Pharmatix's reputation as a responsible corporate citizen and ultimately to maximizing shareholder value. Violation of the Code is a serious matter that could subject you or Pharmatix to legal liability. It's all a part of "doing the right thing"! All employees are required to report suspected or observed violations of the law, the Code, or company policies. Failure to do so may result in loss of company reputation or public trust; serious damage to the health and safety of our customers, your co-workers, or members of the community; financial penalties for the company; and/or serious penalties for individual employees.

Figure 21.2 Code of conduct of Pharmatix

The newly recruited employee's signature has the value of a moral and legal commitment. An employee who witnesses an infraction by another employee is expected to inform the management. In this way, management can protect itself from any claims by third parties and is legally exonerated in the event of non-compliant or "unethical" conduct on the part of an employee. In this respect, the code of conduct fulfils a regulating and regulatory function with legal consequences. In the event of non-compliant conduct, employees face sanctions, which can lead to dismissal in extreme cases. Meriting special mention is the normative, explicitly binding and mandatory nature of the code of conduct as demonstrated in the event we consider now.

2.2 A violation of the code of conduct – a parcel to Spain ...

Our incident happens in the German subsidiary of the American company. One thousand people work in this subsidiary, and its organizational structure is divided into five departments: research and development, production, finance, marketing and human resources. The financial situation of the German subsidiary is seen as healthy.

By chance, a parcel, which was sent to a Spanish address, returns to the company's post room because the recipient in Spain has moved without leaving a forwarding address. As with all letters and parcels which cannot be assigned to a department the parcel goes to the human resources department. It turns out that one of the marketing managers, a very competent, successful and hard-working woman, Maria Müller, a German employee who has been living and working in Germany for some years, sent private post at the company's expense.

The human resources director, Markus Schmidt, invites her for a talk about this. Maria Müller is a little upset and stresses that this was an exception, but after all, working more than 60 hours a week for Pharmatix, from the early morning until late at night, she has no time to go to the regular post office. Investing so much time and energy, she contributes to the well-being of the company. It is difficult to weigh out the appropriate action to be taken in this situation.

Markus Schmidt underlines that Maria Müller's behaviour is a substantial breach of trust and that private and professional matters should be strictly separated, as is written in the code of conduct. Someone who uses the infrastructure for private matters may also take advantage of more substantial resources, which are technically owned by the company. Maria Müller argues that sending a small parcel will not harm the company substantially.

What should Markus Schmidt do? Ask Maria Müller to resign? (According to the code of conduct, Maria Müller would have to leave the company.) Accept the fact that this is a minor violation? Refuse to punish the violation? Markus Schmidt is facing a dilemma.

Figure 21.3 gives some information about the two protagonists:

Markus Schmidt

Markus Schmidt is 55 years old, was born in Hannover, in the north of Germany, went to school there and studied business administration, specializing in human resource management. He worked in the HR department in an American company based in Hamburg and joined Pharmatix at the age of 35. Afterwards he spent three years in the US headquarters of Pharmatix before he became head of the HR department in the German subsidiary. He is a very structured, analytical and principled person.

Maria Müller

Maria Müller is 35 years old. She was born near Lake Constance in the south of Germany and studied business administration with specialization in marketing at the University of Applied Sciences in Cologne. She started her career at the age of 25 with Lufthansatic, became a manager at Dr. Oscar, and then worked for Unilevel, heading various international marketing projects before going on to work for Pharmatix in Frankfurt, Germany. She speaks English and French perfectly. She is a very hard-working and dedicated employee, spontaneous, communicative, and with an infectious smile that is very much appreciated by her colleagues.

Figure 21.3 Characteristics of the two protagonists

3 BACKGROUND KNOWLEDGE

3.1 The authors' point of reference

The authors, Christoph Barmeyer (German national, worked in France for eight years), Eric Davoine (French national, worked in Germany for eight years, working and living in Switzerland since 2003) and Vincent Merk (French and Dutch national, working and living in the Netherlands since

1981) are specialists in intercultural management, human resource management and organizational culture. They have experienced in their daily work the conflicting and complementary aspects of working interculturally. They believe that culture is a system of values, meanings and practices which is socially constructed, so that a new culture – an interculture – can be co-constructed in dialogic reciprocal processes. Often, these system differences, which sometimes include opposed viewpoints, may lead to dilemmas which can be reconciled and resolved and may combine their strengths as a resource.

More information about their approaches (and some articles) can be found on their websites: www.uni-passau.de/barmeyer, www.unifr.ch/rho and www.linkedin.com/pub/vincent-merk/1/6a6/b16.

3.2 Concepts, models, frameworks

Cultural dimensions Based on the work of Parsons and Shils (1951) as well as Kluckhohn and Strodtbeck (1961) and inspired by Hofstede's (1980/2001) cultural dimensions, Hampden-Turner and Trompenaars (2000) suggest different cultural dimensions that help to facilitate and implement a process of reconciliation. All seven dimensions feature opposites in values, concepts and the behaviours that stem from them (Hampden-Turner & Trompenaars 2006). A short overview:

Universalism vs. particularism
What is more important, following universal rules, procedures and protocols, meeting (technical) standards, or, on the contrary, focusing more on particular circumstances and (local) situations involving many more relationships with the people present?

Individualism vs. communitarianism
Do we act in society in general and function at work in particular as an individual or rather in a group (*I* vs. *we*)? How much is teamwork involved?

Affective vs. neutral cultures
To what extent do we show our emotions? To what extent can a show of emotions be a professionally acceptable behaviour?

Specific vs. diffuse cultures
How far do we get involved? Do we segment reality or, on the contrary, do we have a holistic approach to it?

Achievement vs. ascription
Do we have to prove ourselves to receive status by achieving things in our (professional) lives, or is status assigned to us, for example on the basis of birth, family background or gender?

Time perception
How important are past, present and future and their relations with one another? *Sequential* vs. *synchronic* cultures: do we usually do one thing at a time or rather several things at once? Is time a friend or an enemy?

Relation to nature

Internal vs. *external control*: do we want to control our natural, social or professional environment and hence master all kinds of processes in our lives or at work, or on the contrary act and work in harmony with our environment and let things happen by themselves?

For a further description of these cultural dimensions, see Hampden-Turner and Trompenaars (2000).

Dilemmas What is a dilemma? Taking the original Greek meaning, it is a double (di) proposition (lemma) in apparent conflict. A dilemma refers to a predicament in which a person has to decide between several alternative solution proposals for achieving a goal. Bipolar cultural dimensions may give indications to solve social problems in social systems that take the form of dilemmas. However, these cultural dimensions are not to be construed as absolute realities but as virtues that can be brought from a systemic point of view into a harmonious relationship.

How do you best define a dilemma? By defining the issue at stake in terms of opposites, as follows:

On the one hand we need/want to …

While on the other hand we also want/need to …

Here are some illustrations of dilemmas that are relevant for this case study. Using the model above, we can describe them in the following sentences which emphasize the contradictions in italics:

- On the one hand, we need to reach *global consistency* that leads to *unity*, while, on the other hand, we also want to be able to be *flexible locally and thrive on our diversity*.
- On the one hand, we need to develop a *"One company" culture*, implying *treating employees the same* way in all locations, while, on the other hand, we also want to *recognize differences (arising from history) in each local or original organization*, which means that people are *treated differently*.
- On the one hand, we need to *standardize our systems and procedures*, while, on the other hand, we also want to *maintain local systems and procedures* that have been developed, understood and implemented throughout the organization.
- On the one hand, we need to respond to the *particular needs of some individuals*, while on the other hand, we also want to *maintain equity of opportunity and treatment for all.*

These dilemmas are encountered on a daily basis by operations or HR managers, the main protagonists in the case.

Dilemma theory and reconciliation Dilemma theory argues that humans can never develop and grow until we actively strive to embrace the behaviours and attitudes that feel most uncomfortable to us, as opposites. The most effective working practices are those that gently force individuals to embrace the unthinkable. It is the way humans are taught to deal with those tensions of opposing alternatives (Trompenaars & Woolliams 2003).

Dilemma theory considers values as bipolar, in contrast to the cultural dimensions of Geert Hofstede (2001) as dynamic and circular. By reconciling differences it contributes to a less static and more developmental view of cultural dimensions and therefore a more synergistic approach to cultural differences (Hampden-Turner & Trompenaars 2006).

Hampden-Turner and Trompenaars (2000) suggest four different options and positions for dealing with dilemmas where the last is reconciliation:

1. **Ignore other cultures**
   Ignore the other orientation. You stick to your own cultural standpoint. Your general attitude or decision-making style is to impose your own way of doing things, or to reject other ways of thinking or doing things, because you have either not recognized them or have no respect for them. In short, you think "my way is the best way; it has indeed proved so in the past".

2. **Abandon your standpoint**
   Abandon your own orientation and go the other way (go native). Here you adopt a "When in Rome, do as the Romans do" approach. Play-acting or keeping up a façade will not go unseen. You will often adopt a "learned behaviour" which is not yours. People from other cultures may eventually mistrust you for trying to be "one of them".

3. **Compromise**
   Sometimes you do it your way (point 1); sometimes you give in to the other way (point 2). But this is a win–lose solution or even lose–lose solution, because by compromising you also lose some of your identity, values, etc. Compromise cannot lead to a solution in which both parties are satisfied, a real win–win situation.

4. **Reconcile**
   What is needed is an approach where the two opposing views, values or practices in question can come to fuse or blend – where the strength of one extreme is extended by considering and accommodating the other. It is not about an exclusive "either/or" approach (which is inherent to traditional Western/Greek philosophy), but about an inclusive "and/and" or rather "through/through" model. Symbiosis of both opposites needs to be realized.

Implementing this reconciliation process can be done by using the cultural dimensions proposed by Hampden-Turner and Trompenaars (2000). All seven of them feature opposites in values, concepts and the behaviours that stem from them. In order to make the reconciliation process tangible, Hampden-Turner and Trompenaars (2000:349–352) suggest *5 Steps to Reconciliation* which can be linked to the grid (see Figure 21.4) with x and y axes to visualize opposites.

Step 1: Eliciting the dilemma

- Specify who the dilemma holder is
- Explicit the dilemma as perceived by the dilemma holder: "On the one hand, I want to … while, on the other hand, I also want to …"

- Identify which of the seven dimensions as presented on pp. 292–293 are involved here.

Step 2: Charting the dilemma

- Label both axes on the grid with the dimension you chose.

Step 3: Stretching the dilemma

- List the *positives* of position 1
- List the *positives* of position 2
- List the *negatives* of position 1
- List the *negatives* of position 2

Step 4: Finding epithets

- Find descriptive, funny, stigmatizing, labels for the two positions (1,10 and 10,1) and the intermediate one (compromise 5,5).
- As a reference use the positive and negative aspects listed in Step 3.

Step 5: Reconciling the dilemma

- Combine the strengths of position 1 with those of position 2 and vice-versa.
- Think of a solid reconciliation going further than mere compromise.
- Suggest actions to be taken in view of the proposed reconciliation.

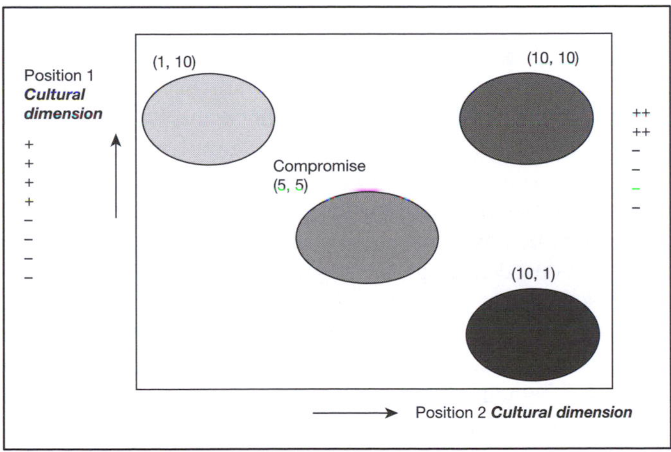

Figure 21.4 The reconciliation grid

3.3 Recommended reading

Barmeyer, C. & Davoine, E. (2011). "The intercultural challenges in the transfer of codes of conduct from the USA to Europe". In: Primecz, H., Romani, L. & Sackmann, S. (Eds), *Cross-Cultural Management in Practice. Culture and Negotiated Meanings*, 53–63. Cheltenham: Edward Elgar.

Multinational companies (MNCs) face the challenge of harmonizing corporate culture throughout their subsidiaries, following the widely held idea that a strong global corporate culture will strengthen the company's identity and image and reduce transaction costs within the MNC. Corporate values and especially codes of conduct can be defined as instruments to implement a normative global organizational culture, proposing orientations for action in order to control and to regulate the employees' behaviours and practices in every subsidiary. A case study of a US-based MNC is used to show the complexity of the intercultural challenges of the implementation of codes of conduct in European subsidiaries.

Edwards, T., Colling, T. & Ferner, A. (2007). "Conceptual approaches to the transfer of employment practices in multinational companies: An integrated approach". In: *Human Resource Management Journal*, 17:3, 201–217.
This article examines the transfer of employment practices across borders within multinational companies. It contrasts market-based, cross-national comparative and micro-political perspectives on this issue and argues for an integrated approach that focuses on interrelationships between markets and institutions on the one hand and the material interests of actors on the other. The argument is developed using data from a multi-level case study of a multinational in the US and Britain.

Hampden-Turner, C. & Trompenaars, F. (2000). *Building Cross-Cultural Competence.* West Sussex: Yale University Press.
The book focuses on the dilemmas of international managers and offers constructive advice on dealing with culture shock and turning it to an advantage. Opposing values can be understood as complementary and reconcilable. A manager who concentrates on integrating rather than polarizing values will make better decisions. Furthermore, the authors show, wealth is actually created by reconciling values-in-conflict. Based on 14 years of research involving nearly 50,000 managerial respondents and on the authors' experience, the book explores six culture-defining dimensions and their reverse images (universalism/particularism, individualism/communitarianism, specificity/diffusion, achieved status/ascribed status, inner direction/outer direction and sequential time/synchronous time) and discusses them as alternative ways of coping with life's – and management's – exigencies.

Hampden-Turner, C. & Trompenaars, F. (2006). "Cultural intelligence: Is such a capacity credible?". In: *Group & Organization Management*, 31:1, 56–63.
Three major objections to the idea of Cultural Intelligence are discussed: (a) cultures are said to be entirely relative in their values, so holding one culture to be more intelligent than another is discriminatory; (b) cultural studies are said to be a form of postmodernism, whereas to have one central definition of culture is modernist – an imposition of our own dominant beliefs; and (c) attempts to categorize cultures are said to be crude stereotypes, lacking

real subjects. The answer to the first objection is the synergy hypothesis: values are relative, but they are more or less synergistic. The answer to the second objection is the complementary hypothesis: cultures are different, even polar opposites, yet they converge in a fuller description. The answer to the third objection is the latency hypothesis: every value is given face value and its latent shadow lies behind it.

Helin, S. & Sandström, J. (2008). "Codes, ethics and cross-cultural differences: Stories from the implementation of a corporate code of ethics in a MNC subsidiary". In: *Journal of Business Ethics*, 82, 281–291.
This article focuses on the cross-cultural aspects of the implementation of an American company's code of ethics into its Swedish subsidiary. Several stories that the receivers in the subsidiary use when trying to explain the parent's code and conceptualize it are identified. The receivers resisted the code by amplifying the importance of national identity. Rather than stimulating a discussion on ethics that might have strengthened the ties between the parent and the subsidiary, the outcome of the code implementation had the opposite effect. The article concludes by stressing the process of implementing codes across cultures rather than code content.

Palazzo, B. (2002). "US-American and German business ethics: An intercultural comparison". In: *Journal of Business Ethics*, 41, 195–216.
The differences between the "habits of the heart" in German and US-American corporations can be described by analysing the way corporations deal with norms and values within their organizations. Whereas many US corporations have introduced formal business ethics programmes, German companies are very reluctant to address normative questions publicly. This can be explained by the different cultural backgrounds in the two countries. By defining these different "habits of the heart" underlying German and American business ethics it is possible to show the problems and questions within the intercultural management of values, but also the possible solutions.

Trompenaars, F. & Woolliams, P. (2003). "A new framework for managing change across cultures". In: *Journal of Change Management*, 3:4, 361–375.
The authors argue that changing an organization's culture is a contradiction in terms. This is because cultures act to preserve themselves and to protect their own existence. So rather than seeing change as a "thing" opposing continuity, it is considered as a difference. A new methodology is centred on diagnosing the tensions between the current and ideal corporate culture. These tensions manifest themselves as a series of dilemmas. The new approach for the management of change is to reconcile these dilemmas. The authors demonstrate with examples and offer a conceptual framework describing how seemingly opposing values deriving from the tensions arising from change imperatives can be integrated to achieve a "win–win" outcome.

4 QUESTIONS ON THE CASE

1. What do you think about the corporate values of Pharmatix? What is striking about them? Compare them with the findings of Mercier in Table 21.1.
2. What is the main dilemma the HR director is facing in relation to the marketing manager? What are the underlying value orientations? Refer to the cultural dimensions of Hampden-Turner and Trompenaars:

   a) What may be the most important value orientations that could drive the attitude/decision of the HR manager?
   b) What may be the value orientations behind the attitude/behaviour of the marketing manager?

3. Try to resolve the conflict and reconcile cultural differences by using dilemma theory, in particular:

   a) the four options and
   b) the five steps to reconciliation.

   Use the reconciliation grid to visualize your answers.

5 REFERENCES

Barmeyer, C. & Davoine, E. (2011). "The intercultural challenges in the transfer of codes of conduct from the USA to Europe". In: Primecz, H., Romani, L. & Sackmann, S. (Eds), *Cross-Cultural Management in Practice. Culture and Negotiated Meanings*, 53–63. Cheltenham: Edward Elgar.

Blasco, M. & Zølner, M. (2010). "Corporate social responsibility in Mexico and France. Exploring the role of normative institutions". In: *Business & Society*, 49:2, 216–251.

Blazejevski, S. (2006). "Transferring value infused organizational practices in multinational companies". In: Geppert M. & Mayer, M. (Eds), *Global, National and Local Practices in Multinational Companies*, 63–104. Houndmills: Palgrave Macmillan.

Brown, A. (1998). *Organizational Culture*. Essex: Prentice Hall.

d'Iribarne, P. (2002). "La légitimité de l'entreprise comme acteur éthique aux Etats-Unis et en France". In: *Revue Française de Gestion*, 140, 23–39.

d'Iribarne, P. (2012). *Managing Corporate Values in Diverse National Cultures: The Challenge of Differences*. London: Routledge.

Edwards, T., Colling, T. & Ferner, A. (2007). "Conceptual approaches to the transfer of employment practices in multinational companies: An integrated approach". In: *Human Resource Management Journal*, 17:3, 201–217.

Foreign Corrupt Practices Act (1977). 15 U.S. Code § 78dd. Retrieved on 16 January 2016, from http://www.justice.gov/sites/default/files/criminal-fraud/legacy/2015/01/16/guide.pdf

Hampden-Turner, C. & Trompenaars, F. (2000). *Building Cross-Cultural Competence*. West Sussex: Yale University Press.

Hampden-Turner, C. & Trompenaars, F. (2006). "Cultural intelligence: Is such a capacity credible?" In: *Group & Organization Management*, 31:1, 56–63.

Helin, S. & Sandström, J. (2008). "Codes, ethics and cross-cultural differences: Stories from the implementation of a corporate code of ethics in a MNC subsidiary". In: *Journal of Business Ethics*, 82, 281–291.

Hofstede, G. (1980/2001). *Culture's Consequences.* Thousand Oaks, CA: Sage.

Kaptein, M. (2004). "Business codes of multinational firms: What do they say?". In: *Journal of Business Ethics*, 50:1, 13–31.

Kluckhohn, F. & Strodtbeck, F. (1961). *Variations in Value Orientations.* New York: HarperCollins.

Mercier, S. (2001). "Institutionnaliser l'éthique dans les grandes entreprises françaises". In: *Revue Française de Gestion*, 136, 62–69.

Palazzo, B. (2002). "US-American and German business ethics: An intercultural comparison". In: *Journal of Business Ethics*, 41, 195–216.

Parsons, T. & Shils, E. (1951). *Towards a General Theory of Action.* Cambridge, MA: Harvard University Press.

Schein, E. H. (1986). *Organizational Culture and Leadership.* San Francisco: Jossey-Bass.

Talaulicar, T. (2009). "Barriers against globalizing corporate ethics: An analysis of legal disputes on implementing US codes of ethics in Germany". In: *Journal of Business Ethics*, 84, 349–360.

Tempel, A., Wächter, H. & Walgenbach, P. (2006). "The comparative institutional approach to HRM in multinational companies". In: Geppert, M. & Mayer, M. (Eds), *Global, National and Local Practices in Multinational Companies*, 17–37. Houndmills: Palgrave Macmillan.

Trompenaars, F. & Woolliams, P. (2003). "A new framework for managing change across cultures". In: *Journal of Change Management*, 3:4, 361–375.

22

Managing Glocally: Resolving Intercultural Challenges in the Management of Local Multicultural Teams in a Multinational Venture

Laurence Romani

1 INTRODUCTION

By definition, multinational companies have to manage a multicultural workforce. For many manufacturing companies starting internationalization, it is expected that they are strong in their home market first, and then start exporting abroad, maybe with an agent. Later on, they establish a subsidiary or a production facility (see the "classic" cases by Johanson & Vahlne 1977). In consequence, the first kind of diversity that is faced with internationalization is between country A (origin) and country B (target country). This leads to bicultural interactions coupled with hierarchy: management is from country A and the executants are from country B.

When organizations continue their internationalization process, they can reach more global forms of operations, increasingly focusing on the resources of the foreign markets. For example, an enterprise can be organized around regions (e.g. Asia–Pacific, North America, Europe). In the regional offices, there will be representatives of several countries in this region working together. In addition, it is likely that there will also be nationals from the organization's country of origin. This leads to multiple intercultural interactions.

Now imagine that a multinational company that is organized around regions is cultivating a strong organizational culture, or, even, is adopting ethnocentric points of view. Simply put, it means that the standards or practices of the headquarters are presented as a reference for the rest of the organization, even if they are in opposition to what is perceived as desirable or good management locally. This adds another layer of culture (this time organizational culture) to the situation. Employees with diverse cultural backgrounds, working in different regions, interact within a framework established in yet another country. In addition, they will implement more or less faithfully their headquarters' ideas of organizational culture and processes (Barmeyer & Davoine 2011; Clausen 2011) and thereby create yet another dimension of culture: the local (regional) interpretation of the organizational culture spread by headquarters.

Let us now imagine that two companies with this profile (international with regional operations, with a strong – ethnocentric – organizational culture) merge. The situation becomes quite complex since there are several strong organizational cultures that need to be renegotiated (Brannen & Salköop 2000) as well as multicultural teams that need to be managed.

This situation is getting quite common, in view of the high number of mergers, international joint ventures and acquisitions currently, as well as increasing workforce mobility. Today, managers have to lead, motivate, reward and manage teams of employees that are from multiple cultures, used to different organizational cultures and operating in a cultural environment they may not be very familiar with. This is so in the case in this chapter.

This case presents a frequently occurring situation in a company active in the service industry. It is a typical challenge for a multicultural team but is coupled here with the difficulty of combining different expectations from different organizational cultures, since the case took place about four years after a merger. Whereas four years may seem a sufficient period of time to create a new (merged) organizational culture, it appeared that for the management team, references to the former organizations were still strong. The names of the persons and some characteristics of the organizations have been changed for the sake of anonymity; the names of the companies are pseudonyms.

2 CASE DESCRIPTION

2.1 The situation: company background

"Hej Malin!" – "Hej Pierre, hur mår du?" asks Malin, salesperson in one of Pierre's teams in PaDam.

"Jag mår bra, tack! Vill du också ha kaffe?" Malin thanks Pierre for offering the coffee that he puts into her A'Dam cup. They drink together, standing at the table of the kitchen area as they exchange remarks about the weather being so cold for April. Pierre, from France, uses his broken Swedish; he has been living in Sweden for two years and spent some time at the beginning of his stay to learn some Swedish. When they reach to the dishwasher to put their dirty cups away, they realize that it is full of clean dishes and they start emptying it together.

"You seem so happy today!" remarks Malin, this time in English. "Of course I am!" replies Pierre enthusiastically. "We are just back from the fair in

Finland where we did excellent, really excellent business! The last three days were perfect, our marketing effort for Finland will pay, I can tell you now! And this is thanks to a few people in the marketing team. They did an outstanding job, really, they went beyond my expectations. I really want to reward them for this."

"How do you mean … you want to reward them? Do you mean you want to have a few people stand out of your marketing team?"

"Yes, I mean, of course; they really did a lot of work, it did make a difference!"

"Well, but what about the team? Maybe it's because these persons were in a supportive team that they could do so much, do you really want to reward them and not the team? What are the others going to think?"

"But …"

"I don't know, but it seems to me that for the team's spirit and group work, it's better not to single out individuals but instead to reward and praise the entire team. Do you really know how much work each and everyone did? And how much they all contributed to enable a few to do outstanding work?"

Pierre looks at Malin in silence, pondering on what she had just said.

"I don't know." She pauses. "I just have a feeling that here, I mean in Sweden, it's important that you value and reward the team; team work is important, and team spirit. Don't you think?"

Later in the day, Pierre, Nordic Sales and Marketing Director of PaDam made up his mind. Malin is probably right; he will treat the entire marketing team to a dinner and thereby celebrate the team spirit and group work. As Simone passes by his room, he walks up to her and shares his idea.

"What are you talking about? A dinner for 20 people? This will cost at least SEK 15,000 [circa € 1,700]. I am not paying for that." And with this abrupt comment, Simone, the head of the entire Nordic operations of PaDam, ended her conversation with Pierre. Despite his disappointment, Pierre smiled: he liked the manners of this dynamic Dutch lady. There was never a doubt about what she thought! He also wondered whether she had always been so direct, and whether this had contributed to her long and successful career.

PaDam is a relatively recent organization that is the outcome of a merger between two former competitors Pant and A'Dam. It is now a multinational company, among the top three world leaders in packaging and delivering services. Pant and A'Dam were organizations with many similar features in their corporate histories which started in two different European countries, all the way back from the period between the World Wars. Over the years, the companies had strengthened delivering and packaging services respectively and their merger in the early 2000s was perceived as the ideal combination of expertise. Located in Sweden, in a suburb of Stockholm, PaDam Nordic operations is the subsidiary of PaDam and centres on activities in the Nordic region (Scandinavia and Finland) as well as the Baltic States. The Nordic region is the second largest market for PaDam.

That evening, once the kids were in bed, Pierre shared with his wife Caroline his impressions of the day, and when he mentioned Malin and Simone's reaction to his proposal, Caroline was surprised: "Comment ca? Mais ils ne sont pas tous suédois dans ton équipe. Et pas ceux qui ont si bien travaillé, si?" Caroline was right, the marketing team was composed of about one third of Swedes, and the others were from other countries, mostly Nordic countries but also South America and South of Europe. Pierre wanted to reward three people: Marco, Janne and Lena. Marco was originally from Argentina and he had been working in PaDam Nordic operations for four years. He was fluent in Swedish and married to a Swede. Janne was originally from Finland. He had worked for PaDam in France and came to Stockholm two years ago. He seemed to be well integrated in Sweden, married to a Dane, and was the very happy father of newborn twins. Lena was Swedish and had started her work for PaDam a few years ago after graduation from a top business school here in Stockholm. Pierre did not know her so well, she was rather private.

Next morning, while Pierre and Caroline left home for work, Caroline reminded Pierre that he had to pick up their daughter Coline from her football training that afternoon. "Oui, oui!" replied Pierre while rushing for the bus.

At 5.30 p.m., when Pierre arrived at the football field, he recognized Per, the father of Emma, another girl playing in the AIK football team with his daughter. As the girls had to stay longer to work on some theory with the trainer, Pierre and Per got talking. During the conversation, Pierre mentioned his situation, his desire to reward the work of a few outstanding individuals in the team, without compromising the team spirit that is such a strong part of work here in the Nordic region.

"You must have this kind of problem all the time at Ericsson, your staff is so international," said Pierre.

"Sure, but we don't manage the 'Swedish way', we manage the 'Ericsson way'', replied Per. "All over the world we have the same organizational culture, and we are very clear about it. We use the same visuals, the same furniture in our offices in Brazil or in Hong Kong. Personally, I think our organizational values have to override the local values and individuals' own values".

"Really?" replied Pierre in disbelief. "So you don't take advantage of the cultural diversity among your employees?"

"What?" replied Per distracted by his daughter giving him a big hug.

Pierre knew that PaDam was trying to promote shared organizational values to give the merger a stronger sense of identity. The problem was that although Pant and A'Dam were previously organized around regions, both companies had a strong organizational culture, fostered and cultivated by their respective head offices before the merger. For Pant, the organizational culture was attached to the country of origin (France). Until the merger, the corporate language of Pant was French, whereas it was English for A'Dam, although the headquarters were positioned in a non-English speaking country (the Netherlands). Compared to A'Dam, Pant had an organizational culture that was more hierarchical, more collectivist and where the metaphor of a family was used almost literally. Pierre had worked 12 years in Pant and enjoyed the spirit of collegiality to be found among its staff.

The following day, Pierre took the opportunity of another informal conversation with a member of the sales team to investigate how the reward of individual team members would be perceived.

"Well, although we are not all Swedish here, we do things the Swedish way. We are also based in Sweden, follow Swedish regulations, have Swedish unions and we all live here, so of course it makes sense to go the Swedish way," commented Gaston, originally from Spain.

Pierre knew what he meant by "the Swedish way". Cultural differences in management style between Sweden, France and the Netherlands were discussed frequently at corporate events in PaDam Nordic. The management team of PaDam was predominantly Dutch and French expatriates, while the other employees were on Swedish local contracts. Pierre heard that compared to the French, Swedes are not hierarchical, prefer teamwork and empowerment, and give stronger values to quality of life and the well-being of employees at work. He remembered how he was shocked, at first, to hear that parents (male and female) share 15 months' paid parental leave per child, and how he realized with time that this was never really a problem for the organization, sometimes even an advantage as it had attracted new talents to replace the employees on leave. He remembers how he felt upset, at first, to realize that most employees were gone by 5 p.m. and how he progressively understood that the employees' productivity was very different, with shorter breaks during the day. "The Swedish way", with consultation with subordinates before decision making, with consensus decision making, with an emphasis on group work, Pierre knew about. But this was not *his* style. Was it because he was French? Pierre did not see himself as a "typical" French manager. In contrast to most of his colleagues back home, he had signed up for expatriation. He spent two years in Senegal, as the head of the Western African Region for PaDam, before he took this position in Sweden. But this kind of "Swedish" leadership was not in his experience of Pant. This was neither his experience of PaDam nor something that stood high in PaDam's corporate values.

"I do think it would be wise to give a collective reward to the team", insisted Pierre in his new attempt with Simone to secure budget for a dinner for the marketing team.

"What are you telling me? I won't pay for a dinner for the team. We value and reward individuals in this organization, not teams. Individuals get promoted, not teams. Give the three a bonus. I have money for a bonus, not for a dinner," replied Simone.

Simone had worked 25 years in A'Dam. She had a tough management style and was known for her direct communication and a strong focus on performance and pragmatism. To some extent, she was right. The same outstanding performance elsewhere in PaDam would be rewarded with a bonus. This means that if Janne had done equally well in France, he would have probably got a bonus. Would it encourage him to work hard in future if he saw that his performance, his extra work, was rewarded with a dinner for the entire team? At the same time, it would be devastating to the team to hear that some of their members had got a bonus. The amount might be small, and half of it might disappear in taxes, but it would be impossible to promote teamwork after that.

"You say that they would rather have it the Swedish way, Simone summed up. We are not a Swedish organization, we are an international organization. And, by the way, why do you ask your subordinates for their opinion? You are the manager, you make the decisions."

2.2 The challenge

"And here I am, with this problem," Pierre, whom I met a few days later, tells me. "This is the kind of dilemma that I am dealing with quite often. On the one hand, my team is clearly influenced by the Swedish way. Of course, they are not all Swedes, but Nordics are in the majority of people who are quite well integrated in Swedish society. One can say that the Swedish way is a common basis of understanding for all of them. And, as far as I can see, it is a shared basis which is regarded positively. The problem, of course, is that the management team does not use this 'Swedish' frame of reference."

"What kind of frame of reference do you use?"

"It should be PaDam, I know, but from what I can see we refer to the organizational culture from prior to the merger. It's also that those who were in Pant think that its culture was more humane than A'Dam's. Those who had their career in A'Dam saw Pant as inefficient and too people-oriented rather than result-oriented. So, among us, in the management team, we are split in our heart between PaDam and our previous organization ... that, we think, was better than what we have now. So, as I said, on the one hand I have the Swedish frame of reference, and on the other hand, I have a vague PaDam frame of reference that is not really lived up to by management, at least here ... But this frame of reference exists and we should be consistent across countries in our way of rewarding individuals."

"OK, but is the PaDam frame of reference something that 'should' be used by management? I mean, something that is perceived as desirable by management and employees to put forward?"

"I guess so, yes. Officially it is, of course. But I am not so comfortable with this 'one way'. I don't want to reduce the cultural diversity of our team, the rich cultural complexity of this interaction to the few corporate values that I can find on a PaDam folder. We have here Scandinavian, Nordic, Latin, Dutch and French people, and I should ignore this diversity and focus on the narrow and few limited values that we have in common? That feels like a waste to me. I am sure I can do better than that."

"OK, I see. So you don't want to do it as your friend Per does it!"

"Nor as Simone is implying. I cannot be the manager of a team here in Sweden and not consult with the employees. I mean, they won't be very happy about it if I start making decisions and just inform them. Simone, she does not consult, I know, and she is not liked among the staff. I heard someone comparing her to Margaret Thatcher. That was funny to hear, I must admit. But when you think about it, this comparison also united the staff against her."

"But you don't have to change your leadership style to make it more directive, do you?"

"No, I know, but Simone is my boss. I am coming to an end of this assignment; I don't want her to write my evaluation without enthusiasm. Moreover, I can't do much without her consent. I don't have enough leeway in my budget to find SEK 15,000 for a dinner! If she disagrees, I am stuck."

"Yes, I understand."

"But the problem is also that I really want to distinguish these three people. If I don't, I won't be in line with what I believe is good management. I won't see myself as a good manager. Praising the team does not feel enough for me."

"Well, have you ever heard of the MBI model?"

"The what?"

"Let me tell you about it."

3 BACKGROUND KNOWLEDGE

3.1 The author's point of reference

I, Laurence Romani, am a specialist in intercultural management, especially in issues linked to leadership and the valorization of cultural diversity. My approach is interpretive and critical. This means two things. First, I believe that how people analyse and make sense of a situation is the most important variable to be considered for the resolution of a case. It means that people's interpretation of a challenge is what I will concentrate on. Second, I believe that people are embedded in unequal power relationships that influence how they analyse a situation, but also how they will react and act upon it. I see cultural differences as a given in our society and in organizations, it is a strength that can contribute to complementary and synergetic ways of working and living together. I see cultural diversity in national culture diversity, but also in the diversity reached by other forms of socialization, for example, gender, sexual orientation, ethnic belonging, etc. More information can be found on www.casl.se or http://hhs.academia.edu/LaurenceRomani.

3.2 Concepts, models, frameworks

Cultural differences are never a problem. They are just a given. We live in a multicultural world; we interact with people who have different life experiences and socializations than we have: it's just the way things are. What can be a problem, however, is the lack of acknowledgement and consideration that we are diverse. In my opinion, it comes down to a rather simple formula for success: identify diversity and manage it in a respectful way. The MBI model is a great tool to achieve this.

The Mapping Bridging Integrating (MBI) model The MBI model, developed by Martha Maznevski and Joseph DiStefano (2000) from IMD in Lausanne, is a simple representation of three critical skills needed in intercultural interactions. The first one is "mapping", that is, identifying and understanding that there are cultural differences which influence a given situation. The second is "bridging", which means communicating about these differences and reaching a true understanding of the other's point of view. The third is "integrating", that is, building on the differences to develop something new, building on these identified and understood differences. These three critical skills are presented as a process (mapping, then bridging towards integrating, see Figure 22.1 and in more detail in Table 22.1).

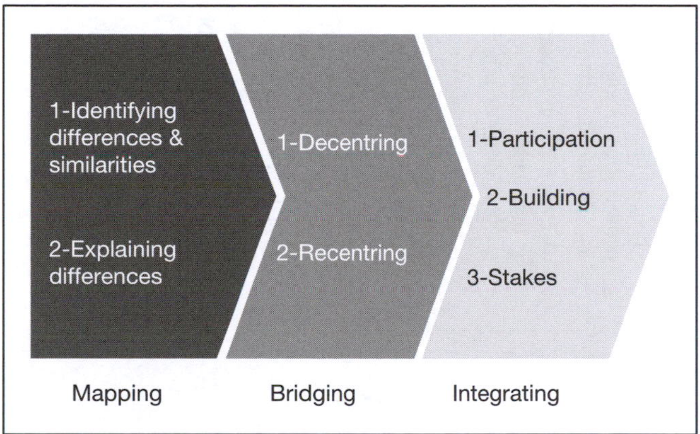

Figure 22.1 The MBI process
Adapted from Maznevski & DiStefano (2000)

A careful presentation of the model in Figure 22.1, illustrated with examples, is available in Lane et al. (2009). In Table 22.1, I build on Lane et al.'s work (2009:65–81) and my own experience of the model to present the prerequisites, actions and consequences of each step of the model in an intercultural situation.

Table 22.1 Components of the three MBI steps

	Pre-requisites and challenges	Actions	Consequences
Mapping	Knowledge about the existence of cultural differences. If the people in interaction are in denial of cultural differences or adopt an ethnocentric position, this will make the task harder. Some knowledge of existing cultural differences (e.g. national culture, professional culture, etc.) between the people in interaction. There must be readiness from the participants to share and listen to the others. In task-oriented environments, it can be difficult to motivate people to "spend time" on this since this is not directly linked to action and tasks.	*Identifying differences and similarities* This can be done in an informal conversation or with the help of tools such as cultural dimensions frameworks. a) The people in interaction discuss what they have in common and how their views differ on other points. b) Topics to cover need to relate to the situation (e.g. decision-making style, views on leadership, etc.). c) Exploring national cultures but also professional, gender, ethnic and generation differences (and more) are relevant. *Explaining differences* a) Avoid stereotyping. Search for nuances and contingent variables. b) Each person is given a voice to present her/his opinion. c) Respectful listening to the others. d) Questions and clarifications are used to better understand others' points of view or experiences. e) Need to consider that all differences brought up are likely to be relevant, thus should not be ignored later on in bridging.	Awareness of the relativity of each person's position. Awareness of alternative thinking and experiences. Awareness of the diversity of the people in interaction. People in interaction have engaged in a dialogue about their differences and similarity. This means they communicate at a meta-level. This will help future communication. Note: Without a good "mapping" "bridging" cannot be reached. Using stereotypes and minimization of differences that are brought up is not a good mapping. Mapping is about identifying differences and similarities, not about finding common ground.

(*continued*)

Table 22.1 (*Continued*)

	Pre-requisites and challenges	Actions	Consequences
Bridging	Willingness to understand and relate to the others. Motivation to understand differences, not just to grasp them. Confidence that the process will go well. Openness and trust between the participants. In a situation with strong differences in status between people, or in a situation where people do not know each other, engaging in bridging can be a challenge. Power inequalities can hamper communication and discussion: if one side believes that "they are doing things right", bridging will be a challenge. It can be useful to have a person moderate this process to guarantee that each voice is heard and respected.	*De-centring* a) Being able to see things from the point of view of other people. b) Being able to explain this point of view without a value judgement (in a neutral descriptive way). Decentring is done when people are capable of suspending their judgement and can explain a difference identified in mapping from another person's point of view. *Re-centring* It means that the people involved are now using their own views of the world to describe someone else's point of view in a way that is found acceptable by him/her.	Understanding of differences. Modification in people's patterns of behaviour since they understand another person's preference or point of view. Creation of an egalitarian interaction (fewer power differences). Creation of a situation where differences are not seen as a problem. Emergence of common views or common rules where differences were first identified. Note: A good bridging leads almost automatically to integrating. Bridging may be needed several times. Bridging is not the same as empathy. It is not enough to know how the other individuals think, it is also necessary to integrate their views into one's own views.

(*continued*)

	Pre-requisites and challenges	Actions	Consequences
Integrating	Belief that ideas and solutions accepted and adopted by all are stronger than those imposed. Value differences. See differences as a potential for increased performance (better ideas, more sustainable solutions, resilience, etc.). Willingness to work harder on finding solutions that really take into account all contributions. Willingness to include everyone. Refusal to go for a middle way or a form of compromise that is not fully satisfactory. In a high time pressure environment, this can be a challenge (unless bridging was very well done).	*Assuring participation* The benefit of bridging can be lost if people stop at understanding each other. It is important that differences and similarities are now built upon, and this is achieved with the participation and contribution of each actor involved. This can be done in different ways (formal, informal, in writing, orally, before meetings or after, etc.). *Building on differences* This is the core of integrating and demands a real respect and consideration of each idea and point of view. By considering each contribution seriously, this is when the interaction reaches new levels of solutions or creativity. *What is at stake, for whom?* Keeping this question in mind helps the group in its interaction to identify potential conflicts and to address them and go beyond differences in points of view to address differences of (work) conditions as well. Focusing on a common stake often helps identify integrative solutions.	Synergy between participants. Higher creativity. Higher trust. Higher satisfaction. Higher performance. Note: Integrating cannot be achieved without a good bridging, otherwise some ideas will be lost or ignored or some participants will not commit. It is not necessary that all participants share beliefs about the value of difference, but the moderators need to.

3.3 Recommended reading

DiStefano, J. J. & Maznevski, M. L. (2000). "Creating value with diverse teams in global management". In: *Organizational Dynamics*, 29:1, 45–63.
This paper presents at length the MBI model, how to do the different steps and the likely outcome for each step, and a concrete example of how a successful team used the model. This paper also presents in appendix the cultural orientations framework with questions for each cultural orientation. This framework can be used in the teams to do the mapping stage.

Hampden-Turner, C. & Trompenaars, F. (2000). *Building Cross-Cultural Competence*. West Sussex: Wiley.
Tensions between different views are presented in this book in the form of dilemmas. What the MBI model calls bridging and integrating is done here with the resolution of these dilemmas. The reconciliation of dilemmas is illustrated with many practical cases for six key dimensions. The powerfulness of the examples and the many topics linked to each of these six dimensions provide rich and multiple ideas on how to reach synergies between differences.

Maloney, M. & Zellmer-Bruhn, M. (2006). "Building bridges, windows and cultures: mediating mechanisms between team heterogeneity and performance in global teams". In: *Management International Review*, 46:6, 697–720.
The authors present strategies to deal with heterogeneity in teams (e.g. bridging faultlines, building swift norms, valorizing diversity) in order to reach social integration and self-verification for each team member. This, in turn, is said to lead to effective performance. This article echoes the ideas and principles of the MBI model and complements them.

Maznevski, M. L. & DiStefano, J. J. (2000). "Global leaders are team players: Developing global leaders through membership on global teams". In: *Human Resource Management*, 39:2&3, 195–208.
This paper is also a presentation of the MBI model with the detail of each step and the presentation of the cultural orientations framework. In addition, the authors develop how this model is linked to leadership.

4 QUESTIONS ON THE CASE

1. Assess the main differences and similarities between the different people (or groups) involved in the situation (the sales and marketing teams, Pierre, Simone, Marco, Janne, Lena, PaDam, etc.). Assess these differences from what has been said in the case, but also in view of what you believe is likely to be similar or different between them. Consider these differences regarding decision making, reward, value of diversity, etc. Do this "mapping" by also considering the origin (corporate socialization, national culture, age, etc.) of these differences and similarities. Use the mapping tables to help you.

Mapping actors' profiles

	Pierre	Simone	Sales & Marketing teams	Marco	Janne	Lena
Generation						
Profession						
Gender/ sexuality						
National culture of origin						
Company of origin/ years in the company						
International experiences						
Languages spoken						
Cultural sensitivity						

Mapping actors' views on management

	Pierre	Simone	Sales & Marketing teams	Marco	Janne	Lena
Hierarchical relationship with others						
Decision making						
Preffered mode of work						
Incentives						
Reward						
Communication style						
Orientation						

Mapping of organizational and country profiles on management

	France	Pant	Netherlands	A'Dam	PaDam	Sweden
Hierarchical relationships						
Decision making						
Reward						
Leadership preferences						
Preferred mode of work						
Orientation						

2. In this case, Pierre is the person facing the challenge. Use the differences identified in mapping and select key issues that you will address in "bridging". Consider Pierre's point of view and how others think about the same topic (de-centring), and then try to re-centre Pierre's point of view. What ideas emerge? Use the tables to help you.

Pierre's possible bridging in regard to four key elements where he contrasts with the team, the organization, or his boss Simone

	Original position	De-centring	Re-centring	Emerging ideas
Reward				
Orientation				
What to prioritize				
Decision making				

3. By now you are probably already seeing synergies between the actors in the case. Work on possible solutions that would satisfy each person and respect their points of view and preferences.

Integrating and solving the challenge of rewarding the three outstanding individuals

Assuring participation	What is at stake? For whom?	Building on ideas and possible solutions

5 REFERENCES

Barmeyer, C. & Davoine, E. (2011). "The intercultural challenges in the transfer of codes of conduct from the US to Europe". In: Primecz, H., Romani, L. & Sackmann, S. (Eds), *Cross-Cultural Management in Practice: Culture and Negotiated Meanings*, 53–63. Cheltenham: Edward Elgar.

Brannen, M. Y. & Salk, J. (2000). "Partnering across borders: Negotiating culture in a German–Japanese joint venture". In: *Human Relations*, 53:4, 451–82.

Clausen, L. (2011). "Corporate communication across cultures: A multilevel approach". In: Primecz, H, Romani, L. & Sackmann, S. (Eds), *Cross-Cultural Management in Practice: Culture and Negotiated Meanings*, 77–88. Cheltenham: Edward Elgar.

DiStefano, J. J. & Maznevski, M. L. (2000). "Creating value with diverse teams in global management". In: *Organizational Dynamics*, 29:1, 45–63.

Johanson, J. & Vahlne, J. E. (1977). "Internationalization process of firm – model of knowledge development and increasing foreign market commitments". In: *Journal of International Business Studies*, 8, 23–32.

Lane, H.W., et al. (2009). "International management behavior". In: Lane, H.W., et al. (Eds), *Leading with the Global Mindset*, 65–81. 6th ed. Chippenham: Wiley.

23

Strategic Alliances and Intercultural Organizational Change: The Renault–Nissan Case

Christoph Barmeyer and Ulrike Mayrhofer

1 INTRODUCTION

Cultural and institutional factors have been largely underestimated by leading managers in international corporations and mergers, which has produced negative financial results, primarily in the automotive sector, e.g. the cases of BMW–Rover, Renault–Volvo, Daimler–Chrysler and VW–Suzuki. The failure rate of international mergers and acquisitions requires *other* organizational forms that might be more successful in an intercultural context. A strategic alliance could be such a form of organization – in the middle of a continuum of a close merger and a loose so-called "one-shot contract".

Facing the globalization of markets, companies need to form strategic alliances in order to remain competitive and to increase their international market presence. Over the past few decades, alliances have developed considerably around the world. They involve organizations of different size, nationality and industry (Mayrhofer 2013; Mayrhofer & Urban 2011). Because of the necessity to achieve critical size and to reduce costs, car manufacturers are even more influenced by this trend.

A strategic alliance can be defined as an agreement between two or more companies that combine resources to pursue a set of agreed objectives, while remaining independent. The collaboration can concern different elements of the value chain: human resources, research and development (R&D), production, logistics, marketing etc. Alliances can take the form of contractual arrangements (non-equity agreements), minority equity stakes or joint ventures. Major benefits associated with partnerships are the sharing of costs and risks, and the development, transfer and combination of resources and competences as well as the accelerated expansion into foreign markets. Despite their proliferation, failure rates of strategic alliances remain relatively high. In fact, companies do not always share similar objectives and strategies, and the coordination of activities appears to be difficult. A major factor causing failure is linked to intercultural aspects since organizational and human issues are critical, especially in a cross-cultural context (Prange & Mayrhofer 2015; Spencer-Oatey & Franklin 2009).

This case study focuses on a strategic alliance formed between the French company Renault and the Japanese[1] company Nissan. This bilateral agreement associates actors and teams from two different national and corporate cultures. Created in 1999, the Renault-Nissan alliance has become the most productive and longest-lasting intercultural alliance among major car manufacturers. The success of Renault Nissan can be seen as a positive exception and a role model for the future in the field of international cooperations such as alliances.

In order to achieve this successful alliance, the two companies went through a complex and broad process of organizational development and change headed by a remarkable, multicultural leader applying transcultural leadership techniques. This process took into account strategic, structural, process-related and cultural factors that can be seen in many ways as holistic, intercultural best practices, combining in a complementary way the strengths of Japanese and French managerial, organizational and national cultures.

So, this case study deals with the management of an international strategic alliance. The objective is to explain the manifold organizational development measures and solutions that have been adopted to overcome and integrate national and corporate cultural differences to develop a new organization in an interculturally synergetic way.

2 CASE DESCRIPTION

Renault and Nissan are among the leading companies in the global car industry. Since its inception, the Renault–Nissan Alliance has included the following five brands: Renault, Dacia, Renault Samsung Motors (RSM), Nissan and Infiniti.

Renault–Nissan and the automotive market Table 23.1 indicates the number of vehicles produced by the top 20 car manufacturers in the world (the nine leading car producers account for three-quarters of the world's total production, which amounted to 54 million vehicles in 2012) and shows that Renault–Nissan are ranked number four. Taken together, the two groups produced

[1]We would like to thank Gabriele Scheuring, PhD, for her valuable contribution on Japanese working culture.

more than 8,3 million vehicles in 2013 (more than 10% of the world's top 20 automotive producers) and thus were close to the market leaders Toyota, General Motors and Volkswagen. The figures show that the world ranking list is still dominated by multinational companies from triad nations (in North America, Western Europe and Japan), even if the growing importance of several manufacturers from emerging markets is becoming more obvious (e.g. the Chinese group Dongfeng Motor, the Indian group Tata after the acquisition of Jaguar and Land Rover). Global competition has considerably increased the pressure on companies from mature markets to reduce costs and to innovate in order to remain competitive.

Table 23.1 The world's top car manufacturers in 2013

Car manufacturers	Number of vehicles (thousands)
1. Toyota–Daihatsu–Hino	9,8
2. General Motors	9,7
3. Volkswagen Group	9,5
4. **Renault–Nissan**	**8,3**
5. Hyundai–Kia	7,4
6. Ford	6,3
7. Fiat–Chrysler	4,4
8. Honda	4,3
9. PSA Peugeot Citroën	2,8
10. Suzuki	2,7
11. BMW	2,0
12. Daimler	1,8
13. Mazda	1,3
14. Mitsubishi	1,0

Source: CCFA – Comité des Constructeurs Français d'Automobiles (2014), The French Automotive Industry. Analysis and Statistics, Paris.

Table 23.2 highlights some of the two companies' key figures in terms of number of employees, revenues, net income and portfolio of brands. In 2012, Renault and Nissan achieved net profits, despite the global economic crisis which deeply affected the automobile industry. Cost savings and synergies developed within their alliance have undoubtedly contributed to these positive results. The companies continue their cooperation and aim to achieve a 10% market share in all markets and accelerated growth in emerging markets, notably in BRIC countries (Brazil, Russia, India and China).

Table 23.2 Key figures of Renault and Nissan (2013)

	Renault	**Nissan**
Number of employees	121,807	142,925
Revenues	€ 40.9 million	€ 78.1 billion
Net income	€ 695 million	€ 2.9 billion
Major brands	Renault, Dacia, Renault Samsung Motors	Nissan, Infiniti, Datsun

Sources: Renault and Nissan websites (https://group.renault.com/en/(last accessed 15 June 2015); www.nissan-global.com/EN/index.html (last accessed 15 June 2015)).

An ambitious international strategic alliance: Renault and Nissan On 27 March 1999, Louis Schweitzer and Yoshikazu Hanawa, the former CEOs of Renault SAS and Nissan Motor Co. Ltd., signed the strategic alliance contract between Renault and Nissan in Tokyo. The aim of this alliance, in which every company should retain its autonomy, was to become one of the five largest automobile manufacturers in the world through a common strategy and exploitation of synergies. Three years later, on 28 March 2002, Renault–Nissan BV was founded in the Netherlands.

In July 1999, shortly after the two companies agreed on the cooperative alliance, an Alliance Charter was created and signed which respects the identity of each party, assures a fair balance between the two partners of the Alliance and establishes rules for operations and confidentiality (Barmeyer & Mayrhofer 2009:122). This Alliance Charter consists of three pillars: (1) cooperative spirit and mutual respect, (2) maintaining a separate identity, but with a performance focus, and (3) learning from complementary cultures.

Since 1999, both partners have significantly reduced costs and developed important synergies, notably in the fields of supply, R&D, production, logistics, information systems, and marketing and sales. The Renault–Nissan Purchasing Organization (RNPO) is the alliance's largest common organization and negotiates prices among suppliers on behalf of both partners. Since 2009, joint purchasing has represented 100% of alliance purchases, compared to 30% in 2001. Shared platforms (from 33 different platforms to currently 10) and common parts have increased economies of scale and reduced both development and production costs (1.4 billion euros since the 2000–2005 period). The launch of the Renault Pulse and Nissan Micra models in India in 2011–2012 marked the alliance's most important passenger car platform-sharing project. The companies have recently adopted a new approach, called "Common module Family" (CmF), a system that makes it possible to apply different sets of parts and derivatives to various car models and powertrains. The two partners have also capitalized on their powertrain expertise: the alliance co-develops engines and gearboxes, and Renault specializes in diesel engines and manual transmissions while Nissan specializes in gasoline engines and automatic transmissions. Powertrain synergies amounted to 280 million euros in 2011.

In the field of logistics, a joint team has developed shared packing, shipping and other functions, achieving synergies amounting to more than 220 million euros in 2011. Another team has been working on the reduction of customs duties and administrative costs connected with trading, allowing cost savings of at least 50 million euros per year. Renault and Nissan also share common information systems infrastructure, data centres and licences. In marketing and sales, the partners won their first fleet contracts in 2012 to supply more than 15,000 vehicles on multiple continents for the French food processing company Danone. Finally, the cooperation has also reinforced the presence of the two groups in international markets (Renault is strongly present in Europe and Nissan in Asia) and accelerated their development in emerging markets.

Cultural change and transcultural leadership As in every international corporation, there are specific cultural and institutional characteristics in the Renault–Nissan alliance, which affect managerial issues. Crucial peculiarities have been, for example, those of language, decision-making processes and labour relations. Nissan followed the Japanese style of decision making by consensus, whereas at Renault decisions were made by senior management. Further differences were to be seen in a European attitude of acceptance of individual responsibility for actions, in contrast to a more group-oriented philosophy in the Japanese team.

The positive transformations that have taken place within the alliance, including those that led to a productive evolution of these peculiarities, are the result of the work of the CEO Carlos Ghosn (see Figure 23.1) – also called "the auto industry's most celebrated turnaround artist" (Emerson 2001).

Born in Brazil in 1954 of parents of Lebanese origin (his mother has French citizenship and his father Brazilian citizenship), Carlos Ghosn was raised in Brazil and Lebanon, receiving a French Jesuit education. He completed his studies at the most prestigious engineering schools *Ecole Polytechnique* and *Ecole des Mines* in Paris.

In 1978 he entered the French Michelin group, Europe's largest tyre maker. In 1985, he was nominated Managing Director of the Brazilian subsidiary and had to turn around a plant of 9,000 employees. Later, he became director of Michelin USA.

In 1996, he joined Renault and became the second in command in the group, reporting directly to CEO Louis Schweitzer. He was in charge of the recovery in Renault's financial situation and recommended the closing down of the Renault plant in Vilvorde in Belgium, resulting in the loss of 3,500 jobs. In 1997, Renault became profitable again. Since this period, Carlos Ghosn has the image of a "cost killer" and "Mister Fix It".

Carlos Ghosn joined Nissan as a Chief Operating Officer in 1999 and became CEO two years later. He was the lead architect of the Nissan Revival Plan, which brought the company out of a severe crisis in the late 1990s and back to profitability in 2000. Carlos Ghosn was nominated Chairman and CEO of Renault in 2005. He also became Chairman and CEO of the Renault–Nissan alliance.

Figure 23.1 Biography of Carlos Ghosn

Sources: Barmeyer & Mayrhofer 2009; Stahl & Brannen 2013.

When Carlos Ghosn came on the scene, he initiated some fundamental cultural changes within the Nissan company, for example dismantling the Japanese tradition of promotion by seniority and breaking open the Japanese *Keiretsu* networks for Western suppliers.

Ghosn changed some unprofitable practices and abolished seniority-based compensation. He ended this Japanese tradition and brought in promotion on merit so that young, able and talented managers could be given accelerated promotion rather than having to wait until those older left or retired. In addition Ghosn changed the recruiting process to end recruitment of only graduates from the law faculties. Nissan's senior management, whose working attitude was extremely bureaucratic, had all been recruited in this way.

Once sufficient knowledge and confidence in the alliance had been built, Ghosn's Japanese predecessor Yoshikazu Hanawa effectively used Renault to present the truth about Nissan to his own executive board, as working with Renault had exposed bureaucratic inefficiency and uncompetitive management in certain fields of activity.

Nissan suffered badly through its reliance on the traditional Japanese *Keiretsu* system (a kind of informal business group), in which several main component suppliers were managed by former Nissan managers. High prices were paid to almost captive suppliers through this system, which was inflated through a distinct lack of cost control. There were more than 1,000 suppliers within the Nissan *Keiretsu* suppliers' network. Even though Nissan was aware of the problem, the key weakness was an inability to reduce costs. It was discovered that, in a number of cases, Nissan did not know exactly what it purchased from some of its leading suppliers, nor what several others actually produced. Inspection showed that it was paying up to 25% more than Renault for components from the same suppliers.

It was decreed that the total number of first-tier suppliers would be cut from approximately 1,300 to around 600 by 2002 and that there would have to be an upwards shift in quality with the doors open to Western suppliers for the first time to increase the pressure on their Japanese counterparts.

Again, Ghosn was able to restructure the suppliers' network without destroying the Japanese laws of loyalty. It breached the Japanese principle of "lifetime cooperation", but at the same time there was a recognition that costs had to be reduced. Cutting the number of suppliers by 50% from 1999 to 2002 helped reduce purchasing costs by 20%. The success of these actions emphasize that cultural changes can make sense economically.

Nissan's desperate financial situation right before the merger with Renault made it easier for the *Nissan Revival Plan* to be accepted even though it broke with significant Japanese values and management practices. The context is described in Ghosn's own words:

> "When Renault people came to Japan, the management of Nissan had from the beginning a very strong consciousness about the severity of the situation. There was no room for bickering or fighting or infinite discussions about whose method or whose process we were going to adopt." (Emerson 2001: 6)

At the beginning the *Nissan Revival Plan* was introduced quite fast and didn't leave room for meditation on the differences about cultures. Was it about neglecting cultures or the survival of the most powerful culture? Its aim was to help the company survive and differences in cultures were used as ways of listening to what the other company could do better.

For Ghosn, the right approach to French–Japanese intercultural cooperation is to accept that people don't think or act the same way in France and Japan (Stahl & Brannen 2013). By accepting this fact, everyone involved would be motivated and mobilized by a very strong objective. Then, the cultural differences can become seeds for innovation as opposed to seeds for dissention. He stresses the importance of cultivating a certain mindset or character that truly enjoys the challenge of living in new environments:

> "If you have to work and particularly do something significant in a country it is much easier if somehow you are connected with the country and you like the country and you respect the people and you are curious about the culture. [...] And try to learn about its strengths, don't focus on the weaknesses, and make sure that all the people you are transferring with you are of the same opinion." (INSEAD 2008)

Based on this experience with Renault and Nissan, he also gives a definition of synergy:

> "Synergy is not only what exists in one company or the other. It is not just about transferring best practices. It's also about creating together something that neither one could have done alone." (Stahl & Brannen 2013:496)

Ghosn's leadership style and use of methods displayed high levels of intercultural sensitivity: "I think one of the basics of transcultural leadership is empathy" he says (INSEAD, 2008). Cultural traditions can be challenged when they are responsible for keeping a culture back from where it really needs to go. It is important that people understand why a tradition is being challenged.

> "You have to explain with what the former tradition will be replaced. People need to know what the prize is. If this is clearly spelled out why some established traditions have to be changed people will be more motivated to follow. Especially in Japan change and risk is never easy." (Ghosn in an interview, Emerson 2001:7)

It is interesting to note that Ghosn's managerial methods are not based on so-called "universal" Anglo-Saxon mainstream concepts. One interesting method he introduced at Nissan to solve organizational problems was simply listening to employees of any level, as Sibylle Rizk (undated, our translation from French), confirms:

> "Instead of applying preconceived plans, he takes the time to listen to everyone and organizes working groups of employees of different grades and different cultures, in this case Japanese and French."

Intercultural structuring and processing The cooperation between Renault and Nissan is governed by the Alliance Board, set up by the two companies. As is shown in Figure 23.2, the Renault–Nissan Alliance Board consists of three Renault (one Portuguese citizen and two Frenchmen) and three Nissan senior executives (of Japanese citizenship) and is chaired by Renault–Nissan Alliance Chairman and CEO Carlos Ghosn. The Alliance Board is supported by the Executive Committee of both companies. The board focuses on the strategic direction, new opportunities for collaboration and the progress of the alliance relative to industry benchmarks. Alliance Board meetings concern major topics associated with the collaboration: mid-term plan progress, the validation of product plans, the commonality of products and powertrains, strategic investments impacting the alliance and strategic partnerships with third parties.

It was in 2009, in a context of global economic slowdown, that the Renault–Nissan alliance created a team of dedicated alliance directors (see Table 23.3) in order to accelerate synergies and best practice sharing and to enhance the performance of associated companies. The 12 alliance managing directors are responsible for the operations of alliance functions for both partners and advice teams in partner companies. They may oppose measures taken by Renault or Nissan that do not contribute to the development of synergies, referring the matter to the executive committee of the company concerned or even, ultimately, the Alliance Board. It is interesting to note that of the alliance managing directors some are French and some are Japanese; one is Franco-American, one is Brazilian of Japanese origin, one is American and one is Belgian. Furthermore, one of them has been working for both Renault and Nissan, four come from Renault, six from Nissan and two were recruited without prior experience in either partner company.

Besides these structural elements, there are important process elements: Renault and Nissan employees had suffered from communication problems and a lack of information flow within the organization. As Ghosn underlines: "Here [in Japan], the lack of communication is the biggest problem. You cannot over communicate. Every time we have respected this basic rule of communication, we have had no problem. This has been my own experience in a country [Japan] that has a reputation of respecting tradition." (Emerson 2001:7)

In fact, there was little information flow between departments and foreign subsidiaries. For this reason, Ghosn set up Cross-Functional Teams (CFT) – as he had done in South America at Michelin – which allow French and Japanese managers to mix and merge their working and management styles, trying to use only the best of each system rather than letting one dominate the other. Ghosn believes in the cross-fertilization between the two companies through employees from different cultural and professional backgrounds:

> "When you have a very diverse team – people of different backgrounds, different culture, different gender, different age, you are going to get a more creative team – probably getting better solutions, and enforcing them in a very innovative way and with a very limited number of preconceived ideas." (Fitzsimmons et al. 2011:199)

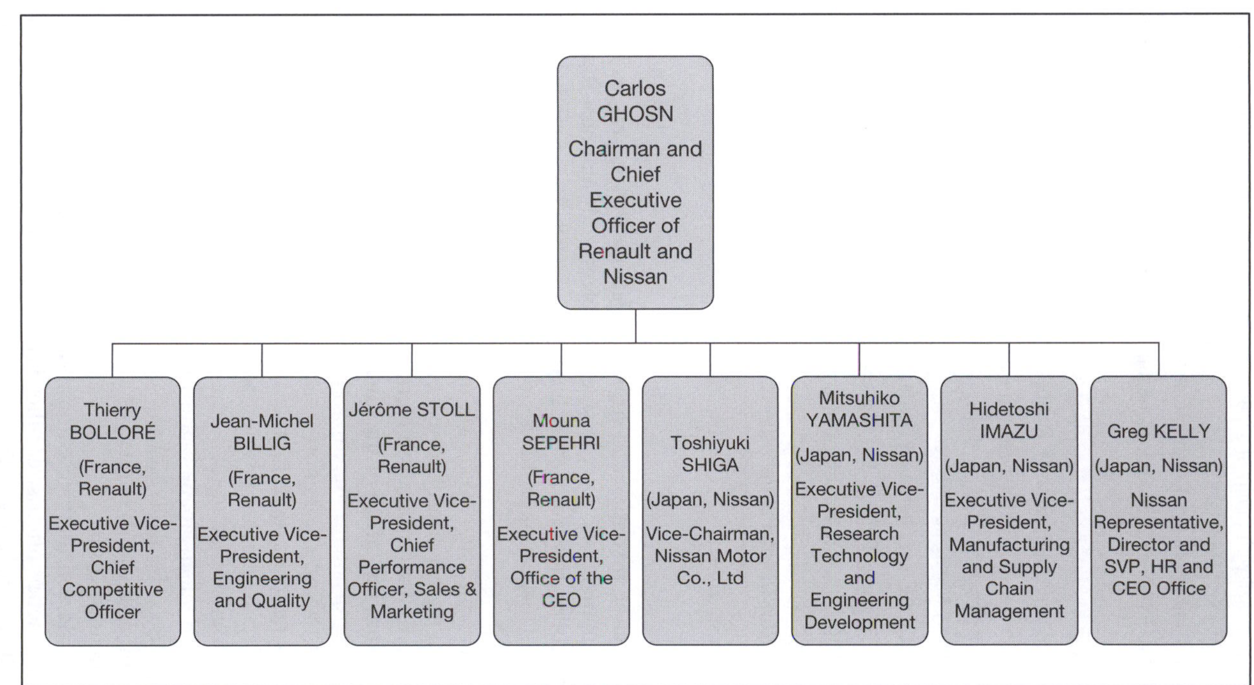

Figure 23.2 Alliance Board of Renault–Nissan

Source: Renault Nissan (2014).

Table 23.3 List of Alliance Managing Directors of Renault–Nissan in 2015

Gérard DETOURBET (France, Renault): Managing Director, A-Segment development unit
Celso GUIOTOKO (Brazil with family of Japanese origin, Nissan): Managing Director, Information Systems & Technologies
Rachel KONRAD (United States): Communication
Christian MARDRUS (France, Renault): Managing Director, Chief Executive Officer Office & Logistics
Toshiaki OTANI (Japan, Nissan): Managing Director, Battery Business
Jérémie PAPIN (France/United States): Finance
Alain RAPOSO (France, Renault): Powertrain Planning
Véronique SARLAT-DEPOTTE (France, Renault): Alliance Global Senior Vice President, Purchasing & Deputy Managing Director
Jacques VERDONCK (France, Renault): Daimler Coordination
Isabelle VIEUILLE (France, Renault and Nissan): Economic Advisor
Tsuyoshi YAMAGUCHI (Japan, Nissan): Platforms & Parts
Yasuhiro YAMAUCHI (Japan, Nissan): Alliance Executive Vice President, Purchasing and Chairman & Managing Director of Renault–Nissan Purchasing Organization

Source: Renault–Nissan (2014).

At Nissan, the CFT first appeared strange to Japanese managers, as Japanese culture prefers managers to solve business problems only amongst themselves, and not with colleagues from other hierarchical levels and functions. In the CFTs middle managers have the opportunity to work with senior managers and executives.

A very challenging step was to set up communication structures and processes. Frustrations occurred because of language barriers that did not allow spontaneous communication; team members always had to go through a translator, which meant that much of the intended meaning was lost. To communicate in a meaningful and resourceful way, the Franco-Japanese Renault–Nissan teams also had to find a common working language: the corporate language English was for neither side its mother tongue, so most of the members of the board had the same starting position as far as language was concerned. But due to the poor knowledge of each other's language, managers communicated in a mixture of English, Japanese and French, although English is the official working language at Renault–Nissan. To help them, a management manual of keywords in English was developed as a common basis for communicating in English at Renault–Nissan.

Because of the considerable cultural distance between Japan and France, research and practice often stress the difficulty of these two cultures working successfully together. Nevertheless, in this case, both parties respected the different values of the cultures involved, considered various interpretations and demonstrated the will to find the best solutions in a complementary way through the use of bicultural teams.

3 BACKGROUND KNOWLEDGE

3.1 The authors' point of reference

Christoph Barmeyer, specialist in intercultural management, and Ulrike Mayrhofer, specialist in international and strategic management, work with a systemic-integrative approach, which takes account of the importance of the context (corporate biography, strategies, structures, processes etc.) and relationships. As a result of their long working experience in France and their German (Christoph Barmeyer) and Austrian (Ulrike Mayrhofer) backgrounds, they have found during their manifold intercultural leadership and management activities in universities and business schools that cultures and cultural actors may be complementary.

More information about their approaches (and some articles) can be found on their websites: www.uni-passau.de/barmeyer and http://iae.univ-lyon3.fr/menus/outils/annuaire/mayrhofer-ulrike-157038.kjsp.

3.2 Concepts, models, frameworks

Organizational development After the participation of the French automotive manufacturer Renault, the Japanese company Nissan underwent important changes, which contributed to the development of both the Nissan company and the international Renault–Nissan alliance. The strategic, structural, process and cultural changes initiated by Carlos Ghosn and his management teams can be understood as – interculturally oriented – organizational development.

What is organizational development? Organizational development (OD) refers to the intentional, controlled and result-oriented change and evolution of structures and processes in organizations with the aim of securing their survival and performance, taking into account the needs and competences of the organizational members. Organizational development helps the planning and implementation of changes both in a target-oriented and holistic way. Care is taken that the organization members are involved in this process and that corporate identity is maintained.

As a result of corporate globalization – as is the case in the automotive sector and at Renault–Nissan – organizational development becomes more and more international; methods and tools such as strategic orientations, organizational cultures, controlling systems or leadership development do not only apply to the domestic context, but also to organizations worldwide.

Consequently, organizational development is increasingly confronted with intercultural challenges, namely strategies, structures, processes and groups that change and evolve in different cultural contexts, without disrupting their own cultural and proven specificity and impairing the effectiveness of the organization. Both development and change approaches and the organizational environment are involved in specific cultural contexts that must be taken into consideration (Barmeyer & Bolten 2010).

What makes organizational development "intercultural"? Interculturally oriented organizational development is defined as a continuous and sustainable process of change that concerns the whole organization, namely its strategies, structures, processes and resources, with the goal of achieving effective and appropriate intercultural behaviour in the organization. Interculturally oriented organizational development should contribute to the development of a value-added organization as well as to respectful collaboration between employees of different cultures.

Organizational development as cultural change has to deal with specific contexts and affiliations (such as national, regional, professional and departmental cultures), with value systems, institutional structures and traditions, as well as cultural practices – in this case Japan and the managerial and corporate culture of Nissan.

Managerial capabilities and ethnocentrism During the implementation of change or development processes, especially with a top-down strategy, a key role is played by the leader, who in addition to his/her leadership competence also possesses managerial capability. Managerial capability is defined as the ability of managers to create a safe workplace and a strong culture to make it easier for employees to participate in business processes (Boeker & Wiltbank 2005). Important components of managerial capability are leadership style, employee development, succession planning and decision making as well as the steering and controlling of a company (Boeker & Wiltbank 2005:124). A successful CEO in multinational corporations should be able to involve the perspectives of all organizational and national cultures in order to avoid a one-sided dominance. As Carlos Ghosn highlights:

> "Everybody has to be a manager of diversity, but especially senior executives because people always look to the top. They look at the top and say, 'OK, is he doing what he is saying?' If employees see top management talking about openness and learning – but they see an arrogant person who is closed down – they will not take it seriously. So the top management in a multicultural environment has an important role: They must walk the talk." (Stahl & Brannen 2013:497)

This managerial capability therefore needs an ethnorelativist view. Ethnorelativism (Bennett 1993) refers to an attitude that questions one's own standards and beliefs and helps to accept the norms and world views of other cultural groups and consider them as equally valuable. Research and practice in intercultural competence development assumes that a change in perspective leads to a relativization of one's own point of view (Spencer-Oatey & Franklin 2009). The challenge is – concerning intercultural organizational development – to transfer individual ethnorelativist attitudes to the collective level of the organization.

Recently, more and more managers in intercultural key positions come from different cultural backgrounds. Applied research designates such persons growing up in these conditions as biculturals, Third culture kids (TCK) (Pollock & van Reken 2001) or third culture individuals (TCI) (Moore & Barker 2012). They acquired and developed specific attitudes and competences during their socialization process: a distinction can be made between primary socialization (childhood, family and school education) and secondary socialization (academic education and working experience). While they grow up in symbiosis with two or more cultures, they develop a new one, from which emerges a new combination:

> Biculturals have a simultaneous awareness of being a member of (and sometimes an outsider in) two (or more) cultures and exhibit a behavioural repertoire that stems from having access to two distinct cultural knowledge traditions, sometimes switching between schemas in response to cultural cues. (Brannen & Thomas 2010:5)

On the one hand, their strength is to be able to confront the challenges of life by referring to numerous cultural orientation systems in which they are integrated (Fitzsimmons et al. 2013). On the other hand, they are also able to adapt and move with greater ease within new and different environments.

Very often, they find outstanding positions in multinational companies as third-country nationals (TCN) (Zeira & Harari 1977) where they use their competencies as human interfaces between different cultural, institutional and language systems (Torbiörn 1985). Since they come from a third culture, which is different from the headquarters' or subsidiaries' culture, they are able to have a more neutral and objective view of organizational strategies and practices, as Ghosn states:

> "When you have a more vague, hybrid, multicultural background, people feel they have a chance to talk to you. They say, 'He is going to listen, he is not taken by one particular concept or representing one particular culture.' So one of the things that I benefited from without knowing it – I discovered it only later – is that people did not see me as typical French. They saw me as a Franco-Brazilian-Lebanese guy. So, they said, 'Hmm, he doesn't come with a typical talk, with a particular approach, he is more open.' That's why I think embracing multiculturalism opens up more opportunities for you than if you operate in a monocultural world." (Stahl & Brannen 2013:499)

Very often, TCN are interculturally competent and sensitive with an empathic attitude of observing, listening, understanding different systems, knowing different cultures and speaking different languages. They are capable of initiating and steering cultural change processes.

3.3 Recommended reading

Barmeyer, C. & Mayrhofer, U. (2008). "Management interculturel et processus d'intégration: une analyse de l'alliance Renault–Nissan". In: *Management & Avenir,* 22, 109–131.
This article contributes to a better understanding of the success of the alliance formed between Renault and Nissan. The authors analyse – with a focus on national and organizational culture – the integration process that has allowed the companies to manage their strategic partnership since its creation in 1999.

Boeker, W. & Wiltbank, R. (2005). "New venture evolution and managerial capabilities". In: *Organization Science,* 16:2, 123–133.

This study examines important factors influencing changes in the top management of new firms. The authors examined several firms for several years after their founding to evaluate the conditions that influence a firm's changes in top management. The results show that power and control of inside and outside constituencies also affect changes in top management. Furthermore, this article goes into detail about strategic change, board independence and current top management characteristics of leadership change.

Brannen, M. Y. & Thomas, D. C. (2010). "Bicultural individuals in organizations: Implications and opportunity". In: *International Journal of Cross Cultural Management*, 10:1, 5–16.
Due to internationalization processes more and more individuals have more than one cultural identity and, as a consequence, employees and managers in organizations will increasingly be bicultural. The article provides a brief review of what bicultural individuals are, points out some implications of current understanding for organizations and identifies opportunities for further exploration of these topics.

Emerson, V. (2001). "An Interview with Carlos Ghosn, President of Nissan Motors, Ltd. and Industry Leader of the Year (Automotive News, 2000)". In: *Journal of World Business,* 36:1, 3–10.
The attitude of Carlos Ghosn in this strategic alliance is shown in this interview where Ghosn puts emphasis on the cultural differences between the two partners and is candid about the fact that these differences can be viewed as either a handicap in cross-border acquisitions or alliances, or they can be perceived as a powerful seed for something new. How Ghosn turned this potential handicap into an effective asset is revealed in this interview – from "mission impossible to mission accomplished".

Korine, H., Asakawa, K. & Gomez, P.-Y. (2002). "Partnering with the unfamiliar: Lessons from the case of Renault and Nissan". In: *Business Strategy Review,* 13:2, 41–50.
This article explains how "odd couples" can effectively cooperate in practice in search of greater geographic coverage and complementary skills. There are quite a few challenges in establishing deep strategic interdependence, especially where intercultural issues are concerned: cultural differences have to be overcome, diverging world views reconciled. By giving a historic overview of the strategic alliance and by presenting and explaining Ghosn's strategy, the authors demonstrate how the initiator of such an alliance process can avoid being seen as too aggressive and how to let knowledge and innovations flow, especially between cultures as different as those of Japan and France.

Mayrhofer, U. (Ed.) (2013). *Management of Multinational Companies: A French Perspective*. Basingstoke: Palgrave Macmillan.
This book offers an innovative perspective of managerial practices adopted by multinational companies that operate in the French economy. It highlights the diversity of responses these companies have developed in regard to the

challenges of market globalization. The authors examine the complexity of the internal organization of multinational companies, namely the management of headquarters–subsidiaries relationships, but also the performance of partnerships and networks they form with actors from other countries. The contributing authors provide explanations illustrated with quantitative data, examples and case studies.

Stahl, G. K. & Brannen, M. Y. (2013). "Building cross-cultural leadership competence: An interview with Carlos Ghosn". In: *Academy of Management Learning & Education*, 12:3, 494–502.
This publication is an interview with the CEO of Renault–Nissan, Carlos Ghosn. It deals with challenges in managing across borders, Ghosn's multicultural background, the mindset and skillsets that managers require to create cultural synergies, and how global corporations can utilize their cultural diversity to build cross-cultural competence in individuals and teams.

4 QUESTIONS ON THE CASE

1. What kind of key factors were essential for the organizational development of the strategic alliance in the case? In what way did they contribute to the success of Renault–Nissan? Please try to distinguish strategic, structural, process and cultural key factors and measures.
2. In what way are the two companies complementary within the strategic alliance? How far do they follow complementary strategic plans? Please refer to the interview of Carlos Ghosn with Stahl and Brannen (2013).
3. How can intercultural cooperation and organizational development be enabled as a result of: the organizational structure adopted; the composition of the alliance board and alliance managing directors; the processes that are implemented?
4. Describe the specific profile of the CEO Carlos Ghosn. Why is he a good candidate to make organizational change happen in a Japanese company?

5 REFERENCES

Barmeyer, C. & Bolten, J. (2010) (Eds). *Interkulturelle Personal- und Organisationsentwicklung*. Sternenfels/Berlin: Wissenschaft & Praxis.

Barmeyer, C. & Mayrhofer, U. (2009). "Management interculturel et processus d'intégration: Une analyse de l'alliance Renault–Nissan". In: *Management & Avenir*, 22, 109–131.

Bennett, M. (1993). "Towards ethnorelativism: A developmental model of intercultural sensitivity". In: Paige, M. (Ed.), *Education for the Intercultural* Experience, 21–71. Yarmouth: Intercultural Press.

Boeker, W. & Wiltbank, R. (2005). "New venture evolution and managerial capabilities". In: *Organization Science*, 16:2, 123–133.

Brannen, M. Y. & Thomas, D. C. (2010). "Bicultural individuals in organizations: Implications and opportunity". In: *International Journal of Cross Cultural Management*, 10:1, 5–16.

CCFA (Comité des Constructeurs Français d'Automobiles) (2014). The French Automotive Industry. Analysis and Statistics. Paris.

Emerson, V. (2001). "An Interview with Carlos Ghosn, President of Nissan Motors, Ltd. and Industry Leader of the Year (Automotive News, 2000)". In: *Journal of World Business*, 36:1, 3–10.

Fitzsimmons, S. R., Miska, C. & Stahl, G. (2011): "Multicultural employees: Global business' untapped resource." In: *Organizational Dynamics*, 40:3. 199–206.

Fitzsimmons, S. R., Lee, Y.-T. & Brannen, M. Y. (2013). "Demystifying the myth about marginals: Implications for global leadership." In: *European Journal of International Management*, 7:5, 587–603.

INSEAD (2008). "The transcultural leader: Carlos Ghosn, CEO of Renault, Nissan". Retrieved on 29 May 2008 from http://knowledge.insead.edu/leadership-management/operations-management/the-transcultural-leadercarlos-ghosn-ceo-of-renault-nissan-1904

Mayrhofer, U. (Ed.) (2013). *Management of Multinational Companies: A French Perspective*. Basingstoke: Palgrave Macmillan.

Mayrhofer, U. & Urban, S. (2011). *Management international. Des pratiques en mutation*. Paris: Pearson Education.

Moore, A. M. & Barker, G. G. (2012). "Confused or multicultural: Third culture individuals' cultural identity". In: *International Journal of Intercultural Relations*, 36, 553–562.

Pollock, D. & van Reken, R. (2001). *Third Culture Kids. The Experience of Growing Up Among Worlds*. Yarmouth: Intercultural Press.

Prange, C. & Mayrhofer, U. (2015). "Alliances and joint ventures". In Vodosek, M. & Den Hartog, D. (Eds), *Wiley Encyclopedia of Management, Vol. 6: International Management*. 3rd ed. [online] New Jersey: John Wiley & Sons.

Renault–Nissan (2014). *Alliance Facts & Figures 2013–2014*. Paris.

Spencer-Oatey, H. & Franklin, P. (2009). *Intercultural Interaction*. London: Palgrave Macmillan.

Stahl, G. K. & Brannen, M. Y. (2013). "Building cross-cultural leadership competence: An interview with Carlos Ghosn". In: *Academy of Management Learning & Education*, 12:3, 494–502.

Torbiörn, I. (1985). "The structure of managerial roles in cross-cultural settings". In: *International Studies of Management and Organization*, 15:1, 52–74.

Zeira, Y. & Harari, E. (1977). "Third-country managers in multinational corporations". In: *Personnel Review*, 6:1, 32–37.

Contributors

Soon Ang, PhD, Goh Tjoei Kok Distinguished Chair and Professor in Management, Nanyang Technological University, Singapore. ASANG@ntu.edu.sg

Fritz Audebert, PhD, CEO and founder of ICUnet.AG, Germany. fritz.audebert@icunet.ag

Christoph Barmeyer, PhD, Professor and Chair in Intercultural Communication, University of Passau, Germany. Christoph.Barmeyer@uni-passau.de

Thilo Beyer, Senior Consultant at ICUnet.AG, Germany. thilo.beyer@icunet.ag

Sylvie Chevrier, PhD, Professor of Management, University Paris-Est Marne-la-Vallée and Deputy Director of the research centre IRG (Institut de Recherche en Gestion), France. sylvie.chevrier@u-pem.fr

Eric Davoine, PhD, Professor of Human Resource Management and Organisation, University of Fribourg, Switzerland. Eric.davoine@unifr.ch

Christine R. Day, PhD, Faculty Member, Management Department, Eastern Michigan University, Ypsilanti, Michigan, USA. cday1@emich.edu

Peter Franklin, Professor of Business English and Intercultural Business and Management Communication, Hochschule Konstanz University of Applied Sciences. Peter.Franklin@htwg-konstanz.de

Anna Gajda, PhD, Consultant, The Boston Consulting Group, Germany. gajda.anna@bcg.com

Petia Genkova, PhD, Professor in Business Psychology, University of Applied Sciences Osnabrueck, Germany. P.Genkova@hs-osnabrueck.de

Veronika Hackl, Marketing Manager, ICUnet.AG, Germany. veronika.hackl@icunet.ag

Ulrike Haupt, Consultant and Coach for Intercultural, Systemic Transition Consultancy, Starnberg, Germany. u.haupt@culturebridge.de

Astrid Kainzbauer, PhD, Assistant Dean for International Relations, College of Management, Mahidol University, Bangkok, Thailand. astrid.kai@mahidol.ac.th

Matthias Kempf, Director HR Emerging Markets, adidas Group, Dubai/UAE. Matthias.Kempf@adidas-group.com

Yih-teen Lee, PhD, Associate Professor, Department of Managing People in Organizations, IESE Business School, Spain. YLee@iese.edu

David Livermore, PhD, President of the Cultural Intelligence Center, East Lansing, Michigan, USA. info@culturalq.com

Jasmin Mahadevan, Dr. Phil., Professor of International and Cross-Cultural Management, School of Engineering, Pforzheim University, Germany. jasmin.mahadevan@hs-pforzheim.de

Ulrike Mayrhofer, PhD, Professor of Management Science, IAE Lyon and Director of the Magellan Research Centre, Jean Moulin Lyon 3 University, France. ulrike.mayrhofer@univ-lyon3.fr

Vincent Merk, Senior Lecturer in Intercultural Management and Advisor for the International Community at Eindhoven University of Technology, Netherlands. v.merk@tue.nl

Christof Miska, PhD, Assistant Professor, Institute for International Business, WU Vienna University of Economics and Business, Austria. christof.miska@wu.ac.at

Evalde Mutabazi, PhD, Professor of HRM and Cross-Cultural Management, EM LYON Business School, France. contact@mutabazi.com

Jenny Plaister-Ten, Founder and Director, 10 Consulting Ltd. jenny.plaister@10consulting.co.uk

Michaela Pleskova, Masters Student in CEMS/International Management, Vienna University of Economics and Business, Austria. michaela.pleskova@cemsmail.org

Philippe Poirson, Professor of HRM and Cross-Cultural Management, EM Lyon and Consultant in HRM, France. ph-poirson@wanadoo.fr

Laurence Romani, PhD, Associate Professor, Centre for Advanced Studies in Leadership, Stockholm School of Economics, Sweden. Laurence.Romani@hhs.se

Tobias M. Scholz, Doctoral Candidate and Research Assistant, Chair for Human Resource Management and Organizational Behavior, University of Siegen, Germany. tobias.scholz@uni-siegen.de

Claus Schreier, PhD, Professor, Lucerne University of Applied Sciences and Arts – School of Business, Lucerne, Switzerland. claus.schreier@hslu.ch

Helen Spencer-Oatey, PhD, Professor and Director, Centre for Applied Linguistics, University of Warwick, Great Britain. helen.spencer-oatey@warwick.ac.uk

Volker Stein, PhD, Professor and Chair of Human Resource Management and Organizational Behavior and Founding Director of University of Siegen Business School, Germany. volker.stein@uni-siegen.de

Craig Storti, Trainer and Consultant in Intercultural Communications, Westminster, USA. craig@craigstorti.com

Fons Trompenaars, PhD, CEO and Owner of Trompenaars Hampden-Turner Consulting, Affiliated Professor, Department of Management and Organization Studies, Vrije Universiteit Amsterdam. fons@thtconsulting.com

Riana van den Bergh, Consultant, Trompenaars Hampden-Turner, Amsterdam. PhD student at the University of Pretoria, South Africa. riana@thtconsulting.com

David A. Victor, PhD, Professor of Management and Director of International Business Programs, Eastern Michigan University, Ypsilanti, Michigan, USA. DVictor@emich.edu

Index